Miss May Sinclair: Novelist

Also by the author:

The Works of Edwin Pugh (1874–1930): A Chapter in the Novel of Humble London Life

Biographical note and critical essay on Stephen Hudson, in *Richard, Myrtle and I,* edited by Violet Schiff

Miss May Sinclair: Novelist

A Biographical and Critical Introduction

By
THEOPHILUS E. M. BOLL

Rutherford • Madison • Teaneck
Fairleigh Dickinson University Press

Associated University Presses, Inc.
Cranbury, New Jersey 08512

Library of Congress Cataloging in Publication Data

Boll, Theophilus Ernest Martin, 1902–
   Miss May Sinclair.

   Bibliography: p.
   1. Sinclair, May.
PR6037.I73Z58 1973   823'.9'12 [B]   72-414
ISBN 0-8386-1156-7

Printed in the United States of America

To
Muriel M. Sinclair
and
To the Memory
of
Harold Lumley Sinclair
and
Florence Bartrop

Contents

Preface

This introduction to May Sinclair began one day when Professor Albert C. Baugh suggested that I explore the possibility of obtaining help from the American Philosophical Society for research in England, which I had not been able to visit for many years. It happened that I had read entirely through the already known works of May Sinclair, as part of my vocation to know the English novelists, and I developed a strong curiosity about any letters or journals that might be awaiting an appreciative reader of hers. I even became host to an obsession, which I was alert enough to confess to Professor Loren Eiseley, that I should find her literary remains, not in a conventional attic, but in a small outbuilding standing near a garden, and far away from any city. How that obsession turned out to be a prophetic vision I have described in an essay, "On the May Sinclair Collection" (*The Library Chronicle,* University of Pennsylvania, Winter, 1961, vol. 27, no. 1).

This book has been delayed much too long by another, but counterproductive obsession, which mounted my shoulders just as I began making progress with the main work. It urged me to make a thorough study of the image that was being drawn month by month by each printed remark about her work and about her as a writer. May Sinclair had saved many cuttings of reviews and interviews, and as I read these I imagined how strong must have been her feelings as she studied each one. It seemed to me a wonderful idea, to weave through my account of her life and works an account of the parallel growth of that piece of many-authored fiction: her literary reputation. After having read her works, I could not understand why she had been denied a place in the main procession of English novelists. The product of my diligent, even enthusiastic double labor was a volume of unconfessable length—and weight—appalling to any publisher who was concerned with his own survival and unmoved by my passionate mission for a revival.

Here is the much-shortened volume, the testament of my faith in May Sinclair, without the history of her image.

For starting me on my vocation, I thank Professor Cornelius Weygandt and Professor Felix E. Schelling, of revered memory. For their encouragement to me to go on with this particular phase of it, I owe profound thanks, beyond those offered in the list of acknowledgments to Professor Albert C. Baugh, Professor Maurice O. Johnson, Dr. Donald S. Murray, Professor Edward Wagenknecht, Professor Nina L. Theiss, Mr. William L. Coakley, Mr. Thomas Yoseloff, Miss Margaret Storm Jameson, and to the three to whom this volume is dedicated.

T. E. M. Boll

The Knoll
Lansdowne, Pennsylvania

Acknowledgments

My search for the copyright holders of the letters that May Sinclair saved came to a less than perfect detection. I hope that I and the many correspondents who tried to help me will be forgiven our failures. I am happy to thank the following:

Curtis Brown Ltd., of New York and of London, for permission to quote from *The Immortal Moment*, 1908, *The Tree of Heaven*, 1917, *Mary Olivier*, 1919, *Mr. Waddington of Wyck*, 1921, and from all other titles whose copyright they acquired from Hutchinson Publishing Group Ltd., from Cassell and Company, Ltd., from Holt, Rinehart, and Winston, Inc., and from Constable Publishers Ltd.

Routledge Kegan Paul Ltd., for clearing the way to my quoting freely from *Nakiketas and other Poems*, 1886, and from *Essays in Verse*, 1891.

Macmillan of London and Basingstoke, for permission to quote from *A Defence of Idealism*, 1917, and *The New Idealism*, 1922.

Macmillan of New York, for permission to quote from *A Defence of Idealism*, 1917, and *The Tree of Heaven*, 1917.

Harper and Row, for permission to quote from *The Judgment of Eve*, 1908, and *The Combined Maze*, 1913.

Constable Publishers, for permission to quote from *Mr. and Mrs. Nevill Tyson*, 1898, *The Divine Fire*, 1904, and *The Creators*, 1910.

Miss Lucy Chauncy, for permission to publish the letters of Anthony C. Deane.

Miss Pamela Hinkson, for permission to publish her mother's letters to May Sinclair.

Mrs. Gillian Williamson, for permission to publish Evelyn Underhill's letters to May Sinclair.

Miss Sylvia Holt, for permission to publish her father's letters to May Sinclair.

David Garnett, for permission to publish the letters of Richard Garnett, Robert S. Garnett, and Edward Garnett to May Sinclair.

Mrs. T. S. Eliot, for permission to publish a letter of T. S. Eliot, and two letters of May Sinclair.

Richard L. Purdy and the trustees of Thomas Hardy, for permission to publish the correspondence of Thomas Hardy with May Sinclair.

Miss Sylvia Moore and A. D. Peters & Co., for permission to publish the letters of Maurice Hewlett to May Sinclair.

Mrs. Dorothy Cheston Bennett, with the kind intercession of Dr. James Hepburn, for permission to publish Arnold Bennett's correspondence with May Sinclair.

Mrs. Barbara Holt, for permission to publish two letters of Edwin Arlington Robinson.

Miss G. B. Stern, for permission to publish her letter to May Sinclair, and Dame Rebecca West for securing that permission.

Alfred C. Gissing, with the kind intercession of Professor Pierre Coustillas, for permission to publish a letter of his father.

Miss Beulah Hagan and Harper & Row, for permission to publish the letters from members of the Harper organization to May Sinclair.

The Committee for Ezra Pound, New Directions Publishing Corporation Agent, for permission to publish the letters of Ezra Pound, copyright 1972 by Ezra Pound.

Ivor Brown, for permission to publish his father's letters to May Sinclair.

Miss Margaret Storm Jameson, for her gift of letters of May Sinclair to Morley Roberts.

Spencer Curtis Brown, for permission to publish his father's letters.

A. P. Watt & Son and the executors of H. G. Wells, for permission to publish a letter of H. G. Wells.

Miss Jane Eustace and Messrs. Hodder and Stoughton, for permission to publish a letter from Arthur St. J. Adcock.

Lord Russell and William Ready, for permission to publish a letter from Lord Russell.

John Farquharson Ltd., for permission to publish a letter from Henry James.

John James, with the kind intercession of Professor Gay Wilson Allen, for permission to publish a letter of his father, William James.

Irving Shepard, for permission to publish a letter from Jack London.

Baron Layton, for permission to publish the letter of Francis Osmaston.

W. Hudson Vincent, Postmaster of Porthleven, for identifying Francis Beresford Osmaston.

William Collins Sons, for their attempts to trace the relatives of W. L. George and J. D. Beresford.

Charles H. Bocking and L. N. Allinson, who tried to trace the relatives of "Zack."

Elizabeth C. McKey, for her efforts to trace the relatives of Ida Hatch.

Rupert Hart-Davis and the executors of the late Sir Hugh Walpole, for use of the letters of May Sinclair to Hugh Walpole.

Miss Phyllis Bentley, for obtaining a letter from W. C. Speirs, of Reeth, and for sending me information about May Sinclair in Reeth.

Dr. Lola L. Szladits, for securing permission to publish the May Sinclair letters in the Berg Collection of the New York Public Library.

Miss Jean Preston and the Huntington Library, for permission to use the letters of May Sinclair to Mrs. Fields.

Jim Underwood and Constable & Co., for permission to quote a letter of May Sinclair from Douglas Goldring's *South Lodge*.

Mrs. Faith Puttick, for her research into the residences of the Sinclairs.

Mrs. Stanley Hyde, for sharing with me her considerable knowledge of May Sinclair at Stow-on-the-Wold, and Mrs. Gladys Woodward for introducing me to her.

Miss Laura Price, for her research in the affiliation of May Sinclair with the Medico-Psychological Clinic.

Miss Pamela A. Rose, for contributing her research into May Sinclair's membership in women's suffrage organizations.

J. Haydon W. Glen, town clerk of Kingston on Hull, for information about William Sinclair, Jr.'s activities in Hull.

Miss E. Higgs, who answered my appeals for information at the Society of Authors.

Reginald A. Place, former headmaster of Reeth School, and James Strachan, for information about the Sinclair prizes.

Professor W. S. Trout, for his gifts of letters of May Sinclair.

R. Burnett, of the National Library of Scotland, for dating "The Frewin Affair."

Miss V. M. Hounsfield, for supplying me with a copy of every item relating May Sinclair to the Cheltenham Ladies College.

Dr. Neda Westlake, Curator of the Rare Book Library, for her guardianship of the May Sinclair Collection and her helpfulness in making it continuously accessible to me.

Mr. Bernard J. Ford, Assistant Director of Libraries, for tracking down the translations of May Sinclair's works.

Mrs. Delphine O. Richardson, head of the Interlibrary Loan Department, for her constant helpfulness.

Miss May Sinclair: Novelist

If I do not keep step with others, it is because I hear a different drummer. Let a man step to the music which he hears, however measured and however far away.

Henry Thoreau
Found in Richard Garnett's handwriting among the papers of May Sinclair

Miss May Sinclair . . . is the most widely known woman artist in the country and America.

Thomas Moult
September, 1920

Miss May Sinclair, the great novelist, the greatest psychological analyst in fiction.
John Farrar
May, 1924

Miss Sinclair knows this England with a knowledge that is remorseless, and she loves it and hates it, as one can hate and love only something that is part of one's flesh. . . . Miss Sinclair is a psychologist of the first order.
Lewis Mumford
September, 1924

"If I don't like to see you celebrated, Jinny, it's because I want to see you immortal."
Spoken by George Tanqueray
to Jane Holland
The Creators

16

Part: 1
HER LIFE

1

The Philosopher at the Summit

When on a Monday evening in London, February 5, 1923, Miss May Sinclair read her paper on "Primary and Secondary Consciousness"[1] to fellow members of the Aristotelian Society for the Systematic Study of Philosophy, she would seem to have reached the summit of a progress on which she had started in the spring of 1882, and to have cause for being proud and happy. John Henry Muirhead, the general editor of the Library of Philosophy for Allen and Unwin, was among those who were impressed, as he showed in the letter he wrote her on March 29, 1923, inviting her to contribute to his projected series of essays by living philosophers, *Contemporary British Philosophy*. He enclosed a list of those who had already sent or had promised papers: "You will notice that there is no other woman writer. I hope you will not object on this ground, and that you will be willing to join."

The audience was a distinguished one. By the end of that year the Society would include sixteen Fellows of the British Academy, ten Fellows of the Royal Society, and two wearers of the Order of Merit. The only other member who had ever written novels was George Bernard Shaw.

May Sinclair had been admitted to membership in the latter half of 1917, after the publication of *A Defence of Idealism*. Her sponsor was probably Professor Herbert Wildon Carr, the Honorary Professor of Psychology at King's College, who in 1925 was to establish a School of Philosophy at the University of Southern California. Since 1920 she had joined in discussing papers read by fellow members on such topics as "Professor Alexander's Concepts of Space, Time, and

---

1. Aristotelian Society, *Proceedings* 23, no. 7 (1923) : 111–20.

Deity," "Cosmic Evolution," "The Idea of Progress," "Realism and Value," "Croce's Historiography," "The Double-Knowledge Approach to the Mind-Body Problem," "Professor Whitehead's Enquiry into the Principles of Natural Knowledge and the Concept of Nature," and "The Problem of Classification in Religion."

The chairman that Monday evening was the Society's president, Alfred North Whitehead, Professor of Applied Mathematics at the Imperial College of Science, who in the following year was to become Professor of Philosophy at Harvard University.

The speaker was about five feet tall, and within six months of her sixtieth birthday. Her features were smooth and plump. Her darkish mouse-brown hair, without a streak of gray in it, was loosely coiled and knotted into a broad, nestlike coiffure. Her audience had only a contracted view of her high, rounded forehead, her Buddha-like immobile face, and her very beautiful nose, and they never met her intensely black eyes during the reading of the paper, because she looked unwaveringly at the typescript, shutting out with her strong will all notice of the organs of primary consciousness that were intent upon her tight, imperceptibly moving lips, her thin, clear, high-pitched and level-toned voice. When she finished her paper she abruptly retired, trotting and shuffling on the balls of her feet to her chair alongside her companion that evening, Miss Aphra Wilson, who was both the editor assigned to her by Hutchinsons, and a treasured friend.

After she had taken her seat, Professor Whitehead commented on her paper, and then recalled her to the platform to reply to questions and comments from Professors Hoernle, Wolf, and Herbert Wildon Carr, and Mr. Joad and Lord Haldane. A young student who attended the meeting as a guest recalled the shades of unhappiness that flickered over the face of the gentle little woman during the discussion period, her state of total disarmament of any proud poise or confidence or of feminine defiance. At every question that was put to her, she turned to Professor Whitehead in a gesture of apparent rout, to ask him most appealingly, "Oh, dear! What ought I to say to *that*?"[2]

Her distress was a surprising climax to her coadunate career in philosophy, which had begun with a note on Descartes, written while she was still a schoolgirl and printed in the *Cheltenham Ladies College Magazine* in the spring of 1882 and which ended, except for the publication of her address, with her second book, *The New Idealism*, published in June, 1922. Her distress was surprising, and yet it was

---

2. The account of the evening came from Miss Florence Bartrop, in conversations; and from Dr. Ruth L. Saw, Honorary Treasurer of the Aristotelian Society, in a letter, September 1, 1959.

foreshadowed in the life of George Eliot, whose eminence as a novelist and a scholar in philosophy May Sinclair most nearly repeated in the first quarter of the twentieth century.

Both women proved their intellectual equality with the most distinguished men of intellect of their time, and were yet conservatively feminine, asking only for an unprejudiced trial of freedom for women to contribute their abilities and their responsibilities to society. Both read Greek and German and French easily. Both were good musicians. Both were in the forefront of the intellectual movements of their time. Both wrote analytic criticism of the highest merit. Both wrote verse and plays in verse as an expression of their minor talents as poets. In their novels, both motivated much of the drama in the lives of their characters with the forces of conscience, compelling, rebelled against, sickly, and healthy. Both were permanently influenced by their emotional relationships to their families and drew upon the themes of marriage and family life for the substance of some of their most important novels. Both wrote about the woman's dilemma of being a daughter and a developing person. Both had an older brother upon whose affection they were deeply dependent. Neither had children. Both were devoted nurses of the ill who were closely related to them. Both believed with an elemental faith that love and duty were the highest motives in personal relationships, and applied their faith equally to humanity and to the art that represented their vision of the spectacle of humanity. Both drove their creative genius to develop innovations in narrative form, although only May Sinclair turned her experimental urge toward style. Both were intellectual rather than emotional rebels against Victorianism.

They were most unlike in the levels they chose for exploring the mysteries of human behavior and the mood they brought to their searching. George Eliot studied life solely on the level of consciousness, and her personal awareness of life was haunted by moral anxieties. The most fitting phrase to describe her mood, suggested by the title of Dickens's last Christmas book, is the Haunted Woman. By contrast, May Sinclair probed the unconscious as well as consciousness for the answers to her curiosity about human behavior. Her own conscience was wholly without personal moral anxieties. George Eliot never resolved her anxiety over departing from the religious fervor of her youth. May Sinclair perfectly resolved the conflict with her mother through her study of philosophical Idealism, in which she found through reason what her conscience rejected as dogma. There could not have been a more wholly emancipated mind, or a more balanced emotional nature than May Sinclair's. She deserves the title of

Emancipated Woman, in the sense in which George Gissing most clearly defined the term *emancipation*.

But on this climactic evening, when she ought to have felt proud of being honored by a very superior group of men, May Sinclair was unhappy and childlike in her confession of unhappiness. It was as if the full meaning of a poem she had published in 1886 had struck in front of her eyes like a flash of lightning. In the poem she had analyzed the dual parts George Eliot had acted, the intellectual masculine and the loving and loved feminine. She had praised her:

> Oh! soul so strong—yet woman weak to lean
> On man's firm heart! that mid its greatness found
> No rest, till fainting life with love was crowned,
> As with its flower.

And she had judged her:

> . . . as not alone in power and brain
> And utterance of knowledge thou didst seem
> Manlike, but wiser in thy womanhood.[3]

In this moment, her intellectual attainment seemed to slip like a mask from her femininity, and her childlike embarrassment seemed like a symbolic confession repeating the explicit one that her idol had made in the closing line of that wistful sonnet series, "Brother and Sister,"

> But were another childhood-world my share,
> I would be born a little sister there.

May Sinclair could not be born again, but she could make a clear break from her philosophical writing and resume with a demonic intensity the free expression of the creative writer.

---

3. "George Eliot," *Nakiketas and other Poems* (London: Kegan Paul, Trench & Co., 1886), pp. 70–72.

2

The Little Sister and Her Family

On September 26, 1850, William Sinclair, twenty-one, son of a Liverpool merchant, married by license in the Parish Church of Belfast the daughter of a Belfast merchant, Amelia Hind, who was twenty-eight or twenty-nine.[1]

William Sinclair became a shipowner with changing offices in Liverpool from 1851 to 1867.[2] From 1850 to 1870 most of his ships sailed from Belfast, their home port. They were not large (the smallest was 142 tons; the largest was 1,558 tons), but their ratings were generally high. They sailed to the West Indies, Bombay, Barbados, the Baltic Sea, Leghorn, Aden, Malaya, China, Ceylon, and Australia. The high point of the company's fortune was from 1861 to 1862, when it sailed twenty ships. In the last year of any registration of ships, 1869 to 1870, there were only five, of which one, the *Beloochee*, 967 tons, running from Belfast to India, was wrecked. The only visible sign of family sentiment in the naming of the ships was the *Saint Clair*, the smallest. There was, significantly, no *Amelia*.[3]

William Sinclair not only changed his business offices in Liverpool, but he also shifted his residences from Lower to Higher Bebington, in Cheshire. At the summit of his residential moves, he lived in Thorncote,[4] a villa in the Rock Park estate in Rock Ferry, where Mary Amelia St. Clair Sinclair was born on August 24, 1863, the last child in the family, and the only sister of five boys. As a forecast of her

1. General Register Office, Dublin.
2. G. Hampson, of the Liverpool Record Office, gave me the information on William Sinclair's resisdential and business addresses, in a letter, April 23, 1960.
3. Lloyd's *Register of Shipping* tells the complete story of William Sinclair's ships.
4. J. Reynolds, Headmaster, Rock Ferry High School, wrote me about Thorncote, January 6, 1960.

revolt in childhood against religion as dogma, she was the only child
of the Sinclairs for whom there is no record of baptism in the permanent register, kept now in St. Andrew's Church in Lower Bebington.
Her oldest brother, William, was born October 18, 1851; Joseph Walter
was born July 29, 1855; Francis Edwin, or Frank, was born March 11,
1857; Harold was born September 12, 1858; Reginald St. Clair was
registered at birth as Frederick Amelius, born January 23, 1861. Her
sister Gertrude, born on July 7, 1853, died on September 24, 1854, after
a month's siege of scarlatina. The children divided into the older and
the younger groups, with Mary Amelia's idol, Frank, heading the
younger group.

Liverpudlians on the rise thought that Rock Ferry, which the steam-
boat had converted from pasture and farmland into a booming suburb,
was the most desirable new residential district to move to. It was just
across the Mersey River in Higher Bebington, Cheshire. The Rock
Park Estate, which was in Rock Ferry, was started in 1835 by a number
of affluent Liverpool businessmen and a surgeon, who bought 112
acres of land of the Manor of Bebington on February 21, 1837, and
drew up detailed articles of agreement that provided a restricted residential park to afford them the amenities of the country gentry and
the practical advantage of a home close to their business. Along the
river side of the estate, they erected an esplanade nearly half a mile
long and six yards broad, to create a public walk for the community.
Inside its boundaries, which were formed by walls and houses, were
ten roads, alternating between straight and winding lines, and serving
as walks and carriage drives. All housing had to be built of stone,
cemented, stuccoed, or rough cast, and could not be higher than two
stories, not counting the attic. The articles of agreement forbade any
boundary division, or party wall, or fence higher than three feet from
the ground to be erected between the properties, and forbade all close
boarding, except along the esplanade, that would prevent persons from
looking through railings and fences.

The owners bought the right of the Rock Ferry to insure their control of transportation, and scheduled convenient departures between
Rock Ferry and Liverpool, beginning at 7:30 A.M. and ending at 9:30
P.M. On Sunday the service began an hour later but otherwise followed the same schedule of intervals. The fare was 2d.[5] One member

---

5. The *Adelphi Hotel Guide to Liverpool* supplied the information on Rock Ferry
transportation. The history of the Rock Park Estate is drawn from a manuscript
put at my disposal by its owner, Mrs. Joy Tanfield, of Rock Ferry. Other materials
are found in Francis White, *History, Gazeteer, and Directory of Cheshire* (1860);
Kelly's Post Office Directory of Cheshire (1857, 1864); and *The Picturesque Hand-
book to Liverpool* (1842).

contributed an acre of land and £500 toward the erection of a church, St. Peter's, spacious enough to seat seven hundred persons on the ground floor, and financially endowed to provide for a perpetual curate. The church left one known mark on May Sinclair's imagination, the family name of the perpetual curate, the Reverend Thomas Fisher Redhead, which she transferred to the heroine of *The Romantic*. Nathaniel Hawthorne, who was consul in Liverpool between 1853 and 1857, stayed four weeks at the Rock Ferry Hotel, which the estate owned, before moving into Rock Park on September 2, 1853, to occupy a furnished home there. He described the police station that had replaced the original porter's lodge at the entrance and the policemen who allowed "no ragged or ill-looking person to pass." The noiseless streets and the woody gardened seclusion of the estate made Rock Park "the quietest place imaginable."[6]

The bankruptcy of William Sinclair, which was not legally registered, must have occurred around 1870, when Mary Amelia was seven; it scattered the family among relatives and friends. Mother and daughter lived in Ilford, Essex, and in Fairford, Gloucestershire. William Sinclair's whereabouts at any particular time are difficult to trace. The Essex Court Directory for 1870 gave his address as Warley Road, Brentford; and from 1872 to 1882 as 5 Park Villas, Great Ilford; and in 1882 as 3 Ethell Villas, Idmiston Road, Forest Gate. The Gloucestershire Street Directory for 1879 listed him as a merchant and a private resident at Mount Pleasant, the villa in Fairford where he died on November 19, 1881.[7] The informant registered on his certificate of death was a Martha Mitchell, who died five years afterward at the age of seventy-one.[8] William Sinclair's death of hepatic cirrhosis, chronic nephritis, and exhaustion spells out the alcoholism that May Sinclair feared as a hereditary curse. Three sisters of the senior William Sinclair, Sarah, Mary, and Elizabeth, were living in the High Street of Saffron Walden, Essex, in 1895.

Florence Bartrop told me that the boys' mother encouraged them to regard themselves as entitled to all of the luxuries to which gentlemen were privileged. She must have had some private means that she sacrified to support their image. The oldest, William Sinclair, was listed in *Lloyd's Register of Yachts* for 1878 as being in business in Leadenhall Street, London, and owner of the yacht *Lilly*. He was listed again in 1882, now living in Hull, as owner of the yacht *Norah*. From

6. *Passages from the English Note Books*, Houghton Mifflin, 1879, p. 39.
7. I owe this information to P. F. A. Puttick, who searched these Directories; letters, February 1, March 3, 1961.
8. H. W. Hedges, resident in Mount Pleasant, Fairford, supplied the information about Martha Mitchell; letter, November 20, 1960.

1884 to 1891 he sailed two yachts, the *Torch* and the *Coralie;* from 1892 to 1895, only the *Coralie.* He was then a manager with the provisioners' firm of Finningley and Company, Hull. He died at Hull in 1896, aged forty-four, of aortic and mitral valvular disease of the heart and anasarca.

His brother Reginald was with Harold when the latter died at the age of twenty-eight, in 1887, at Gresford, in Denbighshire, of Bright's disease and cardiac disease. Reginald sailed the yacht *Nannie* in one known year, 1878, when his address was the Royal Northern Yacht Club, Glasgow. He died in 1891, aged thirty, of cardiac mitral disease, in the house at Brook Hill, Salcombe Regis, which May Sinclair had chosen after Cheltenham proved to have too raw a climate for him. He was buried in the churchyard of Saints Mary and Peter in Salcombe Regis, and his mother joined him there after her death in London on February 22, 1901. Mother and son are buried in a straight line, head to head, under a simple cross one yard high, without any inscription or epitaph of commitment other than their names and dates. May Sinclair ordered it so, and planted her mother's favorite flower, violets, on the grave.

Francis Edwin entered the Royal Military Academy, Woolwich, as a Gentleman Cadet on September 5, 1874, became a lieutenant in the Royal Artillery in India in 1877, and a captain in 1885. He died in Poona on April 18, 1889, in the fourth year of his second five-year tour of duty,[9] in the midst of an uproarious party in the officers' mess, from overstraining his heart in an impressive exhibition of his strength. All the boys, despite their weak hearts, were remembered by their relatives as show-offs in feats of daring and endurance on the water and on land.

Joseph was a volunteer in the first Boer War, served during the Basuto Rebellion, and emigrated to British Columbia, where he died in October, 1905.[10]

The Helpmate represents the marital relationship of May Sinclair's parents, the mother having been religiously antisensual, resisting her husband's natural affection, and the mother using her daughter to avenge herself upon her husband for the infidelity to which she drove him. *Mary Olivier* gives a warm account of May Sinclair's love for her six-years-older brother Frank, and of the tyranny her gentle mother,

9. J. O'Connor, Royal Artillery Institute, Woolwich, supplied the information on the career of Francis E. Sinclair; letter, May 16, 1960.
10. R. W. Sinclair wrote me about his father, Joseph Sinclair; letter, August 25, 1960.

whom her family named "the Lamb," exercised upon her daughter to keep her religiously orthodox, and femininely unintellectual and docile, a tyranny that provoked a stubborn and victorious resistance. A photograph taken in Cheltenham after her widowhood gives us Mrs. Sinclair's full face, sober, classically smooth, lips thin and pressed tightly together. Her ruche-edged widow's cap with a half-veil exposed a generously rounded tip of nose. Below the lips that were so tightly pressed together hung a man's strong chin. There was irony in the reversed allusion to the ancient rhyme, for it was Mary who followed the restless "Lamb." It was her mother's restlessness that caused the two to make so many moves, to Ilford, Wrexham, Fairford, Cheltenham. May Sinclair understood how her own sensitivity, in imagining the pain she caused her mother by resisting her religious rigidity, might betray her will to evolve into an independent self. Wherever they lived, their home was a setting for devotion, conflict, tension, gentility, pride, ambition, and near poverty, whatever fun the boys were having on their yachts. A young friend whom she met in Cornwall, the novelist G. B. Stern, wrote to her on June 15, 1919, about *Mary Olivier:* ". . . I hated little Mamma—hated her from the very first mention of her. I remembered you told me once you had a nervous breakdown because you tried to write in the same room with your own mother. . . . I remembered, too, in the brook-jumping part, how you had jumped the patches of rushes at St. Merryn, and told me you had always jumped like that with your brother. . . ."[11] Nevertheless, May Sinclair dedicated her first novel to her mother, and nursed her during her illnesses with an affection that was modified only by the realization that it was not her utmost, because she needed to hold something back for her writing.

Mary Olivier reveals something of the fear May Sinclair had that her heredity might overpower her will, and something of the shame the family felt over the father's drunkenness. *Life and Death of Harriett Frean* gives a fictional portrait of a father's hypnotic influence over his daughter that reads like an authentic memory, never explicitly confessed. Mr. Frean kissed his daughter with a "kiss-me-awake" goodnight kiss that made her a slave to his will. If the photographs of his sons William and Francis, and of his grandson Harold Lumley are any guide to the appearance of Mr. Sinclair, he must have been a very handsome man. He was a tyrant to his sons, demanding from them a Victorian father's tribute of reverence. He allowed no talking by the

---

11. Quoted by permission of G. B. Stern; letter, n.d.

boys at the dinner table. If any boy talked or even coughed, he was banished from the room. May Sinclair used to provoke her father out of sympathy for her brothers to make him send her from the table; and she always had a book that she was eager to return to.

A Journal of Impressions in Belgium derives May Sinclair's adult resistance to authority, religious and military, from her family experiences with repression: "My world was spoiled with too many ceremonies in my youth; ceremonies that lacked all beauty and sincerity and dignity."[12]

Deepest in its illumination of the shadows of her unhappiness with her family is a poem in *Essays in Verse,* which tells without reticence the harm a family does to a child through the divisions that exist between the parents, and between mother and child. Although the narrator is a man, his feelings are those of a woman.

> Father and mother had slowly grown,
> In the course of their married life, to dwell
> Each in a separate round from each,
> With narrow interests of its own,
> That on all the house the shadow fell,
> And I too came to live alone.[13]

> I—who have memories of thy face
> Stained with swift tears, of hair grown grey
> With petty griefs—my scorn were base
> To touch on weakness such as thine,
> Knowing that all thy narrow way
> Was barred with binding frost like mine;
> And crossed by one whose egotist mood
> Made half thy life a widowhood.[14]

What had caused the binding frost?

> Yet, mother, had your love been such
> That you had kept me by your side,
> And soothed me with the tender touch
> Of nursing hands; nor yet denied
> Of your sad heart—not all—not much,
> But just the little more than due,
> The little over and above
> The common debt between us two;
> My stubborn will had ne'er defied
> Thine, but given love for love.[15]

12. *A Journal of Impressions in Belgium* (New York: Macmillan, 1915), p. 32.
13. *Ibid.,* p. 52.
14. *Ibid.,* p. 51.
15. *Ibid.,* p. 50.

The psychic and physical separation of the parents is silently attested by the separate burials. No matter the poverty of mother and daughter in 1901. There were second cousins in Hull, and relatives in Ireland, and friends in London who would have paid the single fare of the passenger in the coffin, and the round-trip fare of the mourner, so that the second burial could have been beside the place of the first, wherever that had been—unless the wife had decided that the separation that had come before the first death should go on for all of time.

There is no record of any academic schooling that the boys underwent. Mary Amelia was tutored in piano. Her father was a man of books and had a good library in Elizabethan and Restoration literature, and in Victorian literature.[16] Somehow, Mary Amelia had taught herself German, Greek, and French before she arrived at the Cheltenham Ladies College in 1881. She had also read Shakespeare's comedies, Milton's *Lycidas* and *Paradise Lost,* Pope's *Iliad,* Smith's *Classical Dictionary,* Macaulay's *Lays of Ancient Rome, A Child's First History of Rome,* Pinnock's *Catechism of Mythology, Plutarch's Lives,* Pepys's *Diary,* Locke's *On the Human Understanding,* sections in the *Encyclopedia Britannica* on Spinoza and on pantheism, the Oxford Homer, Aeschylus, Sophocles, two volumes of Aristophanes, three volumes of Euripides, the Greek Testament, the Greek Anthology, Mosches, the Funeral Song from Bion, Allison's *History of Europe,* four volumes of Shelley, Plato in Bohn's Library, Hume's *Essays,* Kant's *Kritik.*[17]

Each novelist has his obsessive images and verbal compulsions. All through her creative writing there is one word that flares up out of May Sinclair's controlled volcano of emotion and that gives away the sense of strain she felt as a girl and as a young woman; it is the word *unbearable.* For a considerable part of her writing life, as *Mary Olivier* lets us see so plainly, she relived her experiences with the members of her family, and her anxiety lest she discover in herself the hereditary traits that would be unbearable to cope with: alcoholism, sensuality, heart disease. Of the formal schooling that, had it been sound, ordinarily would have helped her to identify, organize, and maneuver such traits as it would have brought to light, she had none. But her single year of informal study at Cheltenham Ladies College brought her the guidance of one of the most admired educators in England. It was Dorothea Beale who gave her the confidence to endure what she had feared until then would prove "unbearable."

16. Richard Aldington; letter, February 17, 1960.
17. Based on a copy made in May Sinclair's handwriting of a letter she wrote to her French translator and critic, Marc Logé, in which she listed the chapters and sections of the novel *Mary Olivier* that are true to life.

3

With Dorothea Beale
at the Cheltenham Ladies College

When May Sinclair came to the churchlike Gothic Renaissance edifice of Cheltenham Ladies College in the fall of 1881, she was eighteen, the usual leaving age, and the Principal, Miss Dorothea Beale, was fifty.

Miss Beale was born into a wealthy family, and until she was thirteen, governesses taught her. Thereafter she managed her own education, sharing lessons in the classics with her brothers. She then spent a year at an English school in Paris until the revolution drove her home early in 1848. She registered at Queen's College in London when it opened in March, 1848, and a year later she became its first lady tutor in mathematics. In 1854 she taught Latin there. She crossed the path of the Brontës when she became head teacher of the Clergy Daughters' School at Casterton. When she was twenty-seven, in 1858, she was elected Principal of the Cheltenham Ladies College, which had opened in 1853.

There were similarities that were to account for the lifelong influence Dorothea Beale exerted on her brilliant special student. A brother to whom she was deeply attached went to India, although as a missionary of Christ, not of the Empire. She read Latin, Greek, and German easily, and was particularly proficient in German. Only in her intense and professed religious faith did Miss Beale differ from, and with, her pupil. She accepted her family's religion as an embrace of the love she knew was real; Mary Amelia resisted the pressure of a faith urged without love and affecting her like a clamp crippling her aggressive mind. It was the unthinking pressure she resisted, rather than the faith.

Miss Beale was dedicated to duty, and to the particular duty of helping others attain their fullest spiritual growth. She believed the will to be the secret power of the discipline that effects the fullest self-realization, and believed in the rule of silence as the best method of letting the will grow strong by protecting it from distraction. In the morning, the girls of the college might have a twenty-minute period of free communication with each other, but thereafter they might not converse without the permission of a teacher. No talking was allowed in the bedrooms of the pupils' boarding houses.

Miss Beale believed that education was a means to moral training, not for social, material, or intellectual distinction. She allowed no hero-worship of any sort within the school. She did not abolish the custom of giving prizes for the best midsummer examinations, but deprived their winners of all public display, and made them call at the Secretary's office for their awards. She allowed no applause at their concert performances, because she felt that the girls had not developed a refined enough discrimination to render a sound judgment.

She was generous in helping girls to an education, and instituted scholarships to the needy; but she wanted it understood that the help was given to encourage intellectual distinction and not to recognize an intellectual elite. She despised what she called "the modern slavetrade in so-called scholarships . . . the buying up of clever children by rival schools."[1] She thought those who needed help should have the grace and frankness to admit their need. She answered the plea that to be compelled to admit poverty was to be condemned to a trauma by saying, "I think if people are ashamed of being poor, they ought to be ashamed of being ashamed of it."[2]

Her inner life was an intense dedication to God. Every year, from 1877 on, she went into retreat. During the year of Mary Amelia's residence at the college, Miss Beale underwent a long, dark night of anguish over the death of her loving and dearly loved mother.[3] Her good sense in confessing her despair to a sympathetic clergyman led to her recovering her faith and her sanity. The submerged volcano of emotion that was a pure need to love helped her to understand Mary Amelia, and so to win a strong influence over her.

As an educator, she was a proponent, not an agitator, for the education of women. When she testified before the Royal Commission on Education in the 1860s, she argued only for equal opportunities for

1. Josephine Kamm, *How Different From Us* (London: The Bodley Head, 1958), p. 220.
2. *Ibid.*, p. 221
3. Elizabeth Raikes, *Dorothea Beale of Cheltenham* (London: Archibald Constable, 1908), pp. 180–86.

women as women. She was a model for May Sinclair in being feminine rather than feminist.

Miss Beale's regular teaching fields were history, English literature, German, and the Scriptures. During Mary Amelia's year she taught only the Scriptures, in the Library. The prospectus listing the subjects available to regular and special students from 1881 to 1882 was headed, as had been the first prospectus in 1853, by the Holy Scriptures. Other regular subjects were history, literature, English language, geography, arithmetic, geometry, algebra, natural science, physics, physiology, chemistry, French, German, Latin, Greek, and calisthenics. The optional subjects, for extra fees, were music, singing, dancing, drawing, and painting. There was a staff of fifty-six regular teachers. In addition, there were fifteen teachers of music and four teachers of drawing and painting. The girls chose their mistresses in most subjects. Among the regular teachers of modern languages, the girls could choose from among four teachers of French and four teachers of German. University professors from Oxford and St. Andrews, and other authorities in special fields gave single or a series of lectures.[4]

In her year as a student, Mary Amelia lived probably in Miss Draper's boarding house, where she had, like all the other girls, a room to herself. A member of Mrs. Brady's house, at 21 Royal Parade, Base Hill, remembered her as "a nice-looking girl with dark hair." After breakfast, the girls marched to the college, two by two, and once inside the entrance, divided to enter their respective division halls, of which there were three, classified by age groups. The oldest girls, those fifteen and over, entered the First Division hall, where Miss Beale was seated on a sort of throne on the platform, dressed in a long, black dress and a black lace cap, awaiting the girls, to preside over the service of prayers. As each girl entered, and again when she left, she bowed to the awesome figure in black. Instruction began at nine-fifteen.

When the girls left the college at one o'clock, mistresses paraded outside to make sure that each girl wore her gloves. The boarding girls marched back to their houses, and the day girls went home. No day girls were permitted to walk together unless the parents of each girl were known to the parents of the other girls.

In the afternoon the girls who had kept up a satisfactory standing in their classwork were free to engage in their favorite sports or to

---

4. The Prospectus of the college, copies of all publications by May Sinclair in the *Cheltenham Ladies College Magazine,* and copies of all letters from Miss Beale to May Sinclair and from May Sinclair to Miss Beale were presented to me by Miss V. M. Hounsfield, the librarian of Cheltenham Ladies College, and by Miss J. A. Tredfold, the principal.

take their drawing or music lessons. For those students who had not done an assignment well enough, the afternoon was the time when they reported to their class mistresses with their failed essays for special instruction. If they were seniors, their appointments were with Miss Beale. The individual afternoon sessions over "failed" essays were called "returns."

The chief indoor sport at Mrs. Brady's house was toasting buttered bread over the smoky hall fire in the evening. Mrs. Dorothy Scott remembered the enchanting fragrance of the buttered toast of that tranquil evening time, nearly eighty years afterward.

On Sundays the girls attended services at Christ Church, along with the boys of Cheltenham College, who sat on the opposite side of the aisle. Sleight of hand during the seating movements made romantic messages quite possible.

College records were based upon the results of examinations, and because Mary Amelia was a special student, there is no record beyond that of her presence in that one year.[5]

We may imagine that one of the incentives that brought Mary Amelia to the college was the hope of a warranty by a discerning judge of the talents she suspected she had. Miss Beale gave her the sweet assurance that she could think and write lucidly; but she could not grant a desire that was nearly as strong as her hope: to be fully liberated from her mother's religious orthodoxy.

The Principal wrote regularly to the family of each girl, and kept the correspondence confidential. When a girl happened to speak about any friends of hers to her house mistress, or to her teacher, or to Miss Beale, she was immediately asked, "Do your parents know her?" or him, or them. The girls had to report to their class mistress the girls whose parents they knew. Girls of different classes were not allowed to converse with each other unless the parents of the girls were known to each other. So, without giving any orders, Miss Beale taught each girl her duty to conform to her family's wishes and standards, and Miss Beale's confidential communication with the families made her intimately aware of what each family's wishes and standards were. Her exchange of letters with the orthodoxly religious Mrs. Sinclair made any encouragement of an overt rebellion on

5. The account of life at the college in May Sinclair's time was drawn from a letter, July 29, 1959; from an interview with Mrs. Dorothy Scott, of Barnlands, Lindfield, Sussex, on a Saturday afternoon in the summer of 1959; and from a letter of Mrs. Winifred King, of Prestbury, near Cheltenham, March 25, 1960. The secretary of the Guild of Cheltenham Ladies College, Miss Mary Sager, gave me the addresses of the two ladies. Mrs. Scott's neighbor, Mrs. James C. Low, made the interview possible. Also, Kamm, *How Different From Us,* and Raikes, *Dorothea Beale.*

Mary Amelia's part unthinkable. But Miss Beale could guide her in good conscience to read deeply in English and German philosophy so that she might form for herself a rational and therefore acceptable concept of reality that would have the discovery of God as its climax. So she carefully guided Mary Amelia's intellect to make of philosophical Idealism both a discipline for resisting dogma and a mirror for refracting the light of God, and directed her steps onto the course that eventually brought her to the rostrum of the Aristotelian Society. It is true, as May Sinclair later acknowledged, that Dorothea Beale encouraged her to write, but only on philosophical subjects.

Miss Beale was an awesome figure at a distance and as she swept her Victorian skirt over the floor of the corridor and the classroom, but it would be a pity to miss a closer view and the softer lines. She was a keen reader of her pupils' faces, and a remarkably accurate diagnostician of their personalities and their moral faults, usually gentle, and only occasionally caustic in treating each girl as an individual. As a critic of the senior girls who came to her for their "return" appointments or their special papers, she probed tactfully, and then she analyzed the difficulty and taught with memorable thoroughness the lesson that the girl had failed or needed to focus more sharply. She gave exactly the appropriate encouragement to strengthen incentive and to improve performance. But to a girl like Mrs. Dorothy Scott, who was at Cheltenham from 1880 to 1884, pleasure-loving, not interested in any career, the happy-tempered prospective mate of an army officer who served in India, Miss Beale was sympathetic, prescribing no rule of conduct to curb her happiness, inflicting no feelings of guilt upon her for not conforming to her own ideal of a career of service to society. Mrs. Scott was given the freedom to be her own unserious, happy self.

It must have been an event of glory to student Mary Amelia to have had an essay of hers printed in the magazine that Miss Beale edited, the *Cheltenham Ladies College Magazine,* as respectable in its heavy, sand-gray covers as any distinguished quarterly in England, and priced at an impressive two shillings a copy.[6] The essay was one of a series of three student papers that were given the inclusive title, "Short Notes of Professor Knight's Lectures on Philosophy." Mary Amelia's paper, "Descartes," was her report of the lectures that Professor William Angus Knight, Professor of Moral Philosophy at St. Andrews University, had given at the college.

Written with a most unusual schoolgirl's intellectual maturity, the

6. "Descartes," *Cheltenham Ladies College Magazine* no. 5 (Spring, 1882) .

essay tells us that already, at age eighteen, she comprehended experience to be an engagement of consciousness rather than an effect of stimulating the senses. She already believed that it was wiser to discipline the self rather than the environment; that it was a moral duty to accept nothing as true that the self did not positively know to be true; and that the student of life must start his study by understanding the instrument, his mind, with which he resolved the experiences of which he became conscious. She showed an awareness of the crucial question: What is the test of reality? She appreciated the difficulty of solving the relationship between man's ideas and the reality for which they stand; the need for establishing a significant subject-object relationship; the choice of alternative paths the mind could travel, reason and intuition, to arrive at a conclusion about the existence of God. The end of the essay praises Kant for having shown that theoretical reason is inadequate and intuition ample, to provide proof for the existence of God. Her very last sentence is not yet out of date: "The problem of the actual nature of mind and matter and of their mutual dependency, remained to puzzle philosophers, and to furnish ever new subject for speculation."

Miss Beale's own writings let us study at leisure the influence of her mind upon Mary Amelia's. Miss Beale declared her own intense religious fervor, accepted Kant's idealism, and approved of Herbart's modification of Kant. Kant described the ego as the furnisher of ideas from sense dicta; Herbart added the concept that the moral self is important because, by apperception, it converts sensation into subjective form. Miss Beale believed that philosophy, psychology, and religion branched from the same root, and that the old empiricism was on the wane.

Miss Beale conceived a school to be a temple for the worship, exercise, and development of the soul, and conceived its teachers as forming a priesthood trained in psychology, "that marvellous instrument, from which it is ours to draw forth heavenly harmonies."[7] She believed that the common good of the democratic ideal is secured when each individual life is developed to the highest perfection. She recommended the teaching of French and German, and of Greek over Latin. History gives training in the habits of justice and truthfulness, in

---

7. "Preface," *Work and Play in the Girls' Schools* p. vii. The Preface and Section One of *Work and Play in Girls' Schools*, by Three Head Mistresses, Dorothea Beale, Lucy H. M. Soulsby, and Jane Frances Dove (London: Longmans, 1898), were written by Dorothea Beale. Dorothea Beale also wrote the preface to *The Application of Psychology to the Science of Education*, by Johann Friedrich Herbart, whose translation (New York: Scribner, 1891) was by Beatrice C. Mulliner, lecturer at the college. These works have been the sources of my account of Miss Beale's pedagogical principles and methods.

looking for factual corrections to emotionally prompted imbalances of judgment. She saw science as knowledge of a thing or an act known objectively, and the humanities as knowledge known subjectively by personal sympathy.

Mary Amelia had one battle with Miss Beale over the writing of an essay on God. Her excuse for refusing to write it was that she could not finish it by the assigned date. Her real reason was the compulsory nature of the task, the requirement to make a submission that she had not yet evolved out of her own thinking and volition. It was like the battles she had had with her mother. Miss Beale still held the anthropomorphic concept of God, which Mary Amelia's mother had tried to inculcate in her, and that the daughter would not accept without proof. The pupil's defiance did not lodge any resentment in Miss Beale, and may even have influenced her conceptualizing of God. She was to offer her pupil a lectureship at the College in philosophy, not in the Scriptures; but by that time the care of her mother and her career as a novelist occupied May Sinclair's days too fully for any time to be left over for teaching.[8]

The year at Cheltenham from 1881 to 1882 strongly urged May Sinclair's mind forward in its studies of philosophy, psychology, and Greek literature, and helped mold her temperament to honor the precepts of love and surrender to duty, first to the duty she owed her family, and then to the duty she owed the world, to be of service to humanity. Miss Beale had taught her, "One must be prepared to pay rent for his room on earth."[9]

Miss Beale kept in touch with her pupil by correspondence and through May Sinclair's visits to Cheltenham. In December, 1886, Miss Beale wrote to discourage her from reading Spinoza, and to oppose her velleity to adopt agnosticism as a means of circumventing unsolvable problems. She recommended the reading of Martineau's *Types of Ethical History* and Green's *Prolegomena to Ethics*.[10] In January, 1887, she again urged her pupil to read Green's *Prolegomena*, to help her see the unity underlying all possibility of knowledge. She outlined the pattern that May Sinclair was years later to trace in her metaphysics of Idealism and in her novel, *Mary Olivier*. In the same letter Miss Beale supplied a term that May Sinclair was to revive in a very different context after thirty-five years of metaphysical and psychological study and thought. Miss Beale wrote, "There is the unity of consciousness which makes memory possible, and moral judgment pos-

8. Letter, Mrs. Wilda St. Clair McNeile, June 16, 1959.
9. Kamm, *How Different From Us*, p. 228.
10. Raikes, *Dorothea Beale*, p. 389.

sible; and yet there is a secondary consciousness, the 'categorical imperative,' the ideal goodness, ever revealing to man a higher and better."[11]

Miss Beale wrote in January, 1892, to pass along the compliment that the Bishop of Gloucester had paid to a poem about Goethe that had been printed in the *Cheltenham Ladies College Magazine* in the autumn of 1891, and advised her to send the bishop a copy of *Essays in Verse,* in which that and a second poem on Goethe were included.[12]

In December, 1893, Miss Beale wrote of her delight over May Sinclair's essay in the *New World,* "The Ethical and Religious Import of Idealism," in which the author had made use of the reading that Miss Beale had recommended. She asked, "Did I tell you I lunched with Jowett tête-à-tête not long before his death?"[13] May Sinclair celebrated that meeting with two sonnets in memory of Professor Jowett; they appeared in the *Cheltenham Ladies College Magazine* in the spring of 1894. Miss Beale sent her a copy of Mary Pulling's *The Teacher's Text Book of Practical Psychology,* and May Sinclair wrote a brilliant review of it that appeared in the spring, 1896, number of *Cheltenham Ladies College Magazine.*

Some time in 1896 Miss Beale reassured the poverty-pinched and yet anxiously sympathetic May Sinclair, who had written to apologize for being unable to send a contribution to the College Guild, which Miss Beale had founded in 1890 for old pupils as an organization to sponsor social welfare: "You *ought not* to give anything. I am sorry even that the notice was sent you."[14]

In January, 1897, Miss Beale faintly praised a romantic short story, "Not Made in Germany," published that month in *Macmillan's Magazine.* She advised against any further dissipating of her talents, but also confessed her pleasure over the serious mood of her pupil's first published novel, *Audrey Craven.*[15] She helped her pupil by writing a review of the novel and obtaining a second, very perceptive review written by a teacher of English literature at the College, Amy Lumby, for the autumn, 1897, number of the *Cheltenham Ladies College Magazine.*

An undated letter strongly pleaded with May Sinclair not to let herself be diverted altogether from philosophical study. Miss Beale's aforementioned letter of December, 1886, expressed her last plea pressing religious orthodoxy upon her pupil; thereafter she argued in

11. *Ibid.,* p. 391.
12. *Ibid.,* p. 392.
13. *Ibid.*
14. *Ibid.,* p. 393.
15. *Ibid.*

purely metaphysical terms. Perhaps the firmness with which her pupil resisted her efforts to prepose the orthodox image of a manlike God for worship had something to do with effecting a change in the teacher's concept. At any rate, Miss Beale had given up her belief in the resurrection of the body when she wrote her will, in which she ordered that her body be cremated. Her ashes found rest in the Lady Chapel of Gloucester Cathedral.

Forty years later, May Sinclair's body was cremated at Golders Green Cemetery. Her ashes were placed in Hampstead churchyard.

4

The Eighteen-eighties: First Poems

Mary Amelia was at the College when her father, separated from the family, died in Fairford on November 19, 1881. She left in the late summer of 1882, strengthened by her friendship with Miss Beale, but with only her talent and her resolution to carry her forward to her first ambition: to be a poet. Where she lived with her mother can only be hazarded by occasional hints. She said that she and her mother lived in Fairford, presumably in the house where her father had died, Mount Pleasant. Her niece Wilda visited Aunt Mary May and her mother in 1886 somewhere in Cheshire.[1] She nursed her brother Harold in Gresford, Denbighshire, before he died on August 28, 1887.

She published her first book, a book of poems, in 1886: *Nakiketa and other Poems,* and hid herself under the effectively masking pseudonym of "Julian Sinclair," pretending to be a man. The volume of eighty pages contains three long narrative poems and six short poems. Her friend, C. A. Dawson, wrote that she sent a copy to the prime minister, and that Mr. Gladstone wrote her a card to assure her that he was "sensible of the merits" of the poems.[2]

In its somber pages, her art tried to shape feelings to music, and her intellect searched both for the authority to justify her agnosticism and for some kind of reconciliation between the Greek worship of vitality and the Eastern worship of death. The *Katha Upanishad* obviously inspired the title poem and its theme: the search for God in death. The longest poem in the volume, "Helen," six hundred lines in blank verse of iambic pentameter, is a realistic narrative about a loveless and failed marriage. The husband, Emile, a superficially clever person who turns cruel when he fails in business, is a first sketch of

1. Letter, Wilda McNeile, June 16, 1959.
2. *London Bookman,* October, 1920, pp. 7–9.

the Maurice Jourdain who appears in the novel *Mary Olivier*. The emphasized traits in the character of the wife, Helen, are her capacity for love, her swift aptness for learning, and the strength of her will in suppressing love for another suitor, from a sense of the higher good of her duty to her fiancé and husband:

> for I know
> That love is not the whole of woman's life,
> Nor yet of man's, but there are higher things—
> Devotion—honour—faith—self-sacrifice.[3]

The finest poem in the volume is an ode to "George Eliot." The last poem, "Christapollo—In Memorian Percy Bysshe Shelley," suggests the antinomic breadth of May Sinclair herself. It lauds Shelley for challenging

> all sceptered ignorance,
> All mitred falsehood, crowned hate
> Whate'er. . . .[4]

and for revering the greatest while remembering the best, for waking love in the loveless and hope in the despairing.

The volume was launched upon the literary pool of 1886 without stirring a ripple in current literary records.

In 1889 the autumn number of the *Cheltenham Ladies College Magazine* contained "A Custance of Today," a lyric of 112 lines, in rhyme, whose theme is the poet's fear that her potential gifts might never be fulfilled because she was sacrificing her life—"oh, death in life!"—for the sake of others, and her resignation to the fact of nature that the unfulfillment of one creature is a stage in the natural progress toward a greater fulfillment of a greater creature.

A lyric published in *Essays in Verse*, in 1892, but dated November, 1889, hopes for sympathy for a poet's misery of heart: "This death-in-life of pain." Again it rises to an acceptance of sorrow as a preface to better things: "Were there no sleep, would there be wakening?"

The poems of this decade, which have merit as music and for their skillful variations of rhythm without disturbance to the rhythmic flow, mean most for us as they tell us about May Sinclair's straining to form some kind of religious belief, even in self-destruction, struggling her utmost to fulfill the duty that she acknowledged she owed her family, and carrying on with assertions of hope for the creative self against the waves of despair, the urgings to surrender.

---

3. *Ibid.*, p. 37.
4. *Ibid.*, p. 79.

5

The Eighteen-nineties:
From Poet to Novelist

The 1890s were for May Sinclair a twisting maze that she entered blindly as a poet and from which she came out as an exceptionally open-eyed novelist. At the beginning, there was a great advance in quality, but no abrupt break from the 1880s in her lyrical and philosophical verse, until she tried verse drama, at the start of which she was rather heavy-footed, but in which she soon became ethereally light in her music and movement. She worked hard at philosophy and psychology, and at the translations from the German that helped her support her mother and herself. She then tried short stories, a character sketch, and a long story; and she signaled her escape from the maze as a novelist by publishing in 1897 *Audrey Craven,* and in 1898 *Mr. and Mrs. Nevill Tyson.*

Essays in Verse

The first address we have for May Sinclair in this decade, dated July, 1890, is 6 Royal Parade, Cheltenham, her address when she was elected to membership in the Guild of Old Students.[1] Former students proposed, members of the staff seconded, and the Principal passed the approval that constituted election. Each member was required to send an annual report describing what useful work in life she was undertaking. Austere housekeeping forbade these reports being kept for biographers. This formal tie with her old school was a sign of her beginning to weave herself into the fabric of literary history after her

1. Letter, Miss V. M. Hounsfield, April 1, 1960.

family had pulled her away from the fabric of society. The climate of Cheltenham proved too harsh for Reginald, who had left Gresford with his mother and sister after Harold's death. In the same year, May Sinclair found a house on Brook Hill,. in Salcombe Regis, an agricultural parish about five hundred feet above sea level, reached from Sidmouth by a steep road that runs east by north for some two miles and ends in red sandstone cliffs. Its church, of Saints Mary and Peter, is Norman. It had never held either a public house or a dissenting chapel inside its boundaries.[2] Her niece Wilda remembered visiting her there in 1890, and the long, two-storied thatched house in which the Sinclairs had lived.[3] It was called "The Quest,[4] and was still standing in 1964.[5] Reginald died there on January 31, 1891.

Through her association with Miss Beale she made the first of five important friends who were to help her find herself in the critical 1890s: Janet Elizabeth Hogarth, who was to marry in 1911 her former teacher at Oxford, the editor of the *Fortnightly Review*, W. L. Courtney. On the basis of her having won a First Class in Philosophy at Oxford in the Honors Examination, Janet Hogarth was appointed a part-time teacher of Greek at Cheltenham Ladies College from 1889 to 1890.[6] It must have been that year that Janet Hogarth remembered when she told in her autobiography, *Recollected in Tranquillity,* published in 1926, how she and May Sinclair spelled out *The Phaedo* and *The Apology* while lessons on every sort of subject went on around them.[7] In a later book, *The Women of My Time,* published in 1934, she said that when she met her at Cheltenham, May Sinclair had two loves, Goethe and Plato. She visited May Sinclair later at Salcombe Regis, where her host vaulted lightly over stiles, read voraciously, and turned scenes from Goethe's life into verse.[8]

The poetry she wrote in the new decade was better than that she had written before. *Essays in Verse,* a volume of eighty-six pages, dated 1891, published in January, 1892, bore the confident signature of May Sinclair, and its contents tell us that the poet had entered a new stage of energetic inquiry, profound examination and resolution, toward

---

2. *Deacon's Court Guide Gazeteer and County Blue Book; White's Devonshire Directory; Kelly's Directory of Devon and Cornwall.*
3. Letter, Wilda McNeile, June 16, 1959.
4. Harold Lumley Sinclair.
5. Found and painted by Mrs. P. F. T. Puttick. The house is the one appearing in a photograph in the *Book News Monthly,* February, 1908.
6. Letter, Miss Mary Sager, Guild Clerk, January 1, 1963.
7. Janet Hogarth Courtney, *Recollected in Tranquillity* (London: Heinemann, 1926), pp. 117–18.
8. *The Women of My Time* (London: Lovat Dickson, 1934), p. 52. Miss Laura Price called both of these books by Janet Hogarth Courtney to my attention; letter, September 4, 1962.

the subjects that meant most to her: religious faith, the discovery and use of the self, and the mystery of the creative process. "Guyon, a Philosophical Dialogue," is a lively and lightly handled Platonic dialogue in blank verse, twenty pages long, prefaced by two epigraphs, one from Parmenides, and another from the Upanishads. It gives us a segmented survey of the philosophy that May Sinclair was compounding out of the sources of Greek, Buddhist, German, and English Idealism that were her reading, and out of the Christian orthodoxy that Miss Beale and her mother had taught her. The five Oxford classmates who hold a reunion seven years after leaving the university, talk about reason and faith, good and evil, sense and reality, the individual self and the universal self; and the partial resolution of their differences is very much like the thesis that May Sinclair offered the following year in the sober, restrained prose of her article on "The Ethical and Religious Import of Idealism." Guyon, the writer, most nearly embodies May Sinclair's resolved and organized thinking.

"Margery" contains a good deal of what Disraeli called "psychological autobiography" in its confession of the poet's (a man) unhappiness at home, his self-doubt over his reality, and the solution of his doubt, a surrender of the self to become one with the universal all.

The best whole poems in the volume, "Two Studies from the Life of Goethe"—the first, 270 pentameter lines in blank verse, the second, only 120 lines—reveal, with the beauty of disciplined music, Goethe's original rapture of absorbed love, the subsequent play of his critical intellect upon the laden self, his standards of artistic beauty, his belief in his right to strive for the complete fulfillment of his creative genius, and Frederica's gratitude for the quickening of her life, which Goethe's love and patience had made possible.

Essays in Verse caught the notice of London reviewers. On June 11, 1892, the *Academy* found "Guyon" to be decidedly clever, the two poems on Goethe of dramatic intensity, and "Margery" "full of eloquent, passionate, and musical writing" worthy of being compared to "Maud." The *Spectator,* a year later, on July 29, 1893, lamented the author's having chosen metaphysical and philosophical thought as her subject, and found the verse to be "decidedly meritorious" but "wanting the charm which would attract." The sickly critic had a sure jugular touch, as he showed by quoting twenty of the weakest lines in "Margery," confessing the author's self-doubting phase. Two lines will sample the critic's skill in bloodletting:

> Though all the truth shine clear within my mind—
> Myself still subject to a mastering doubt.

Anthony Charles Deane: "The Friendly Critic"

The one person responsible for May Sinclair's conversion from a poet to a novelist, Anthony Charles Deane, was a name unknown to her family, a name never mentioned to the many interviewers who used every technique of interrogation they were equipped with by instinct and by experience to tear off the veil covering the eternal mystery of what causes genius to flower. It was a name May Sinclair never mentioned to her companion for twenty-seven and more years, Florence Bartrop. The sixty-nine letters from him that she kept in their order for over fifty years are well worth reprinting in full some day for the story they tell, a story Deane did not hint at in his autobiography, *Time Remembered,* which was published in 1945, a year before his death, which occurred the same year in which his protégée died.

The son of a successful barrister, Anthony Charles Deane attended Wellington College, which was also Stephen Hudson's school, when the Reverend E. C. Wickham was master, and entered Clare College, Cambridge, in 1889. He had wanted to read for honors in the Classical Tripos, but instruction in the classics at Clare was so dessicated that he chose instead to read law. His real ambition was to learn to write and speak well. He became an editor of *Granta,* and in his third year at Cambridge he published a volume, *Frivolous Verse,* which Andrew Lang praised in a whole leading article in the London *Daily News.* Lang recommended him to the editor of *Punch,* Francis Burnand, and after only a month of contributing verse, Deane became a regular member of the outside staff and sent his verse directly to the printer, an arrangement that lasted during the whole fifteen years that Deane wrote for *Punch.*

At Cambridge, Deane reacted to the intellectual atmosphere of aggressive agnosticism by deciding to discover for himself if Christianity is true or false by the most thorough examination of the evidence. In the second term of his third year, that is, in 1892, a profound spiritual experience, which he acknowledged without describing in his autobiography, convinced him that he had a calling for Holy Orders. This experience I place during his early acquaintance with May Sinclair.

As tenants of The Quest in Salcombe Regis, the Sinclairs were not even listed in *Lethaby's Sidmouth Journal and Directory,* the *Sidmouth Directory and General Advertiser,* or in *Deacon's, White's,* or *Kelly's* gazetteers and directories, which included Salcombe Regis.[9] They be-

---

9. Mr. P. W. W. Ninnes, Director of the Sidmouth Museum, kindly made all the materials available to me.

came important enough for official notice only when the Salcombe Regis Parish Register was opened so that the vicar could record the burials of two members of the family, each four days after death. The Reverend W. J. Baugh, the vicar, held the services over the body of Reginald on February 4, 1891, and a relative of Mrs. William Sinclair, the Reverend William Hind, held the services at her funeral ten years later, on February 26, 1901.[10]

The Deanes were long-time summer residents of the town of Sidmouth, and somehow became friends with Mrs. Sinclair and her daughter. Mrs. Deane had studied the piano with Sir Charles Hallé and other teachers. The first of the surviving letters of Anthony Deane, dated January 1, 1893, is so intimate in all its tones of communication, so obviously in the high tide of friendship as to imply a long preliminary period of progressively closer understanding, but wholly free from any explicit romantic tenderness. If the disturbing experience of 1892 that Anthony Deane alluded to—the experience that turned him from the law to theology—had at its root an episode of tempting passion, the woman who most plausibly might have excited it would have been the emotionally intense, love-and-friendship craving, and perfectly disciplined May Sinclair. Any letter of his written in the course of any purely conjectured episode of passionate madness, she would have destroyed with the same perfect discreetness with which she must have destroyed, years later, the letters of Charlotte Mew.[11]

Anthony was nine years the younger, but May looked much more youthful than her years. From the beginning the letters revived their talk about philosophy, religion, and literature. It was a mutually stimulating friendship between a very gifted and socially self-possessed young university student and graduate and a woman who hoped some day to be able to make a living beyond poverty for herself and her mother, in spite of being buried away, unlisted, in a South Devon summer resort all the year round. Perhaps intuition told her that Anthony Deane was destined to help her find her way into the world's view. He had all the qualities that her genius needed to become an independent traveler to the so very different real world outside the cocoon world of her imagination. He was such a man as she could love, and must have loved, from sheer joy in finding a companion and a complement to her laboriously evolving and desperately unfulfilled self. His mind was orderly, lucid, calm, subject now to the

---

10. Salcombe Regis Parish Register, Bishop's Transcript. Transcribed for me by the Rev. H. B. Clark.
11. See New York Public Library, "The Mystery of Charlotte Mew and May Sinclair: An Inquiry," *Bulletin* vol. 74, no. 7 (September, 1970).

instant control of his will. Some instinct made him see her as the rare material for his rare, creative criticism. He was a George Henry Lewes inspiring a Mary Ann Evans. He probed with instant accuracy into her mind and moods, and what his insight saw forced him to feel responsible for shaping her rare potential with his practical outlook and intelligent and balanced temperament.

The qualities that he employed to advance her he applied as well to his own advancement. After he chose the Church as the field of his career, he made only one exception to his closing all outlets of emotion that might tempt him into competitive channels of exploration: the one exception was May Sinclair. He managed his life with the single purpose of becoming an entertaining writer and an eloquent clergyman in the active service of Christianity. Toward May Sinclair he was a patient, thorough, tactful critic of her verse, an intelligent counselor in guiding her to understand herself and to turn her involuted personality outward so that she could free her creativeness to face and address a real social world. He was a generous, even a devoted middleman who helped market her not conspicuously attractive early literary wares. He taught her to prepare her art for the marketplace in the very act of creating.

In that first letter, a very long one, he agreed with her that it was impossible to write fiction before age thirty. On October 21, 1893, he offered to send any of her verses to Andrew Lang for *Longman's Magazine*. He advised against writing blank verse and to try something *leviore plecto*. He read her *Essays in Verse* and thought that "Your Muse looks at things rather too exclusively from the subjective standpoint, perhaps?" On October 25, he wrote to her that he had forwarded her verses on Jowett to George Bentley, at the *Temple Bar*. He kept sending a poem, "Song," to periodical after periodical until *Pall Mall Magazine* printed it in March, 1895. He sent a poem, "Sonnet," to the *Cambridge Review,* for which he wrote, and in which it appeared on November 23, 1893.

He kept up his patient analyses of her verses. On October 30, he advised her to look for ideas in nature, outside of herself. "Introspection is like opium-eating, both in its growing fascination, and in its deadening effect upon the mind, if overmuch indulged in." He recommended that she get hold of Richard Jefferies's *Life of the Fields.*

On December 21, 1893, Anthony Deane was ordained at Chichester by Bishop Durnford. The realistic shrewdness that he tried to inculcate in May Sinclair he practised in answering the examination questions that the bishop's chaplains had prepared. One question set up a violently ringing alarm in the young man's brain: "What do you mean by sacerdotalism?" Deane knew that one of the examiners was advanced, and the other was an Evangelical who distrusted all men of Cuddesden—Deane's college—as papists. To steer safely between the two opposing chaplains, he gave two separate answers to the question, each satisfying one of the extremists, and then added the note, "Both the above views are sincerely held, and it seems impossible to combine them in one answer." Immediately after 'he was ordained, he took up his first curacy in the rural village of Barcombe, near Lewes, in Sussex.[12]

On January 20, 1894, he asked her to let him see the result of her trying a "Turnover," like the one he had sent her, a light familiar essay or descriptive sketch, which occupied the last column on the first page and about a third of the first column on the second page of the London *Globe*. Deane could turn one out as cleanly and effortlessly as he turned out verses for *Punch*.

In a very long letter written February 5, Deane, among other matters, described Christianity as "a mode of life rather than a mode of thought," a statement we should recall when we come to the novel *The Rector of Wyck*.

"Decadence," a verse sequence of five monologic stanzas, appeared in the *Academy* in March, 1894, in a form superior to that which Deane had seen before he had begun to suggest improvements, every one of which May Sinclair accepted.

While the sensitive counseling of Anthony Deane was sharpening May Sinclair's critical focus on her verse, her restless creativeness was trying the broader keyboard of drama in verse. Deane referred in a number of letters to the play that she was engaged in writing. Finally, on February 15, 1894, he wrote to her that he had received the play. He returned it with his analysis on February 21, and on March 1 answered the defense she had put up against his criticism.

The new medium of verse drama, which May Sinclair added in 1893 to her lyrical and reflective verse writing marked an advance toward her eventual fulfillment as a novelist, because it forced her to think in narrative patterns of personal involvements. She must have considered the move at least a sign of growth, or she would not have recorded her conviction, in *The Divine Fire,* that a poet must pass from lyrical to dramatic poetry if he is to mature.

The play that Deane read was *A Debt of Honour: A Tragedy in Three Acts,* in blank verse. It exists in a manuscript of one hundred blank-book pages. *A Debt of Honour* dramatizes certain thoughts that

---

12. *Time Remembered* (London :Faber and Faber, 1945) , pp. 69-70.

May Sinclair had already expressed in her verses: the determination to give up the writing of poetry and to dedicate her life to helping the underprivileged urban masses; a belief in the essential identity of the noumenal reality and its phenomenal form; and a creed of enduring loyalty to an unresponsive beloved. But the play is naïvely feeble in its characterization, in its grasp on the practical matter of using a stage for representing life, and even on the complexities of motivation, the last being the area in which May Sinclair was to become a master.

The play's protagonist, Walter Brandon, after seeing a city savage beat a poor woman to death, has given up being the poet that his wife Honoria loved in him; he thinks that he had caught himself acting the passive spectator of cruelty to glean material for his poetry. Instead of writing any more of the poetry he now despises, he has spent his inherited wealth building people's colleges, free libraries, and housing units that have replaced slums; but he refuses to manage the housing estates for the profit that would maintain them. He is insanely callous toward Honoria's need for affection and asks her to give him her own money to support his charities. A poet-friend of Brandon and Honoria, Davenant, becomes Brandon's secretary. Deprived of love for her husband, Honoria breaks off her loyalty, and offers her love to Davenant, who rejects her offer and defends Brandon's sacrifices as having the ultimate improving effect of art. After Honoria has yielded to Davenant's argument and has agreed to give all her money to her husband, Brandon shoots and kills her as the hated obstructor of his schemes.

The play is so intensely and sincerely, if naïvely, drawn from the depths in which personal emotions engender even rhetorical power, that one must look for a personal situation in its story. May Sinclair was tied to her mother, who had a general love for humanity but a specific callousness toward her daughter's need for love in return for love, and a voracious greed for her daughter's sacrifices. Anthony Deane shared with May the love for culture that was her great passion, but he proved to be more loyal to her mother's generalized philanthropy than to her daughter's need for a personal affection; and he even urged her to pay her debt of honor to her tyrannously greedy mother. In paying that total sacrifice without any reward of love, she felt that she was letting her mother kill her. The letter of February 21, 1894, in which Deane told her why the play was unconvincing, was a masterpiece of sympathetic tact and truthfulness.

After one feeble attempt in a letter to Deane, May Sinclair gave up the defense of the indefensible, and started on a second verse play, which was never finished: *Tancred of Adan: A Lyrical Drama in Five*

Acts. One fragment was printed in a small periodical that experts have not been able to identify from the tear-out that the author saved. The play is a mixture of rhymed and blank verse, and its touch is often as light as Deane begged her to keep it. Many of the verses are pure feeling; the songs are especially sweet in their melody.

Its hero gives up the narcotizing life of the poet to become a leader in action, and the heroine, who is not his wife, loses her life through helping him fulfill his sense of duty to his land. At the profoundest level of urgency, its motive for creation seems to be May Sinclair's sense of having been for too long a victim of the fear that she would suffer the same doom that had struck down the men in her family, and her summoning her will to fight her fear and free herself from its hold. She is Tancred, the prince and poet who has been too fearful of the specter of doom to fight for his country's independence, and she is also Sora, Tancred's illegitimate half-sister, who loves Tancred and who faces the specter at the risk of death, so that Tancred shall gain the courage to lead his restless army to certain triumph and his people's independence. An immediate message of *Tancred* could be May Sinclair's impatience with her relative futility as a poet. Tancred, stirred by the example of Sora's courage, breaks out of his dream-habit of writing dreamy verse, to fight a prosaic battle that ends in his winning political freedom for his people and a personal freedom from the fear of death. Freedom for Tancred's people meant freedom for people to emerge from May Sinclair's imagination into the open life of a novel.

There is evidence of an embryonic symbiosis between *Tancred of Adan,* which was being written in 1894, and the novel *Mr. and Mrs. Nevill Tyson,* which was not published until 1898. If this evidence, tending to show that *Mr. and Mrs. Nevill Tyson* was finished by 1894, should represent the truth, May Sinclair had already been trying to break the long compulsion of her verse-writing before she began *Tancred* and, of course, before she published *Audrey Craven.* After *Tancred,* her verse became the smallest part of her writing.

The Young Philosopher

Along with her writing increasingly melodious verse in dramatic form, May Sinclair carried on with the scholarship in philosophy that Dorothea Beale had first encouraged, an expression of which was to attract still another personal influence to her.

Beginning with 1893, "Three Studies in Plato" appeared in successive spring issues of the *Cheltenham Ladies College Magazine.* The first, "Was Plato a Dualist?" argued that Plato's dualism approached

a monistic system. "Platonic Sociology," in 1894, related Plato's prescribed society to his whole philosophy, and passed it under an ad-
versely critical review. "The Philosopher-King," in 1895, found Plato's
requirements of a political leader to be in fact a prescription for the
individual.

The first paid-for article in May Sinclair's career was "The Ethical
and Religious Import of Idealism," which was published in December
of 1893 in *The New World,* a Boston publication edited by Harvard
University professors. The essay brilliantly interpreted Thomas Hill
Green's Idealism and described what was to be the foundation of her
own philosophy of Idealism. Its core of developing the case for idealism
proceeds by showing that self-consciousness makes knowledge possible;
that consciousness makes nature possible; that the principle common
to knowledge and nature is will; and that religion guides man's developing individuality into serving the universal needs through moral law.

Professor Henry Melvill Gwatkin

The article in *The New World* came to the attention of the Emmanuel Fellow and Dixie Professor of Ecclesiastical History at Cambridge, Henry Melvill Gwatkin—fifty and married, but not to an
intellectual mate—when he visited Sidmouth in the summer of 1894.
He climbed the steep hill to Salcombe Regis to call upon the young
philosopher who had written it. In her unpublished "Reminiscences
of Professor H. M. Gwatkin" May Sinclair wrote that his visit "ended,
for me, in one of my happiest friendships." She visited Professor and
Mrs. Gwatkin in Cambridge in October, and hugely enjoyed "the
walks through the town, in the Backs; the lecture at Emmanuel . . .
best of all, the long talks in his study in the house in Scrope Terrace."
This friendship led to her obtaining the work of translating Rudolf
Sohm's *Kirchengeschichte im Grundriss* (6th edition, Leipzig, 1893)
as *Outlines of Church History,* which Professor Gwatkin edited and
Macmillan published in 1895.

Anthony Deane became worried over the professor's interference
with his own plan to rescue May Sinclair from her introverted verse
and philosophical writing, and to set her free for an outwardly directed
view of real people. On August 1, 1894, he sandwiched his irritable
comments about the professor between proddings toward creative
writing. "And where is the 15 chaptered story? Has Professor Gwatkin
interfered with its progress?" And "I hope you won't make yourself
ill over that wretched German book, the pay really isn't good enough

for that. And I shall be very interested to see how that story turns out, the beginning seems to me to promise exceedingly well."

Sohm's point of view on Christianity was Evangelical, and May Sinclair's translation catches his animated faith, even to his rejecting, in his final sentence, the intellectual approach of the academic philosophers to the highest good: "It is not our culture that will save us, but the Gospel alone."

Although it is possible that Sohm's ardent Evangelicalism may have contributed some elements of perspective to her two novels of clerical life, her feeling values had already accepted compassion toward all humanity as the highest human attribute. Her unpublished memoir about her friendship with Professor Gwatkin, particularly a holograph correction on the typescript, seems to me to account for two characters in *Mary Olivier:* the very scholarly and very wise Mr. Sutcliffe, and his wife, who worries over the personal results that might follow from her husband's intellectual intimacy with Mary.

The Poet Turning to Prose Fiction

Anthony Deane's letter, written on May 25, 1894, to Hull, where May Sinclair was visiting her brother William and his family, dates the progress of the writing of *Tancred of Adan.* Four surviving manuscript pages of *Mr. and Mrs. Nevill Tyson,* parts of chapters twenty and twenty-one, written in black and red ink, carry evidence that they were written even before *Tancred,* for on their backs are fragments of *Tancred,* written in pencil. A song sung by Molly in chapter fourteen of the novel was written out on a separate slip and found in a copy book that contains advanced fragments of *Tancred.* The evidence of the economically double manuscripts circumstantially implies that May Sinclair had been working on her novel during or even before 1894, and had kept the secret from Anthony Deane.

One of the manuscript pages carries on its back an address in the author's handwriting, "Miss May Sinclair 1 Ormond Terrace Regent's Park N.W.," which suggests that not long time after the exciting meeting with Professor Gwatkin at Salcombe Regis and the return visit to Cambridge, May Sinclair took her mother to London, as early as 1894.

But she was still writing verse, although the verse she published seems willed rather than released. "Three Singers," appearing in the *Pall Mall Magazine* in October, 1894, is a sonnet reverting to the pallid theme of a vague death wish. May Sinclair had sent a copy of it to Deane before its publication, and on August 16 he had indulged in some harsh dissuasion. "To be odiously frank, it doesn't seem to me a favorable specimen of your powers, its language is so exceedingly involved and obscure. However, it will lend itself to a picture of poppies and an opposite verdict to mine is implied in its acceptance."

"Helen in Leuce," another sonnet, was published in the *Temple Bar Magazine* in August, 1895. It is a joint tribute to Achilles the warrior and to Helen, "that phantom of the heart's desire," who caused the war. It reappeared in *The Divine Fire* as a sample of Rickman's genius. A sonnet, "Know that the Love who is my Lord most high," dated 1894 in typescript, is so vague in its worship of love as to be taken as either Christian or pagan. It was first published in *The Divine Fire,* where Rickman recites it to Poppy Grace while he is very drunk, and he confesses that he stole the idea for it from Dante and Rossetti. A sonnet, "I asked the ministering priests who never tire," dated October 7, 1895, in manuscript, was printed in the *Cheltenham Ladies College Magazine* in the autumn of 1897 and reappeared in *The Divine Fire.*

"The Last Decade," a sonnet published in *Temple Bar* in April, 1895, is sternly Hebraic and Christian in its rebuke to a world that has gone mad in its corruption of beauty and decency. The short story whose title was a tribute to Anthony Deane, "A Friendly Critic," published in *Macmillan's Magazine* in October, 1896, contained two light-hearted quatrains. "A Fable," appearing both in the *Cheltenham Ladies College Magazine* in autumn, 1898, and in the *Hampstead Annual* of 1902, offers a cloudily diffuse Vedanta-Yeatsian version of the Narcissus tale.

The unpublished verse in this decade of competing experiments in verse and prose are mostly about a love that is not returned and is yet undisheartened. Only one poem refers to a love that was mutual before it was disjoined. There are poems that express a love for Christ and others that lament the corruption of the age, the falling away from faith in Christ. One sonnet (whose first manuscript version Dorothea Beale found fault with in her letter of July 4, 1898, for implying a fusion of irreconcilables) was changed in the final version to show Christ the successor to Eros as the God of Love. Eleven of the sonnets were collected in a typescript and entitled "Sonnets, Verses, etc." It must have been the collection that May Sinclair showed to a new friend she had made when she settled down in London, Richard Garnett, whose advice she asked about their publication.

Beyond her original verse, she did two translations from the Greek in this decade. One, a translation of a fragment of "On Nature," by

Parmenides, was published with a note in the *Cheltenham Ladies College Magazine* in the spring of 1896. She also paraphrased a "Hymn to Apollo," which was printed, alongside the original text arranged by Dr. A. Thierfelder, in *Literature* on February 10, 1900, and in the autumn number, 1901, of the *Cheltenham Ladies College Magazine*.

The published and unpublished poems of this period betray May Sinclair's failure to expand her emotional range and to grow into a freely assertive poet. The forms and the imagery she employed with pride in the intellectual distinction they gave her forced her to allegorize and conventionalize her emotions. In spite of the assurance with which she passed some of them off in *The Divine Fire* as proof of Savage Keith Rickman's genius, in spite of the fervent admiration with which her ideal other self in that novel, Lucia Harden, ranks them as the work of genius, they are really not distinguished verse, and quite as bad as she confided, possibly insincerely, to Morley Roberts, years later, that she thought them. Their one important service was that they helped her to write truly distinguished prose. Professor Cornelius Weygandt put it this way in his *A Century of the English Novel:* "It was not for nothing that Miss Sinclair wrote verse in her youth."[13]

The first sign of May Sinclair's having thought about writing fiction is the letter from her "friendly critic" dated January 1, 1893: "With what you say about fiction, and the impossibility of writing it before 30, I agree fully." On October 30 Deane began his campaign to turn her inward-viewing mind in an outward direction, but not until he had analyzed and commented on the verses she had sent him. She had apparently tried to follow his advice in a "Village Sketch," which he complained on March 10, 1894, he had not yet received. On March 13 he returned it after an imaginative reading and a sensitive, conscientious correcting of its amateurish faults. She snapped back with her usual defense, and Deane replied with his usual apology. He kept prodding her about the fate of the sketch, suggesting *Longman's Chambers' Journal* as a place to send it to.

On June 24 he wrote that his mother had informed him of an imminent novel—or at least "a story in 15 chapters." On August 1 he prodded her again on her "Reminiscent Rustic" and on her "15 chapter story." The sketch had been sent to *Temple Bar* and had been forgotten there. On August 3 Deane urged her to raise the roof at *Temple Bar,* and advised her to join the Society of Authors, which Besant had founded in 1883, so that she would have a strong champion against editors and publishers.

---

13. New York: The Century Company, 1925, p. 368.

On January 28, 1895, having read her story "A Hero of Fiction" with his customary conscientiousness, he returned it with specific editorial corrections and wise general advice: it would have a better chance with the editors "if it were wrought with a rather lighter touch —and this criticism extends, I suspect, to other things of yours, besides this particular story."

On February 20 he patiently replied to the objections that she offered to his constructive criticisms: "I don't agree with your view, by the way, that lightness and deftness of literary touch are the gifts of nature rather than the results of art. 'True ease in writing comes from art, not chance, As those move easiest who have learned to dance,' said the ingenious Mr. Alexander Pope, and it's very true." May Sinclair followed Deane's every editorial advice in preparing "A Hero of Fiction" for publication.

In the meantime, *Black and White,* one of the magazines to which Deane was contributing, had accepted a surprisingly sophisticated narrative sketch, "A Study from Life," but delayed publishing it so long that May Sinclair had to write a brusque demand to the editor to hurry it into print. On June 21, 1895, Deane congratulated her on her triumph over the editor's sloth, and the story appeared on November 2. May Sinclair had at last started on the course that led to her mastery of both the short story and the novel forms. "A Study from Life" has the distinction of being the only published work to be signed with its author's complete initials: M. A. St. C. Sinclair, which Deane hailed on November 12 as "a new and impressive signature," and about which he asked, "Has this been adopted to circumvent the other Richard in the field—the spurious 'May Sinclair'?"

Deane's magnetic eloquence moved him in 1896 to Bath, and in his letter of November 6, 1896, he confessed his delight over having "a congregation of eleven hundred or thereabouts to preach to every Sunday." He gave a course of sermons on Sunday evenings in Advent and a series of nine lectures on Ecclesiastes on Wednesday evenings. But he was never too busy to follow the career of his protégée: "I read 'A Friendly Critic' in *Macmillan,* and liked it very much. It is a pity they wouldn't let you sign it. Have you finished your novel, and are you doing any more short stories? I hope you're not going to desert fiction in order to translate dull Teutonic treatises." He busied himself to help her in another direction. "When I was last in town I made one or two inquiries about reviewing, for your benefit, but couldn't find any vacancies. The literary market is desperately overcrowded nowadays." Mostly, the letter confessed Deane's happiness in his new parish. "We've just had electric light put in our church, and it is in use today for the first time. There's a very good organ in it, on which —how very idiotic; I'd clean forgotten that you've both seen and heard it."

There was a reason for his dissociation, as we learn from his letter of January 17, 1897, thanking May Sinclair for her "very kind letter of congratulation" answering the announcement of his engagement to a young lady in Bath. (The announcement was not among the literary remains.) "Her Christian name is Maud, and she will insist on reciting the last two verses of 'The Prayers of Coelebs' from *Leaves in the Wind*[14] from time to time. Then there are great scenes. However, I point out that the proposal was made not 'on some lovely summer's eve' but on a rainy winter's night, which, of course, makes all the difference." If May Sinclair's was the face the poet remembered from a lovely summer's eve, that would make all the difference, as she would understand so well.

Toward the end of that same letter, Deane praised another story, "Not Made in Germany," and told her of his pleasure in hearing that her first novel had been accepted. "I always felt certain that you would succeed as a writer of fiction, and it is a great pleasure now to me to recollect that I helped in some small degree in making you take seriously to that branch of literature."

Miss Beale argued her case as tactfully as she could in her letter in January, 1897. She thought "Not Made in Germany" prettily written, but not worthy of May Sinclair, and monotonous in its romantic theme. "I wish we, like the Greeks, had things written which turned on other problems. These things are very well as a diversion."

May Sinclair was thirty-three, desperately poor, imprisoned with her difficult mother and still an unknown when, in May, 1897, Blackwood published her novel *Audrey Craven*. She saved two letters that record the judgments and feelings of people whose opinions mattered deeply to her. Anthony Deane, writing a very long letter on May 19 from Bath, called it "exceedingly clever. Technically, in the matter of style and workmanship, it shows an enormous advance upon your earlier work." He thought the heroine "the most detestable young lady I have ever met between the covers of a book." The clergyman in the novel, Flaxman Reed, he called a caricature; and he may have had a personal reason for his detestation. The dialogue he found extremely well done: "terse, and epigrammatic and biting—sometimes almost too good, because all the characters talk so well."

The other letter she saved was dated July 23, 1897, and came from Epsom as an answer to the author's presentation copy:

---

14. Published in October, 1896.

Had you not told me it was your first novel, I should have thought it came from a hand already practised. . . . For the work—if you will let me say so—is very well written, in sound, careful, often polished English, assuredly such as one does not meet with every day. Moreover, the characterisation and construction seem to me decidedly good. Audrey herself arrested and held me throughout. . . . There is a quiet balance about the thing which suggests an artistic conscience and more than the beginning of artistic powers. I like, too, the taste of irony on this page and that. . . . I hope the critics will give it the attention it deserves.

The letter ended with the exciting signature of George Gissing, whose literary creed held that "Irony meant intellect."

Deane in this year sponsored her application for membership in the Society of Authors, and calmed her fears about not being able to write a good second book. On October 24 he wrote, "Every writer, I think, feels them in some degree, every writer in moments of depression is apt to read former work of his own with a kind of incredulous wonder, and a dark belief that he has reached his highest point once and for all in what he has already done. But presently he does something else incomparably better." On December 29 he retired from the post of literary advisor, now that A. P. Watt had become her agent and had placed her second novel with Blackwood. He added the advice that short stories were more immediately profitable, "but they are not so in the long run; for one thing, they use up such a lot of material."

A new friend who was to be of great importance to May Sinclair in raising her often drooping morale was "Zack," really Gwendoline Keats, short story writer and novelist of Devon, whose first book of stories, *Life is Life,* appeared in the year in which her first surviving letter to May Sinclair was dated, February 25, 1898, addressed to 1 Ormond Terrace, Regent's Park, Primrose Hill. In it Zack made much of her friendship with Mr. Blackwood and of employing it to blandish him into showing May Sinclair the greatest possible favor. Apparently, Blackwood was hurt by May Sinclair's having employed an agent to place her second book with him. Characteristic of her cheery motif, Zack complimented her on a chapter of the new book she had read. "There is a lot of reserved strength about it; and all the characters so sharply drawn that I feel as if I understood them from heart to act— after reading those three short pages."

Blackwood demanded some revisions, and May Sinclair complied promptly, and heard no more. Zack wrote on April 13, "I am sure you will hear from Blackwood soon; and I am sure he will accept your story; even, if he thinks that you have handled a ticklish subject with a touch strong, as it is delicate."

On May 2 Zack wrote, "I can't quite understand B—— shying a little at the £100; but believe that he will eventually buy it, or he would have returned the book outright." On July 5 she wrote, "Am awfully glad old Blackwood has been brought to the nail—dear Beggar—he must believe it is going to be a success." An undated letter soon after to "Dear Duffer" brought Zack's comfort to the anxious May Sinclair. "How can you dream of worrying over the fate of your book—B—— must have thought it extraordinarily good;—for he was evidently in no mood to do you a favour when he accepted it.—Mr. Colvin is very anxious to read it, and many others that I have not told you about." Zack added the information that Blackwood told her about her own collection of stories, *Life is Life,* that only 633 copies had been sold, 344 of them belonging to the Colonial Edition. And that Blackwood kept sending her packets advertising the book, asking her to place them advantageously. "I stuck them all down a certain place and wrote and told him if he only knew where I placed them he would think the spot anything but advantageous."

On the fifth of July, 1898, Deane and Miss Edith Maud Versturm were married at Christ Church, Bath, in a wedding that was a social event. The *Gentlewoman* for July, the Bath *Herald,* and the Bath *Journal* gave it full coverage: the ladies' dresses, the guests, the list of presents sent and the names of the donors. There were plenty of names of distinguished guests "who recognised the occasion." May Sinclair was not there. There was one coincidence that related Maud, as Deane called her, to May: she had five brothers, of whom all were in the army. Maud also had four sisters. Before going to their new parish, Gnosall, in Staffordshire, the happy couple honeymooned in Lyme Regis.[15]

It was from the honeymooners' cottage, 2 Library Cottages, Lyme Regis, on July 10, that Deane wrote to thank May Sinclair for a gift not listed in the official list, a volume of Tennyson: "It seems strange now to think of your first tentative efforts in the direction of fiction, and your success is doubly pleasant to me—because, for one thing, one's friends' success is always pleasant, and, for another, I feel that satisfaction which a prophet experiences when his predictions happen to 'come off.' I always said that you had it in you to write good fiction, and events have more than justified my faith."

In a letter postmarked July 24 and redirected to 2 Vittoria Walk, Cheltenham, where May Sinclair was visiting, Zack thanked her for

---

15. Miss Lucy Chauncy, literary executor of Mrs. Deane, not only gave me permission to print Anthony Deane's letters, but also contributed the cuttings of the accounts of the wedding.

what was so characteristic a consideration, the sending of a copy of *Life is Life* to Miss [Janet Elizabeth] Hogarth. In August, Zack confessed that she was "awfully gratified that Miss Hogarth likes my book."

In a letter postmarked October 10 and sent to May Sinclair's new address, 13 Christchurch Road in Hampstead, Zack wrote encouraging gossip: "Mrs. W. K. Clifford came to see me yesterday; I told her about your book; she said she had reviewed *Audrey Craven,* and had come to the conclusion that the woman who wrote it had a future before her.—Said she would also have the Tysons to review; that she had been struck by the name." In a letter from Florence postmarked November 10, Zack confessed that Mr. and Mrs. Nevill Tyson had moved her to tears: "I think that your drawing of Mrs. Nevill Tyson is marvelous for subtlety, insight and human tenderness."

On November 19, Zack had to console her: "I am sure your book will not be a failure—as for Beatrice Harridan's [sic] criticism I don't think much of it or her for making it—: the book is *not* lacking in heart—and on that score Zack is a good critic."

The only letter out of the sixty-nine that the fastidious Anthony Deane left undated confessed his bewilderment and disappointment over *Mr. and Mrs. Nevill Tyson,* which had been published in Novemver of 1898. The author had sent a copy to her old-time "friendly critic," but now he confessed that the reviews of it that he had read and the comments on it that he had heard from his friends, whom it disgusted, convinced him that he would dislike it and therefore would condemn it if he were asked his opinion. He believed that there were certain aspects and certain problems of life, "especially on the animal side, which undoubtedly exist, but to have them dealt with in fiction is, to the average clean-minded man or woman, intolerable." It was a long and a kind letter, and its general philosophy, that a writer should remember his readers to be other selves, with other associations and responses than the writer's—a knowledge that May Sinclair had already applied in her splendid review of Mary Pulling's *The Teacher's Text Book of Practical Psychology* in 1896—was a healthful one for her to relearn. It was as long as most of his letters, and contained good advice. He wished that she lived in the country.

> In town, I think, one's sense of proportion is weakened, and, instead of literature being the expression of life; life, for a writer, becomes the expression of literature. Beyond a certain point, the more one dwells upon one's literary work, not only the worse is it for one's mind, but the worse too for the quality of the work. I wish you were living here, and I could set you to work among my rustics, who probably never heard of Shakespeare in their lives. After an afternoon with

them, you'd go back to your pen with a resurgence of the old divine optimism which, though town-life nearly kills it, still lurks with each one of us, and you'd set to work again with clearer eyes and a truer perception of life. But, while you're in London, try and keep your literature to work time, and absolutely refuse to allow yourself to think about it outside those limits.

He begged her to keep in touch with nonliterary people, who did not know what proof or copy means. He was concerned to benefit her work and her health. Apologizing for his homily, he begged her to use her gifts rightly, so that "the world will be better for your books." He counseled her to write to make friends, to give cheer and courage, not to gain the admiration of a literary set, or the praises of a few reviewers. He had not really resigned as her literary counselor.

She fought a secret battle against despair, as she had confessed only to Zack, who, writing on February 16, 1899, from Maderno, cheered her with an account of the critical praise that she had read of the book and added, "I believe the Nevill Tysons has made a far deeper impression than you are aware of—; and I know that you will one day make a great name for yourself.—Goodbye old pessimist without a cause."

On August 1, the safely married Deane wrote again from Gnosall, but in a sentimental mood, recalling Sidmouth days. "I wondered if anyone was toiling up the Salcombe road, and so I thought of you and the old days—the days of sonnets on classical themes and blank-verse tragedies." He asked about the new novel she had been engaged on; she had even told him the name of the hero: Rickmann. "I discussed your work with H. W. Lucy, who reviewed Mr. and Mrs. N. T. in *Punch,* and who shares my longing for a cheerful work from your pen. I didn't say anything to him about Mr. Rickmann, as perhaps that is a secret at present." It is such a shame that Deane was a neat housekeeper, and kept only one letter of May Sinclair's of a much, much later date. "By the way, your letter (in reply to my dreadful criticism of the book I hadn't read) gave me the very greatest pleasure. This isn't a politeness, but solid truth." She must have pointed out to him the depth of Molly's love that caused her to act as she did—and shamed the censorious preacher.

On July 14, Zack wrote from Ireland: "Why are you so downhearted, dear Beggar—Your work is GOOD and that is all that really matters in the long run." Another letter from Throop, Dorchester, on August 6, responded to May Sinclair's account of her nursing her mother: "Dear old Duffer. How good of you to nurse other folk instead of caring for yourself."

On October 12, 1899, still, Zack comforted May Sinclair in her despair over Blackwood's report on the scant sales: "Oh my dear Beggar what absolutely infernal luck—Don't lose heart just when you are on a good thing—You have more stuff in you than 9/10 of the writers have now a days. I know you must succeed in the long run—there is absolutely no other end possible for you—Hang that B—— with his loss of £ 13 odd—I bet the final reckoning between you and that firm will have a different look. . . . Don't be a fool and give in—the real big 'uns always have to face hell first of all."

On November 28, Anthony Deane, at the end of a very long letter, asked, "And how is the Arcadian Mr. Rickmann? I was so sorry to hear that you've been out of sorts. But the new book will appear in 1900, I hope?" He had met an enthusiastic admirer of her works at the Authors' Club, Eveleigh Nash, who wanted to know all about her.

"The Village Sketch," the direct outcome of Deane's having sent May Sinclair some of his *Globe* "Turnovers" years ago, was given a new title, "A Servant of the Earth," and was published in 1899 in *The Woman at Home,* as written by "May Sinclair, Author of *Mr. and Mrs. Nevill Tyson.*" Two full-page and three half-page illustrations spared the readers of this popular magazine the fatigue of a continuous attention over the eight pages of the sketch. It is simply written as an account of the author's visit to the cottage of a disabled farm laborer, renamed Elisha Bole, and of her success in luring the prematurely aged man out of his cell of bitterness to a fresh pride in his house. It is not strange that May Sinclair should have chosen in this sketch to play the heroine of such a freeing of a trapped self as Deane had accomplished, with equal cunning, and gentleness, and patience. The stages of the author's friendship to the death of Elisha Bole are told with the most imaginative compassion. Every one of the amateurish faults that Deane had pointed to in the first draft and corrected had been cleared away. Obeying Deane's command, given in October of 1893, May Sinclair had created in Elisha Bole, first named Holmes, her first original character outside of herself. This single trial at the sort of sketch that Deane could turn out effortlessly taught her that it was a genre for which she lacked the light touch. Her literary remains show that she tried again, but she gave it up.

The nineteenth century came to an end. Its last twenty years laid a firm foundation for the career of Miss May Sinclair, novelist.

6

Exposure on Parnassus: 1900-1910

At its opening, the decade from 1900 to 1910 held no prophecy of a better tomorrow for May Sinclair. She was still in desperate need of money and anxious over the health of her mother, who required constant care. Mother and daughter still lived in lodgings at 13 Christchurch Road, west of the Ponds, in Hampstead.

In the hope of receiving encouragement and advice on its publication, she sent a collection of her sonnets, with a bodyguard of some of her published pieces, to Mr. Richard Garnett, who lived at 27 Tanza Road, on the east side of the Ponds, by Parliament Hill Fields. The Keeper of Printed Books at the British Museum from 1890 to his retirement in 1899 responded to her appeal with sympathy and respect, and so joined the small group of friends whom May Sinclair needed to hearten her and to help her with practical aid.

The open ties between Mr. Garnett, who was sixty-five, and May Sinclair, who was thirty-six, were their common practice of the sonnet, their love for German literature in particular and for literature as a whole, and their respect for Samuel Butler, who had dedicated his *Unconscious Memory* to Richard Garnett and shown him the manuscript of *The Way of All Flesh*.[1] Less obvious, but surely as strong a reason for his admiration of her was her having, like himself, driven superior abilities to acquire a solid scholarship without the help or the privilege of a university training.

On March 20, 1900, he gave May Sinclair his opinion that her sonnets were worth publishing for their "very great merit." "We who have

1. Caroline G. Heilbrun, *The Garnett Family* (London: George Allen and Unwin, 1961) , p. 47.

written sonnets know the technical difficulties only too well." He was more tolerant of her divagations from technical orthodoxy than was Deane.

Her appeal to him for help in finding a nurse for her mother brought an answer, postmarked August 8, that recommended her applying to a Mr. W. M. Rossetti for the name of the unprofessional nurse who had attended the late Miss Christina Rossetti. Mr. Garnett also helped her to obtain the translating of a manuscript by Theodore von Sosnosky, an Austrian who advised a drastic reform of the British army to cope with Germany's expanding strength. To help her with the translating of military terms, Garnett consulted with his friend Major Singleton. Chapman and Hall published her translation in 1901 as *England's Danger, the Future of British Army Reform.*

On May 2, 1900, Anthony Deane prodded her on her new book ("Is Mr. Rickmann still in abeyance?") and sympathized with her ("I do hope you're better again in health"). Zack wrote her sympathy from Carlow on August 24: "How terribly hard for you and sad. I can't think of anything to say, damn it. That it should come when you need all your strength, pluck and time for your work—Am glad though that this last book of yours is your best—Must be uncommonly good. . . . If you could only leave your mother I wish you would stay with me and Gertrude Godden and (Tommy) Miss Whitehead for a week. . . . The tragedy of it all makes my heart ache."

The summer of 1900 brought a new friend, a novelist, whose insight into May Sinclair's loneliness called up a tender affection for her. Katherine Tynan Hinkson first learned of her existence when she reviewed *Mr. and Mrs. Nevill Tyson* for the *St. James Gazette* in 1899, and the women met at the annual Woman Writers' dinner through Mrs. Hinkson's introducing herself. Mrs. Hinkson remembered her as a "pretty, refined-looking, mousey little girl, not in the least like what might be expected of the author of Mr. and Mrs. Nevill Tyson and Two Sides of a Question."[2] The epithet "little girl" betrayed Mrs. Hinkson's not dreaming at that time that May Sinclair was only two years younger than herself. The tenderness she felt toward the "little girl" was a motherly blend of pity and regret that so sensitive a lady was bedevilled by an imagination that drove her to write about phases of life that shocked Mrs. Hinkson's feelings of a gentlewoman.

In November, Zack sent congratulations upon the acceptance of a new book, *Two Sides of a Question,* which contained two long stories. On February 22, 1901, the difficult patient, her mother, died of

---

2. Katherine Tynan Hinkson, *The Middle Years,* Houghton Mifflin, 1917, p. 292.

heart disease, at age seventy-nine, the survivor of her younger, playful husband by almost thirty years. May's sister-in-law, Eleanor, the widow of the younger William Sinclair, who had died in Hull five years before, had come from Liverpool to help with the nursing.

On March 23, Zack sent a message of sympathy over Mrs. Sinclair's death and confessed an unwarranted disgust from reading the proofs of her latest book, *The White Cottage*. She "felt so sick over its rottenness that I have written to Messers Constable offering them back £ 40 out of the £ 150 they gave me for it." She neurotically underrated her powerful, if morbid, novel.

March was the month in which *Two Sides of a Question* appeared. Richard Garnett rated the second of the stories, "Superseded," a masterpiece. "There can be no doubt of your success, if only your invention and experience of the world are sufficient to guard against self-repetition. See as much of life as you can. Your book is advertised today at the head of Constable's list in *Literature*." Tactfully, Mr. Garnett was giving her the same anxious advice that Deane had given her: to turn her mind more to outward interests. On April 11, he wrote to her about a translation she was engaged on which I have not been able to trace. It was a "bright and wholesome story," probably in German, and it was for an American publisher.

A few days before Easter in 1901, Deane invited her to stay more than the one night that she had promised to stay at Gnosall on her way to visit relatives in Ireland. On Easter Eve, he wrote to praise the same story that Garnett had liked, calling it "simply a little masterpiece." He went on, "I pat myself on the back when I remember my belief of many years ago in your capacity for writing fiction, a belief which this last book of yours justifies so splendidly.—Now do, if you possibly can, hurry on Mr. Rickmann. . . . If you produce a novel no oftener than once in two or three years, you are practically making a fresh start—so far as public recognition goes—each time. It is exasperating to conceive you translating grisly German books for starvation wages when you can produce original work such as this. . . . 'Superseded' is *magnificent*. . . . Yes, three cheers for 'Superseded!' "

May Sinclair must have written to Zack out of a depression over the poor sales of *Two Sides*, because Zack answered on May 12, "You always take such a gloomy view of your own prospects but that will not prevent your prospering."

Mrs. Hinkson wrote on December 30, 1901, joining in the praise of the latest book: "Very humbly and sincerely I say that it is *great* work. . . . No wonder you take time to it, while I and such as I are turning out our poor ephemeral stuff." Her plea for the privilege of friendship must have been answered, because on January 2, 1902, Mrs. Hinkson invited May Sinclair to come to supper the next Sunday to meet the poet Louise Imogene Guiney.

In the January issue of *Blackwood's* appeared a short story, "The Return of the Prodigal." Mrs. Hinkson wrote about it in her letter of January 10, but her real concern was over May Sinclair's poor health and lonely life. She penetrated to the secret of May Sinclair's sadness, the futility of her lonely life, and she tried to dispel a mood that did not affect the quality of May Sinclair's writing but that eclipsed her hopefulness that others would like it. "I wish you were not such a lonely little person. Perhaps it is good for the work, but it is bad for the human creature. And I have learnt to love her; began to love her from the first.—Will you come to us often on Sundays? We are always here Sunday evenings, and always want you to come to supper." "Here" was Wrentham, Longfield Road, Ealing, W.

After May Sinclair confessed that she had written some poems, Mrs. Hinkson used both that confession and her excuse that she herself could not go out to tempt her into a visit. Mrs. Hinkson always found some means of making her persuasion effective.

In this year of 1902, the circle of May Sinclair's friends and critics gained a new member, Edward Garnett, Richard's son, who discerned in her a partial discipleship to Henry James. In the letter he wrote on March 11 from The Cearne, Kent Hatch, near Edenbridge, Kent, he congratulated her on both stories in *Two Sides*, and recognized the painter in "The Cosmopolitan" to be Henry James's favorite young man, "*plus* some additions." He invited her to send him any of her work that she thought might suit the Greenback Series that Messrs. Duckworth were publishing. On March 16, he wrote to her that she was "in a sense, a born writer," but that she had written *Mr. and Mrs. Nevill Tyson* romantically rather than from nature. Elaborate as his analysis was, he failed to get at what it was in the novel that made him reject it. He could not have read her *Audrey Craven* to have written, "If you were to work in the spirit of a modern Jane Austen you would make your own field; it would be *yours*. You have a very delicate gift of expression, and you have a great deal of insight, where you decide not to go out of your depth. Our depths are not of our making, so don't try to make yours." Meanwhile, he recommended Turgenev's *Smoke* as a sample of "how deep natural depths are."

She must have defended the plausibility of Tyson against his objections, because on March 21 Garnett objected less vehemently and more helpfully, by showing her how she had failed to build a foundation of cause to persuade a reader to believe in so complex a person as Nevill Tyson. The lesson was a valuable one.

On April 16, Anthony Deane sent news of an important elevation, to the editorship of the *Treasury,* a new monthly owned by the *Church Times* and aimed at a popular rather than a literary public, half of its matter to be "church," the other half fiction, verse, and miscellaneous articles. He was busy writing *Church Times* leaders, reviewing books, writing something for *Punch* "nearly every week," and writing "a good deal of light verse for the *World*." And yet he did not forget to prod her to finish her novel about "Mr. Rickmann," and to invite her to contribute something to the *Treasury*. She must have sent him a fragment of her old verse drama, *Tancred,* because he wrote in a later letter that " 'The Sword' doesn't quite go."

Deane was sincere in inviting her to contribute short stories to the *Treasury*. On August 30, he asked for a story of about three thousand to thirty-five hundred words, "and I beg for a cheerful ending!" He also asked about the poems that she had apparently promised to send. But the magazine was never to publish any poem, story, or sketch of hers. Deane let no sentimental notions bemuse his editorial ambition to make his magazine a popular success. A reader going through the *Treasury* with Dickens's motto for *Household Words* in mind would conclude that the editorial formula was "Keep it cheerful, keep it moral, keep it trim"—the philosophy of a born professional who could discipline his temperament so that its controlled spontaneity would steer him toward popular success.

On May 10, Mrs. Hinkson deprecated May Sinclair's praise of her novel *The Handsome Quaker*: "I am sure the finest thing in the book is your name on the dedication page. Yet, feeling as I do about you, you will know that your praise is sweet."

On October 12, Mrs. Hinkson mourned the death "of dear Lionel Johnson. We went to his funeral on Wednesday. Every day I seem to feel a sharper pang because I hadn't seen him for so long before he died. It was very hard to get hold of him, though he loved us, and one has a way of taking one's time about things. As though one ever had time in this world. I wish you had known him."

In *The Middle Years* Mrs. Hinkson set down more impressions of her friend than any other novelist has left us. Even when she had no money to spare, May Sinclair was generous and hospitable. Her freedom from pettiness and malice and envy was a trait that Mrs. Hinkson recalled with as much admiration as did the priceless housekeeper, Florence Bartrop. May's shy and dainty femininity was joined to a

masculine competitiveness that she showed off to her greatest joy when
she ran races on Hampstead Heath with a small boy. Even in her
forties she was "swift as Atalanta." Her artistic conscience drove her
to acquire a mastery of the living actuality of all the material she was
transmuting into her fiction, "so that her books should be true human
documents." Mrs. Hinkson once teased her by telling the outline of a
story that she would write about a lady novelist who, despite her
loathing for drink, made herself drunk so that she could give a truthful
description of how one of her characters felt, and ended by saying it
had been May Sinclair herself who gave her the idea for the story.
The novel that May Sinclair had started by 1897 became the topic of
planning conferences that were held at the Hinksons' house: "She
debated the possibility, the probability, of the incidents with us one by
one. She was delighted when she struck the title. I believe she made
a special pilgrimage to Ealing to share the joy of the discovery with
us."[3] This joyously articulate May Sinclair was the same woman whom
Mrs. Hinkson had described in her first book of autobiography as a
woman of notable silences.[4] May Sinclair was not silent with those who
knew her confessed hunger and who gave themselves to still it.

Zack wrote in a state of depression from Amersham, Bucks, on September 30, 1902: "Very glad you're so fit and doing good work—I have
had a racking time this year, and have just had another turn in with
the flue—My head feels like a rotten apple." She suggested that May
Sinclair visit her about the seventeenth of October for a couple of
nights. That visit seems to have been put off, and on November 2 Zack
wrote her grief over the illness of her dog, which howled night and day.
An undated later note carried the news that Zack had been obliged to
destroy her dog, "and having to do so has knocked [me] pretty flat. I
think it would be better if you came and saw me in the Spring—even
the 7 chapters of my book I had written I have chucked as so much
bad work." The book was *The Roman Road.*

On April 15, 1903, Mrs. Hinkson sent a note that her husband, also
an admirer of May Sinclair's work, had initialed: "When can you come
to us for an evening? . . . We don't want you to immolate yourself over
that book. You are finer than the finest book. We send our love."

Zack was in better health on May 26; *The Roman Road* was either
out or was coming out that week. On June 13, Zack's spirits were down
again; *The Roman Road* was "only a makeshift book." She also confessed that a blow that she had somehow gotten on her eyes had almost

3. *Ibid.*, pp. 292–93.
4. Katherine Tynan Hinkson, *Twenty-Five Years* (London: John Murray, 1913),
pp. 189–90.

blinded her. On November 14, postmarked, Zack wrote in great despair: "Life hit me so terribly hard this year, and till I can jamb the pieces together again I shan't be able to write. I must just have patience and wait. One can't write when you've had such a blow in the eyes you can't see straight." She suggested that May wait until spring to visit her in Derbyshire. "Indeed, now I am no company, I have thought so much about one thing that I feel as if I had worn a hole in my brain." What calamity it was that made her feel so distraught, Zack never confessed in her letters. And this, the last that May Sinclair kept, left the mystery unsolved. I have found no trace of any later residence, or of anything at all about this writer, whose writing has such an elemental, earth-rooted power. She could well be the model for Nina Lempriere in *The Creators*.

On May 27, Mrs. Hinkson wrote that Eveleigh Nash had been to dinner and had been very enthusiastic about May Sinclair's work. On June 22, she asked for another book of Zack's. "She made a great jump in artistry after *Life is Life*. That book made me feel as though I must scream out." On June 28, she asked May Sinclair to meet Ella D'Arcy, a writer of short stories. On October 2, she asked, "How does the novel go? This is only a line to say that we love you and look forward to meeting." On November 15, 1903, Mrs. Hinkson expressed her sympathy over an accident: "I feel that you endured a lot of pain, a burn is horrible,—although you are too heroic to talk about it. I kept expecting you every fine day, and if you didn't come that time, I felt sure you would the next. I hope you'll soon have the book off your mind: and that it will bring you into your kingdom."

For a time long enough to alarm Mrs. Hinkson, *The Divine Fire* was keeping its author from visiting and even from writing her friends. On December 20, Mrs. Hinkson pleaded: "Dearest May,—Have you vanished into vapor and shadows over that book? I confess I grudge your too great absorption if it wears you out so much. I love your books as you know, but I love you even better. Dear, will you come to us for Christmas, from Christmas Eve till after the Christmas Tree on December 28th? The children will make you forget all the sadness of Christmas. . . . We have missed you this Autumn." A note gives us to understand that May Sinclair waived the ordeal of Christmas Eve.

On Valentine's Day of what was to be the wonderful year of 1904, Mrs. Hinkson invited her to dinner on February 23 to meet Eveleigh Nash. The only reference to May Sinclair's well-being on the day of that visit is preserved in Mrs. Hinkson's note of May 3, "I'm so sorry you were tired."

May Sinclair had found the time and the energy to attend the annual dinner of the Society of Authors at the Hotel Cecil on April 20, with Mrs. Hinkson, Violet Hunt, Mrs. Belloc Lowndes, Mrs. Gertrude Atherton, H. G. Wells, Beatrice Harraden, and many more whom she knew well. She missed the women writers' dinner on June 20.[5]

About two months before Constable published *The Divine Fire,* a letter typewritten in New York, dated July 13, 1904, and carrying a printer's device of an owl perching on a book with its right claw, and proffering another book with its left claw, arrived to give May Sinclair a writer's thrill of being courted by an American publisher, and offered fame, provided that she took his advice on matters of style and form. He had published one novel, anonymously, with Macmillan. Henry Holt's letters deserve to be read, every word of them, for their story of a publisher who fell in love with a feminine genius and wished to help her outshine her original glory, without fully realizing that author's critical genius and the strength of her will. Henry Holt did not know that the young and promising author he was addressing was a woman of forty with a mind whose rights were not for sale. The final result of Holt's detailed directions on how she could improve her book was the deletion of some fifty lines from chapter thirty-seven and less than a line from chapter sixty-one. A comma that Holt inserted in the first paragraph of chapter thirty-seven betrayed his insensitivity to the meaning that the author had intended. He urged his new author to use more punctuation marks in her book to spare him from stumbling over meanings and from rereading sentences. The letter of R. Holt, the vice-president of the company, written on September 30, carried out the firm's policy by referring to the English publisher of *The Divine Fire* as "Archibald, Constable and Co."

Many years later as a grumbling autobiographer, Holt rapped the knuckles of publishers and agents who had stolen from him authors whose fortunes he had founded with his admittedly lower percentage of royalties. He argued that he had benefitted these authors through his vigorous promotion and his greater respectability, and he growled at authors who were so weak as to be lured away from him by the ephemeral bait of higher royalties.[6]

Mrs. Hinkson knew the exhaustion and apprehension from which May Sinclair was suffering now that *The Divine Fire* was launched in both England (in September) and America (in October), and she sent a note on October 10, urging her to come for a visit. On October

---

5. *Author,* May 1, July 1, 1904.
6. Henry Holt, *Garrulities of an Octagenarian Publisher* (Houghton Mifflin, 1923), pp. 211–12.

24, Edward Garnett wrote, asking if he might call to talk about her book, which he had reviewed in the *Speaker*.

The abrasions that Henry Holt inflicted with his clamoring for more commas and more cutting were soothed by the dreamlike courtship of publishers and editors that began in November, 1904, after *The Divine Fire* had captured readers who were hungry for literature and for a novel about the mysteries of literary creation. One can understand the feelings of Miss Matty of *Cranford* as one reads the faded letters that May Sinclair saved, from periodicals whose circulation has long since expired with the coming of radio and television. On November 9, Harrison S. Morris, editor of *Lippincott's Magazine*, asked for stories of three thousand or thirty thousand words. S. S. McClure praised *The Divine Fire* on November 29, and hoped for short stories or a longer piece for *McClure's Magazine*. A. L. Sessions on December 10 asked for a serial, for novelettes, and for short stories for *Ainslee's Magazine*.

Even while the most exciting encouragements were arriving from America, May Sinclair was still drudging away in London at a textuary. On December 1, Richard Garnett wrote sympathetically, "I am glad to hear from Mr. Mayle that your Goethe book is nearly ready for issue." Sydney C. Mayle was a bookseller at 70 High Street in Hampstead, who published *The Hampstead Annual* (in which May Sinclair's poem "Fable" had appeared in 1902) and the Priory Press Booklets, at three pence each (in Japanese vellum nine pence each, and in leather binding, one shilling six pence each). The "Goethe book" was *Thoughts From Goethe,* an anthology of passages from already published translations, of revised translations, and of fresh translations by May Sinclair, who also wrote the Introductory Note. It was published in the Priory Press Booklet series in August, 1905.

On Christmas Eve of 1904, Anthony Deane wrote from the vicarage of Holy Trinity at Malvern, promising that he would read *The Divine Fire* as soon as he had seen to all his pastoral Christmas duties. Humorously, he described how busy he was being the editor of the *Treasury;* but his ordeal of continuous strain rested upon the cushions of domestic comfort that his self-effacing wife supplied with devotion to his program of the cozily strenuous life.[7]

On December 28, in the course of an uncompressed letter, Henry Holt let his young and promising author know that he had "given the booksellers no peace, and made it impossible for them to escape taking a few hundred." He was confident that the book would reach

7. Letters from Miss Lucy Chauncy, February 14, March 14, 1960.

"most of the comparatively limited class capable of appreciating it."
He thanked her for letting him have the refusal of the next book, and
then complained, "All books are too long, and the author's craving
for elbow-room is most always an unregenerate craving. Some of the
very best books, including 'The Divine Fire,' would be still better
if they were shorter." One wonders what Henry Holt would have said
about the compactness of *The Romantic, Life and Death of Harriett
Frean,* and *History of Anthony Waring.* Perhaps May Sinclair did
owe something to the nagging of Henry Holt, as well as to the gentle
hints of Anthony Deane, and, most probably, to the example of the
imagists. She could surely have written a delightful mini-comedy,
tracing an author's long-delayed response to its resisted origin as the
cause of her later adoption of a drastically compressed style.

One of the letters that Henry Holt sent on to her on December 28
was from R. J. Cross, a brother of George Eliot's husband, who was
gratified that May Sinclair's characters speak English, and not New
York slang.

In a letter dated January 6, 1904, instead of the correct 1905, Henry
Holt pleaded with her to take advantage of the services of a Miss
Bate, an agent who, because she was working out of his office, would
not charge her any commission; and he further suggested that she
could send any of her work directly to Miss Bate without bothering
to use an agent of her own. "You know these gentlemen very naturally
want to extend their functions beyond finding a publisher for an
author, into conducting all subsequent negotiations." Some agents,
he complained, even have an unpleasant way of shifting an author
around among the publishers. "I firmly believe it to be to the author's
best interests to concentrate on one publisher—of course only if satisfied
that that one is a good one."

May Sinclair's Christmas visit to the Hinksons was not the success
she had longed for, because Mrs. Hinkson had heard there was some
vulgarity in *The Divine Fire.* Whatever she said to her guest, regret
gnawed at her humanity and made her apologize on January 24, 1905,
for her want of sympathy, and assure her that the book had the divine
fire and was a book of genius. She admired the Devon scenes for having
the vitality that Hardy gave to his places. "It is a big book, worthy
of the little woman of genius to whom I have always taken off my
hat." The letter disclosed the habit of reticence that had kept May
Sinclair from talking to Mrs. Hinkson about such parts of her book
as would rouse a demurral by the socially timid.

But Anthony Deane, on January 31, 1905, writing from Holy

Trinity Vicarage in Malvern, atoned for his demurral over *Mr. and Mrs. Nevill Tyson* by congratulating its author on *The Divine Fire* as being miles and leagues beyond her previous best: "no longer promise, but achievement—and quite splendid achievement, too." He had mentioned the book to Morley Roberts, who was staying with him at Malvern, and Roberts too was "quite enthusiastic about it." Deane praised her book, "for the first time, isn't it? to congratulate you with no sort of reservation or qualifying criticism." He also called her attention to the next day's issue of *Punch,* "and you'll find in it an Al notice of *The Divine Fire,* written by Owen Seaman. I rejoice that he is so discriminating."[8] It is quite possible that, growing more and more sentimental over the far away Sidmouth days, "with the friendly, frumpy, gossipy residents; . . . the Sunday climb to Salcombe Church,— the walks on Mutter's Moor and, best of all, the misty evenings on the Esplanade, with the last of the light tinging the red cliffs, and the gentle wash of the full tide on the stones—" Deane, an old contributing member of the *Punch* staff, may have suggested the book for review to Seaman, the assistant editor, and have stirred him into his hot indignation over England's apathy toward a new genius. It would have been only characteristic of Deane's helpfulness.

A friend of George Meredith, Seaman was aware of that giant's scorn for the stubborn resistance that the English reader could put up against any novel that dared to proffer brain stuff with its entertainment; and that *The Divine Fire* most certainly had dared to do. There was a personal reason, too, why Owen Seaman could take fire over the book. A graduate of Shrewsbury School and Clare College, Cambridge, and himself a sound classical scholar, he was perfectly equipped to appreciate Rickman's—and May Sinclair's—mastery of the Greek poets; and he could thrill with empathy over Rickman's social leap from shop-keeping to classical scholarship and literary fame, for Seaman's father had been a ladies' haberdasher.

The last sentence of Deane's letter echoed through the years: "Once more, then, three cheers for Rickman—all together—Hip, Hip, Hurray!"

Through two of its members, Mr. Kyllmann, and William Maxse Meredith, the son of George Meredith, the firm of Archibald Constable kept watch over May Sinclair's interests, particularly as Henry Holt affected them. Mr. Kyllmann was a friend of a close friend of May Sinclair's, Dr. William Carnegie Brown, the father of Ivor Brown. At Kyllmann's suggestion, William Maxse Meredith invited her on January 23, 1905, to talk over the agreement with Henry Holt, which

8. February 1, 1905.

Kyllmann thought "rather a hard one"; but Kyllmann also thought that Holt's interest in her work appeared to be so great that it would be unwise to upset him.

In February, James B. Pinker, who had a prejudice for backing certain winners, began paying her the compliment of writing repeatedly to offer his services in placing her work. She never accepted him as her agent. On March 25, George William Blackwood wrote on behalf of his uncle to inform her that there were still seven hundred copies of *Audrey Craven* in sheets, which the firm would be pleased to sell to any prospective American publisher at sixpence per copy. On March 28 Henry Holt wrote another one of his very long, annotated letters rejecting *The Tysons* for publication as "relatively so slight a thing" and giving a reader's report on *Audrey Craven* that agreed with his own objections. May Sinclair ignored every single one of the numerous suggestions that Holt fondly believed would improve *Audrey Craven*. She read again his warning against "letting anybody interfere with your publisher," and his regret that *The Divine Fire* was not shorter, because he had heard "much croaking, even from its friends, on that account."

It was apparent from the letter that he wrote on March 29 that Curtis Brown was winning May Sinclair's confidence in his ability to handle the difficult Mr. Holt in figuring out royalties and advances, and to extend her market to Canada. He must have pleased her with his "keen delight in reading The Divine Fire."

On April 11, the firm of William Heinemann made its bid for manuscripts through its Sydney S. Pawling, who wrote under the letterhead of *The World's Work*.

In a letter written over April 6 and 7, Henry Holt made suggestions for changes that he forecast would improve "The Cosmopolitan" in *Two Sides of a Question*. His ideas must have been as unacceptable as ever, because he ended by publishing in a separate volume only the second story, "Superseded," the favorite of others besides Holt. On April 14, waning in fervor and waxing in defensiveness, he wrote her that *The Divine Fire* was flourishing in the United States, and denied the allegations that he had heard that he was smothering the book with inadequate advertising. He admitted that its sales had not been large, and consequently "the advertising that is possible for it, of course, contrasts very unfavorably, to some judgments with the booming that is done here for books selling anywhere from a hundred thousand to half a million copies, and this contrast is what has aroused the anxiety and condemnation in the heart of your amateur friend.—I think I need not assure you that I have done everything for you which

I can afford to do: for I appreciate very highly the attitude you have taken in regard to me." On April 23 he wrote again: "Your 'smothered' book somehow or other keeps selling. . . . You will be amused to know how our figures stand on the money that has so far come in. For every $7. that the publishers have above their expenses, you have $20. and the advertising people have $22. What do you think of this sort of smothering?"

Dodd Mead, through their literary agents in London, inquired on May 1 if she had any new novel in hand. Witter Bynner, only three years out of Harvard, began his correspondence on May 9, writing not only as the assistant editor of *McClure's Magazine* and as a literary advisor to McClure, Phillips and Company, but also as a poet and a scholar who admired May Sinclair's work ardently. He thought even more highly of the Tyson book than of *The Divine Fire,* which he ranked along with his set of Meredith. He thought the Tyson book sent "a crystal bullet straight into the heart of modern social and domestic conditions. I never knew a book to go in a straighter, surer line from start to finish." On May 11, S. S. McClure offered her the bait of serial publication in *McClure's Magazine* to multiply the final sale of the novel that she had contracted for to Holt and Company. He was certain that "such a finely conceived and finely executed story as *The Divine Fire* would have been in the hands of almost every novel reader long ago" had it received the preliminary advertising and the monthly sampling that serial publication gave to a novel. "I want to lose no opportunity of a chance of presenting to the public writing of so high an order."

On May 5, James MacArthur, founder of the *Bookman* of New York, started Harper Brothers' courtship with a rhapsodic letter in praise of *The Divine Fire.*

> For me it is a matter of joy and pride to be able to write to you as one who hails and names a star. . . . The creative vision and power are rare gifts and the oasis in the desert is no more welcome to the traveller than is the real worth of genius to the passionate lover of literature. . . . I don't know when I have received so much deep enjoyment from a book; it is a long time since I was kept up late and made to rise early to follow with absorbing interest any story. . . . Your vision, your insight, your realization of human hopes and fears and joys and woes is so true and poignant, so manysided; the little comedies and tragedies, the heights and depths of moral struggle, the passion of loving, the joy and the sorrow of it—it is all so real so searching that it baffles one to comprehend or define the power that has conceived and created it. . . . the balance struck is so fair and proportionate, so embued with sanity and wholesome

humor. The art of the book is admirable, but one feels that the personality of the artist, hidden though it be, is a mighty pulse and a winning power behind the art.

Robert Underwood Johnson, associate editor of the *Century Magazine,* was greatly interested in her work, Miss Florence E. Bate of Holt's wrote her on May 31. Witter Bynner wrote again on June 5. He repeated his wooing of her literary work, and praised the enduring readability of *The Divine Fire.* On June 7, Harpers' eloquent James MacArthur offered her the publicity of his firm's periodicals, the *Magazine,* the *Weekly,* the *Bazar,* and the *North American Review* for whatever work of hers they would have the good fortune to publish. "It helps an author immensely toward recognition to be enrolled among the contributors of a magazine that is known for its high and rigorous standard, and the distinction of its company of writers." In his letter of May 5 he had told her how well he knew the places in London that she had described in her novel; in this one he told her that he remembered the Christchurch Road where she lived, and thought he knew just where number 13 was.

Rutger Jewett, New York manager for John Lane, the Bodley Head, made his bid for her favor on June 12 by recounting the history of his appreciation of her genius, since he had been reader for the house that issued *Two Sides of a Question* in New York, J. F. Taylor & Company. He told her that one effect of *The Divine Fire* was a marriage so amazing that it had "out-Meredithed Meredith."

William Morrow, associate editor under Ellery Sedgwick of *Leslie's Magazine,* took his place in the line of suitors on June 13 with a compliment on *The Divine Fire.* "Not in years have I read a book that gripped me as powerfully as this has done. I felt that the book had meant a great deal to you; that you had lived with it for a long time." He asked for anything that she might have to offer, short story or novel. He enclosed the cutting of a note on *The Divine Fire* that his friend William Aspinwall Bradley had contributed to *Leslie's*: it perfectly sums up the intent and the performance of the novel.

Elizabeth Jordan, the novelist, and editor of *Harper's Bazar,* made a special appeal on June 15 to obtain short stories, novelettes, or a novel from the woman who had shown in *The Divine Fire* and in *Two Sides of a Question* a special capacity for writing for women. On June 15 also, Leonard P. Moore used his charm to try to coax May Sinclair into James B. Pinker's "stable" of authors, by giving her the news that "one of the best known publishing houses in the United States" had approached him to win for it the American rights of her book. This offer James Pinker himself verified, and again May Sinclair declined on July 10, expressing her faith in Mr. A. P. Watt's good offices.

On July 10, Margaret Heitland, of the *Queen*, asked for her portrait and for "some biographical particulars to be published in that paper"— a dreamlike adumbration of the invitations to the garden parties at Buckingham Palace that were to come many years later. Witter Bynner wrote on July 16 on behalf of *McClure's*, to plead for a sequel to *Audrey Craven* that would complete the story of Katherine and Ted Haviland, and to ask for permission to dramatize *Mr. and Mrs. Nevill Tyson*.

Harpers' faithful courtier, James MacArthur, wrote voluminously again on August 1, pleading for short stories for the *Magazine*: "The note in your work so far as I've read is *Distinction*, and we have so little of that, and we want it—crave it so much for the Magazine. Then I am kept in amazement at your characterization: the subtlety, the wonderful divination, the insight *and* the humor—humor gives your work its individuality. . . . One thing I am sure of (and I'm a staid and sober critic as well as a lover of literature) there is a singular charm and individuality, a power peculiar and magnetic in your work which with the growing years ought to rank you with the very few living novelists." He pleaded that the new novel ought to be serialized in the *Magazine*; there was especial urgency because an author had defaulted. "As you know we are careful to maintain a high standard in the Magazine, especially in our serial writers, so that it becomes difficult at times to find them in succession. Now I have bethought me of *you*. You have the qualities that are essential to a serial in the *Magazine*." It was probably the persuasion of James MacArthur that brought to Harpers two novels, *Judgment of Eve* and *The Combined Maze*, and five stories of the highest merit for the *Magazine*.

The first cachet of praise from a widely known novelist admitting May Sinclair to the rank of the celebrated came from an American, whose *Call of the Wild* had so short a time ago, in 1903, written his name in the literary skies. Jack London wrote from Glen Ellen on September 20: "My dear May Sinclair:—The Divine Fire—it is colossal! I have read every line of it, and re-read many lines of it. I take my hat off to you. I sit in the dust at your feet."[9] A careful reader of *Martin Eden* must strongly suspect that that novel about a crude genius of a sailor and his inspiring lady must have been conceived or at least encouraged during the reading of *The Divine Fire*.

---

9. Published by permission of Mr. Irving Shepard.

"The Lounger" in the November issue of the *Critic* announced that May Sinclair was coming to America and prophesied that the welcome to her would be a warm one. Of *The Divine Fire* he said, "Few books have made such a profound impression as that book upon the American reader. I do not know how it has been received in England, but over here it has made a veritable sensation." Sometime in November she arrived. "Pendennis" reported in the *New York Times* on November 12 that he had interviewed her. He puffed *The Divine Fire* by declaring it was in its fifteenth printing. More modestly, Henry Holt was to announce on December 1 a tenth printing. Foremost in his perception, "Pendennis" recognized that he had met "the modern Charlotte Bronte."

May Sinclair stayed in New York City at the home of Miss Winifred Holt, the sculptress and philanthropist daughter of Henry Holt. She wrote on November 19 to that most sympathetic and imaginative of readers and that most encouraging friend of writers, Mrs. Annie Fields, that she planned to arrive in Boston with Miss Holt sometime between the eighth and the eighteenth of December.[10] Miss Holt took her guest to her father's house, Fairholt, in Burlington, Vermont, from where the travel-weary May Sinclair wrote again to Mrs. Fields on November 29, to confess that she had forgotten when she was expected. The Burlington *Free Press* gave its readers notice on December 2 of the presence of the English visitor at Fairholt. It carried the often journalized story that Miss Sinclair had spent two years in school, instead of the actual one year; and the truth that her unusual attainments were the result of self-instruction.[11]

The visitor contributed to the *New York Times* of December 1 as gaily bubbling a puff of persiflage, "Man and Superman: A Symposium," as anyone who had overlooked her music-hall verses in *The Divine Fire* would have thought wholly beyond her powers for lightness and humor. Winifred Holt rushed her from Burlington back to New York in time for her to be a member of the most illustrious gathering of writers in American literary history, with which Harper's honored the seventieth birthday of Mark Twain.

The souvenir number of *Harper's Weekly*, dated December 23, tells the full story of the magnificent occasion, a dinner held at Delmonico's Restaurant on December 5, the closest that Colonel Harvey, the editor of the *North American Review* and the manager of the affair, could approximate to the actual birthday, November 30. The most striking

---

10. Letters, courtesy of the Huntington Library.
11. The curator of the Wilbur Collection, University of Vermont, Mr. T. D. Seymour Bassett, sent me transcripts of the *Free Press* items.

fact about the evening to which Colonel Harvey referred was that fully
as many women as men were present. In his opinion there was no
measurable weight of prestige favoring either sex. As pretty a face as
any among the women in the great gathering of writers was the face
of May Sinclair, and as deserving a dinner companion as could have
been found in America was James MacArthur, of *Harper's Weekly*,
who sat to her right. Another who sat at her table that evening was
the Minerva of etiquette, Mrs. Emily Post. The *Washington Evening
Star* for December 6 reported that each guest received as his principal
souvenir a bust of Mark Twain, half life-size. Neither the material
nor the method by which the guests got their memento home was
revealed.

Two days after the exciting dinner to Mark Twain, May Sinclair
wrote from Miss Holt's home in New York to make certain that Mrs.
Fields would expect her. The anxiously viewed visit to Boston took
place from the eighth to the eleventh of December. On Christmas Eve,
back at 44 East 78th Street in New York City, May Sinclair wrote to
Mrs. Fields, regretting that her "little Christmas cards (Katherine
Tynan's 'Poems' and 'The Grey World' [by Evelyn Underhill] will
not arrive in time to greet you and dear Miss Jewett. Meanwhile, I
send you both my love and all possible good wishes for Christmas and
the New Year.—It is now settled that I am going home after the middle
of January, so my next visit to Boston must be put off a little longer."
On January 12, 1906, May Sinclair wrote again from Miss Holt's
residence, hoping that "Miss Jewett will like the 'Grey World' as
much as I do."[12]

Some time during her American visit, May Sinclair was a guest of
that unusual man of letters at the White House, President Theodore
Roosevelt, and went automobiling with him. Perhaps it was during
this call that she acquired the joy in moving by motor car that was
to last to the very end of her life. Not the president's appointment
books, not his letters to his son at Harvard, not the Washington newspapers or libraries of Washingtoniana, not the embassy's files of Ambassador Durand, who, of course, would want to meet England's finest
export of the year, give us news of this treat and tribute, but a letter
that Richard Garnett wrote her on January 18 of the new year 1906.
"The last news we have of you, later than your letter to me, is of your
having been at Washington, driving with the President. We shall expect
a full account of your impression of this remarkable man when you
return." He had heard about her adventure "through a Californian

---

12. All letters to Mrs. Fields by courtesy of the Huntington Library.

newspaper, which had borrowed a paragraph from New York." Richard Garnett wrote that Dr. Gilder and Professor Trent, to whom he had sent letters of introduction, had written to him about her "in very warm terms." He also referred to her having enjoyed the hospitality of Professor Norton.

Garnett died on April 13, 1906. He had given May Sinclair an authoritative reassurance of her worth that she had sought as a girl and found first at the Cheltenham Ladies College; and he had given her direct help in finding and in perfecting translating from the German so that she might survive and grow as an artist good enough to write an internationally admired novel. He gave her the affectionate fatherliness, too, that she needed to balance the tender motherliness of Mrs. Hinkson.

On April 28, May Sinclair wrote to Morley Roberts. Part of her news was that her address, after May 5, was to be 8 Willow Road, Hampstead. She wrote from Liverpool, where her brother William's widow had died. On May 15, at home again in London, she wrote to Morley Roberts about *The Divine Fire,* about her discovery of Gissing, and about herself. Characteristically, she defended herself from all of Morley Roberts's strictures, and also blamed her typist. She confessed that she could not correct proofs, and "the friend who angellically undertook to correct them was so preoccupied in putting huge crosses against all my 'improprieties' that many things escaped her all-too-vigilant eyes." He had caught an error in yachting terminology in "The Cosmopolitan." She confessed that she dreamed of form day and night. Of *The Divine Fire* she wrote:

> I sketched out the whole of the novel before I began it. I sketched out each chapter before a line of it was written, and tried *hard* for form and I missed it. I won't miss it again. You should see the opening of my new novel, where I've gone straight to the roots of the matter and cut preliminaries [*The Helpmate*]. You've no idea how you've helped, though. That's just what I wanted, not the wail of the bewildered amateur, complaining of the weary length, but the judgment of the craftsman who can put his finger on the flaw.

About the "pomes" she wrote:

> [I] never meant them to be taken for Rickman's best. But I think I can defend each one in its place. They *do* give an impression of Ricky's lyrical feeling at the time, they are not dragged in to show what *I* can do! The first I consider effective, spouted in Poppy's drawing-room by Rickman drunk. That instance disarms criticism. The second is avowedly a failure, and Ricky is justly annoyed when Lucia finds it. (He was very young when he wrote these, and the

first is by no means a bad sonnet, and it's not suggested that it was great.) Of the last I think your criticism holds fairly good, though it is a good sonnet. But it does give an impression of more behind it, and above all, it suggests a mood of love, a spiritual atmosphere which was what I wanted. . . . Luckily for me, only two unimportant reviews flung their obvious jibes at the "pomes."

Of Gissing she wrote that she had never met him, but she could tell from her reading that he had put more of himself into *Born in Exile* than even into *New Grub Street*: "I think I was born in another sort of Exile and that makes me understand."[13]

Truthful reporting would have to say that Rickman does *not* feel unhappy over Lucia's finding and reading his "Helen in Leuce." He thinks so well of it that he dares to ask for her opinion; when she limits to the first dozen lines her appraisal, "extremely beautiful," he retorts that *every* line in a sonnet should be perfect.

In 1906 the public image of May Sinclair was gaining the substance of the permanent. In June, Holt published *Superseded,* one of the two stories in *Two Sides of a Question,* and in August *Audrey Craven. Ainslie's Magazine* ran *Mr. and Mrs. Nevill Tyson* in two numbers, May and June, and B. W. Dodge published it as *The Tysons.*[14] "The Eternal Child," an essay on the children's books of her friend Mrs. Allen Harker, appeared in the American *Bookman* for July, and an essay, "Three American Poets of Today," considering Moody, Robinson, and Torrence, was published both in the *Atlantic Monthly* and in the *Fortnightly* in September.

In January of 1907, *The Helpmate* began its serial run in *The Atlantic Monthly.* Holt took over *The Tysons* from B. W. Dodge and published it at the end of March; and at the end of August he published *The Helpmate,* which Constable put out in London in the same month. *Everybody's Magazine* for September contained *Judgment of Eve,* and in London in the same month the first essay in a brilliant series of Brontë criticisms introduced the Everyman Library edition of *Wuthering Heights,* May Sinclair's favorite Brontë novel. *The Lady's Realm* offered *Judgment of Eve* as a supplement in December.

Another close friend of May Sinclair's, Evelyn Underhill, poet, novelist, authority on mysticism, sent a picture postcard from Arizzo on April 12 with a message of concern: "I do hope you are better now— I was dreadfully sorry to hear how ill you had been."[15]

13. The letters to Morley Roberts were presented to me by Miss Storm Jameson.
14. Mr. Henry J. Dubester, of the Library of Congress, identified the serialization.
15. See the most thorough and perceptive study by Sister Mary Xavier Kirby, *The Writings of Evelyn Underhill,* Dissertation, University of Pennsylvania, 1965: It contains a biographical introduction.

From America Mrs. Fields and Sarah Orne Jewett wrote their praise of *The Helpmate,* and May Sinclair answered their letters on August 29 at her new address in Kensington, 4 The Studios, Edwardes Square: "I was very glad you thought *The Helpmate* bore up to the end. I am not now *quite* sure whether the last chapter is more than inwardly and essentially right, whether Anne and Majendie *could* say as much to each other as they do. They would, I'm convinced, have felt or thought like that—but there would not, I'm afraid, have been quite so much conversation. I wish I could do that part again. . . . I *am* very anxious about it in this country. My reviews have been as bad as bad could be. However, it has gone into a second edition in spite of them, which looks hopeful."[16]

One of the very few mementos of friendship shown for May Sinclair is a beautiful white marble portrait, a silhouette bust of May Sinclair, sculpted by Winifred Holt and inscribed by her on November 5, 1907, as a gift to "Gaston from Alphonse."[17]

Nineteen hundred and eight bore two novels, three short stories, and three more critical essays in Brontëana. In March Harper's published her short novel *The Judgment of Eve.* In June Constable published *Kitty Tailleur,* which Doubleday Page issued in October under the title *The Immortal Moment: The Story of Kitty Tailleur,* with illustrations and decorations by a forgotten master of the blow brush and feminine flesh tones, C. Coles Phillips. Her short stories this year were "The Fault" in the January issue of the *Century Magazine;* "Wilkinson's Wife" in the February *McClure's* and in the April *Fortnightly Review;* and "The Gift" in the August number of the *American Magazine* and the September issue of the *Fortnightly Review.* She wrote the introductions to the Everyman edition of *Jane Eyre* and *Shirley,* both in February, and of Mrs. Gaskell's *Life of Charlotte Brontë,* in June.

Two letters to another friend, Violet Hunt, tell of party-going and party-giving. On June 26 she accepted an invitation to her second party on July 5, the first being at Evelyn Stuart-Moore's. On July 12, she wanted "Dear Miss Hunt" to hear a short recital that Mr. Vincent Thomas was giving at her flat on Friday, July 17. She hurried the affair to have as a guest an American musical critic, not named, who was leaving England early the following week. The Ernest Rhyses were joining her as hosts.[18]

---

16. Letter, courtesy of the Huntington Library.
17. I last saw this exquisite portrait in stone in the home of Mr. and Mrs. Harold Lumley Sinclair.
18. Letter, courtesy of the Berg Collection.

Professor William James, whom she must have met in the winter of 1905, when she was a guest of Mrs. Annie Fields, answered her last note with a drolly frank one on May 12, while he was at Oxenford Hall. He asked her if she wrote her books in the same noble hand in which she had written her note. "I don't see how you keep it up. How could you ever believe a pack of psychologists? Of course I couldn't go to their meeting—the dismalest of pseudo-sciences!" He included the best regards from his wife and assured May Sinclair, "we shall both be very happy to see you again," when they came to London.[19]

Through the mediation of Edward Clodd, May Sinclair arranged a meeting with Thomas Hardy to introduce an American critic of both Hardy and May Sinclair, Miss Mary Moss. On September 9, 1908, Hardy sent a formal unsigned note from Max Gate to say that he would receive the guests any afternoon about four o'clock.

On September 19, May Sinclair wrote to Mrs. Fields that she could not visit America that year because she had had some heavy expenses. She had enjoyed a holiday yachting with friends in Scotland and motoring with others in Normandy, and she looked forward to taking her friend Miss Moss to visit Hardy in October and be guided by him on a tour of his country. She mentioned having come back from a visit to Oxford with Professor Jastrow and his wife. "She was so good to me when I stayed with her in Philadelphia and it is pleasant to see her over here and 'show her round.'" She wondered if Mrs. Fields would like her new novel, *Kitty Tailleur*. "It is so different from my others that you may not care for it." She was now planning a "long— really very long—novel. It will be harder to write than anything I've done since The Divine Fire, and I must not talk about it—in case it doesn't 'come off.' It is one that I've had in my mind for years and I have not felt ready for it till now. Please give my dear love to Miss Jewett."[20] The allusion to *The Creators* helps a little to explain the tenseness and depth of that second novel drawn from the life of writers. "It is one that I've had in mind for years" is a tiny hint that its germ may go back to her years of intellectual intimacy with Anthony Deane, her "friendly critic."

May Sinclair and Mary Moss put up at the Black Bear Hotel, Wareham, Dorsetshire, and Hardy addressed a letter to the former on October 7, suggesting the plan by which the ladies would leave Wareham for Dorchester with their bicycles by the 11:39 train and meet

---

19. Published by permission of John James, with the gracious intercession of Professor Gay Wilson Allen.
20. Letter, courtesy of the Huntington Library.

him at the station on Friday at one, if it did not rain. As Hardy wrote to his wife,[21] rain on Friday caused a postponement of the cycling trip to the next day. After the meeting Hardy wrote a note on October 12 to Edward Clodd: "I bicycled to Weymouth with Miss Sinclair last Saturday, and found her a charming companion." Clodd was so thoughtful as to send the card to May Sinclair, with an *adscriptum* in red ink: "You may like to keep this certificate of character. E. C."

On January 9, 1909, May Sinclair wrote to Mrs. Fields: "I am so glad that you liked my poor Kitty [Tailleur], who seems to have offended so many of my American reviewers. You *always* understand just what I mean in everything I've written, and you can't think how dear your approval is to me.—I wish you could give a better account of yourself, I can't bear to think of your being ill." Mrs. Fields's letter had reached her "in the country, in the cottage I go to under the Sussex Downs. It was very lovely and quiet all the time, and I got through some work. I've finished about one-third of my new novel, which will be longer than 'The Helpmate;' *nearly* as long, I'm afraid, as 'The Divine Fire.' It has been more joy to do than anything since the days of Ricky, but it is different, though more like him than his successors." She had met Mrs. Wharton at the home of Lady St. Helis, and "liked her very much indeed."[22]

A young poet who had arrived from America in 1908 struck up a gay camaraderie that must have been a fountain of joy, and, at times, a sprinkler of embarrassments, to May Sinclair. In 1909 she became forty-six, and Ezra Pound was twenty-four; but he more than made up in brashness what he lacked in years and considerateness. In a series of letters written in March, 1909, from 48 Langham Street, London, flourished the lightheartedness with which, so differently from May Sinclair, he plunged into the war of letters.

She had invited him to call on a Tuesday, which was inconvenient for him; would she have any spare time on Friday? He thought he had no special joys to promise her except for "a most blood-curling sestina, which I think I have divested of the air of superficiality supposed to haunt that form." In his answer to her permission, he denied her certainty that the sestina was beautiful, and declared it "gore-bedabbled as the head of Coligny, or Marlowe's horses in Tamberlaine. Carol would have amended your adjective to 'brutiful.' "

In an undated letter relating to a tea party given by May Sinclair in November, Pound assured her that he had survived the party, and that "the vision of praeterhuman glowry sawed two little verses out of

21. *Dearest Emmy* (London: Macmillan, 1963), pp. 79–80.
22. Letter, courtesy of the Huntington Library.

my arid carcass, to deprive me of hours of repose." He sympathized
with her diligent attendance on her novel, remembering three horrible
days in March when he wrote "an interminable beginning of a novel,"
and then desisted. "I am man and mortal, the feminine power of
endurance is beyond me." The last paragraph in a letter of pyro-
technical cleverness, in the course of which he marveled at her disciplined writing hours in the morning, read: "Believe me, Socrates, the
symposing would not approve your course, nor would his assiduous
Bozwell, Messire Plato. The already superfluous length of this document—the only excuse for which—or rather for which the only excuse—
none-extant, or to be more clear—which might have a faint reflection
of a cause for pardon—if there were the slightest possible of your being
able to decipher it, compels me both to end the document itself and
my reminiscence of H. James, his style."

On April 6, 1909, May Sinclair wrote to Ford Madox Hueffer that
the International Suffrage Delegates Dinner was being held on Sunday
April 25, at the Lyceum Club. She also alluded to a party that he
had given: "In fact I don't know when I've enjoyed a party more, as
you might tell by my squeals of happy laughter."[23]

On April 13 (postmarked), Ezra Pound wrote, "Your 'Helpmate'
is I think the finest, strongest, etc. not to be expressed from the 3 ring
circus wherein I write this."

May Sinclair was among those who upheld the position of the
Society of Authors in signing in May an understanding not to publish
an edition of any novel first issued at six shillings in a cheap form any
time within two years from the date of the first publication.[24]

A sign of the respect that her fellow and competing authors had for
her was her being chosen to write the eulogy to George Meredith
for the Society of Authors. Black borders framed its five pages in the
Author on June 1. The *Outlook* published the essay in America on
June 19.

Thomas Hardy wrote to her on July 12 from the Athenaeum Club.
Since she was yachting in the Channel, probably with Evelyn Underhill, he directed his letter to the Southampton post office, which sent
it on to Portland. He wrote to her that he was in London, looking on
at the rehearsals of a novel of his that had been transubstantiated
into an opera: "It is Tess—Think of a Wessex Dairymaid singing in
choice Italian. But when the first sense of incongruity is past it seems
natural enough—especially to me who can accept musical conventions
to any extent. . . . Why do you say, no more cycling? I can't believe

---

23. Letter, courtesy of the Berg Collection.
24. *Author,* June 1, 1909.

that Doctor. I knew another lady who said she had been forbidden to cycle any more, but after two or three years she began again, and keeps it up now." On August 1 Hardy was back at Max Gate, and May Sinclair was again in her studio flat at Edwardes Square. He was deeply interested in her account of her nautical adventures, and thought it a pity that "Tess" should have come on the very week when he might have had luncheon with her and her friends at Southampton. If she should be in Dorset during the summer, Mrs. Hardy and he could put her up "for a night or two *en passant,* with pleasure, if you would come to stay at such a dull house, where there would be nobody else."

A letter from Mrs. Hinkson dated August 4 acknowledges a typical kindness, to which no other reference appears on record: "Dearest May,—How can I thank you? You are a dear, good little friend, God bless you! You know I needed just some such encouragement and it made my heart sing.—not only for what Mr. Bliss Perry said, but for the kindness and love of your heart towards me. . . . When I have another volume of poems you must accept the dedication. . . . We have just had an unsigned telegram to say that 'we' are coming down tomorrow. I take it to be Alice Meynell and Ezra Pound." She invited May Sinclair to come to Chipperfield, King's Langley, in Herts, if she should feel in need of a rest or a change.

Hardy wrote again from Max Gate on September 16 (postmarked), asking when she was coming to Dorset. "Ever since your piquant invitation—which, alas, I could not accept—I have felt that you must give me another opportunity of showing you about this country—and the sooner the better."

She was never so concerned with her own difficult progress that she did not have the will and the interest to help others succeed. She had known Ford Madox Hueffer so far back as 1905, when the flames of *The Divine Fire* were still recent and she lived briefly at 13 Pembroke Gardens in Kensington, for he remembered how annoyed she had been because he wore a fireman's hat at a party that the Garnetts gave in Highgate, to symbolize her novel. She did not speak to him during the whole ten miles of their ride in a carriage from Highgate to her home.[25] To help Ezra Pound become known in London, she introduced him to Hueffer with a flamboyant speech to the effect that she wanted to introduce the greatest poet to the greatest editor in the world. The meeting led to Hueffer's publishing three poems by Pound in the October, 1909, number of the *English Review,* apparently the

25. Ford, *Return to Yesterday* (London: Gollancz, 1931), pp. 326–27.

first poems of Pound to appear in a magazine since 1906, when the
Book News Monthly, a remarkable literary magazine published by
John Wanamaker in Philadelphia, carried his "Burgos: A Dream
City of Old Castile." Ford recalled that after the meeting, Pound
went on to take charge of Hueffer, the *Review,* and London.[26] There
is no record of Pound's ever disclosing the secret of the material aid
that May Sinclair gave him out of the kindness of her motherly heart.

The Creators began its serial run in the November number of
Century Magazine, and Evelyn Underhill wrote to her to prophesy that
it was going to be SPLENDID: "I suppose by the way you are prepared
to hear everyone say that Jane [Holland] is you? Because I'm sure that
they will! . . . It's going to be a *gorgeous* book: I can see and am
convinced of it. Much love and many congratulations. . . . Don't forget
Nov. 25 is the Cruising Club Dinner. Herbert will send you the formal
card later."

As a lesson to herself, May Sinclair kept a letter from a correspondent
signing herself "Betty," praising the first portion of the serial issue of
the novel and pointing out a unique lapse in grammar: "My darling,
would a literary genius say 'Of our generation—mind you—who counts
except you and I?' Doesn't 'except' always take an accusative in the
same way as 'but'? If he hadn't been literary I could understand it—but
it offends the ear—perhaps, or rather probably, it's a misprint." I suspect that May Sinclair did not remove the error in the book version
because she had heard a contemporary model say it and stubbornly—
loyally—retained that form.

On December 14, she admitted in a letter to Mrs. Fields that she
had been ill "for some time in the summer, and it was not till long,
long afterwards that I heard of your great trouble." Mrs. Fields's great
friend, Sarah Orne Jewett, had died. "I shall never forget Miss Jewett's
sweetness and kindness to me when I was with you. It is a great loss—
and we feel it over here—to American literature; her work stands alone,
so simple, so beautiful, so perfect."[27]

In February, 1910, the fifth item of Brontëana appeared, the introduction to *The Professor* in the Everyman Series.

On June 4, Thomas Hardy, writing from Maida Vale in London,
proclaimed her dignity with his own form of homage when he addressed his envelope to "Miss May Sinclair (Novelist)" at the Lyceum
Club, 128 Piccadilly, and invited her to visit him and his wife. On

---

26. *Ibid.,* p. 371; Eustace Mullins, *This Difficult Individual, Ezra Pound* (New York:
Fleet, 1961) , p. 40; Charles Norman, *Ezra Pound* (New York: Macmillan, 1960) , p.
44.
27. Letter, courtesy of the Huntington Library.

June 23 (postmarked), still in London, he had to regret being ordered by the doctor to stay in, and so having to miss the "pretty lunch (as I know it will be)"—to which she had invited him in return.

In the summer of 1910, Harriet Monro stopped in London on her way around the world and visited with May Sinclair, who introduced her to Elkin Mathews in his Vigo Street shop. Talk about Ezra Pound, who was then in the United States, led to her buying Pound's *Personae* and his *Exultations* and to her enjoying them on her Siberian journey.[28]

On August 3, May Sinclair wrote to Mrs. Fields, to thank her for a "lovely coral pin," which she would wear as a charm against evil eyes, and to recall Mrs. Fields in her beautiful room: "Always it stands out as the happiest and most *living* thing that happened to me in America. I loved you from the minute you asked me (you won't remember, but *I* do!) to give you my arm when you went across the room; and I can feel yours now, as it touched mine—very light and very gentle. Somehow I knew that you wouldn't have taken my arm if you hadn't liked me a little." She looked forward to living with her again by reading her *Letters of Sarah Orne Jewett*. She was happy that she had finished *The Creators* and glad "to have said good bye to all the horrible, interminable proofs. They made me hate it, poor thing. . . . I think it is since I last wrote you that I went abroad and saw the Riviera, and Rome, and Florence and Venice for the first time. Unfortunately I couldn't stay long enough to know them well; though doing enough to remember it all as long as I live!"[29] *The Creators* ended its serial version in the *Century Magazine* in October.

On October 27, Mrs. Hinkson wrote her praise of *The Creators* and condoled with her over some stinging reviews: "Anyhow many of them are very appreciative. Of course the book is packed full of splendid things and so generous like yourself. . . . Don't wear yourself out. No matter how splendid your work is, personally you count more for me, which I am sure you will think a wretched attitude in me. But there it is. I love the little human woman and would not have her sacrificed for a book, no matter how great. Let me know when you will come to us. . . . You are a splendid little girl with the generous qualities of a very generous man in addition to the others."

On October 28, May Sinclair wrote to Ford Madox Hueffer, who was in Germany, to congratulate him on his novel *The Call*.[30]

Maurice Hewlett joined the circle of her friends when he thanked

---

28. Norman, *Ezra Pound,* p. 60.
29. Letter, courtesy of the Huntington Library.
30. Letter, courtesy of the Berg Collection.

her for writing sympathetically about his *Rest Harrow*: "I don't care a snap what critics say, and never see their criticisms. They have no time to think, and no knowledge by which to judge. Nobody who knows me, or reads that book, (with knowledge) could think that it came from anywhere but the heart. I am incapable of writing at all unless I feel what I am writing." He assured her that he admired her book profoundly, and invited her to dine with him and two others he would invite: "You can't talk properly with more than three people at a time." She, a proper lady, gave a proper lady's reply, inviting him to dinner, and on November 1 he answered, "It seems very absurd that I should ask *you* to dinner, and that the only way of getting my desire should be to dine with you,—but I bow." He insisted that she accept his return invitation so that she could "consider the merits of a new cook I have just purchased."

When he thanked her on November 7 (he was home again at Max Gate) for the gift of her latest novel, Thomas Hardy disclosed his private curiosity as a reader of novels, reiterating what he had already proclaimed as a test of a novel's merit in his essay, "The Science of Fiction," in the *New Review* of April, 1891: "I am much interested in learning from the female characters the things that go on at the back of women's minds—the invisible rays of their thought (as is said of the spectrum) which are beyond the direct sight or intuition of man. I recollect Leslie Stephen once saying to me that he liked women's novels for that reason: they opened to him qualities of observation which could not be got from the ablest of novels by men.—Poor Rose: I have arrived at a critical point in her career. I have not peeped (I would scorn the action) so I don't know at all what is going to happen."

On December 9, May Sinclair confided to Mrs. Fields that she was exploring a new territory imaginatively. "I am busy writing short stories—stories of all queer lengths and all queer subjects; 'spooky' ones, some of them. I like doing them!"[31]

An activity of this decade whose influence upon her art has been exaggerated by both partisan and unfriendly historians was the modest, unmilitant part she played in the current struggle for women's suffrage. R. H. Gretton gave a heavy-handed account of her help to feminism when he suggested that she loaded her literature with propagandic explosions.[32] The records of the Women's Freedom League show that

---

31. Letter, courtesy of the Huntington Library.
32. R. H. Gretton, *A Modern History of the English People, 1880–1922* (London: Martin Secker), p. 730.

May Sinclair was a member of that militant organization for only one year, 1908.[33] She left a typescript among her literary remains, telling how she entered the feminist movement:

> What clinched my own conversion to the cause of women's suffrage was not the brilliant pleading of my friend, Miss Evelyn Sharp (though that began it). It was Mr. John Burns's benevolent but not quite so brilliant scheme to prevent married women working. That scheme, when it was explained to them, converted the wife of the hall-porter of the Studios where I live, and the hall-porter himself and his charwoman; it may be trusted to convert every working woman when she has once grasped it. It is a very simple scheme and it does not take much intelligence to grasp it, but it is only one amongst a thousand simple schemes of the same kind. What woman, what charwoman would have been responsible for the blunders of the Insurance Act, a well-meant scheme if ever there was one?"

The Women Writers Suffrage League was a nonmilitant organization to which May Sinclair belonged, When she joined, and when she separated from it, I could not find out.

Her earliest written contribution to the movement appears to be a letter, one of four letters by distinguished women, printed in *Votes for Women* on March 1, 1908: "I can only say that it is impossible to be a woman and not admire to the utmost the devotion, the courage, and the endurance of the women who are fighting and working for the Suffrage today." When in March of 1908 Mrs. Pethic Lawrence called upon the members of the Women's Social and Political Union to join in a week of self-denial to raise funds for the cause, May Sinclair, with Evelyn Sharp, Violet Hunt, and Clemence Housman, stood outside the Kensington High Street Station of the District Railway, where they were photographed as they rattled their collection boxes in the wintry cold weather, like Salvation Army lasses.[34]

Votes for Women on December 24, 1908, carried a second signed statement, entitled "How It Strikes a Mere Novelist," of her sympathy with the movement and of her hope for the glorious change its success would produce for England: "The coming generation will, I believe, witness a finer art, a more splendid literature than has been seen since the Elizabethan Age. . . . The Nineteenth Century was an age of material cocksureness, and of spiritual doubt. The Twentieth Century

---

33. Letter, Miss Laura Price, January 20, 1963.
34. Estelle S. Pankhurst, *The Suffragette Movement* (New York: Longmans, Green, 1931), p. 279; Emmeline S. Pankhurst, *The Suffragette* (New York: Sturgis and Walton, 1911), p. 208; Violet Hunt, *The Flurried Years* (London: Hurst and Blackett, 1926), pp. 41–42.

will be the age of spiritual certainty.—And this thing, this desire of all the ages, this spiritual certainty will, I believe, come through the coming revolution, by the release of long captive forces, by the breathing in among us of the Spirit of Life, the genius of enfranchised womanhood."

When Mrs. Elsie Hueffer tried to make her husband's life with Violet Hunt a couch of legal thorns, Henry James timidly sentenced the two lovers to a moral quarantine,[35] but May Sinclair stayed fiercely loyal, as she proved in a letter to Hueffer in April, 1910: "I'm sick of the world we live in, with its cowardice and hypocrisy, and abominable, sham morality. . . . Do come, both of you, to a little tea-party on Tuesday 19th 4–6. (It's got to be early, because of the Tax-Resistance Dinner.) —I do hope you'll both come."[36] In *The Flurried Years* Violet Hunt appropriated that letter as written to herself.

An undated letter that May Sinclair did write to Violet Hunt apologized for abstaining from the too heady convivialities of the Cave of the Golden Calf,[37] the nightclub run by Mademe Strindberg in a basement in Heddon Street, where the vorticists danced the turkey trot and the bunny hug, and found good food and good wines and steep prices.[38] This letter gives the first hint that she may have found Reeth as a perfect sanctuary for her writing: "I want to be in Yorkshire, all alone, writing my novel. But I'm very, very tired, and don't know how I'm going to do it. I haven't been able to bear stuffy rooms since I got back!"

On Saturday, June 18, 1910, May Sinclair joined with her friends Mrs. Alice Meynell, Miss Alice Zimmern, Mrs. Belloc Lowndes, and others, to march in a procession as a member of the Women Writers unit—identified by a special black and white scriveners' banner that Mrs. Cicely Hamilton and Mrs. Gascoigne-Hartley held up in front of it. Each of the women writers carried a goose quill and a black-and-white bannerette, summoning up the spirit of an English woman writer of the past: Elizabeth Barrett Browning, Fanny Burney, George Eliot, and many more.[39] The leader of the procession was Lord Lytton. At its head was a banner whose slogan Laurence Housman had phrased: "From Prison to Citizenship." Forty bands inspired the rhythm of the marchers in a column of fours. Seven hundred banners

35. Hunt, *The Flurried Years*, p. 88.
36. Letter, courtesy of the Berg Collection.
37. Letter, courtesy of the Berg Collection.
38. Edgar Jepson, *Memoirs of an Edwardian and Neo-Georgian* (London: Richards, 1937), pp. 154–55.
39. Miss Pamela A. Rose, M.A., discovered this account in *The Vote*, June 25, 1910, and sent me a transcript.

waved; more than six hundred women carried staves, each staff holding a broad arrow to symbolize an imprisonment.

May Sinclair signed a Writers' Memorial that was sent some time in June to Mr. Asquith, to urge the claims of a women's suffrage bill. Bernard Shaw, John Galsworthy, Arnold Bennett, and Joseph Conrad were among the fellow-signers.[40]

It was probably their common interest in the cause of women's suffrage that formed the friendship with Dr. Jessie Margaret Murray, who was to interest May Sinclair in a unique medical venture early in the next decade. Dr. Jessie Murray and Mr. H. N. Brailsford headed an inquiry into the physical effects of police action upon women who took part in a suffrage demonstration on November 18, 1910. Two women died of the injuries they had received then: Mrs. Pankhurst's sister, Mrs. Clarke, and a Miss Henrietta Williams.[41]

Sometime in this year May Sinclair, perhaps in memory of her brother Frank, became a founding member of the Royal India Pakistan and Ceylon Society. There is no record that she took an active part in its affairs, but she evidently subscribed to the publications that the Society commited itself to undertake, like the reproductions of the Ajanta Frescoes, in 1915.[42]

The decade from 1900 to 1910 had built a sturdy foundation to a literary career that had raised her close to the top of Parnassus and was to raise her even more spectacularly in the following decade.

---

40. Miss Pamela A. Rose, letter, August 17, 1962.
41. A. E. Metcalfe, *Woman's Effort* (Oxford: Blackwell, 1917), p. 165; Estelle S. Pankhurst, *The Suffragette Movement*, pp. 343–44; London *Times*, December 6, 1910.
42. Letter, Frederick Richter, C. B. E., Honorary Secretary, August 6, 1959.

7

The Decade of Vortices: 1911-1920

The new decade, which opened when May Sinclair was in her outwardly undetectable forty-eighth year, was to let her enjoy in the
company of the young imagist poets the excitements of a postponed
youth. It would introduce her to the theories of psychoanalysis, make
her a charter member of the first English medical clinic to include
psychoanalysis in its therapy, and through her association with the
clinic lead to her acting a healing part in civilization's severest disrup-
tion, war. It was to let her take part as a writer in a lesser war, for
women's suffrage, honor her for her literary genius, and admit her to
a ranking with England's best minds in philosophy. It was a decade
during which, while her personality lived a pattern of varied interests
(of which a strenuous one was the encouragement and promotion of
younger writers), the artist's self tirelessly explored and experimented
to reach always a heightened level of originality and merit, while
around her great social vortices dashed against the foundations of
literary, social, and political mores.

The torn half of a letter, whose writer I tried but failed to trace,
implies the conscious sacrifice that May Sinclair offered to the god of
her art so that she might win his favor. The letter, addressed at The
Florence 19 and 20 Lancaster Gate, W., dated January 15, 1911,
discusses the central theme of *The Creators*: if a woman can be a good
wife and a good novelist at the same time. The essential fragments
of the letter, in answer to her letter or letters, give us our clue: "My
view is with yours in so far as you believe the actual life of love and
of home [for a woman] is incompatible with the life of work—that is if
the work is to be great . . . and her power of saying something of

actual value to humanity is of real account, her forte lies in the creation of high and beautiful types of children and of ennobling and charming everyday life of the imagination." Her real belief, which she fictionally refuted in creating Jane Holland, survives in this half of a torn letter that a second impulse made her keep..

On March 11, 1911, Ezra Pound, when he had read 163 pages of *The Creators*, wrote: "The book is a perfect sign of the decadence which makes me stay out of London." He implored her to burn her correspondence and come to Paris, "before whatever holy feast day you had set for your possible pilgrimage." In another letter under the same date he iterated, "I wish to divorce you from London—at least for a seasonable space."

Mrs. Hinkson wrote from Southborough in Kent on April 10, sending the latest news about her family and her writing: "I must manage the Woman Writers where I see you are to preside." As always, there were a warm welcome and an assurance of love: "Do come and stay at the Hand and Sceptre and let us see a lot of you and give you your meals. What are you working at?"

Sometime in April Evelyn Underhill wrote from Campden Hill Square her opinion of the manuscript of *The Flaw in the Crystal*, and queried some of the phrasings. The mystical, psychic theme had a special appeal for her, of course; her own book, *Mysticism*, had just come out in March, and she had already published three mystical novels[1]: "I still think your most brilliant bit is that vision of the evil world. I wonder whether you have ever *seen* that disagreeable piece of evidence of the existence of the devil. If not, it is an *extraordinary* piece of imaginative reconstruction. I saw it once for 24 hours (this piece of information is for you *alone*!) and it was awfully like that, allowing for difference of landscape. You reminded me of it again with horrid vividness!!!" May Sinclair considered the queries, but kept most of her own phrasing.

During a cruise on the yacht *Nepenthe*, Evelyn Underhill wrote a letter that she dated May 2 and posted a month later at Westmersea, thanking May Sinclair for valuable criticisms of a poem of hers that had appeared in the *Nation* and in the *Living Age*. She confessed: "I knew *nothing* about the technique of poetry unfortunately and wrote it in a casual sort of way and 'hope for the best.' But now you've told me, I see exactly that the weight in these irregular verses does fall on the long lines and that I must pay more attention to their con-

---

1. See Sister Mary Xavier Kirby, *The Writings of Evelyn Underhill*, Dissertation, University of Pennsylvania, 1965.

struction! Rhymes in 'y' are an awful snare into which I am always tumbling." She returned to the subject of *The Flaw in the Crystal*: "It's simply *amazing* about the evil vision of the world, and makes me quite afraid of you! I've never heard of any one else having it in that violent form, though the other day a man I know rather well told me that after a year of intense spiritual exaltation he lived in a modified state of that kind, in much misery for 2 years. My own belief is that where not associated with insanity it is educative and ought to be endured as long as possible. I wonder whether the description in the *Crystal* will bring to light any other cases. The heavenly vision seems to be much commoner, doesn't it?" From Evelyn Underhill's reference to a letter that was not saved, it may be assumed that May Sinclair had confessed to her first what she later wrote to Mrs. Fields: that she had actually experienced the vision that she had described.

On May 15, Evelyn Underhill wrote to May Sinclair after having read the manuscript of a short story, probably "Between the Lines," the single farcical character story that she wrote in 1911:

"Dearest May—I think this is perfectly *delicious*—so exquisitely touched off—not a word too many or too few. I read it right through to one long underground giggle! . . . You've never done anything better in your light vein. As to originals I feel convinced you are absolutely safe——the connection would never even have occurred to me if you hadn't suggested it. Somehow I see him as quite a different looking person, and you've got him so splendidly alive that he just couldn't be anything but himself. Oh, it is really too lovely! I do congratulate you on it! . . .—I'm writing verse, of all absurd things, and nothing else. Isn't it idiotic? However, the *Nation* says it can take all I can send so it's not utterly profitless.

Arnold Bennett's *Journal* records his having had dinner on May 22 at Pagani's resturant with Austin Harrison, May Sinclair, and an American couple. The dinner ended after midnight, Bennett took a taxi, and after letting Austin Harrison get out at Davies Street, Bennett saw May Sinclair home to her studios in Edwardes Square. He liked "this prim virgin" who had such great sense and who lived alone, not even having a servant. On June 8, Bennett and Irving Brock of the *New York Times* were dinner guests of May Sinclair at the Albemarle Club. Bennett must have enjoyed himself, because on June 14 he wrote from the library of the Authors' Club, where he did a good deal of his writing, asking her to persuade another member to join her in putting him up for membership. It was going to be his fate to be in London in August, and his wife was not coming until later.

"It appears to me that a mixed club might be useful to me, especially in a month like August. . . . I only ask you as you kindly offered, you know."

The *Spectator* contained on June 24 a letter from May Sinclair protesting against a declaration in its pages on June 10 that it would suspend notice of the *English Review* until it discontinued its policy of printing such invitations to moral leniency as Frank Harris's "Thoughts on Morals." While wholly agreeing with the *Spectator's* particular condemnation of Frank Harris, she fervently defended the supreme principle of the freedom of the press and defended the *English Review* from the charge of dumping garbage on the national doorstep, when it had been publishing the work of Henry James, Arnold Bennett, Joseph Conrad, H. G. Wells, Maurice Hewlett, and John Galsworthy.

Two more short stories of hers appeared before the winter, "Appearances" in the August *Good Housekeeping*, and "Miss Tarrant's Temperament" in the August and September numbers of *Harper's Magazine*. She accepted Mrs. Hinkson's invitation to visit Southborough that summer, and she stayed at the recommended Hand and Sceptre. She accompanied the Hinksons on many expeditions and to dinners in the Pantiles in a gallery overlooking the promenade, with a band supplying the dinner music. Mrs. Hinkson left this impression of her during that summer of 1911: "She was a quiet little mouse-like lion for Southborough to stare at; and we took her to some local functions, where she was very amiable, but more interesting than interested."[2]

Arnold Bennett wrote again on August 14 from Avon-Fontainebleu to say that he would be in London in August, but the rehearsals of his play *The Honeymoon* had been postponed until September. Since his wife was ill and not coming on until later, he hoped that they would be able "to manage a conviviality of some discreet kind."

On September 22, 1911, from Granville Place, W., Ezra Pound wrote an invitation to luncheon on the twenty fifth. The handmade rag paper, faded now to a lavender blue, Pound deprecated: "For this passionate paper blame us not, it is not our original sin." On September 29 (postmarked), he gave his opinions, on plain paper, of Miss Hilda Doolittle and Margaret Hannay. About Hilda Doolittle he wrote: "Hilda is—in her lucid intervals—rather charming"; and about the latter: "Margaret Hannay has always impressed me as a young person of some stolidity to more or less common sense." He suggested that May Sinclair write to Margaret Hannay, "introducing Hilda as a stray American who paints— (or better 'draws') a little, writes a

---

2. Katherine Tynan Hinkson, *The Middle Years*, p. 401.

little, may be stopping on at the 'Slade,' or may not be doing anything of the sort, etc." He also suggested that she write to Miss Hilda Doolittle at 30 Bernard Street, W. C., to ask her to bring Miss Frances Gregg to tea: "If you write at once it may be there for her arrival and the quicker the effect of hospitality is produced the less hospitality will be needed to produce the effect." Ezra Pound ended with "Salaams and prostrations."

On December 8, May Sinclair shared the distinction of the High Table of the annual dinner of the Society of Authors at the Criterion Restaurant with Lady and Sir Arthur Conan Doyle and Ezra Pound.[3]

The fourth short story of the year, "Between the Lines," came out in the December *Harper's*.

An unsigned attack upon literary and dramatic agents, which had appeared in the October number of the *Author,* prompted her always alert sense of fair play to make a lengthy rebuttal on December 1. She described the varieties of an author's problems with publishers and defended her agent in a masterpiece of analysis and argument.

Maurice Hewlett on January 11, 1912, invited her to dinner on the twenty-second at his home in Northwick Terrace, N.W., to help celebrate his birthday. "I can't help it," he pleaded.

A letter of hers appeared in the London *Times* on April 4, advancing the argument that she was to incorporate into her pamphlet *Feminism*: that women's suffrage would support her right and power to compete with men in the economic market.

On April 13, she wrote to Hugh Walpole to praise *A Prelude to Adventure* as his best work to date. She had happened to meet Henry James when she was three-fourths through with reading it, and he had said that "it was far and away the best and *'closest'* thing you'd done, but that it wasn't 'close' enough." At first she thought that the Master had meant "close-knit"; but after finishing the novel, she realized that James had meant "close to reality." She thought that Walpole had gone astray when he made Mrs. Craven murder her husband, producing not only an improbable anticlimax, but also a serious distraction from the tragic interest that should have centered, without any rival, in Dune: "This seems to me exactly the same sort of error that led you into melodrama in 'Mr. Perrin and Mr. Traill.' " In some of his earlier books she saw that his danger lay in falling into "a certain vein of fantasy which beautiful in itself, was not of a piece or on the same plane with the reality you were treating."[4]

On April 16, 1912, she informed the still importuning James Pinker

---

3. *Author,* January, 1912.
4. Letter, courtesy of Rupert Hart-Davis.

of her agent's satisfactory arrangements for her next three novels, the reason why she was making no change in agents. She told him also that Constables had broken their contract with her for *The Three Brontës* because they had heard that she had offered her next three novels to Hutchinsons, who would publish her Brontë book too. "Simple fury, nothing more."[5]

The surviving part of a letter written by Curtis Brown on April 22 at his office in Covent Garden tells us that he had at last taken over her literary business from A. P. Watt & Son. Its tone reminds us of the clangs and clamors of buyers that had sounded in 1905. He sent her an acknowledgment of her having returned the contract with Hutchinsons for *The Three Brontës,* and sent her the contract with Duttons to publish *The Flaw in the Crystal,* which was appearing complete in the *English Review.* That contract gave her the right to republish with other stories after three years, and required that the first offer to publish a book of short stories in the United States would be made to Duttons: "If, when the time comes, you don't want them to publish it, all you have to do is to put a high price on it."

The pamphlet, whose writing May Sinclair had said in a letter on April 13 to Hugh Walpole was swallowing up her time, was published by the Women Writers Suffrage League, Women's Press, in May under the title *Feminism.* It was the ninth publication of the League since its founding in 1908 by Miss Cicely Hamilton and Miss Bessie Hatton. May Sinclair was not listed among the founding members. In October, 1912, when Florie Annie Steel succeeded Elizabeth Robins as president, May Sinclair was one of twelve vice-presidents, along with Sarah Grand, Mrs. Belloc-Lowndes, Margaret Woods, Edith Zangwill, Mrs. Baillie-Reynolds, and Miss Symonds (George Paston) .[6]

The pressure under which May Sinclair was hurrying her gently reasonable apology for feminism into print was the increasingly violent behavior of the suffragists, whose heroines were later so modest in revealing in their memoirs the unladylike feats with which they wrought their heroism. The reader who is not satisfied by the paltry evidence in the memoirs must turn to the daily newspapers for supplementary reporting of the original facts. On March 1, several hundred women effected a smashing attack on plate glass shop windows in London. W. W. Jacobs was one of those arrested for window-smashing on the first of March. Eight women were arrested on March 7 for smashing windows in the Buckingham Palace Road and in Oxford

5. Letter, courtesy of the Berg Collection.
6. A. J. R., ed., *The Suffrage Annual and Women's Who's Who* (1913) , pp. 134–37.

Circus. The windows of Selfridge's and Robinson's stores escaped all damage.[7]

Why Robinson's windows were spared I do not know, but the *Suffrage Annual and Women's Who's Who* for 1913 bears witness to the insurance Selfridge's took out. The hard front cover advertises that Selfridge and Co., Ltd., is "The Modern Woman's Club Store," and every single page, from page 1 to page 405, carries one or two lines of Selfridge advertising, like "The needs of the modern woman are carefully studied at Selfridge's," and "Selfridge Policy: To make every passing customer a permanent friend." The line "Selfridge's is the ideal store for the busy man" was so palpably overwhelmed by its staunch feminine environment as to be almost ridiculous.

Feminism, whose completion was dated March 31, appeared as a prompt refutation to a letter that had occupied three columns in the London *Times* on March 28, 1912, and was written by a physician, Sir Almroth Wright, who diagnosed the feminists as sufferers from hysteria.

May Sinclair was a woman, not a swinger of hammers, and *The Tree of Heaven* was to confess her renunciation of the violent causists. But when her clear mind saw an inconsistency, she had to speak up or write out. She was to be just as fearless in pointing out gaps in the thinking circuits of established, prestige-gowned philosophers as she now was in pointing out an inconsistency in the government's disposing of criminal suffragettes. On June 19 the *Times* carried a letter that she had dated June 17. It ridiculed the government's acknowledging the leaders of the militant suffragist movement as political prisoners by removing them to the first division, and so practically admitting the justice of their claim, while classifying the obedient rank and file as common criminals. In terms of the logic of comparative guilt, the militant leaders would probably plead "more guilty," because they must be held more responsible than the rank and file. On July 6, after serving only about four months of their six months' sentence, the still imprisoned members of the Women's Social and Political Union who had taken part in the March gale of window smashing were released.

The year 1912 was blessed by some calmer days and evenings. There was an evening in June when William Lyon Phelps was a dinner guest at the home of Mrs. W. K. Clifford near Paddington Station, his only fellow guests being May Sinclair and Henry James. Professor Phelps described the overwhelming impression of reality that *Tess of the*

---

7. London, March 2, 5, 8, 11; April 13; June 17.

D'Urbervilles had left upon him. Perhaps to test the professor's flexibility, or to tease Henry James, May Sinclair said that she had undergone the same experience with Mrs. Humphry Ward's novels. Henry James took the bait by pontificating, "May Sinclair, May Sinclair, such a remark may do credit to your heart, but where does it leave your head?"[8] Phelps's designation for James's style of conversing as of his writing should be preserved for the history of terse criticism: "verbose reticence." Phelps was lucky too in catching sight of Arnold Bennett accompanying May Sinclair to a matinee performance of Bennett's *What the Public Wants* at the Coronet Theatre at Queen's Gate. May Sinclair gave a tea party on June 4, for which Henry James accepted on June 3 on the stationery of the Reform Club. The note must be startling to students of the Master for its laconic economy.

A treasured friend whom May Sinclair may have met as early as 1906 was Dr. William Carnegie Brown, who had taken his regular degrees in medicine and surgery at Aberdeen in 1881 and his Doctor of Medicine in 1884, had practiced in Penang until 1905, and after bringing his family to Hampstead, specialized in Oriental diseases at 32, Harley Street. He published a volume on amoebic dysentery and another on sprue, the disease of which he died in September 1913. His son, Ivor Brown, believed that Mrs. Allen Harker, a writer of children's stories (who was at Cheltenham Ladies College while May Sinclair was there but did not meet her then), had introduced his family to May Sinclair when she lived in lodgings at 8 Willow Road, Hampstead. May Sinclair took an interest in Ivor Brown when he was a schoolboy at Cheltenham College, when he went on as a classical scholar to Balliol in 1909, and afterward when he was building a distinguished career in journalism and in literature.[9] Dr. Brown's residence in Malaya, his familiarity with the countries and the philosophies of the Orient (including the India where her brother Frank had served and where he had died twenty-three years before) must have affected her with a claim like that of a relationship, which she could reciprocate by becoming a godmother to his daughter, Hazel Urquhart Brown.

Evelyn Underhill wrote about the just-published *The Three Brontës* on June 20: "My present impression is one of the wildest enthusiasm. I think it is perfectly *splendid*—magnificently written and full of insight—it looks like being one of the *very* finest things you have done.

8. W. L. Phelps, *Autobiography* (Oxford University Press, 1939), pp. 551–52.
9. Letters, Ivor Brown, August 14, September 16, 1962.

If you come by your own, as you should, you will walk up to a top place among the literary critics." On June 25 she wrote again: "It seems to me a perfectly wonderful achievement—every line and word of it carries conviction, and I can never again believe the Brontës to be other than what you have described—or revealed. The thing simply throbs with life. . . . Of course, I *entirely* agree with you about Emily—you seem to me to have proved it up to the hilt. . . . This is really a great book you've done, dear May, and you have my deepest and humblest respects for it."

Mrs. Hinkson wrote from Ireland on July 2: "I've done The Brontës for the *Pall Mall*. . . . I read it from cover to cover, finding it more fascinating than any novel."

May Sinclair's early interest in Buddhist religious literature prepared her to admire a contemporary poet whom India was offering to the world's taste. William Rothenstein's encouragement had led to Tagore's arrival in London in the summer of 1912 with the translations he had made of some of his Bengali poems during his passage from India. Rothenstein then induced Yeats to come from Normandy to read aloud some of Tagore's poems to a gathering of his friends. Among the listeners were Tagore, who left a record of the silent suffering with which he endured Yeats's mannered barding,[10] and May Sinclair, who enjoyed the performance. The very next day she wrote to Tagore, who answered her on July 10: "When I wrote my songs I never for a moment thought that they could be translated. In fact, I never looked upon them from the point of view of literature. What made me feel glad in your beautiful letter was not so much at the appreciation of the literary merit of these writings of mine as at the evident sign of response they had awakened in your heart which is the richest reward that a poet can ever expect."

At Rothenstein's instigation the India Society printed a selection of Tagore's translations under the title *Gitanjali,* which the London *Times* lauded on November 7. Rothenstein then persuaded George Macmillan to publish a popular edition of the poems in 1913, and in that year *Gitanjali* won the Nobel Prize. May Sinclair wrote an enthusiastic essay on "The *Gitanjali*," which appeared in the *North American Review* for May 1913. She also helped Jo Davidson, the young American sculptor, whose studio was directly below hers at 4 Edwardes Square, when he was trying to do a bust of Tagore. The sculptor found Tagore's habit of slipping into meditation and thereby

---

10. Edward Thompson, *Rabindranath Tagore: Poet and Dramatist* (Oxford University Press, 1926), pp. 231–32; William Rothenstein, *Men and Memories, Recollections, 1900–1922* (New York: Coward-McCan, 1932), pp. 262–82.

draining his face of all expression very baffling, just when he had hoped to catch a significant expression. He finally implored the tenant upstairs, the notably silent one, to leave her work and try with her conversation to lure. the mystic poet into restoring liveliness to his features.[11]

On July 16, 1912, May Sinclair thanked Mrs. Fields for her praise of *The Flaw in the Crystal,* and confessed her ambition to write some more "uncanny Tales" like that one, because

> They fascinate me; but I think they should be kept to themselves in their own atmosphere.—The queer thing about this tale is that it really happened—at least the uncanny part of it did. Only of course I let myself play about with the possibilities of the things and added the man Rodney Lanyon and his wife Bella to "thicken" it.—Since I last wrote to you I have had the very great pleasure of making Mr. James's acquaintance, and I have quite lost my heart to him. I dare say I shall never see him again, but it is something to have seen him even these few times. He came out to see me in my funny flat, and I think I provided him with a new sensation in "interiors."[12]

The abbé Ernest Dimnet wrote from Paris on July 19, thanking her for an inscribed copy of her *The Three Brontës.* She had challenged a number of opinions that he offered in his *Les Soeurs Brontë* in 1910, and on his part he defended M. Heger from what he believed to be her unjust treatment of him. The abbé thought Heger had "realised the powers of his pupils better than anybody had done before and than most people did afterwards, and he respected them deeply."

May Sinclair's alert sense of fairness was provoked by Cicely Hamilton's essay "Man" in the April number of the *English Review,* into sending a rebuttal "A Defence of Men," which was published in the July number, and which acted as a counterweight to another rebuttal, her pamphlet *Feminism.* Engagement in literary and political controversy must have been as exhausting as it was exhilarating, for her friend Dr. William Carnegie Brown wrote from Scotland, on August 20, that he was sorry to hear she had been ill, and that she was doing the right thing in getting herself looked after.

In October of 1912, May Sinclair stayed at the Victoria House, kept by Miss Mary Wallis,[13] in Reeth, a gray stone village set in the grandly sweeping Swaledale in North Yorkshire. Reeth had become

---

11. May Sinclair, *A Journal of Impressions in Belgium* (London: Hutchinson, 1915), p. 91.
12. Letter, courtesy of the Huntington Library.
13. Letter, Phyllis Bentley, August 31, 1961.

both the center for exploring new country that was to furnish her with a new setting, and a sanctuary for uninterrupted writing in the midst of heavenly normal, unliterary people. Evelyn Underhill's letter to her there, written in London on October 15, hints that May Sinclair dreamed of finding a cottage and someone to keep house for her.

Dutton issued *The Flaw in the Crystal* in October in the attractive form that Curtis Brown had expected. Fourteen point type and tasteful decorations gave the book a dignity for the eye to linger over. The review in the *New York Times* on September 8 was so inadequate that the editor of the Book Section invited her to contribute a letter of explanation, and this letter appeared on the first page of the book section on Sunday, November 3. The American investigator of psychic phenomena, James H. Hyslop, did not read the book, nor the review, but he did read the letter and on the same day, November 3, requested (under the streaming scientific banner of a letterhead that ran "The American Institute for Scientific Research—Section B—American Society for Psychical Research, New York") a *scientific* account of the genuine experience: "It is the cold naked facts we desire without color of imagination or fear of ridicule. I hope I may have a detailed record of the facts which gave rise to the book." Her answer has been lost.

On October 15 and on November 7, Evelyn Underhill wrote of the joy that she shared with May Sinclair in Tagore's *Gitanjali*.

The annual dinner of the Society of Authors, held at the Hotel Cecil on December 7, 1912, gave new evidence of the changing, sensitive stratification of literary prestige when Maurice Hewlett, May Sinclair, Hugh Walpole, E. Phillips Oppenheim, and the Hon. Mr. Justice Darling were among those who sat at the High Table, while W. W. Jacobs, Mrs. Belloc Lowndes, and the fellow Cheltenhamite Beatrice Harraden sat at smaller and lower tables.[14]

Ezra Pound wrote a thank-you note on New Year's Eve to the always generous woman: "Dear M. S.—It is very good of you to send me sinful luxuries, and very bad of me not to have thanked you sooner." On January 28, Dr. William Carnegie Brown thanked her for the tulips that she had sent to cheer him during his illness. His strong, clear handwriting records the courage with which he was advancing toward the end of a road that his professional vision had already sighted.

After reading *Fortitude*, May Sinclair wrote Hugh Walpole on January 28, 1913, to give him the harvest of her discernment. She was confessing the continuation of her experiment in a lean style when

---

14. *Author*, January 1, 1913, p. 124.

she wrote: "I wish you could have kept it a bit tighter and cleaner, but that's merely personal taste, and you know the particular little craze I've on just now, which may wreck me utterly!"[15]

The atmosphere of this time lingers on in scattered references. Richard Aldington told us in his *Life for Life's Sake* that it was the stuffiness of formal entertaining in the world before 1914 that drew him to the magic circle of the informal, exciting people like Ezra Pound, Hilda Doolittle, May Sinclair, and W. B. Yeats. The *Gitanjali* poems stirred up Ezra Pound, May Sinclair, and W. B. Yeats, whose bachelor quarters in Woburn Place were the center of many meetings of young poets. Aldington was not thrown to his knees by Tagore, and was amused to watch Tagore rise to popularity and to a knighthood, and then slide into neglect because, as Sir Rabindranath, he espoused Indian nationalism. Aldington was one of the group of poets whom Ezra Pound, uttering the term T. E. Hulme had minted, called the imagists (meaning Pound, Hilda Doolittle, T. E. Hulme, Aldington, Hueffer, Harold Monro, and D. H. Lawrence). And Aldington (although he smiled at such a howler of translation that turned "nocte canes" of Propertius into "night dogs," instead of "thou singest by night") was the first to esteem the scope of Pound's mind, to appreciate the full comprehension of the European tradition of literature in spirit and in critical standards that Pound tossed into the common fund of new poets in England.[16] Another observer of London's revolution in poetry, John Gould Fletcher, told the story of Ezra Pound's rebaptizing *The Freewoman* as *The New Freewoman* and then reincarnating it as *The Egoist,* with Aldington as its literary editor.[17]

May Sinclair was an intensely interested member of the groups who were collectively blaring and nursing new ideas in literature: Tagorephiles, imagists, and vorticists; yet how many remembered her when they came to recall names second in fame to their own? Her mind was certainly as well stored as the mind of any member of these groups; her critical genius was as perceptive as any. She was generous in giving financial aid to those who needed it and in pleading with her friends and others in positions of power to help the writers in whom she believed. She was nearing the summit of life that is marked "fifty," and was exchanging the best offerings of her brain and her purse for the society of youth and the atmosphere of intellectual zest.

After spending an evening as a guest of May Sinclair's, Arnold Bennett wrote a note of apology, which we should recall when we read

15. Letter, courtesy of Rupert Hart-Davis.
16. *Life for Life's Sake* (New York: The Viking Press, 1941), pp. 134–38.
17. *Life is My Song* (New York: Farrar and Rinehart, 1937), chap. 11 and 12.

Tasker Jevons again, because of the lightning glimpse it gives us of the conflict between the primitive Bennett and the civilized Bennett, a conflict that May Sinclair elaborated, with some possible help from her observations of Ezra Pound, into a portrait of a popular novelist and playwright. Bennett wrote from an address in Putney on February 1, 1913: "I have a most singular and unhappy faculty of leaving hostesses without thanking them for having entertained me and put me in the way of nice distraction. I always think of it in the street! Please pardon me. It is only my barbaric manners! Heart of gold etc., I assure you. I had a fine time."

A copy of *The Combined Maze* went to Evelyn Underhill, who wrote on February 18, to praise the novel as a "wonderful triumph,—the way in which you have made all the little incidents and the whole life in that ordinary little house seem so supremely important and absorbing. . . . On the whole, this is by far the most tragic book you have done isn't it? But it is the noble sort of tragedy, the immortal and purifying kind."

Reading *The Combined Maze* prompted an unknown poet who was seven years younger than May Sinclair to write to its author in March. May Sinclair answered graciously, and after meeting Charlotte Mew became her vigorous champion, encouraging her to believe in herself, securing the publication of her poems in periodicals and in volume form, and rounding up sympathetic reviewers among her friends.[18]

In answering May Sinclair's letter about his recently published book of poems, *Helen Redeemed,* Maurice Hewlett wrote bravely on March 4, 1913: "I don't mind much the present neglect of my rhyming when I get letters like yours. If I am anything of a poet, or come anywhere near the place I claim, one of these days, it will be found out. Meanwhile it doesn't do to be nervous about public recognition."

Evelyn Underhill wrote from Norfolk on March 26, to answer May Sinclair's commentary on her *The Mystic Way.* The letter implies that May Sinclair had defended the metaphysics of the Brahmins and Buddhists. In a cheery, friendly rejoinder Evelyn Underhill exposed the life-denying aim of Hindu religions: "The Christian method of describing Union may be paradoxical and open to attack—yet I'm convinced it's nearer reality than any description, however logical, which involves total obliteration of the subject-object relation, or the achievement of a point at which, as one Hindu philosopher explained to me with pride, 'The word Love becomes meaningless.' "

In May the *North American Review* carried May Sinclair's essay

---

18. For the story of their relationship see "The Mystery of Charlotte Mew and May Sinclair: An Inquiry," *N.Y.P.L. Bulletin* vol. 74, no 7 (September, 1970) .

on the *Gitanjali*. Her other literary article of this year was her fretful notice of "The New Brontë Letters" in the *Dial* for November 1. Four short stories appeared in 1913: " 'Khaki' " in the *English Review* for September, "Compensation" in the October *Good Housekeeping*, "Appearances" in the *Fortnightly Review*, and "The Wrackham Memoirs" in *Harper's* in December.

The *Suffrage Annual and Women's Who's Who* defined in 1913 the limits of the Women Writers' Suffrage League, to which May Sinclair belonged: "its methods are those proper to writers—the use of the pen."[19] The further boundary that she drew around her participation is implied by the absence of her name from the Biographies section, which reaches from page 167 to page 405.

In the summer of 1913, May Sinclair got away again to Reeth. She stayed at Victoria House, writing at a new novel. She was back in London in October to attend the inaugural meeting of the Medico-Psychological Clinic of London. This was the brainchild of Dr. Jessie Margaret Murray, graduate of the University of Durham Medical School and student of Pierre Janet at the College de France. It was the first clinic in England to include psychoanalysis in an eclectic array of therapeutic methods.[20] May Sinclair's financial sacrifice to assure the clinic a successful start aroused anxiety in her solicitor and friend, Robert Singleton Garnett (the son of Richard Garnett), who wrote to her on January 27, 1914, to protest her having given £500 at so early a stage: "What was it wanted for and where is it?" He advised her that the clinic should adopt some policy of responsibility, and "I think you should know more of the liabilities of Directors before you go much further." She wrote the Prospectus that was discussed at a meeting of the subscribers of the Memorial of Association on February 5 and was elected as one of the twelve founder-members and as a member of the Board of Management.

May Sinclair's publications went on, helping to revive her depleted bank account. "The Collector" appeared in the January *Century;* Hutchinsons published a second edition of *The Three Brontës* with a fretful preface deploring the publication in the preceding June of the letters of Charlotte Brontë to M. Heger. In April Hutchinsons also published a collection of one long and seven short stories, *The Judgement of Eve and other stories,* which was dedicated "To the Staff of the Medico-Psychological Clinic," and contained a preface, dated February 13, 1914, in which May Sinclair made her first public

---

19. P. 137.
20. See American Philosophical Society, "May Sinclair and the Medico-Psychological Clinic of London," *Proceedings* vol. 106, no. 4 (August, 1962) .

announcement that she was considering the employment of a sheared narrative style and form. The last introduction to a Brontë novel, Everyman's *Tenant of Wildfell Hall,* came out in April, and Macmillan of New York published a collection of stories, *The Return of the Prodigal* in June, identical with the English volume *The Judgement of Eve and other stories,* except that it substituted "The Cosmopolitan" for "Judgement of Eve" and omitted both the dedication and the preface of the English collection.

Sometime early in 1914 May Sinclair moved out of her studio flat in Edwardes Square, because it was being drowned in sounds of practicing musicians, and into 1 Blenheim Road, St. John's Wood. There she suffered from a deep shock. Her cat, Tommy, was too ill for hope of recovery, and the veterinarian left the lethal dose with May Sinclair. She herself gave it to Tommy and cuddled him in her lap while he fell into his last sleep. In this difficult time she hired Nellie Bartrop, one of twin sisters born in 1886 on a farm near Waltham Abbey in the Upshire district of Essex and trained as practical nurses, to be her companion and nurse as well as housekeeper. When Nellie went on a two weeks' holiday in 1916, her twin, Florence, acted as her temporary substitute. When Nellie came back from her holiday, Florence left for Canada, where she became engaged to an army flyer, who was shot down over Freiburg during the war, and killed.

On May 14, 1914, May Sinclair was proposed by Sir Lawrence Jones, Bart., and elected a member of the Society for Psychical Research, but she never contributed to either the *Journal* or the *Proceedings.*[21] She had an artist's interest in the occult story as a creative exercise, and in the mysteriously happening psychic phenomena in life, but she had no patience with the assumption that psychic phenomena were matters for scientific exploration according to a scientific methodology. She told Florence Bartrop, who was to join her in 1919, that she had not been convinced by any of the testimonials that she had heard and read positing the continuance of a psychic consciousness after the death of its body. Her friend, Mrs. C. Dawson Scott, was a believer who, after she was widowed, wrote what she was convinced was a communication from her husband. She persuaded May Sinclair to write an introduction to the volume that she hoped to publish; and the introduction existing in typescript form, offers four assumptions to account for the alleged communication from beyond the grave. It ends: "If there is anything in it at all—between the first and last of these four assumptions, I suspend my judgment."

---

21. Letter, E. Beale, Secretary General, August 6, 1959.

In that spring of 1914, May Sinclair was an intimate observer at the private meetings of a group of symposiasts who were booming the new movements that would first shatter and then replace all the conventional forms of all the arts: architecture, home furnishing, literature, music, painting, and sculpture. Ezra Pound and Percy Wyndham Lewis were the leaders, and Lewis close the appropriate title *Blast* for the magazine that was to serve as a manifesto of what the pair had christened—if the use of that verb is not sacrilege—"Vorticism." Such observers of the prophets and producers of the new order as John Gould Fletcher,[22] Richard Aldington,[23] and Ivor Brown[24] could not make much distinctive sense out of the blasters and vorticists. May Sinclair enjoyed herself hugely with Ivor Brown at the dinner that John Lane gave on July 15, 1914, at the Dieudonné Restaurant in Ryder Street, St. James, to set off the *Blast;* but she probably gave her final opinion of what it all amounted to through the mind of Matty Crawford, the rector's wife in *The Rector of Wyck.*[25]

A vortex that disrupted and pooled all other vortices struck England when war was declared in the first week of August. A specialist in psychotherapy who was on the medical staff and on the Board of Management of the Medico-Psychological Clinic, Dr. Hector Munro, enrolled a volunteer medical unit for war service. His idea took the final shape of a motor ambulance corps that, after British, American, and French government and Red Cross bureaus had refused him, was approved by the Belgian Red Cross. After this agency accepted the idea, the British Red Cross agreed to furnish the ambulances. May Sinclair, the only other member of the clinic to join Dr. Munro, became the secretary, treasurer, banker, donor of finances, and publicist to the ambulance corps. It left London on the morning of September 25, arrived at Ostend on the same evening, and went on to Bruges and Ghent. In her "Day Book" May Sinclair listed the thirteen members of the corps by their actual names, which were disguised in the serialized version of her experiences appearing in the *English Review* and in the volume published as *A Journal of Impressions in Belgium,* both in 1915. Beyond the duties she had accepted to start with, she became packer to the commandant, waitress to the masses of refugees in Ghent, assistant to the doctors, stretcher bearer searching for wounded, and nurse to the wounded. She was with the corps when

22. *Life is My Song* (New York: Farrar and Rinehart, 1937), chap. 11 and 12.
23. *Life for Life's Sake* (New York: The Viking Press, 1941), chap. 9.
24. In letters to me.
25. Chapter 15. See also Geoffrey Wagner, *Wyndham Lewis* (New Haven: Yale University Press, 1957), p. 144; and Douglas Goldring, *South Lodge* (London: Constable, 1943), pp. 67–70.

it was forced by the advance of the Germans to retreat from Ghent to Bruges, from Bruges to Ostend. After the money for running the corps had dropped to one week's budget, the commandant asked the secretary to return to England to replenish the funds. On the thirteenth of October she was shocked to learn that he had already chosen her successor. In England she learned to her deep humiliation that the commandant had requested the War Office not to allow her to rejoin the corps.

Dr. Munro was still alive when I began to try to weave together the truth about what had happened in Belgium, and I wrote to him in a sympathetic mood; but he declined to answer my several appeals. *A Journal*, even without the support of the more emotional and frankly written "Day Book" and the manuscript version of *A Journal*, permits us to believe that Dr. Munro's order was not unreasonable. Although she admired his fearlessness under fire and even became his patient after the war and his financial, unreimbursed patron,[26] she did not subordinate her strongly critical mind to the disciplinary phase of the military machine, which was as fundamentally abhorrent to her as was institutional religion. At any rate, the order that imprisoned her body for the duration in England did not prevent her memory from reviving for creative use the war scenes that she had witnessed. She suffered no physical harm from her seventeen days of war duty, and she did gain a knowledge of man's opportunity for experiencing reality to the most intense degree. This, she felt, man could not have without being exposed to the threat of imminent death. She had swum in the vortex of war and had not been dragged down by it. She had been freed from it against her will, and came out alive and sane.

I am sorry I was not able to ask Dr. Munro, the psychotherapist, if he had spotted just such a death wish in her as appears to have gripped Charlotte Redhead in *The Romantic* after the death of John Roden Conway, and saved her from its being realized, just as the fictional psychotherapist, modeled, I believe, on Dr. Munro, saved Charlotte Redhead. The theory which Mrs. Belloc Lowndes advanced in *A Passing World*[27] that May Sinclair avenged herself on Munro for his preventing her return to the corps by recreating him as Conway, a psychopathic coward, is silly both as a misinterpretation of May Sinclair's personality, which could not harbor revenge, and as a failure to recognize the fictional portrait of Munro in the psychotherapist.

The reader of May Sinclair's *A Journal of Impressions* will be

---

26. Florence Bartrop told me this.
27. (London: Macmillan, 1948), pp. 196–97.

interested in another war memoir, *The Cellar-House of Pervyse,* by
the Baroness T'serclass and Mairi Chisholm, published in 1916. The
authors were members of the original Ambulance Corps that left
Victoria Station for Ostend, renamed in *A Journal* "Mrs.
Torrence"
and "Janet McNeil." The Baroness joined the corps as a young widow
named Mrs. Knocker, which was how she was listed in the "Day Book."
The Cellar-House wholly authenticates the accuracy of May Sinclair's
characterizations and her reporting, and balances their greater exact-
ness in mechanical matters, which the authors would be expected to
have as the motoring experts that May Sinclair acknowledged them
to be, against May Sinclair's superior discernment into people and
her gift for drawing out of them truths they did not volunteer to
confess. *The Cellar-House* names May Sinclair and mentions her
Journal approvingly.[28]

The Three Sisters, which owes something to her study of the Brontës,
and to her exploring Swaledale and its surroundings, was published
in October simultaneously by Hutchinsons in London and by Macmillan in New York. *The Queen* published her charming wartime
story, "Red-Tape," on November 14, and *Colliers* on November 21
contained her article "Women's Sacrifices for the War." Ezra Pound
must have told May Sinclair himself what he wrote to Harriet Monroe
on November 9, 1914, that *The Three Sisters* was her best book so far,
and he deplored that she was not getting newspaper publicity, although
everybody else had been getting it with large photos.[29]

As the war began to look as though it would last an age, May
Sinclair became more deeply concerned with its effects upon the
human spirit. A biographical note in the *Dial* on September 13, 1917,
said that "May Sinclair was one of the few women writers to sign
the British authors' declaration of loyalty to democratic ideals of
government."[30]

When in 1915 Dr. Jessie Murray established a separate organization
related to the Medico-Psychological Clinic to teach the practice of
psychological therapy, May Sinclair coined the keyword in the name

28. Miss Jessie Howman, of Stow-on-the-Wold, who knew May Sinclair, told me
about this supportive book. David Mitchell, *Women on the Warpath* (London:
Cape, 1966), pp. 125–35, supplied information about Dr. Munro which the discreet May Sinclair withheld; for example, that he was the founder in 1914 of
Britain's first nudist camp, and practiced his creed in Belgium, with a shock-
effect on the queen's nervous system.
29. D. D. Paige, ed., *The Letters of Ezra Pound* (New York: Harcourt Brace, 1950),
p. 46.
30. Neither the Society of Authors, Miss E. Higgins, letter, October 31, 1963, nor
the Public Record Office, R. E. Lather, letter, December 9, 1963, could trace the
materials verifying this statement.

of this school: The Society for the Study of Orthopsychics Laboratory, and she also wrote that Society's *Prospectus of Educational Arrangements,* which was published to aid the Society's drive for funds in 1919. Its quarters were in the building of the Clinic, 30 Brunswick Square. Its first president was Professor T. Percy Nunn.[31]

May Sinclair's meeting Professor H. Wildon Carr, "one of the few remaining Idealists in philosophy,"[32] in the course of his lecturing at the Society for the Study of Orthopsychics restimulated her interest in philosophical Idealism and encouraged her to go forward with the book *A Defence of Idealism,* which appeared in August of 1917 in both London and New York.

Harper's carried her story "The Pin-Prick" in February, 1915, and her *Collier's* article, "Women's Sacrifices for the War," reappeared in the February number of *Woman at Home.*

On April 22, 1915, May Sinclair wrote from Reeth to Charlotte Mew to admit that Henry James "has influenced *me* considerably, and I'm not a bit ashamed of it. He is a good master, if you're strong enough not to be totally swamped by him." The country did not mean freedom from the dangers of war. "Reeth is prepared for Zeppelins. No lights allowed to show in the village or the country round!"[33] She was still in Reeth when she wrote her article "Two Notes" for the *Egoist* of June 1, 1915. To the manuscript of her article she appended the note, "I am in the wilds of Yorkshire with none of the literature of Imagism to refer to but the current number of The Egoist."

In a letter written on June 9, 1915 at 1 Blenheim Road, St. John's Wood, she confessed to Charlotte Mew her private opinion of the shortcomings of the imagists:

> About the Imagists—I'm not so stupid, really, as I seem. Remember, I'm defending H. D. against what I know to be an unfair and rather spiteful attack from a writer who isn't fit to lick her boots. H. D. is the best of the Imagists (You'll observe that I don't say very much about the others.). I used the word "passion" in the limited sense of that which tears its hair—and a lot, not all, but a lot of the Victorian "passion" was hair-tearing. The precise criticism that I should have applied to the Imagists if I'd been out that day for criticism— is that they lack strong human passion. That is one of the things which, as I say at the end of my Notes on Imagism, can be said against them if one *was* saying things.—In writing to Richard Aldington I said "Some day you will have an emotion that the 'image'

---

31. Title from the copy saved by the secretary, Miss Laura E. Price.
32. Dr. Ruth L. Saw, Honorary Treasurer, Aristotelian Society, letter, September 1, 1959.
33. Letter, courtesy of the Berg Collection.

will not carry; then where are you?—" . . . I see that these young poets are doing something that *at its best* is beautiful; and it is intolerable that they should meet with ridicule and contempt because they are not doing something else. You don't despise Meleager because he isn't Sapho—though, if you had to choose between them you know whom you would let go.—I do not think that the hearts of these Imagists beat strong enough to carry them to great heights and depths. They will never be *great* poets, but I never said they were. And I think that some of them are very small indeed, and of these I have said nothing.—If I were writing about poets who had strong passion in them I should have written very differently.[34]

In May, June, and July a first version of her Belgian war experiences, called *From a Journal*, ran in the *English Review*. An impulsively written footnote in the June installment, intended to honor a member of the corps, given the alias "Miss Ashley-Smith," who had, after the ambulance corps had been forced to retreat from Ghent to Eclos, heroically returned to Ghent to stay with one of her patients until he died, was misread by the lady alluded to as an accusation of cowardice for retreating. The lady, furious over the fancied insult, wrote such vile letters to May Sinclair, to the mother of her patient, and to the editor of the *English Review*, Austin Harrison, as to outrage May Sinclair and send her to her solicitor for protection. The considerable documentation filed as "Mrs. McDougall v. E. R. Correspondence" is evidence of the slings and arrows of outrageous trivia that can excoriate the pride of genius.

But there were many pleasant hours of social mixing with good company that did not have worrying after-effects. Douglas Goldring remembered the dinner club at Bellotti's restaurant in Soho that Ezra Pound dominated. T. S. Eliot, Arthur Waley, Violet Hunt, G. B. Stern, Wyndham Lewis, and W. B. Yeats were among her companions there.[35] The group later moved, during wartime, to spend Thursday evenings at a Chinese restaurant in Regent Street, to be joined by Ford Madox Ford, Richard Aldington, H. D., Mary Butts, and Edgar Jepson. An occasional guest who deserves immortality for taking special notice of one of the immortals is Iris Barry: "A small lady, almost always dressed in raspberry pink, with acute dark eyes and a crisp way of speech and sharpness of phrase that, somehow, one would not have expected from her at first sight, was May Sinclair."[36] A smaller group met on Mondays to sit at Yeats's feet in his flat at 18 Woburn Build-

34. Letter, courtesy of the Berg Collection.
35. *The Last Pre-Raphaelite* (London: Macdonald, 1948), p. 203.
36. "The Ezra Pound Period," *New York Bookman*, October, 1931.

ings.[37] Ford gave a going-away party on August 16, 1915, at South Lodge before leaving for France. Douglas Goldring remembered that Wyndham Lewis, Ezra Pound, W. L. George, Ethel Colburn Mayne, and May Sinclair kept Ford and Violet from quarreling, at least until they had to leave.[38]

Aldington recalled an instance of war hysteria that he guilelessly precipitated during dinner at May Sinclair's house when the Aldingtons and Ezra Pound were her guests. Pound must have been enacting some archetypal fantasy of primitive hunting, because he speared potatoes with his fork from a dish in the middle of the table, and lolled back to munch his capture. Aldington saw that their hostess was shocked, and to cover Pound's gaffe he said he did not believe the current stories about Germans crucifying Canadian soldiers. The maid who was waiting on the table, Nellie Bartrop, broke into the guests' conversation to insist that it was true; a nephew in the army had told her so.[39]

On August 4, 1916, May Sinclair wrote to Charlotte Mew from Reeth to say that she had "come up here to work violently for two months. I'm breaking my neck over a small book on a psychological and metaphysical subject that seized me some weeks ago. I'll be very lucky if I get a publisher!"[40] The "small book" became the brilliant study, *A Defence of Idealism.*

On August 25, still in Reeth, she wrote to Charlotte Mew again to express her sympathy with H. D.: "Poor H. D.! She has been so fine in the way she's taken her husband's being conscripted. It isn't *her* country's War, and yet she behaves as if it were. I wish he could have been spared for her sake as well as his own. I can't imagine anything more awful than being sent into the trenches to fight for a cause you don't believe in—unless it is the state of mind that doesn't believe, and that can imagine that anything that's been thought and written (within the last twenty years, anyhow) more important than the winning of the War!"[41]

Tasker Jevons, the first novel to come out of her brief but intense partaking in the war, appeared in February 1916 under Hutchinsons' imprint. In New York Macmillan entitled it *The Belfry.*

On March 3, May Sinclair attended the funeral of the Master at Chelsea in the Old Church, and on the next day, after crossing out the letterhead of the Albemarle Club stationery, wrote to Hugh Wal-

37. Ford: *Return to Yesterday.*
38. Goldring: *The Last Pre-Raphaelite,* p. 184.
39. *Life for Life's Sake,* p. 164.
40. Letter, courtesy of the Berg Collection.
41. Letter, courtesy of the Berg Collection.

pole to praise his *The Dark Forest* as "the best war-novel, in its own way, that has been written yet. . . . You, alone, of all the writers I know who've touched on the War, have seen and felt it as it is. . . I don't know anybody but you who has realised the ecstasy and joy that came whenever you got into what they call 'the danger zone'—that's the nearest to perfect happiness we're likely to reach in this world. It *is* perfect happiness, and it has nothing to do with 'doing your duty,' (I'm not at all sure that my duty wasn't to stop at home lest I should get ill and become a nuisance) it's deeper than all that." Of Henry James she added, "How proud he would be of you if he knew about *The Dark Forest*. It was a good time for him to die. He loved our soldiers and he has gone over with a glorious company."[42]

Her first writing on psychoanalysis was the two-part article appearing in the *Medical Press* on August 9 and 16: "Clinical Lecture on Symbolism and Sublimation."

Sometime in this year of 1916 the Royal Society of Literature elected her a Fellow, just eight years before her patient critic and honorary agent of Sidmouth days, now Canon Deane, was elected.[43]

The January, 1917, number of the *Century Magazine* carried her short story, "Portrait of My Uncle," and *Woman at Home* carried the short story "The Frewin Affair."

On July 25, her review of Dr. Charles Mercier's book *Spiritualism and Sir Oliver Lodge* in the *Medical Press* gave offense to Sir Oliver. His letter of remonstrance and her apology for her errors of fact and emphasis appeared together on August 8. She wrote an introduction for a book of indifferently poor poems in French, *The Closed Door,* by the Flemish illustrator Jean de Boschere, with an English translation by F. S. Flint. John Lane published the first edition, illustrated by the author, in September, 1917, and a limited edition in March, 1918.

Sometime in mid-1917 May Sinclair was elected to the Aristotelian Society of London, sponsored by its president, Dr. H. Wildon Carr, a lecturer at the Laboratory for the Study of Orthopsychics. In August Macmillans of London and of New York published *A Defence of Idealism.*

On October 8, 1917, appeared "A Special Appeal in Time of War," a pamphlet explaining the need for financial aid to the Medico-Psychological Clinic.[44] In October Cassell published *The Tree of*

---

42. Letter, courtesy of Rupert Hart-Davis.
43. Letter, J. M. Patterson, Secretary, February 5, 1960.
44. See the American Philosophical Society, *Proceedings* vol. 106, no. 4 (August, 1962), for a full account.

Heaven in London, and in December Macmillan published it in New York, in time to let it grow to a stature fully as imposing as that of *The Divine Fire*, before the end of the war should bring about an abrupt, though not a lasting, malaise over books about the Great War.

News that Hugh Walpole had returned safely from Russia excited a happy letter from May Sinclair on January 30, 1918. She invited him to dine with her at the Albemarle Club on February 6: "Lady Hamilton and Sir Dan are coming, and I'm asking Mrs. Lowndes and Dr. and Mrs. Page."[45] Dr. Page must have been the American ambassador.

On March 5 she wrote to him again from somewhere in Bucks. She praised his *The Green Mirror* as the best thing that he had done except for *The Dark Forest*. She found "only here and there a faint trace of your old love of the symbolic and fantastic; the one thing that used to put me off. But whereas it used to be part and parcel of the main scheme, here it is only a mere decoration. Some day the decoration will go, and you'll concentrate on plain reality. At least, I seem to see an increasing tendency. (Don't hate me.)"[46]

She was a member of the War Emergency Committee of the Society of Authors, whose object was to help writers to whom the war had brought financial distress. Sometime in 1918 she enjoyed an experience which a fellow member of that committee, F. Anstey, described in his autobiography, *A Long Retrospect*.[47] The committee received an application for relief from, apparently, an old friend of Anstey's, a fellow contributor to *Punch*, a Major Kendall. Anstey, master of magic that he was in fiction, doubted that his friend could be well off and busy in a military office in Ireland and in financial trouble and in London at the same time. He noticed that the handwriting of the letter of application was unlike the major's and that it included a misspelling that was improbably the major's. W. J. Locke, the chairman, May Sinclair, and F. Anstey welcomed the non-Major Kendall and lured him into feeling confident of relief. The committee listened to his proud statement that he was not drawing army pay in spite of his war wound, and that he was not asking a man of Sir George Alexander's low social status for an advance on royalties for a comedy of his that the St. James Theatre had accepted. When the committee members tired of the amateur trespassing on the field of their professional practice and threatened the live fiction with arrest, he acted

45. Letter, courtesy of Rupert Hart-Davis.
46. Letter, courtesy of Rupert Hart-Davis.
47. Thomas Anstey Guthrie, *A Long Retrospect* (Oxford University Press, 1936), pp. 349–51.

a professional amazement that his sincere representations should incur such discourteous incredulity; and when he left he was obviously saddened by their little faith.

In April, May Sinclair's essay calling attention to a younger novelist, "The Novels of Dorothy Richardson," appeared in the *Egoist*. In June the *English Review* carried a short story of the supernatural, "The Intercessor." *The Tree of Heaven* had three printings in New York.

On May 12, 1918, May Sinclair wrote to Violet Hunt from Reeth: "I'm up here working like a gang of navvies on my book." She was also expecting the Baroness von Hutten.[48] The baroness listened to her account of the people who were in the world of the new heroine, Mary Olivier, and in the presence of Reeth's favorite doctor exclaimed, "What terrible people!"[49] Sometime in the autumn of 1918, May Sinclair was at St. Merryn in Cornwall, where G. B. Stern found her not in good health and pressing hard to finish her book. On November 6, she was back in London, inviting Hugh Walpole to have dinner with her at 1, Blenheim Road.[50]

By 1919, May Sinclair's first companion-housekeeper, Nellie Bartrop, had gotten other employment, and her twin sister Florence, back from Canada, still mourning the death of her fiancé in the war, was working as companion to a German woman living in Swiss Cottage. The woman developed an obsession that Florence was her dead daughter and at the same time treated her with a fierce hostility. Florence appealed to May Sinclair, who was without a companion or housekeeper, to give her relief from her mad employer until she could find a permanent place. May Sinclair took her in on a temporary agreement, and never let her go. Florence Bartrop gave to her employer the lifelong loyalty that the war had deprived her of giving to a husband and family. She was a brisk, warm-hearted woman, a very good cook, a born carer-for-others. She stayed as companion, housekeeper, cook, and emissary to arrange for access to places that May Sinclair wished to study as backgrounds for her novels.

When she relived the golden time of her life with May Sinclair, at 1, Blenheim Road, St. John's Wood, she described the daily routine that began with her bringing up tea at eight in the morning. At eight-thirty May Sinclair came down for her stout breakfast of porridge, fried bacon, prepared eggs, buttered toast, and marmalade. She gave a half hour to her *Daily Mail,* and at nine-thirty she went into

48. Letter, courtesy of the Berg Collection.
49. Letter, Dr. W. C. Speirs, of Reeth, July 15, 1964.
50. Letter, courtesy of Rupert Hart-Davis.

her study. She sat in her wheelback chair of oak, and used a plywood board held on her lap as a writing surface. If the day was fair, sunlight shed some of the color from the magenta silk curtains upon her paper.

At one o'clock Miss Bartrop called her to luncheon: a soufflé, soup, fish, a milk pudding, and green China tea, which May Sinclair believed contained no tannin. The tea was bought in five-pound tins. When there was no "at home," tea was brought into the study at four o'clock: bread and butter, cake, biscuits, sandwiches. The dishes she was especially fond of at dinner at seven were curries, rice curries and lentil curries, perhaps in memory of her brother Frank, who had once sent home an iron trunk, never thrown away, filled with curry. When eggs were served, they had to be prepared in neat forms, because May Sinclair as a child had once been revolted by seeing a nanny eating an egg untidily.

No alcoholic beverage was ever served. Memories of her father's and brothers' excessive drinking, of her mother's and her own childhood shame, and her fear that she had a tendency to alcoholism that might become an addiction kept her abstemious. She must have been wholly unaware of the look of wines, for once, in Edwardes Square days, she served what she took to be sherry to her guests, but they recognized it to be ketchup. Florence Bartrop would never have made that mistake; she liked her occasional, and single, glass of sherry. She had heard the story of that error. May Sinclair told her that a friend once gave her a bottle of sloe gin, which she opened on a holiday. She reported her experience in these words: "I liked it going down, but not after it got there"; and it was the last experiment of the kind.

She was dainty, fastidious at table. If she made a spot on the tablecloth she would either cover it quickly or rub it briskly to clean it off, and she would apologize for the extra work she had caused, "So sorry, Florrie."

On Monday, Tuesday, and Wednesday of the first week in every month she had "at home" teas, to prepare for which Miss Bartrop marketed and baked the weekend before. The closest friends that Miss Bartrop remembered calling at teas and coming to dinner were Rose Macaulay, Evelyn Underhill, John and Ada Galsworthy, Mrs. Belloc Lowndes, Algernon Blackwood, Ezra Pound, Mrs. Dawson Scott, Rebecca West, G. B. Stern, Clemence Dane, Hugh Walpole, Richard and Mrs. Aldington, and Dorothy Richardson and her husband. Miss Bartrop knew how greatly May Sinclair had befriended Ezra Pound, but did not think she really liked him. She may have been influenced by her sister Nellie's strong dislike for what she regarded as Pound's outrageously boorish manners. Once, on one of his many visits to luncheon, he whistled downstairs to Nellie and then yelled at her to bring him a second helping of dessert. The spirited Nellie answered back, and if her voice had the same low crisp enunciation and vibrant timbre of Florrie's voice, her reply was sharply audible upstairs: She was not a dog to be whistled at; and she would *not* bring up a second helping. May Sinclair abided by Nellie's decision. Richard Aldington's memories of Ezra Pound's table manners bore out Miss Bartrop's impression of the youthful spectacular who was Ezra Pound.[51]

Miss Bartrop remembered Dorothy Richardson coming to dinner one evening at Blenheim Road wearing her dress backwards. Miss Bartrop took her to a bedroom and redressed her properly. She remembered Dorothy Richardson's husband, Alan Odle, a frail figure topped by long straw-colored hair that hair clips held together at the back of his neck. He wore plimsoll slippers when he called once to recover a portfolio of sketches that he had left for May Sinclair to examine.

Sinclair Lewis used to call after sending Mrs. Lewis to Paris, and Upton Sinclair made much ado claiming relationship to May.

Miss Bartrop remembered Netta Syrett, a novelist whom Mrs. Atherton would not have faulted, as she did May Sinclair, for not leading the unorthodox passionate life that reaps raw material for fiction. The only slightly malicious remark that Miss Bartrop ever heard May Sinclair make about any of her friends was her question about Netta Syrett, "I wonder whose protection she is living under now?"

Mrs. Dawson Scott, later the founder of P. E. N., was a friend who, with her husband, enjoyed conversing about departed souls. They had a shrine in their home, and photographs of the controls who were their mediums to the Beyond. One evening May Sinclair brought home to Florence Bartrop the news that Mrs. Dawson Scott had held a conversation with May Sinclair's favorite, and long-departed, brother Frank. She had asked him how he was using his infinite time, and Mrs. Scott said that he had told her, "Oh, I'm engaged in sorting of souls." May Sinclair's unvarying comment on transoccult communication was, "They couldn't convince me."

Another friend, John Bohun Lynch, brought his wife to dinner once and treated her very nastily while he devoured the salted almonds. After his divorce he came again to dinner, this time with his mistress. Miss Bartrop read the novel that he wrote about his love affair with this woman and recalled the scene of the lovers swimming in the nude.

May Sinclair used to tell Florrie of Richard Garnett's immense

---

51. *Life for Life's Sake*, p. 164.

l elpfulness to her when London was for her still a literary jungle allowing only a precarious livelihood to the civilized among the competitors. His son, Robert Singleton Garnett, watched over her financial interests with a lovingly anxious guardian's devotion. We have seen how concerned he was in 1914 over her generous gift to Dr. Jessie Murray to help establish the Medico-Psychological Clinic. He must have been equally anxious when she spent her savings to finance Dr. Hector Munro's Ambulance Corps.[52] May Sinclair was wholly indifferent to, and ignorant of, money matters. Florence Bartrop paid all her bills and kept all the accounts, and May Sinclair never examined the accounts or questioned any expenses. She explained her attitude: "If I didn't trust you, Florrie, I wouldn't ask you to live with me." Miss Bartrop always bought the presents May Sinclair wished to give her friends.

May Sinclair was chronically anxious that she should be fair to everyone. When Ernest Williams was still her chauffeur she would ask, "Florrie, do you think we pay Ernie enough?" Paired with that anxiety was the eternally human calm about the person closest and most necessary to her. She never asked Florence Bartrop if *she* was getting enough. I suspect that it was Robert Garnett who had to remind her that she had not yet provided for Miss Bartrop; at any rate, on December 4, 1928, her will, drawn originally on November 11, 1918, was amended by a codicil whose only provision was that "I give to my servant Florence Bartrop in recognition of her services to me and providing that at the time of my death she shall not be under notice to leave my services whether given or received the sum of One hundred pounds free of legacy duty and in addition to any moneys which may be due to her."

May Sinclair was very modest about her body. Only after Florence Bartrop had been with her for five years was she allowed to bring morning tea into the bedroom before May Sinclair was fully dressed, and then only because her laming leg needed to be massaged. She was as wary of revealing her age as was Dorothy Richardson, who never confessed to her husband that she was fifteen years older than he.[53] She would not tell Miss Bartrop how many books she had written: "Oh, no, I won't. If I tell you that, you'll know how old I am."

May Sinclair had two compulsive habits. She had a compulsion for tapping on a table with her left hand. She also twisted a curl of her hair with the fingers of her right hand whenever she was bored. The

---

52. Mrs. Belloc-Lowndes, *A Passing World* (London: Macmillan, 1948), p. 196.
53. Mrs. E. V. Odle, Dorothy Richardson's sister-in-law.

older brother of Harold Lumley Sinclair, her nephew Frank, had exactly the same habit. Frank told Miss Bartrop that it was a Sinclair behavior pattern.

After her cat Tommy died in 1914, she said that she would never have a cat again. But while she was writing in her wheelback oak chair, a stray cat holding a kitten in her mouth found a door open and slipped into the house, made her way into the study, dropped the kitten on to the page on which May Sinclair was writing, and then glided out again into the street. The black kitten became the sleek pampered Jerry of the published sketches, whose death late in 1927 was a tragedy. The only pet in childhood days that she ever mentioned was a live monkey that was her playmate, but that did not appear in her novels.

She never spoke to Florence Bartrop about her father's financial mysteries, nor about his library, but she recalled his excessive drinking, his love for yachting, and his yacht *Windward,* which he sailed on the Mersey from Rock Ferry. She described her mother's belief that owning a yacht canceled out the shame of being in business, and her mother's seeing to it that her sons had their chance of each owning his yacht. Her mother's severe dogmatism was a trial that she often recalled, and the irony of her mother's showing the greatest pleasure and approval of her little daughter when she darned her brother's socks. May Sinclair blamed the frequent moving upon her mother's restlessness, which erupted after three years of residence in any one place that May Sinclair had chosen for their home. She talked often about her favorite brother Frank, and she and Florence Bartrop would go out to Woolwich and walk slowly across the broad drill ground of the Royal Artillery Institution, because Frank had trained there before being sent out to India.

May Sinclair dreaded the physical pressure of crowds, and was very shy in public whenever she noticed curious eyes. But Florence Bartrop would not agree with the impression commonly formed by interviewers that she was a withdrawing person. She explained her lack of volubility as simply her "being on the quiet side. She had no time for small talk." Florence Bartrop did not see her laugh much.

An American gentleman once called to take May Sinclair out to dinner, and he worked hard to make her talk. When the American brought his dinner guest home in his car, Miss Bartrop could tell that he had not succeeded; he had tried too hard, and too obviously. Later Miss Bartrop read a short story, whose title she could not remember, in which she recognized, with May Sinclair's help, that the baffling feminine dinner partner had drawn an interesting narrative portrait of her host. She had lived over again her first short story, of 1895, "A Study from Life." She did not like to be the object of planned curiosity. An interviewer had to be as soundly prepared as were Willis Steell and Burton Rascoe and Margaret Walter to relax her into talking frankly and seriously about herself.

So little withdrawn was she when she was not the object of curious eyes that she still could give rein to her tomboy impulses in her fifties. Sometime around 1920 she and Florence Bartrop were hurrying for a train in the St. John's Wood station on the Metropolitan Line to get to Baker Street. Florrie padded faithfully behind her, but they would have missed the train that had glided into the station if May Sinclair had not slid down the banisters to the platform and signaled the guard urgently to hold the train until her companion could descend in the conventional manner to board with her.

Athletic as she had been as a girl, and as superbly as she could describe rhythmic movement, May Sinclair never went to the ballet. She enjoyed visiting churches and cathedrals, and learning their histories. Motion pictures gave her the greatest pleasure of the publicly entertaining arts, plays the next greatest pleasure. Florence Bartrop remembered that two novels had been filmed: *Mr. and Mrs. Nevill Tyson* and *The Immortal Moment,* and she believed that H. G. Wells had a hand in the scenario of the second film. Riding in a motor car gave her the greatest physical delight. She owned three cars from 1919 to her death: a Morris, an Austin 12, and an Austin 15.

She ruled out all public symbols of class distinction in her household. Her chauffeur, Ernest Williams, she equipped with an evening suit, and she fitted out Florence Bartrop with evening dresses, so that wherever the three went, no one could make an instant judgment to set apart employer from employee. If there is a real direction, she moved the symbols up, not down.

Miss Bartrop remembered only two occasions of frettings with publishers to match Henry Holt's attempts to make May Sinclair shorten *The Divine Fire.* The first came when a publisher urged her to put more love action into her novels. She defended herself by explaining that she was not leading the kind of life that some of her friends led to pick up the spicy details that the publisher asked for. The second was a publisher's finding fault with her phrase *the little bitch* as too coarse and making her remove it. She changed the phrase to *the little cat.*

I asked Miss Bartrop if she had known May Sinclair to have been in love with anyone. She thought that she could have loved, but in perfect physical innocence, Richard Aldington in the years when he

had a studio in London, and, of course, was married. He often visited
her, and Miss Bartrop felt an atmosphere of emotion between the
two. Mrs. Aldington called too, and invited Miss Bartrop to call on
her. She thought Mrs. Aldington "a very pleasant woman," but she
never called on her. "I did not go because I did not want to be drawn
into May's private affairs," she wrote me when I asked again.[54] Miss
Bartrop got the impression that Aldington was too poor to do anything
so expensive as divorcing Hilda to that he might be free to remarry.
She did not like Aldington; she thought him to be, like Ezra Pound,
a taker, not a giver by nature. She too had noticed the resemblance
between Richard Aldington and Richard Nicholson in *Mary Olivier*,
but not his resemblance to Victor Rendal, the poet in *The Dark Night*.
Dame Rebecca West was in a more authoritative position to answer
the same question. As a very young friend and confidante of May
Sinclair she learned that May Sinclair had once been in love and
might have married but for "some very obscure grounds of scruple."
It was obvious to her that May Sinclair had felt the renunciation very
deeply. The time of the recollection was during the first World War,
and the reference was to the very distant past and to a brother-officer
of a relative of hers in the service, probably a friend of her brother
Frank. Richard Aldington she could have loved only in fantasy.[55]

Early in 1919, Aldington was demobilized. Back in London once
more, he stopped short in front of a book stall in the Charing Cross
Road, startled to be facing a row of books every single one of which
he had read. He opened them, one after the other, and found that
they were his own books. The Bloomsbury intellectual who had roomed
in his home had stolen and sold his stored books for money for drink.[56]
May Sinclair did her best to reconcile him to his loss by making him the
gift of a life subscription to the London Library, an invaluable help
to the serious literary work to which he had dedicated himself. The
life subscription, based on an actuarial scale, cost thirty-eight guineas,
since Aldington was 27 in 1919.[57] In December of 1919, he took over
D. H. Lawrence's cottage in Hermitage, Berkshire, and profited by the
London Library's system of lending fifteen books at a time to country
members.

A letter written by Professor William Gardner Hale, head of the
Latin Department at the University of Chicago, to the books section
of the *Chicago Daily Tribune* on March 29, 1919, set off a volcanic

54. Letter, August 23, 1961.
55. Letters, October 24, November 3, 1962.
56. Aldington, *Life for Life's Sake*, pp. 264–65, and letter to me, February 17, 1960.
57. Letter, Stanley G. Gilliam, librarian of the London Library, March 3, 1960.

eruption by Ezra Pound, which May Sinclair helped to contain and whose voluminous materials she preserved. Professor Hale objected to the fantastic ignorance of the Latin language that Pound had displayed in his "Poems from the Propertius Series" appearing in the March number of *Poetry:* "Mr. Pound is incredibly ignorant of Latin He has, of course, a perfect right to be, but not if he translates from it. The result of his ignorance is that much of what he makes his author say is unintelligible." He chose ten passages to illustrate his indictment, like Pound's "devirginated young ladies" to represent what Propertius had intended to mean "my lady touched by my words." Pound exploded in a very long letter to the editor of the *Chicago Daily Tribune,* denouncing Professor Hale for not appreciating the essential atmosphere of the time and the mood of the poem, which he had tried to recreate by deliberately discarding the "mask of erudition" that Professor Hale had accused him of putting on. Instead of forwarding his intemperate defense, May Sinclair wrote an essay, "The Reputation of Ezra Pound," which she let him read for his constructive suggestions. She accepted every one of his changes, and the essay appeared in the *English Review* in April, 1920, and in the *North American Review* in May.

On April 8, 1919, she invited Hugh Walpole to dine at the Albemarle Club on the seventeenth with her friends Mrs. Belloc Lowndes, Mrs. Harker, and Richard Aldington, to help her celebrate the finishing of her new book, *Mary Olivier.*[58] It could have been at this dinner party that Hugh Walpole annoyed Aldington by depreciating James Joyce and Marcel Proust, writers whom Aldington thought "vastly more important than their critic."[59]

On April 27, after having finished Walpole's *The Secret City,* May Sinclair chided him again for having let his obsession for fantasy distract him from the real thing: "Is Reality *never* going to be good enough for you? Good—I mean—all the time? . . .—Can't you see that your real strength is in your observation and your *intuition* of reality, and *not* in your fantastic imagination? It isn't really imagination, it's only fancy; it creates nothing; when you drag it in it spoils what you've created.—Cut if off and cast it from you."[60]

May Sinclair commemorated her gratitude to the magnificent Swaledale region for having inspired her to her most passionate nature writing by presenting to the Reeth Friends School Trust fifty pounds, the interest on which was to furnish two annual prizes for the best

---

58. Letter, courtesy of Rupert Hart-Davis.
59. *Life for Life's Sake,* pp. 215–16.
60. Letter, courtesy of Rupert Hart-Davis.

essays on English history and on natural history, respectively. The first award was made in 1919, and the Sinclair prizes are still awarded.[61]

By 1919, May Sinclair's health was beginning to show a decline. During her last known visit to Reeth in that year, when she stayed at the Buck Hotel, Dr. W. C. Speirs noticed how dependent she was for help at table upon her nurse-companion, Florence Bartrop.[62] Her invalidism forbade her continuing to take those long trips to Richmond and to Reeth for the silence, the seclusion, and the relief of outdoor exercise that her habit of intense concentration demanded for her writing and her recuperation. Sometime in 1919, she discovered Stow-on-the-Wold, and chose it to replace Reeth as a more accessible writing-home-away-from-home. The Cotswolds, so much less inward-turning than the Dales in their mood, gave her the restful surroundings that she needed and a subtle encouragement to her suppressed sense of comedy that the Swaledale could not give her. At the beginning, she rented permanent lodgings at the White Hart Hotel. When she was in London, she let her friends enjoy the room that she had furnished herself.

The *Little Review* serialized Book One of *Mary Olivier: A Life,* in four issues: January, February–March, April, and May, 1919. Cassell published the complete volume in June, and Macmillan in New York published it in July. Letters from friends and acquaintances reported the effects of the book upon them.

H. G. Wells, a closer friend in earlier days, when her mother was still living,[63] wrote at Easton Glebe, Dunmow: "Mary Olivier is delightful and wonderful. I would write you a long letter about it if I had not got myself involved with an endless task that I grudge every letter I write. You will understand that exacting egotism of the writer though it never seems to afflict you."[64] Gladys B. Stern, using the intimate signature "Peter," wrote on June 15 from The Lizard in Cornwall to compare Mary Olivier with Miriam Henderson:

> Of course the reason why she's so infinitely more wonderful than anything Dorothy Richardson has done, is that Mary herself matters, and Miriam didn't—Heavens, how Miriam bored me! . . . —I wondered at what point of it you got so despairing, at St. Merryn last Autumn? I hated little Mamma—hated her from the very first mention of her. I remembered you told me once you had a nervous

61. Letters from Reginald A. Pace, retired headmaster, Reeth School; A. John Rowntree, of Reeth Friends' School Trust; James Strachan; and the winner of the award in 1951, Mary Brown Pratt.
62. Letter, July 15, 1964.
63. Dame Rebecca West, letter, October 24, 1962.
64. By permission of A. P. Watt and Son, and the executors of H. G. Wells.

breakdown because you tried to write in the same room with your own mother. . . . I remembered, too, in the brook-jumping part, how you had jumped the patches of rushes at St. Merryn, and told me you had always jumped like that with your brothers. . . . —Those flash-moments of reality you speak of, Mary's, they do come—very rarely, but quite clear. Only they're usually about places, or bits of places. And although they're so sudden and distinct, they don't link themselves up to one's life at all, or help one through a bad time. Will they—later on? . . . P.S. My name now is Holdsworth—you said you didn't know it.[65]

On June 19, a daughter of Lord Ponsonby, Betty Montgomery, wrote about *Mary Olivier* from Ireland: "It is deeply impressive and makes me shiver with admiration. It is on the great lines of the Greek drama which Mary loved so well. I love its relentless gravity and courageous facing of life. (I thought the Times Lit. Sup. review so *smugly stupid* and cowardly,—how I hate that sort of sham 'optimism' with its smear of white-wash—but we won't talk about that.) "

May Sinclair was hurt by the unkind reception given the book. On June 20, she wrote to Hugh Walpole that she was going to Stow-on-the-Wold to settle into her room later in the month, and would be there a week: "P.S. I wonder if you saw the *Times* review of my book? It is a poisonous libel! That sort of thing ought to be indictable—but it isn't." Soon after, she wrote again to thank him "for defending me from *The Times's* gross and beastly attack. It gave me great pleasure to know that you thought such nice things about me. . . . Just finished a long article on Flint's Poems—another poet who hasn't had justice done to him!"[66]

W. L. George wrote a thoughtful and encouraging letter about *Mary Olivier* on June 22:

> I think the comparison with Joyce, in the enclosed criticism (*Ob-server*) absurd, but it does resemble Dorothy Richardson, with this difference: I was very much afraid you were going to fall under her influence, which I think bad, to adopt her method, which is the negation of all selective art; I think she is a fraud and a stunt. But where Mary Olivier distinguishes itself from her pretentious sim-plicity is that Dorothy Richardson records impressions of pure futili-ties, whereas you have recorded impressions of the most cruel human drama. Papa, Mark, Mama, Dan, are true and unhappy.

Betty Montgomery wrote again on June 24:

Such stupidity and "ontulds" in the reviewers fills me with bitter

---

65. By permission of G. B. Stern, letter, n.d., Mill Brook Cottage, Blewbury, Berks.
66. Letters, courtesy of Rupert Hart-Davis.

indignation.—I told you before quite honestly that I was half afraid that, out of your real interest in Freud's Psycho-Analysis, your new book *might* be disproportionately sexual!—*How* wrong I was in my misgivings.—The book tends to the other extreme, and thereby, I think, increases its beauty and greatness. Mr. Sutliffe never saying a word of his love to Mary (let alone not "making love" to her) is such a beautiful figure in the book—and when we come to Richard, the real love of her life, the reserve and reticence is perfect in its wonderful "good taste"—I have *never* come across such restraint before—not one kiss described. And that is the book that the reviewers condemn as sex-obsessed!! I *am* disappointed in what you tell me of R. Lynd—it is unworthy of him—I am still hoping the *Athenaeum* with its young writers, K. Mansfield etc may show more discernment.

A Cheltenham Ladies College graduate about seven years older than May Sinclair, Mrs. Mary Skrine, a novelist of child and country life, wrote from an Oxford vicarage, St. Peter in the East, on July 2 and 12 to praise *Mary Olivier*: "Long indeed is it since I met anybody so alive. She is a real woman, not one of Miss Richardson's meticulous maidens, who make my inferior mind ache. . . . And 'Little Mama' . . . too is so terribly real that (as you see) I can't think of her as not alive still. . . . Every one of the terrible 'family' lives."

On June 17, Hutchinsons contracted for the next three novels: to be not less than eighty thousand words each, to be published within three months of the receipt of the completed manuscript, and to sell at not less than six shillings. Royalties on the published price of twelve out of every thirteen copies sold would be twenty-five percent up to ten thousand copies, and thirty percent on all copies sold over ten thousand. Advance payments on the first novel would be £600, payable on the day of publication; on the second £650, and on the third £700. The contract covered also the publication of a volume of stories on which the advance would be £250 and the royalty twenty percent up to five thousand copies; thereafter it would be twenty-five percent. Curtis Brown had not done badly by her.

Katherine Tynan Hinkson left Ireland some time in 1919 to live once more in England and was May Sinclair's frequent guest at the Albemarle Club, along with Rose Macaulay and Mrs. Belloc Lowndes.[67]

On September 1, May Sinclair wrote to an American visitor in London, to thank her for thinking so well of *Mary Olivier* after a second reading. She sent a photograph of herself: "It is the nicest one to have, because it is the only one in which Tommy appears; and if

67. Katherine Tynan Hinkson, *The Wandering Years* (Houghton Mifflin, 1922), pp. 92, 101, 107, 111, 262.

the silly photographer hadn't been so keen on stage-properties—you'll observe the serious tome he has shoved into the foreground—Tommy would have showed more.—He is as he settled himself after his wild leap into my arms when he saw the camera."[68]

Another American, Ida M. Hatch, of Tamworth in New Hampshire, complained for a reason with which Canon Deane would have sympathized: "Give to the world a new 'Mary Olivier,' one who is not surrounded by sin, ignorance, and weakness, nor hampered by Heredity —one who will hold us on the Heights in full strength—and light, and love—A Book to help shut-ins like myself, because you have the Power— don't misuse it.—In all loving kindness." May Sinclair sketched a gentle answer to the bedridden woman: an author is subject to the vibrations emanating from objects and from every consciousness and striking upon every consciousness, and in his book transmits the impressions of the vibrations he has received. "It is all a question of vibrations."

Her generosity is witnessed by a document that she laid away for its moment of truth, a record of a gift disguised as a loan, never repaid.[69] It was an acknowledgment of a loan for £25, "which I undertake to repay directly my estate comes into my hands, and upon which until then I will pay you 6% per annum as from Jan 1st, 1920." It was signed by Mary Rodker and witnessed by her husband John on January 8, 1920.

Toward the end of March in 1920, May Sinclair confessed to a grandnephew, Harold Sinclair (the grandson of her brother Joseph Walter who had emigrated to Canada), the ill health that she kept from her friends. She was ashamed to have left his letter of January 18 unanswered so long.

Flu and pleurisy and neuritis—for two months in this winter; and all my correspondence got into arrears, and the *act* of writing was very difficult at first because of the neuritis. Then I had my book to finish as soon as I could write; and it was very exhausting. I hated the thought of pens and ink when my day's work was done: so again my correspondence suffered.

To Harold's complaint of the cost of living in Canada she replied:

I can quite believe what you say about the cost of living with you. But except that wages are generally lower here, which makes it harder, things are every bit as bad; food, clothes, everything. But one gets used to it. It's frightfully hard for the people who had only

68. Letter, courtesy of Professor W. S. Trout. I have not seen that photograph, but one by E. O. Hoppe of Jerry has survived.
69. Harold Lumley Sinclair. Mary Rodker was Mary Butts.

just enough to live on before the war, though. However, wages are going up and up in most essential things, and I suppose some day the clerks' and shop-workers' wages will rise. Increased cost of living *and* taxation falls hardest on professional men with families and "appearances" to keep up.—I hope you will like your work at the Cannery. I suppose it will be beginning now.[70]

She sent the typescript of her new novel to Collins, whose reader, the novelist J. D. Beresford, wrote her about it from Winslow in Bucks on April 28, 1920, with the perspicacity in psychological matters one would expect of him. He hoped that Collins would accept it. "If I may take all the preliminary appreciation for granted,—any book you write is sure to be interesting in detail and cleverly planned—I would say that what made the book for me was the amazing completeness of the summary in the last chapter." J. D. Beresford saw how essential was the psychotherapist's clearing up of the mystery of the character of John Roden Conway, who had up to that moment of revelation been viewed through Charlotte Redhead's mind.

On July 14, May Sinclair wrote very happily to Hugh Walpole from the White Hart Hotel in Stow-on-the-Wold: "I'm at Stow till Monday: very happy, writing short stories, motoring and cycling and walking. But I must come back to London and find somebody to talk with.— Will you come and talk some evening next week after Tuesday? Dinner 7.30."[71]

An article in the August number of the *English Review,* "Worse than War," called atttention to the postwar suffering in Europe that England's blockade had helped to bring about, and appealed for aid to the relief organizations, in particular to the Save the Children Fund.

The first poems that May Sinclair published since the poem that served as a dedication to her *A Journal of Impressions,* saluting the Hector Munro Ambulance Corps, appeared in the September number of *Voices,* a magazine of poetry that Thomas Moult edited. The set of poems, called "Childhood," recovered some memories of far-distant Rock Ferry days and nights.

Macmillan of New York published *The Romantic* in September, and Collins published it in London in October. A Jacobean short story, "The Bambino," appeared in the *Athenaeum* for September 24.

Personal sadness overcast professional pride when Dr. Jessie Murray died of cancer on September 25. Besides losing a friend who talked psychoanalysis with her, May Sinclair saw the beginning of the end of the Medico-Psychological Clinic, in whose founding and promotion

70. Letter, courtesy of R. W. Sinclair.
71. Letter, courtesy of Rupert Hart-Davis.

she had been so prominent. In August, 1922, the first public clinic in England for psychoanalytic treatment and the first school in England for the training of students in that method of treatment were closed. Some of the students whom the clinic and its school had trained brought their valuable endowment with them to the Tavistock Square Clinic and to the Institute of Psycho-Analysis.[72]

On September 30, May Sinclair wrote to Hugh Walpole from the White Hart Hotel in Stow that she had been reading *Jeremy* and loved him: "It's one of the best things you've ever, ever done. Congratulations.—Let's exchange books—I'll send you The Romantic when it's out next week.—Till we meet among the Fishmongers."[73]

An invalid in Leicester who was no sensitive critic of merely the aesthetics of a novel wrote on October 19 to confirm the truthfulness of *The Romanic*. The writer, Joseph I. American, testified to parallels between happenings with which he was personally acquainted and incidents in her story: "not only is there a similarity of incident but the geographical points covered by, and the occupations of the principal characters of, your story coincide with the personal experiences I write of."

And a sophomore at the University of Wisconsin, Margery Bodine Latimer, who was to return to her home in Portage and become a member of a literary group revolving around Zona Gale, wrote on November 1 from Madison, in appreciation of *Mary Olivier*. Her letter arrived at the White Hart Hotel on November 15: "I loved *Mary Olivier* so much that I don't want anyone to read it who doesn't 'know.' I don't want them to even touch the pages.—No, I don't mean that at all. No one can mean—really mean such a thing.—I love all of it; it makes one new again."[74] A letter offering such a fountain of true feeling and understanding as that from Margery Latimer could refresh May Sinclair's mind by soothing some of the bruises inflicted by unperceptive reviewers, although it would not reach the public screen on which the author's historical image was being thrown.

The attacks on *The Romantic* provoked the sense of fair play of a good friend of May Sinclair's, an Irishman who was once known as "the modern Pierce Egan" when he was the boxing correspondent for *Field and Sport* and for the *Dramatic News*. Bohun Lynch wrote on November 8:

72. I owe a great debt to Miss Laura Price for help in recording the history of the clinic, and to Dr. John Rees for directing me to her.
73. Letter, courtesy of Rupert Hart-Davis. I have not been able to trace the occasion referred to.
74. Vivien Morgan Hone of the News Service, University of Wisconsin, identified the writer; letter, March 27, 1964.

Please don't think it great cheek of me to say how very, very greatly I admire *The Romantic*. I can't begin to say what I think of it—wonderful style, construction and technique which could not be surpassed. . . . It's an amazing book if only because there is not one word too much or too little: a terrible story most imaginatively and sympathetically told.—When I think of some of the penny-a-line notices I've seen of it—when I think of some books like that being at the mercy (in a manner of speaking) of what are called "reviewers," I am speechless with anger.—Dear Miss Sinclair—do please accept my deepest thanks for this most impressive and distinguished piece of work.

May Sinclair did not mind an interview related to her work, but any probing for personal facts terrified her. An American interviewer who visited her at Number 1 Blenheim Road late in the afternoon of a day in November, 1920, did not print the report of her visit until January 23, 1921, in the *Free Press* of Detroit. Margaret Walter must have questioned her with most unusual tact to have gotten such a truthful insight into the real person.

After Margaret Walter had pressed the bell button a number of times, May Sinclair opened the front door herself. "My maid must be dressing for tea," she offered as a smiling apology. They talked about *The Romantic*: "I don't bother when people say I'm obsessed by the war, or that I've gone in for psycho-analysis. I don't go in for things. But if you care for what is in people's minds, it's bound to come out in your books. You've got to get down to real things." According to Victorian standards, Charlotte Redhead fell, went wrong, and would have to suffer and be branded. Charlotte did suffer, but suffering made her strong, increasingly able to face facts. She began by romancing, but she grew more honest, more courageous. "She could not lie or funk—not even love could make her tolerate that or blind her to it."

Margaret Walter asked her if an author had to go through experiences to write about them—of course, not: a novelist's business is to represent; the materials may be personal to him or to someone else, to anybody.

The Divine Fire had taken her a long time to work itself out. She put it aside for seven years, and wrote other things until she could take it up to bring it to an end.

She wrote out everything twice in her own handwriting, the second copy being plain enough for her typist to read. She did not always admire her heroines, but she admired Charlotte Redhead for being brave and honest. She admitted that her standards of honesty had changed: "Years ago I would not have admired a girl who did what Charlotte did in the beginning of the story [have a lover], no matter what her subsequent achievements. I should have felt that something was essentially wrong with her. In those days an honest woman meant only one thing. Now, to be an honest woman means a great deal more than that." The war had made us see the things that really mattered in the characters of men and woman. It made them take risks as a matter of course, as women had always done in risking childbirth. Miss Walter noticed the rainbow ribbon with a tiny silver rose, her only ornament on her plain black dress, the Belgian government's decoration for her services with the very first field ambulance to reach Belgium from another country in 1914.

May Sinclair would not talk about her wartime experiences, and yet she had been persuaded to reveal her awareness of a change in her moral viewpoint. That new liberal viewpoint was not her last. As moral relaxation lapsed into laxity, she moved to restore the balance without which life would lose meaning. Clear is the portrait that Margaret Walter drew: "This small, well-rounded woman with her piled up soft brown hair, her small healthy brown face, lit up by bright, observant brown eyes, and a low monotonous voice, does not encourage intimacy. She would, I think, be capable of sitting quietly before her fire in her wind-swept drawing room saying nothing at all, for a very long time, and an inquisitive visitor might squirm and squirm unheeded."

During the Christmas season of 1920, May Sinclair surprised the students of the Society for the Study of Orthopsychics by attending their performance of Yeats's play *The Countess Kathleen,* which they gave in their lecture room at 30, Brunswick Square at the end of the Christmas term. She was the only founder member to attend, and after the performance she praised the cast and asked to be introduced to the students. She chatted with them in the friendliest way, asking questions that made the young people thrill to her interest in their activities. They had not read her latest novel, but *The Tree of Heaven* still lived in their imaginations with an awe-inspiring power.[75]

The sales statement from Hutchinsons for the second six months at the year's end was discouraging. No copies of *The Three Brontës* had been sold. Twelve copies of the Colonial edition of *The Combined Maze* were sold at the royalty of fourpence each for a total royalty of four shillings. Of the two-shilling edition, 666 copies had been sold at a royalty of three halfpence for a total royalty of four pounds, three shillings, and three pence. The figures for *Mary Olivier* (Cassells) were: 55 copies of the seven-shilling edition sold, for a royalty of

---

75. Letter, October 23, 1959, from Laura Price, student and part-time secretary of the society, who attended the performance.

three pounds, sixteen shillings, and two pence. The royalty on five copies of the five-shilling Colonial edition was one shilling seven pence.

The writing, nevertheless, had to go on. The accent was on life when *Life and Death of Harriett Frean* opened hopefully in the December number of the *North American Review*. Now the decade of vortices was over. The decade of calm was to offer the relief of an ironic balance; it would raise May Sinclair's writings to a new plane of original achievement, and betray her body to a slow decay, endured with a spiritual giant's cheerfulness and courage.

8

Afternoon and Brilliant Sunset: 1921-1930

Despite the evidence that Dr. W. C. Speirs noticed in Reeth in 1919 that May Sinclair's body was failing her,[1] her creative light burned during most of the 1920s with unlowered brilliance. She worked with a demoniacal concentration, publishing ten excellent novels, nine in prose and one in free verse, a brilliant philosophical treatise, and a small shower of critical essays, reviews, and short stories. Her writing continued to hold its bravery of spirit, to grow in depth and subtlety of motivation, to work toward the utmost leanness of form and litheness of movement. W. L. George set her image for this decade when he met her at a garden party in Campden Hill, probably at Evelyn Underhill's, and described his impression of her at the time as "the burning twilight of May Sinclair."[2]

In this decade her imagination confirmed and carried to a pitch of exaltation the revolt that she had revealed in person to Margaret Walter and which she declared in *Mary Olivier* against the moral dogmatism that would confine love to either a physically unconsummated devotion or to a religiously consecrated marriage. Her mother-inspired —or perhaps her innate—moral orthodoxy she held onto as the fixed and natural rule governing her own bodily life. Only to her imagination did she give the freedom to rebel; and even then she alternated passionate assaults upon conventional morality with lulls for worshiping the heroism of sacrifice by the wanting self, from book to book, and even within the same book. She was no more stapled to a fixed dogma than was one of her masters of revolt, Samuel Butler.

---

1. Letter, July 17, 1964.
2. *A Novelist on Novels* (London: Collins, 1918), p. 101.

In these years there was one falling-off that hurt: of a rewarding affection from the younger writers she had assisted financially and had brought tirelessly to the notice of patrons, publishers, editors, critics, and readers. As her protégés climbed by the rungs to which she had lifted them, they lost sight and touch of her. Her cat Jerry became the surrogate object of the affection that she had endlessly given, and became the imagined respondent of an emotional return that the young writers once had carelessly given her by letting her enjoy the radiations from their youth.

Mark Meredith recognized her eminence when he interviewed her, along with other writers, on the *Future of the Novel*. The interview was printed in the *Pall Mall Gazette* on January 10, 1921, and reprinted when the series became a volume in that year. She modestly silenced her consideration of *Mary Olivier* but generously praised James Joyce and Dorothy Richardson for the impetus they had given the development of the psychological novel when they chose to tell a story through a single consciousness instead of following the traditional method of enacting the role of God Almighty. To the objection that a novel of action could not be told from this viewpoint, she answered that that depended on the kind of consciousness that did the telling. If a man of action did the telling, all his actions would be in his consciousness, the only place where they could be immediately and intimately.

At the instance of St. John Ervine, the Society of Authors met in April, 1921, to decide upon which younger writers should be invited to sign a presentation that would be given Thomas Hardy at a dinner honoring him on his eighty-first birthday. When Hugh Walpole submitted the name of May Sinclair, certain members objected that she was too old to be classified as a younger writer. Walpole knew how passionately she held onto the image of youth, for herself and for her art, and insisted on her being invited: "She must be asked. It will hurt her dreadfully from every point of view if she is not." He won his argument to have her included among the hundred writers who were picked to sign the letter of homage.[3]

If she read Fort Madox Ford's *Thus to Revisit* after it came out in May, she noticed her name among the sixteen whom the editor of a "serious American journal" had listed in his invitation to Ford to write an account of the current English literary world. Robert Bridges, Thomas Hardy, W. H. Hudson, T. S. Eliot, Arnold Bennett, H. G. Wells, W. B. Yeats, D. H. Lawrence, George Moore, Mrs. Meynell, and

---

3. Rupert Hart-Davis, *Hugh Walpole,* London: Macmillan, 1952, p. 207.

Lord Dunsany were among those who kept her company. Ford believed that May Sinclair, G. B. Stern, and Ethel Colburne Mayne were the likeliest innovators who were able to assume the burden of carrying the arts forward.[4]

In the summer of 1921, Mrs. C. A. Dawson Scott, resting on the hill-ridge of a moor near Padstow in Cornwell, conceived the idea of a world fellowship of writers who would' meet with each other in a spirit of kindness and work for international friendship. May Sinclair was a foundation member present at the first meeting, which was held on October 5, 1921, at the Florence restaurant in Soho. John Galsworthy was elected the first president. The name that was chosen for the fellowship, P. E. N., stood for the eligible: poets, playwrights, essayists, editors, and novelists of established reputation. Present also as May Sinclair's guest was Kate Douglas Wiggin, who later formed a center in New York.[5] In the winter of 1921, May Sinclair persuaded Ernest Rhys to join, and took him to a P. E. N. dinner.[6] In November she planned, and on Christmas Day she finished, an article on Violet Hunt's novels.[7]

The only novel to appear in volume form in 1921 was *Mr. Waddington of Wyck,* which Cassells in London and Macmillan in New York published in August. The *English Review* published two critical essays, "The Poems of F. S. Flint," in January and "The Poems of Richard Aldington" in May, and also a short story, "Lena Wrace," in February, which the *Dial* reprinted in July. In May *Harper's* published a short story, "The Return," one of the best of the series of tales told by Simpson, and omitted, but for no aesthetic reason, from the published collection.

Sometime in February, 1922, the Universal Film Manufacturing Company of New York tempted May Sinclair by offering her ten thousand dollars for a story with the theme of the song, "Love Me and the World is Mine." Her answer was predictable. She greatly appreciated the recognition of her work that was implied by the offer, but "unfortunately I never can do anything with a suggested theme, and in this case I am particularly certain that nothing I could write would fulfill your requirements." A long flourish made the tail of the high-flying kite of her defiant signature.[8]

---

4. *Thus to Revisit* (New York: Dutton, 1921) , p. 56.
5. C. A. Dawson Scott, "The First International Club of Writers," *The Literary Digest International Book Review,* November, 1923, pp. 47, 54.
6. Ernest Rhys, *Everyman Remembers,* pp. 302–8.
7. Letters to Violet Hunt, November 17, December 18, December 25, 1921, courtesy of the Berg Collection.
8. Letter, courtesy of Professor William S. Trout.

The editor of the gestating *Criterion* sent an invitation and an appreciation. On March 17, May Sinclair thanked T. S. Eliot for liking her *Harriett Frean,* and offered him "one of my best ghost stories," which had not yet found a home in England. Of the *Criterion* she wrote, "It is time a really good quarterly was started, and I can't think of anyone better fitted to edit it than you. At last there'll be a chance for the people who matter most to get a hearing; and for the *London Mercury* not to have it all its own way."[9]

Edwin Arlington Robinson wrote on March 19, 1922, to thank her for her praise of his *Collected Poems,* and to surprise her with his knowledge of her writings. He knew that she preferred *Mary Olivier,* but he begged for another novel in the "more leisurely and discursive method of The Divine Fire . . . in something of the same mood and along something of the same lines."

She was one of three sympathetic spirits (Richard Aldington and Ezra Pound were the others) who organized a scheme that they called "Bel Esprit," for supporting a dedicated and highly talented author whose having to earn a living by uncongenial means was robbing him of creative energy and time. The idea was that thirty donors would pledge ten pounds a year, no more, for life, or as long as the beneficiary needed support. The total of pledges for the support of any one writer was set at three hundred pounds a year. Bel Esprit's first choice was T. S. Eliot, and its purpose was to ransom him from the slavery of clerking in a branch of Lloyd's. The project was never completed, although twenty-two subscribers gave three hundred pounds.[10]

In August of 1922, *The Romantic* was published in Paris as *Un romanesque.* The translator, Marc Logé, had the good fortune to obtain May Sinclair's help with the proofs.[11]

On May 10, 1922, Samuel Roth invited her to become a contributing editor on a literary quarterly that he planned to start in New York, *Two Worlds.* His idea was that every issue would contain a complete novel, a play, a short story, verse, and reviews of books and plays. He offered to a writer the directness of a private publication and the freshness and flexibility of a magazine, and baited his invitation by confiding to her that he had also invited Aldous Huxley, Ezra Pound, and Arthur Symons to be editors. *Two Worlds* existed from September,

9. Letter, courtesy of Mrs. T. S. Eliot and the Houghton Library.
10. D. D. Paige, *The Letters of Ezra Pound* (New York: Harcourt Brace, 1950), p. 175; and Ezra Pound, "Credit and the Fine Arts," *The New Age,* March 30, 1922.
11. C. Mottot had already translated and adapted *Kitty Tailleur* as *L'immortel moment* in 1912. *Tasker Jevons* was published in Paris in 1916 without credit given to any translator. I owe my thanks to Mr. Bernard J. Ford, librarian at the University of Pennsylvania, for tracking down the French publications.

1925, to June, 1927. Parallel with it was a *Two Worlds Monthly*, which began with the quarterly and ended in September, 1927. Her only contribution was a short story, "The Intercessor,'" which had appeared in the *English Review* in July, 1911; and this the editor of *Two Worlds* reprinted exactly in September, 1926, except for the title, which became *The Intercession: A Novel* by May Sinclair.[12]

Through 1922, she served on the council of the Society of Authors. Her friend of Sidmouth days, now Canon A. C. Deane, was a member of the Pension Fund.

In May, T. S. Eliot returned "The Finding of the Absolute" but accepted "The Victim" for the first issue of the *Criterion*.

May Sinclair was very happy in beautiful, kindly Stow-on-the-Wold, which she had adopted as her writing-home-away-from-home when, in 1919, she had found the long trip to Reeth in Yorkshire too tiring to keep up. A Mr. and Mrs. Groves owned the White Hart Hotel, where she had a permanent room at the top, furnished by herself. She stayed there during spring, summer, and autumn; the winter she spent in London. She liked to look out of the window of her room. When she found the window space left by the curtains was too narrow for comfortable viewing, she had a long curtain-rail put up, so that the curtains could be drawn back from the window against the wall. She liked the inn sign of the Queen's Head, across the Market Square; it was painted in a soft shade of faded blue. After the innkeeper improved the sign by having it painted over in black, and the town fathers tarmacked the square, the ugliness of the double improvement upset her deeply.

She rented a strip of field along the Evesham Road, and had a carpenter build on it a hut, which she fitted out with a table, a chair, a reclining chair, and other conveniences for making this retreat for writing comfortable. The bailiff who rented her the strip of field was the same man who coached her in the agricultural science that she applied in *Anne Severn and the Fieldings*. When I asked Miss Bartrop about the amorously occupied hut in a field in *The Allinghams*, she admitted its resemblance to the writing hut, but assured me that May Sinclair never stayed in the hut at night without having Florence with her. The field on the Evesham Road was owned by a Mr. Mark Fenwick of Abbotswood, and the tenant who let the strip of field on which the hut was built was a Mr. Foster. Rugby players began to use the field, and their noises of competition distracted her; so Mr.

12. I owe the location of *The Intercession* and the history of these periodicals to Robert H. Land, chief of the Reference Department, Library of Congress.

Foster let her have the hut moved to the corner of his garden, close to the wall along the Evesham Road, and had it fenced around. The large window of the hut still faced Upper Swell.

The dream she had never realized in Swaledale, of finding a cottage, came true in Stow when she was able to rent Hillsides, on the Cheltenham Road, the house owned by her friends Arnold and Alys Hannay. Now she could bring Florence Bartrop down with her from London. She still kept her room at the White Hart for her guests. When Richard Aldington took a walking tour through the Cotswolds, May Sinclair gave him a letter to the landlady of the White Hart, and he was able to rest in her permanently rented room.[13] Hillsides still stands, opposite the Unicorn Hotel. A map in the Gloucester Records Office in Shire Hall named it Swell Villa No. 1, in the parish of Lower Swell. Its present owner, Mrs. Biggane, a doctor's widow, commemorated a family place in the new name that she gave it, Beverston. The distance between the cottage and her writing hut gave May Sinclair a brisk warming-up walk to the Evesham Road, and a leisurely cooling-down stroll back to the Cheltenham Road.

The rector of St. Edwards, Stow-on-the-Wold, from 1898 to 1935 was John Evans, who played a large part in having the War Memorial placed inside the church instead of in the Market Square, which the majority of the townspeople thought a more appropriate site. The rector's winning the argument caused some ill feeling, but there was no other resemblance between the rector and Canon Chamberlain of *A Cure of Souls.* John Crawford, the clergyman in *The Rector of Wyck,* was regarded as a portrait very like Mr. John Evans.

The scenery of the Cotswolds novels was positively identified by its townspeople as that of Stow. A group of trees on the top of Bourton-on-the-Hill really looks from Stow like a ship in full sail. The road from Stow's railway station, described in *The Romantic,* climbs a mile and a quarter uphill on Burford Road to Stow through a tunnel of beech trees. It is a lovely sight in spring and autumn and a welcome shade on a hot summer's day. Many of the old country houses, most of them built by wealthy wool staplers of Cotswold stone, are described in the novels, although not in their actual setting. One of the houses in *Anne Severn and the Fieldings* is the Old Manor Farm at Upper Swell. People in Stow were rather shocked by the frankness with which May Sinclair described sexual behavior, particularly in *Anne Severn,* but they also had a marvelous time finding the local people whom the fictional characters might match. May Sinclair used many of the local

---

13. Letter, February 17, 1960.

names, like Minchin, Scarrot, and Febery, but she took great care that people should not be easily recognized.

Stow people found May Sinclair precise in manner, small, and neat. One woman remembered her slightly halting walk; another described her as tripping along and about, reminding one of a bright-eyed robin. She had a small, plump figure, a small appetite, and simple wants in food. Her complexion was pale, her expression serious. Her dark brown hair was always worn in a plaited coronet on top of her head. Her eyes seemed dark brown and were alertly observant. Her voice was low and quiet, her personality quiet, self-contained, kind, sympathetic. She did not often smile, but people heard her laughing when she was with intimate friends. Her dress was unremarkable, usually black, sometimes mauve. She took herself seriously and gave an impression of great personal dignity. People noticed what they thought was a lack of interest in dress, but did not suspect a physical decline as its cause. She loved to talk about cats, especially about her cat Jerry, who stayed in London. People remembered the hut in which she wrote, and envied the wonderful view of its window upon wolds, fields, and woods.

When she chatted about her own books, she would eventually say that Americans were keener on them than were her countrymen. A fellow resident at the White Hart remembered how shy she was, how very little she had to do with the other guests at the hotel. Some of her friends were remembered as having been Mr. and Mrs. McMurdie, Mr. and Mrs. Hannay, and a Mrs. Evans. Mrs. McMurdie was a successful artist who painted under the name Grace Demain Hammond and exhibited at the Royal Academy and the Royal Institute of Water Colours. Mrs. Alys Hannay was remembered too as an artist.

May Sinclair's favorite entertainment for her friends was taking them on drives in a car whose chauffeur was the son of the local garageman, Mr. Stanley Hyde. The prime favorite place to which she asked him to drive was Fairford, for a look at St. Mary's Church, its lovely old stained-glass windows, and the cottage where Mary and her mother had lived. The party would have tea at the Bull Hotel in the Square, and then go on to Lechlade and Burford, for visits to the churches there.

Another trip was to Northleach and Cirencester, with tea at the King's Head. A third was to Stratford-on-Avon. Once she gave her guests a special thrill by pointing out Marie Corelli, then one of the best-known writers, walking not as a tourist come to worship but as a resident in Shakespeare's native place. A fourth tour was of Chipping-Camden, Mickleton, Broadway, Stanton, and Stanway. Some tours lasted two or three days: these would include the Forest of Dean,

Speech House, and Lydney. Bath and Wells made another tour, the night being spent at the Pump House at Bath. The Wye Valley to Symonds Yat gave the party still another view of Gloucestershire. May Sinclair had the highest confidence in Mr. Hyde's driving. When a friend once betrayed her nervousness on a steep hill that was bisected by a crossroad, May Sinclair assured her, "Stanley values his life quite as much as you do yours."

Florence Bartrop once accompanied her to the Point-to-Point races. She asked Miss Bartrop if she wanted to put any money on a horse, and Florence answered that she would not think of placing a bet without knowing something about the horse. Eagerly May Sinclair ran about, looking at each horse to gather as much information as she could to guide Miss Bartrop's betting; but she herself never bet. The wife of Stanley Hyde, Dorothy, an artist whom May Sinclair chose to design the jackets for *Far End, The Allinghams,* and *History of Anthony Waring,* identified the Point-to-Point meeting as the one held at Bledington, three miles from Stow, where the local hunt, the Hetrop Hunt, held its meeting at the end of the fox-hunting season.[14]

It is very possible that May Sinclair left Stow permanently in 1929 because Florence Bartrop resented Alys Hannay's taking advantage of May Sinclair's gentleness and generosity. The two women contracted to share the expenses of maintaining a car that May Sinclair had bought, but Mrs. Hannay used the car most of the time, and let May Sinclair pay the expenses all of the time, until Miss Bartrop was outraged enough to tell Mrs. Hannay off. When May Sinclair reexamined the question of keeping a car, she asked Miss Bartrop, "Can we afford a car, Florrie?" Miss Bartrop answered, "Yes, if you are allowed to use it."

After this diversion into the social pleasantries of Stow, we must return to the story of the professional writer. In the summer of 1922, she was working hard on her *Anne Severn and the Fieldings* at Stow, when she mistakenly thought that she had taken a copybook of "Farming Notes" with her to London and left it there. She asked her friend Eleanor to look for it, and on June 1 Miss Whitehead wrote back that she had not been able to find it: "Are you being good and taking care of yourself? *Do* rest that leg and give it a chance.—Tomorrow you will be having your visitors. Now don't be tempted to walk!"

In June, *The New Idealism* appeared, and Bertrand Russell wrote from Penzance to say he would probably review it in the *Nation,*

---

14. Through their interest in literature and the resourcefulness of Mrs. Gladys Woodward and her son Lionel, of Stow-on-the-Wold, I was able to draw upon the recollections of a number of people who remembered May Sinclair: Miss Jessie Howman, Mrs. Jefferies, Mr. Stanley Hyde, and Mrs. Dorothy Hyde.

which he did. He was frank in writing: "I am sceptical enough to think that not only are the arguments in favour of a philosophy generally fallacious, but those against (as opposed to refutations of arguments for) are usually equally so. I therefore approach your book with an open mind, and with great respect for your patience in mastering views with which you disagree."[15]

When she knew she was to read her paper to the Aristotelian Society on February 5, 1923, she wrote for advice on meeting possible objections to it. The man to whom she turned was the biographer of Tintoretto and translator of Hegel's *The Philosophy of Fine Art*, Francis Plumptre Beresford Osmaston; and she began her preparations early, for he replied to her on October 13, 1922, in a publishable treatise of forty-six pages, expressing the greatest enthusiasm for the two volumes on Idealism that she had written, and his appreciation of the novelist's imagination which she had brought to the exposition of philosophical concepts. He assured her that her two volumes were "superior to any previous achievement of the kind by an authoress."[16]

In November appeared the second novel of the year, the defiantly romantic *Anne Severn and the Fieldings*. On November 22, Evelyn Underhill wrote of the enchantment that she experienced during the reading: "I've just finished your Anne, and why you should have been frightened about her I can't imagine. I think she is superb. I devoured her almost without stopping. I am so glad you have escaped from the thralldom of the 'single-consciousness' daemon. . . . I think this is one of the finest spiritual dramas you've done, if not *quite* the finest. All the last chapters are perfectly wonderful, almost unbearably so."

May Sinclair was anxious because this novel rebelled against the deepest urges of her psyche to submit to orthodox morality. Evelyn Underhill was not the only friend to whom she confessed her panic. The sketch of a letter to Richard Aldington ended, "Love—Always yours—May—Anne Severn and the Fieldings is out and I'm frightened." The sketch of a letter to her French translator, Marc Logé, also ended, "Anne Severn and the Fieldings is out and I'm frightened."

On December 16, 1922, May Sinclair confessed to Violet Hunt about *Anne Severn:* "The thing suffers from my liking my people so much. You're quite right—I do 'do better when I hate them.' I'm even fairer to them." She was apparently dissatisfied with the orthodoxy of her technique, because she wrote, "It's the last I shall do of this sort of thing. I must keep to the method of 'Mary Olivier,' even if I

---

15. Quoted by permission of Lord Russell and William Ready.
16. The identity of the writer of this letter was solved by the postmaster of Porthleven, Cornwall, W. Hudson Vincent, and his qualifications were described for me by his son-in-law, Baron Layton.

must pass from mind to mind."[17] Despite her statement of firm intention, she was to return to the ampler method that readers as different as Edwin Arlington Robinson and Evelyn Underhill applauded.

The harvest of publications for 1922 included two critical essays, "The Novels of Violet Hunt," appearing in the *English Review* in February, and "The Poems of H. D.," which appeared in the same month in the *Dial*. She reviewed Sinclair Lewis's *Babbitt* for the first page of the *New York Times* book review section on September 24. She published three short stories: the cautiously entitled "Heaven: A Story" in the *Fortnightly* in September; "Where Their Fire is not Quenched" in the *English Review* in October; and "The Victim" in the first number of the *Criterion,* also in October.

A circular sent out from the *Criterion* offices at 17 Thavies Inn, Holborn, commemorates the publication date of the first number as October 15, and lists among the contributors to early numbers May Sinclair, T. S. Eliot, Hermann Hesse, Roger Fry, Stephen Hudson, George Saintsbury, Leonard Woolf, Virginia Woolf, and Richard Aldington.

On the Monday evening of February 5, 1923, which has already been described, May Sinclair reached the height of her recognition as a philosopher when she lectured to the Aristotelian Society on the subject that aroused the most interest in the reviews of her *The New Idealism,* "Primary and Secondary Consciousness."[18] On March 29, Professor John Henry Muirhead, the general editor of the Library of Philosophy for Allen and Unwin informed her of his projected volume of essays on the general line of Dr. Raymond Schmidt's *Die Deutsche Philosophie der Gegenwart in Selbstdarstellungen,* and invited her, the only woman writer he was inviting, to contribute an essay. The project appeared in two volumes as *Contemporary British Philosophy,* the first series in 1924, the second series in 1925. Apparently, after the excitement of February 5, she had had her fill of struggle and attainment as a philosopher, for she did not accept Professor Muirhead's invitation. Yet, she did save the letter that gave her the comfort of knowing that she was esteemed as a philosopher above all the women of England in her time.

She contributed to a symposium on "Dreams, Ghosts and Fairies" in the December number of the *London Bookman*. She rated "The Turn of the Screw" as the most perfect and convincing ghost story that she had ever read, and expressed her own attitude of creative interest with actual disbelief when she wrote, "The ghost-lover is on the

17. Letter, courtesy of the Berg Collection.
18. Published in the Aristotelian Society, *Proceedings* 23, no. 7 (1923) : 111–20.

lookout for his own special thrill, which is, or may be, independent of any belief in the supernatural."

The only new volume to come out in this year was *Uncanny Stories*. It was a good year for reissues: *The Romantic* in March; *Kitty Tailleur* in July; *Two Sides of a Question* in August. The two new short stories in 1923 were "The Nature of the Evidence" in the May *Fortnightly*, and "Jones's Karma" in the *Criterion* for October. "Lena Wrace" was included in *The Best British Short Stories of 1922*, issued in January, 1923.

She wrote reviews of three books in this year: Jung's *Psychological Types* for the May issue of the *English Review;* Grant Watson's *The Desert Horizon* in the June issue, and Henry James Forman's *Sudden Wealth* in the November number of the *Literary Digest International Book Review*.

Early in 1923, E. P. Dutton in America reissued the works of the Brontës in a set of six volumes with May Sinclair's introductions and Edmond Dulac's illustrations. Dent had reissued them in 1922. Mrs. Humphry Ward became a competitor as a Brontë critic by writing the prefaces to the volumes in the Haworth edition, published in 1924.

Three new novels made 1924 a richly productive year. In January, Hutchinsons in London and Macmillan in New York published *A Cure of Souls*. In May, Cape published a limited signed edition of a novel in verse, *The Dark Night,* which Macmillan in New York issued in a regular edition. The *Home Magazine* had begun its ten-part serialization of *Arnold Waterlow* in October, 1923, ending it in July, 1924.[19] In September, Hutchinsons brought out this novel in London and Macmillan published it in New York.

Arthur St. John Adcock wrote on March 3 from his office in the *London Bookman*. He had just read "The Grandmother" in the *Criterion,* and thought it "the most poignant and beautiful thing I have read in poetry for a long while. Perhaps because my mother now (at 86) sits waiting just in that way, I know how wonderfully true the picture is." He begged her to let him include this section of *The Dark Night* in *The Bookman Anthology of Living Poets*. Wyndham Lewis likewise contributed a fragment of a long work, *The Apes of God,* to the *Criterion*. He suggested in a letter to the editor, T. S. Eliot, that he hand it to him personally at a party that May Sinclair was giving early in February.[20]

---

19. Robert H. Land, of the Library of Congress, located this serialization.
20. W. K. Rose, *The Letters of Wyndham Lewis* (Norfolk, Connecticut: New Directions, 1963), p. 139. His footnote to the letter proves W. K. Rose to be remarkable as a bestower of appreciation: "The novelist May Sinclair . . . a friend of Eliot, was helpful to writers in the modern movement."

In April, the headmaster of Reeth Friends School in Yorkshire, Mr. Shepherd, suggested to May Sinclair a broadening of the terms of the prizes that she had founded. She opposed his idea in something of the spirit in which Dorothea Beale would have replied: "I meant the prizes to be given for the best papers in Natural History and English History, so that the boys might be interested in the country life around them, and that they might have an idea of the larger life of England in which they have a part. . . . I am grieved to think that the competition should have degenerated into a sordid affair of money-getting."[21]

May Sinclair accompanied Mrs. Dawson Scott to New York in April as a fellow delegate of the founding English branch of P. E. N. to the Second International Congress, which was scheduled for the middle of May and was managed by the American center in New York. She stayed at the National Arts Club, 15 Gramercy Park, where a tribute of flowers aroused her detective ingenuity to discover the anonymous sender, who turned out to be Elizabeth Holden Webb.[22]

A letter of introduction that W. L. George had written for her enabled May Sinclair to meet Carl Van Vechten. In her letter enclosing W. L. George's, she mentioned her adoration of *The Tiger in the House*.[23]

One of the regalements of the P. E. N. congress was a performance of Anne Nichols's popular play, *Abie's Irish Rose*. John Farrar, as the master of ceremonies, filled the interval between the first and second acts by introducing various members of the congress. He identified May Sinclair as "the great novelist, the greatest psychological analyst in fiction." A reporter for the *New York Telegraph,* Alice Rohe, recorded May Sinclair's response (June 8) : "What seemed to be a piece of plush upholstery rose from the sixth row. But soon we distinguished a pair of small, keen eyes beneath a fringe of hair, lowered in recognition of the salute."[24]

The editor of "The Gossip Shop" for the *New York Bookman* noticed May Sinclair and the special favor that she showed to Miss Grace George at the reception given the P. E. N. members by the Painters and Sculptors Gallery Association. The editor talked to May Sinclair and found her to be the shyest woman he had ever met. She sat quite still, seeming not to look at anyone; when she spoke, she seemed to be addressing a far distant person.[25]

21. Letter, courtesy of R. A. Place, retired headmaster of Reeth School.
22. Letter, courtesy of the Library of Congress.
23. Letter, courtesy of the Berg Collection.
24. The cutting was kindly loaned me by Mr. David Carver, General Secretary, International P. E. N., and its source was identified by Mr. Gilbert A. Cam, of the New York Public Library.
25. *New York Bookman,* July, 1924, pp. 637–38.

Willis Steell interviewed her in New York. Like others, he noticed the darkness of her eyes, eyes darker than her hair, which had no thread of gray in it. She confessed to him having written two novels before *Audrey Craven*. Her saying that she hoped that they would never come up to torture her could mean that they had been published, and were not *Mr. and Mrs. Nevill Tyson* and *A Hero of Fiction.* She said that her favorite and, she thought, her best book was *Mary Olivier*. She could not bear people saying, as they constantly did, that they preferred *The Divine Fire* over any of her books. The only family she had left was nephews and nieces. She talked about her cat Jerry, who was black and shiny as a black looking glass, had yellow eyes, and hunted birds. She said that when she was in Belgium writing *A Journal of Impressions,* she remembered that Charlotte Brontë had once lived in Belgium, and had let Charlotte Brontë's vivid style influence her to set down her crude emotions boldly, with few strokes and no afterthought. She described *Life and Death of Harriett Frean* as an experiment: "I went with her over the road I had already gone with Mary Olivier and put her to similar tests. I think that I succeeded technically, and *Harriett Frean* is one of the best books I have done." *Arnold Waterlow* she described as "a male *Mary Olivier*. I have a sort of obsession for making these experiments, and watch the result eagerly." *The Three Brontës* was to her the hardest of hard work, despite the pleasure it gave her. She mentioned among her London writer-friends G. K. Chesterton, Dorothy Richardson, Rebecca West, Arnold Bennett, Rose Macaulay, and W. L. George. Willis Steell found her voice to be quiet and level, her speech not very fluent, but precise, the direct expression of her "firm, tight, little character." She spoke of her maid as "a faithful creature who is there now looking after Jerry."[26]

Burton Rascoe also left a record of his impressions of May Sinclair during her stay in New York. She dominated any group less heterogeneous than a noisy banquet with her Buddha-like calm and charm. He felt her charm to lie almost wholly in her intensely black eyes, which reflected no emotion. Her face was immobile, her lips did not smile. Not her mouth, but tiny muscular contractions at the corners of her eyes displayed her amusement. The composed little woman had a quaint Victorian look. He noticed her very beautiful nose and her tightly pressed-down upper lip. Her clothing was of very richly embroidered materials, mostly brown, and she wore interesting neck chains.

When she addressed the P. E. N. Club dinner she offered her simple,

---

26. *Literary Digest Book Review*, June, 1924.

formal message of goodwill in a high-pitched, thin, clear, unaccented and uninflected voice, speaking in a low monotone. Her lips were eerily without movement, as if they were the mouthpiece of a ventriloquist. Only when she talked about cats did the cadence of her voice rise to an excited pitch and her face warm to animation. She listened to Jules Romain, the French delegate, recite a long poem of his own at the Grand Central Art Gallery without letting any emotion play on her face. She told Rascoe, as she told others, that the favorite among her books was *Mary Olivier,* a masterpiece she thought it likely she would never surpass. She disclaimed being a poet, and yet Rascoe felt that her experiments in fiction had been tending toward the method she employed in *The Dark Night.* He even thought it more than possible that the challenge of the difficulties of narration in free verse, and the union of maximum effect with the greatest economy of means with which it rewarded success, would lead her to adopt that form. He thought her an artist who had always imposed upon herself severe tasks in form. She always kept abreast of literary innovations and was sympathetic with young experimenters.[27]

Edwin Arlington Robinson was as deeply impressed by *The Dark Night* as had been Burton Rascoe. From New Hampshire on June 5, he sent a note that Florence Bartrop forwarded to Stow-on-the-Wold, thanking her for the copy she had sent him, and confessing that he had doubted the effectiveness of telling a story in free verse until "your poignant and gripping narrative" proved him wrong. "Therefore I congratulate you, and thank you once more.—It was a great pleasure to see you again."

The editor of *Poetry,* Harriet Monroe, wrote her congratulations on June 9: "I love your book. I think it makes a beautiful use of a form new in narrative—or at least it uses the form very individually and with new effect. Also it keeps in tone, and does not forget that it is a poem and not a novel and there are beautiful lines and phrases in it. . . . It is really a lovely thing."

Another editor, T. S. Eliot, wrote about the book on June 19 on *Criterion* stationery: "I liked 'The Grandmother' so much that I am certain I shall like the whole poem. . . . It seems to me a very remarkable thing to have accomplished, and perhaps too an important step in the transition of the novel into some other form, which I feel is an inevitable development already foreshadowed in some of your own work as well as in that of Joyce and a few others."[28]

A savage review of *Arnold Waterlow* by Henry Cecil Harwood in

27. "Contemporary Reminiscences," *Arts and Decoration,* July, 1924.
28. By permission of Mrs. T. S. Eliot.

the *Manchester Guardian* drew an indignant reply from the chivalrous Hugh Walpole that was published on October 6. He called the review "surely both arrogant and unfair," in doubting that May Sinclair had produced anything memorable in the past or showed any sign of producing something memorable in the future: "Memorable! Well, he alone knows what he means by that word, but for many of us 'The Three Sisters,' that most beautiful book 'The Tree of Heaven,' 'The Combined Maze,' 'Anne Severn' are memorable enough. And as to the future. Is not your reviewer a little too omniscient in his prophecies? When, further, he says, 'Who ever reread any novel of hers with anything of excitement or recreation?' there are many, I am sure, who could answer him.—From 'The Divine Fire' to 'Arnold Waterlow' Miss Sinclair has steadily produced for us her store of beauty and passion, humor and insight into human nature. One reader at least must chronicle his gratitude."[29]

May Sinclair must have suffered from the wound. So moved was she by the restorative that she dropped formality for the first time to address her champion on October 12 by his given name: "My dear Hugh." She praised his *The Old Ladies* and thanked him for his "generous defence" of her in the *Manchester Guardian*.[30]

It was balm of a sort, too, to be invited by E. V. Lucas, its editor, to contribute some poems to *The Queen's Doll House* of this year, 1924. He chose "Fright" and "Visionary" out of the series that Thomas Moult had printed in his *Voices* in 1920.[31]

May Sinclair wrote two reviews in this year: of Alice Law's *Patrick Branwell Brontë*, in the *London Bookman* for May, and of Henry Justin Forman's *Wealth*, in the December *Literary Digest International Book Review*.

Some reprintings kept up her spirits and sustained the public image: the sixth edition of *Anne Severn and the Fieldings* appeared in April, an edition of *Life and Death of Harriett Frean* in June, an edition of *The Creators* in September, and an edition of *The Helpmate* in October.

In April, 1925, the *London Bookman* ran an epistolary symposium on "Unpleasant Fiction." The editor introduced the letters with the statement that actors and actresses were complaining of the unpleasant plays in which they were called upon to act, and members of the public had been similarly complaining of unpleasant books that the

---

29. I owe the discovery of this letter to the patient research of Miss Kathleen Nisbet, librarian of the *Guardian*.
30. Letter, courtesy of Mr. Rupert Hart-Davis.
31. I owe the discovery of this item to Miss Ellen Shaffer, then curator of Rare Books, Free Library of Philadelphia.

novelists had been writing for them to read. The main subject of unpleasantness was sex relations, a subject that was not really news to adults and that was treated without the imaginativeness and originality with which the Victorians had written, but instead was served up as a mess of facts. May Sinclair's letter headed the fifteen communications from the authors who had been invited to give their opinions. Among those who trailed her were W. B. Maxwell, Frank Swinnerton, Rose Macaulay, W. L. George, J. D. Beresford, Ernest Raymond, and Michael Sadleir. May Sinclair was liberal, terse, unbelligerent in declaring that "the attitude of the modern novelist toward sex relations is more enlightened and more sane than that of those Victorian novelists who ignored this fundamental aspect of human nature. I don't deny that his work is sometimes 'unpleasant'; but it need not be."

A book that could never be classed as "unpleasant" appeared this same April in both London and New York, and helped to prove that the movement of the wheel is not unknown to the traffic of time. May Sinclair could send a copy of *The Rector of Wyck* to the old friendly critic without any fear that he would find it the repelling book that he had once judged *Mr. and Mrs. Nevill Tyson* to be. He had plenty of opportunities to meet his former protégée of Sidmouth days through their common memberships in the Society of Authors and the Royal Society of Literature, but he wrote to her about this book. Only her reply, dated May 23, 1925, was saved. If there is a hint of primness in its tone, a reader may soften it by remembering the youthful excitement with which its author had written to Anthony Deane once upon a time: "My dear Canon Deane—Many thanks for your delightful letter. I do not think it is my best book—I have never done anything better than Mary Olivier—but it has the humble merits of simplicity and truth to life. And I have an affection for John and Matty. . . . —I shall look forward to seeing you at the Royal Literary Fund Dinner on the 9th."[32]

Walter Tittle wrote of his impressions over a number of years in an article that the *Illustrated London News* published on June 27, together with a charming sketch of the author and her cat Jerry. Interviewers had varying success with this acutely sensitive lady, but Walter Tittle's warm felicity with cats encouraged her to be her most unguarded, revealing self. He recalled their first meeting at a dinner of the P. E. N. Club in London, when she looked very diminutive and quaint, and her black eyes scrutinized him with an intense inspection of his humanity. She seemed to be upstage until the childlike sweetness of her smile signaled to him that he had passed her scrutiny. After

---

32. Letter, courtesy of Miss L. A. Chauncy.

he got to know her well, he noticed that she subjected all persons at a first meeting to a defensive appraisal. With her friends she was gentle, warm-hearted, simple, an attentive, comfort-providing hostess, a joyful companion.

When he called at her home in Blenheim Road to draw her portrait, she depreciated herself as a model, but was radiant in her concern that he should draw her splendid black cat, Jerry, a stray she had adopted, actually, a mother's offering of her kitten. Tittle wrote, "Any child would be rich in possessing the amount of love that the famous novelist lavishes on this animal. Her face shone with happiness as she talked about him. . . . Her interest in the representation of herself was casual to the last degree. It was only the cat that mattered!" The impression Tittle recorded was a far sadder revelation of May Sinclair's loneliness than most cat lovers are likely to admit.

She told about her writing hours in London, from half-past nine in the morning until one o'clock, when she stopped for luncheon. If she continued writing in the afternoon she limited herself to a maximum of five hours a day. She never forced herself. She talked about the "shed" she used and the little cottage she resorted to in the Cotswolds, which gave her the joyful union of a retreat for work and freedom for recreation. She said that writing came so easily in the later years that she needed to do very little rewriting, a task she hated. She was hurt by caricatures of her that had been made and published in American newspapers during her visit to the International P. E. N. Congress in New York. She showed him two cuttings and asked with serious concern, "Tell me, really, do I look like that?"[33]

Her satirical success, *A Cure of Souls,* was the one novel reissued in 1925, in January.

One new novel, *Far End,* was published in 1926, in August, both in London and New York. *Uncanny Stories* went into its third edition in September. "Villa Desirée" appeared in Lady Cynthia Asquith's *The Ghost Book: 16 New Stories of the Uncanny,* in October.

Although she worked very hard at it, May Sinclair never realized her ambition to become a successful playwright. Before 1900, she wrote *A Debt of Honour, a Tragedy in Three Acts,* the fragmentary *Tancred of Adan, a Lyrical Drama in Five Acts,* and probably also *The Pilgrim's Way, a Musical Drama,* to the last of which she signed the pseudonym "D. Elliot." After 1900, she transmuted two of her novels and one short story into plays: *The Divine Fire, a Play in Four Acts; The Immortal Moment, a Tragedy in Three Acts;* and *Miss Tarrant's Temperament, a Modern Comedy in Three Acts.* She also

---

33. A mutilated version of this article was printed in the *Review of Reviews* in August.

collaborated with Louis N. Parker in dramatizing another novel, whose title she retained, *The Helpmate, a Play in Four Acts,* the typescript and scenario of which are dated October 3, 1907. I have found no evidence that a single one of these was produced.

The versatile Frank Vosper made a play in three acts out of *The Combined Maze,* which the Repertory Players of London performed on a Sunday night, March 13, 1927, starring Richard Bird as Ranny Ransome. It was next produced by Aubrey Mather and the Forum Theatre Guild at the Royalty Theatre in Dean Street, opening on May 30.[34] Richard Bird continued in the leading role, Jean Forbes-Robertson played Winnie Dymond, Mary Grew played Violet Usher, and Gordon Harker again played Violet's father. The reviews were very favorable.

When May Sinclair and Florence Bartrop went to the dress rehearsal at the Royalty Theatre, May Sinclair was too shy to identify herself to the doorman. Only after the invited guests had been admitted was she recognized and, with Florence Bartrop, escorted to her box. At the end of the performance the audience called for the author. She sat still, but Frank Vosper, who was a large man, led her from her box onto the stage and kept an arm about her while she stood too choked with ecstasy to be able to speak a word to the cheering and hopeful audience. Her glory in the theater that night was so much more thrilling than had been her pride in her intellectual eminence among the Aristotelians only four years before. The two women went again on the first night. Once more the pleased audience shouted for the author, but this time Frank Vosper did not come for her, and she sat paralyzed, unable even to make a bow of acknowledgment.

The short run of the play proved that at that time there were not enough novel readers in London who were also theater-goers to give her compassionate truthfulness a run with their patronage.

At the dinner that the P. E. N. Club gave to Lion Feuchtwanger on December 6, 1927, Arnold Bennett chatted with May Sinclair, whom he had not seen since he and Irving Brock of the *New York Times* had been her guests at the Albemarle Club sixteen years before. Bennett read in her manner the tragedy that she had suffered from the recent death of her cat Jerry.[35] Florence Bartrop told me that the death of Jerry was the blow that broke her will to live.

Hutchinsons published two new novels in 1927: *The Allinghams,*

---

34. The play program erroneously dates the first performance, the single one given by the Repertory Players, as March 28.
35. *The Journal of Arnold Bennett* (New York: The Literary Guild, 1933, Entry for December 6).

in March, and *History of Anthony Waring*, in August. Macmillan issued both in New York. May Sinclair's creativity was sustained at its high level to the end; and this, nineteen years before her death, was the end.

The only critical essay appearing this year was "The Poems of H. D." in the *Fortnightly* for March; it was a fuller, original version of the cut article that had been published in February, 1922 in the *Dial*.

Sometime in 1928, the Royal Society of Literature appointed her to the Academic Committee.[36]

An American reader, a Mrs. Taylor, of York, Pennsylvania, wrote so appreciatively about *Anthony Waring* that May Sinclair replied with a revealing response on February 22: "It was very amusing to do. I delighted in the elimination a story of that length—or want of length entails.—I am down in the country in my beloved Cotswold village, motoring about and enjoying myself immensely."[37] The handwriting, clear and firm as it was when Professor James complimented her on it, betrayed no hint of the decline that was to reduce her life to an almost minimal existence.

In that "sometime" of an otherwise undated reference to 1928, May Sinclair gave up Stow to rent a cottage in the village of Constantine on the coast of north Cornwall, beyond Padstow. The cottage bore the name of her once-enthusiastic American publisher, Holt, and adjoined the cottage in which lived Dorothy Richardson and her husband Alan Odle. G. B. Stern had lived in it once, and Rupert Croft-Cooke was to live in it during 1930.[38]

The only new publication in 1928 was an introduction to Romer Wilson's first novel, *Martin Schüler,* which Knopf published on February 17.[39]

Far End was reissued in February, *The Allinghams* in April, and *Uncanny Stories* in June. Dorothy Sayers included "Where Their Fire is not Quenched" in her anthology, *Great Ghost Stories of Detection, Mystery and Horror,* published in October and reprinted in 1929 and 1930.

On December 4, 1928, May Sinclair signed a codicil to the will that had been drawn up in 1918, on November 11, leaving to Florence Bartrop one hundred pounds and any moneys that might be due her.

---

36. Letter, J. M. Patterson, secretary, February 5, 1960.
37. Letter, courtesy of Professor W. S. Trout.
38. Rupert Croft-Cooke, *The Last of Spring* (New York: Putnam, 1964), pp. 104–06. Rupert Croft-Cooke is one of the genuine enthusiasts for the novels of May Sinclair.
39. Letter, Katherine Hourigan, Editorial Department, January 21, 1965.

In January, 1929, *History of Anthony Waring* went into a new edition. A short story, "Fame," was reprinted as Number Thirteen in the Woburn Books, a series of slender volumes, each limited to five hundred signed copies, published by Elkin Mathews and Marrot. Another short story, "Lena Wrace," was reprinted in Edward J. O'Brien's *Modern English Short Stories,* published in February.

Sometime in February, 1930, May Sinclair attended a dinner party given by H. G. Wells. The main topic at dinner was a dispute between Wells and the Society of Authors, and the guests sympathetically agreed to call for a special meeting of the council in March. The especially convened meeting brought together again May Sinclair and some of her particular friends, Hugh Walpole, Marie Belloc Lowndes, J. D. Beresford, and, of course, Wells, as well as Arnold Bennett.[40]

In May, Hutchinsons in London and Macmillan in New York brought out *Tales Told by Simpson,* which strangely lacked a very well-told story, "The Return," perhaps because its principal was too easily recognized. It was not her last volume, but the last book of hers that won wide current attention.

There was to be some afterglow in the opening years of the next decade, but with the passing of 1930, the brilliant sunset of May Sinclair as a person and as a writer faded away.

---

40. Reginald Pound, *Arnold Bennett* (London: Heinemann, 1952), p. 342.

9

The Long, Dark Night: 1931-1946
With Some Impressions

The years from 1931 to the end of 1946 held few moments of May Sinclair's life that were visible to eyes other than those of her companion, Florence Bartrop, her chauffeur, Ernest Williams, and her close relatives, her nephew, Harold Lumley Sinclair, his wife Muriel, her nieces Agatha Ayre, Wilda McNeile, and Nora Assinder, and her grandnieces and grandnephew. Friends and acquaintances gossiped, and heard that Miss Bartrop was keeping her a prisoner, and gave up trying to call on her. Her family knew better, for Miss Bartrop kept taking her on a round of visits to her nephew and nieces, to whom she took on the image not of a writer who had won honors, but of an old woman with a lolling head whose body and mind had devoluted toward the Nirvana that once had fascinated her imagination. Had death come now, as the shock administered by the passing of a recently honored artist, it might have caused the stream of sentiment that flows just below the surface of public apathy to have spouted up and washed the dusty image, exposing its appealing portrait, and won for it an easy admittance to the corridor of fame. But her useless life would not yield up her body.

She became so reckless in giving her money away that Miss Bartrop appealed to Robert Garnett, her lawyer, who arranged matters so that all disbursements and withdrawals of money were jointly carried out by Miss Bartrop and Mr. Garnett. Dr. Edward Spencer Scott intervened in 1931, warning Florence Bartrop that May Sinclair was not well enough to attend the parties and functions in London to which she was always being invited, and which she eagerly hungered to attend, either because she seemed unaware of her illness or because she was willful in ignoring it. Miss Bartrop thought she was not aware of how ill she was. Dr. Scott advised Miss Bartrop to find some place far enough from London to make the trip back difficult enough to prevent it. She found a house in Little Tingewick, in Buckinghamshire, whose address we see for the first time on the second codicil of May Sinclair's will, dated November 7, 1932. The signature to that codicil started clearly, but the surname ended up in a scrawl that bravely tried to approximate the flourish of her time of strength. At Little Tingewick May Sinclair acquired an Alsatian dog that was named after the legendary Gelert. The chauffeur, Ernest Williams, had personal care of the dog and the feeding to him of his rich diet of butter, eggs, and milk. Sometime in the thirties Ernie drove Florrie and May Sinclair through Wales, and they stopped at Beddgelert to visit the grave of the original Gelert.

She was living in Tingewick when she attended her second and last garden party at Buckingham Palace. To confer upon a local auto-hire garageman a conversation piece that he migtht use for the rest of his life, she went all the way in a taxi.

Hutchinsons published her last volume in September, 1931, *The Intercessor and other Stories,* and reissued *Tales Told by Simpson.* Macmillan of New York waited until 1932 to publish *The Intercessor.* Ernest Rhys and C. A. Dawson Scott included "The Collector" (which had originally come out in the *Century Magazine* in January, 1914) in their anthology, *Thirty and one Stories by Thirty and One Authors,* published in February, 1931, by Thornton Butterworth. In 1933, Hutchinsons reissued *The Three Brontës* in their Booklovers Libary.

On February 6, 1934, May Sinclair accepted the invitation of the president of the Institut Littéraire et Artistique de France, the Marquis de Champvans de Farémont, to become a Corresponding Honorary Member. The admission fee, one hundred francs, amounted at the time to one pound six shillings. On the same day, Hutchinsons issued another edition of *The Three Brontës.* The *Golden Book* reprinted *Life and Death of Harriett Frean* in its Janaury and February numbers of 1934.

Little Tingewick turned out to be too remote, and Miss Bartrop resumed her searching for a place where her charge could be both out of sight of either prying or pitying eyes, and yet within range of medical help from London and of a good local hospital. At last she found the ideal house: The Gables, 96 Burcott Lane, Bierton, two miles from Aylesbury, and only a few miles further from Wendover Hospital. She chose the house for its distance from the country lane, its shade trees, the ample garden, fenced in, and the long side porch, trellised and tapestried with purple clematis, which in spring and summer brought the sky right down to earth as a curtain of flowers. Here May Sinclair could sit, looking at the garden, and dream of her garden in St. John's Wood. To the rear of the flower garden was the vegetable garden, and behind the house were a single-story brick drying room with a ceiling of thick plate glass, and the brick stable that was used as a garage. In the spring of 1936, The Gables became May Sinclair's last home.

Sometime in the late thirties Ernest Williams drove the two women of the household through Yorkshire. They visited the Brontë Museum in Haworth, and when May Sinclair saw Emily's piano, whose keyboard was protected by a glass casing, the compulsion to play on the piano that Emily had played overcame her sense of actuality. Her hands dropped heavily to strike a resounding chord, and instead crashed through the glass, to her immediate horror. She wanted so much to play again, without understanding that her fingers would no longer obey any precise command. At home again, Florence Bartrop fobbed her off with the excuse that there was no space in The Gables to hold a piano. She had not foreseen this pathetic thrust against frustration.

When she was the chief passenger in an automobile, she intensely disliked seeing any cars ahead of hers. She was being driven from Aylesbury to London to see Dr. Edward Spencer Scott. Somewhere between Tring and Beckhampton May Sinclair begged her chauffeur, "Can't you pass him, Ernie?" "I will, as soon as I see my chance," he replied. Dr. Scott told Miss Bartrop that being driven about was a great comfort to May Sinclair, because when she was riding, the shaking of the car kept her from noticing how her hands trembled.

From his office in St. James's Palace, the Lord Chamberlain, whose handwriting was very like May Sinclair's, sent out in a hand-addressed envelope an engraved invitation into which the name of May Sinclair was handwritten, to an afternoon party in the garden of Buckingham Palace, from 4 to 6:30 P.M. (weather permitting). Morning dress was requested. A second enclosure changed the date from July 21, 1938, to July 18, "in view of the alteration in the dates of the State Visit of the King and Queen to France." She could not go. She must have noticed that the envelope was faintly embossed just under the top edge of the flap with a name that looked familiar: Waterlow & Son.

In the summer of 1939, May Sinclair craved a sea trip; so Ernie drove the women to Southampton, from where they were ferried to the Isle of Wight.

Florence knew four of May Sinclair's doctors. She never met Dr. Jessie Murray. She knew that May Sinclair had forgiven Dr. Hector Munro his heartbreaking dismissal of her from the Motor Ambulance unit, and even went to his office once to ask about the lameness that was bothering a leg. She tried out the clay pack that he prescribed, and she obtained no benefit at all from it. Miss Bartrop's voice took on a buzzy edge when she told of Dr. Munro's borrowing forty or fifty pounds. When May Sinclair reminded him of the loan, he answered that he was too financially embarrassed to repay it; and he never did repay it. Edward Spencer Scott treated her over the longest period. He had offices at 59 Fellows Road, Hampstead North, when he was called in to treat Miss Bartrop in 1919. May Sinclair nursed her devotedly, giving up all her writing, until Miss Bartrop was well again. Dr. Scott's address remained the same until 1945. May Sinclair's niece, Mrs. Wilda McNeile, saw him in Aylesbury in the last weeks of her aunt's life in 1946, when he came to visit his old patient.[1]

Another doctor who treated her was Dr. Esther Rickards, who had an office at 39 Fellows Road, N. W. 3, in 1923, and who settled at 150 Harley Street W. 1 in 1925. When Dr. Rickards suffered a coronary, Florence Bartrop, in 1945 or 1946, found Dr. Violet Hilda Minster, of Aylesbury, who was the last physician to attend May Sinclair. By this time May Sinclair would admit only a nominal need for a doctor: "I don't trouble him very much, do I?" she asked Florrie. She did not seem to know that there was anything wrong with her.

The first clear sign of the end came when Florence Bartrop, in another room, heard her cry out. Miss Bartrop came at once. That compulsive tapping on a table with her left hand had failed her. She had tried to tap the table, as she had tapped all her life, and she could not make her hand obey. The thwarting of the reflex frightened her. There came another day when she was shocked into still deeper insight, and a confession of it. Florence Bartrop had broken off her reading to her—for her eyes had lost their ability to focus on print—to prepare their tea. She left May Sinclair sitting back in her chair. When she returned, she saw her dribbling and frothing at the mouth. Florence ran out, got a neighbor to help her carry her to bed. There, May Sinclair confessed her waking from her childish bliss when she said to Florence, "I guess you know this is the end?"

And Florence answered truthfully, "I know that."

Violet Minster, her doctor, came, and brought the district nurse with her. May Sinclair's nephew, Harold Lumley Sinclair, and her

---

1. Letter, Wilda McNeile, January 10, 1963.

niece, Wilda McNeile, were called in too. To her nephew she appealed, "Do anything you like, but don't part me from Florrie."

During the six weeks it took her to die, her mind focused on the point of light that had shared her life since 1919. When Dr. Minster tested her mentation by pointing to the district nurse and asking, "Who is that?" May Sinclair answered, "Florrie." When a relief nurse came in, Dr. Minster made the test again. "Who is that?" May Sinclair answered, "Florrie."

When she was certain that she would never again get up, she became anxious over only one thing: Florrie must be sure to see to it that her body would ride to the funeral in a motor car, and that a motor car would transport her ashes to the burial place. She forgot that she had specified the burial place in her will, and kept asking Florence Bartrop, and kept forgetting the answer to her question, where would Florrie bury her? It was then that Florence Bartrop remembered how often May Sinclair had said, "I would die motoring."

She died on November 14, 1946. The funeral service was held in the chapel of Golders Green Cemetery, on November 18, and it was followed by her cremation. Her ashes were enclosed in an oak chest and buried in the Hampstead Parish churchyard. The B.B.C. announced her passing and her burial, and the obituaries played their solemn part in applying a fixative to what remained of the image that was May Sinclair.

The portrait that Florence Bartrop retained to the years when I talked to her, 1959 and 1960, showed not a gray hair in the head of the body that had been May Sinclair. Its color was still a dark brown, and there was not a wrinkle or a freckle on the sleeping face that she saw in memory.

The obituary in the *London Times* on November 15 appreciated her as "a novelist of keenly analytical intellect, a careful and finished stylist, and the possessor of a comprehensive and imaginative grasp of character." It paid tribute to her respected studies in metaphysical thought, her Brontë scholarship, her interest in the methods and processes of the novelist's craft, and her sympathy for the feminist movement and other progressive causes. It recorded the truth about her continuous growth: "Her later novels were, perhaps, more finely contrived, surer in delineation, more subtle in character drawing, than anything she had done before." It called attention to what many critics could not appreciate—her sense of humor: "The short book 'A Cure of Souls' is a delicious, mildly ironical portrait of a lethargic, comfort-loving rector, which perhaps shows Miss Sinclair at her best. It is complete, rounded, and humorous." It understood her interest in new trends and her strong independence as an artist: "Like many another serious craftsman she saw the significance of Miss Dorothy Richardson's technical innovation in 'The Tunnel' and other books, but Miss Sinclair herself made no violent departure from orthodox form. . . . Her style did not obtrude itself, but her prose was evocative, well-wrought, and distinguished."[2]

Many people still remembered her, all with fondness, as I have already shown, when I began to think of writing her memoir. The oldest child of her oldest brother William, Wilda St. Clair Sinclair, who became Mrs. Alan Hugh McNeile, remembered a visit of her aunt to Hull in 1887, when Wilda was seven. May Sinclair occupied Wilda's bedroom and happened to break a tiny ornament: "Her distress was almost absurd. She couldn't bear hurting anyone or their feelings." Wilda's mother tried to find out what people she might want to meet, and tried to coax her to accompany her to tea parties, but May Sinclair generally chose to stay in the library. Mrs. McNeile thought that her aunt's visits to Hull gave her an insight into the only family life that she knew after her childhood. She had a great knowledge of music, and her playing, while not up to a professional standard, was still very beautiful. She encouraged her niece to study classical music seriously. Wilda's mother, who died in 1906, told her daughter that May Sinclair had been very much in love with someone, but never identified him.

As the wife of a Regius Professor of Divinity, and as an author in the field of philosophy herself, Wilda McNeile knew her aunt's philosophical works and their relationship to religion. But she could only speculate on her personal attitude toward religion: "I don't know if she would have called herself an agnostic, but I never knew her to take kindly to any orthodox clergy."

Wilda McNeile was very much aware that the dominant tone of May Sinclair's mother, who was very orthodox in her religious attitude, was one of disapproval. "Mary May's" referring to her mother as "the Lamb" was only one of the manifestations of her gift for irony.

When there was illness in the home, or the disaster of death, "No one could have been more sympathetic, or nicer to have in the house." May Sinclair and her mother were with the family in Hull in 1896 when William died, and it was May Sinclair who came ten years later to nurse his widow through the last weeks of her life. Wilda recalled that her brother Harold had been released from a German prisoner of war camp after the war, and had collapsed from pneumonia at his

---

2. The cutting was kindly sent me by Storm Jameson.

aunt's house in London. She gave up everything to nurse him until he recovered.

Aunt Mary May was "so very lovable" that the family always wondered at the great unlikeness between the person and her works, her personal and her published outlook on life. There were three distinct facets in Aunt Mary May's life: "One for her family, one for her books, and one for her author friends and others." She never introduced any of her literary friends to her family. The only explanation that she ever gave for what seems to have been a simple reservation of her innermost family life from her professionally curious friends was that she "wouldn't want to introduce my youngest sister to H. G. Wells."

When sclerosis forced Professor McNeile to retire from Dublin University in 1929, the couple took a farmhouse high up on the Wiltshire Downs, where May Sinclair and Florence Bartrop visited them. Of the period from 1929 to 1934 Wilda McNeile wrote of her aunt: "Her friends had left her, and all she wanted to do was to drive about the country. It was not possible to have a real conversation with her, she did not appear to feel it or know about it. . . . She would make little bustling steps to her car or a chair. After my husband died [1934] and we moved to Bedford and Dulwich for the schools, she drove over to see us in both places. The driving seemed to soothe her." Wilda McNeile was with her aunt during the last weeks: "Just before her death I think she saw her little cat again. She told me once that a friend said she had seen clairvoyantly the cat jump on her lap. But as far as I know she wasn't especially interested in E.S.P." "I think some people leave this life in parts and not in one piece." That was how Wilda McNeile saw her aunt fading out of life.[3]

Richard Aldington, who met May Sinclair in 1912 or 1913, thought first of the slightness of her figure: "She could not have been much if any over five feet tall. She was always very neat but not oldmaidy. Once we played a foolish game which consisted in suggesting some object symbolizing each of us. Ezra suggested for her 'an acorn.' 'Oh!' she said, really rather hurt, 'You mean little and tight.' " Her face was oval, very gentle, sweet in expression. "She was conscientious in preparing her novels—she spent a lot of time watching a girls' gymnasium society when she was writing The Combined Maze."

"She was extremely generous, and must have given away a lot of her income, though she lived in modest comfort." He thought that the

3. Letters, June 16, June 24, July 16, 1959; February 20, March 13, 1960; September 3, October 7, 1961; January 10, February 11, 1963; January 2, August 3, 1964.

nearest illustration of the kind of person she was would have been "some of the Quaker ladies of the last century in Philadelphia. She had all their reckless benevolence and somewhat unfounded belief in the goodness of human beings."

"She was a bit touched by mysticism, oriental and otherwise, and must have had some superstition. I remember her saying that for years they (she and her mother) had peacock feathers and were very poor. 'At last I took courage and burnt them, and The Divine Fire began to sell in America.' " She told him that she never made more than about fifteen hundred pounds a year by her books. He knew of her interest in medicine and in medical friends. Her gift to him of a life-time subscription to the London Library, and her lending him her permanently rented room in the White Hart Hotel in Stow-on-the-Wold have already been mentioned.

Ivor Brown lived in Hampstead when, as a boy of about sixteen and a student at Cheltenham College, he met May Sinclair, who came to supper at his home from time to time. When Ivor Brown went up to Balliol College in 1909, he had already decided that he would become a writer. May Sinclair generously read and criticized his trials at story-writing, and told him that she felt that his stories were "too grey in colour" for him to make fiction his career. He accepted her judgment. She invited him to her dinner parties at the Albemarle Club and to discussion evenings at the Sesame Club, a women's club. At the Albemarle Club he met H. G. and Catherine Wells, H. W. Nevinson, Gilbert Cannan, and Phyllis Bottome.

He remembered May Sinclair's moving from her Hampstead lodgings to a studio flat in Edwardes Square, and her retreats to Reeth. His principal memories were of the period of 1910, "when she was very happy with her success and as a hostess of literary dinners at her club. She had a quiet animation, with very bright and lively eyes." She took him to a luncheon that John Lane had arranged to publicize *Blast,* the organ for propagating vorticism. "I don't know how far M. S. was impressed, but at that period she liked to go about and be in the midst of literary goings-on."[4]

A friend who was a full generation younger than she, Rebecca West, and who lost touch with her after the First World War, sketched her as "a very pleasing little person physically—prim, small, plump, soft-voiced, neat." "A delightful human being." "She was uncommonly athletic for her age and compact build," as her ease in jumping five times back and forth to elude a passionate poetess once proved. "Her integrity was visible in every movement and audible in every word she said." "Her manners were of a forgotten age. All this fascinated

---

4. Letters, August 14, September 16, 1962.

me in its contrast to her desire to be tough and masculine." "She was an anachronistic figure—in spite of her desire to be of the Enlightenment. She belonged to the age of the Lady and the Romantic Movement. She was at once La Princess de Clèves, and the Brontës—and wished to be D. H. Lawrence. On top of all this—and underneath it too —great, great sweetness." "She was extremely kind to young writers and particularly young women writers, and G. B. Stern, Sheila Kaye-Smith, and I all benefitted by it." She had "a sympathetic interest in our work and our doings, which was what we needed." "There was something Cranfordlike about her charming house in St. John's Wood Park."

When I complained to her that Ford Madox Ford and Violet Hunt had left no record of appreciation of May Sinclair, the most loyal of their friends, Rebecca West cautioned me to remember that "they were considerably older than she was." But if their vital records are to be believed, Ford was ten years younger, and Violet Hunt was three years younger. The innocence of May Sinclair made her seem so much younger than her age.

"She amused a great many people. H. G. Wells, who liked and admired her, always used to ask her why she was leaving her parties so early, for the sake of hearing her answer, 'I must go now—mother always leaves the lights on.' (They had to be put out for some other reason than economy—they disturbed someone if they weren't turned out.) "

"I had an enchanting feeling about May Sinclair that she liked admiring people—that it was a pleasure to her." Sometime she heard that May Sinclair had had some disabling physical crisis and that her friends could not see her easily: "Strange to say this was foreseen by Ernest Thesiger, the actor, when he read our hands after a Dinner given by Ford Madox Ford and Violet Hunt. He told my fortune in vague terms which came fairly near the mark and on leaving the house said, 'I saw for May having a long illness in the twilight, going on for years—and great isolation.' "[5]

"The memory of her goodness and her innocence and her selflessness is very much alive in my heart, fifty years later." "I may say that the contrast between May Sinclair's athleticism and her prim little physique was very amusing—she looked as if she couldn't take a stride longer than six inches."[6] Rebecca West also passed on to me Noel Coward's memory of her encouraging him when he was a very young writer: "and he remembers her great charm and simplicity."[7]

---

5. Letters, October 24, November 3, November 13, 1962.
6. Letter, April 15, 1970.
7. Letter, October 24, 1963.

Gladys Storey supported Rebecca West's and Noel Coward's memories of May Sinclair's kindness to young writers. She attended an at home at Violet Hunt's and started with May Sinclair toward a table of ices. May Sinclair at once gave way. "Youth should be served first," was her gracious phrasing of a conviction that was an imperative of her character. She was a sensitive reader of reviews. At another party Gladys Storey overheard May Sinclair asking Mr. Melville why he did not give her last book a good review.[8]

In the early twenties Storm Jameson met her at a P. E. N. party in London, and judged her to be deliberately aloof: "She was sitting alone, and I summoned up courage to speak to her and tell her how much I admired her work. She was no more interested in the opinion of an unknown young woman than she should have been, and I don't think she listened to my, I am certain, foolish words."[9] The modest young writer could not know how deeply her humility and beauty and praise were affecting her stolid-seeming idol, whom loneliness was already beginning to entomb in reticence.

In the 1930s Phyllis Bentley sat beside her at a literary banquet. By then she had entered her retreat from life: "I tried to express to her my admiration for her novels, but she made no response; she seemed to be far away in a dream world of her own."[10]

These are personal memories. A solid volume would be needed to gather together the already published comments—interpretation of her works and her aims—forming an aesthetic and a historical evaluation of May Sinclair's writings; like those of William Lyon Phelps, *The Advance of the English Novel,* 1915; Cornelius Weygandt, *A Century of the English Novel,* 1925; Abel Chevalley, *The Modern English Novel,* 1925; Walter L. Myers, *The Later Realism,* 1927; Janet Hogarth Courtney, *Women of My Time,* 1934; Frank Swinnerton, *The Georgian Literary Scene,* 1934; Reinald Hoops, *Der Einfluss der Psychoanalyse auf die englische Literatur,* 1934; Malcolm Elwin, *Old Gods Falling,* 1939; Fannie Elizabeth Ratchford, *The Brontës' Web of Childhood,* 1941; Walter C. Frierson, *The English Novel in Transition,* 1942; the anonymous author of the article in Kunitz and Haycraft, *Twentieth Century Authors,* 1942; and Edward Wagenknecht, *Cavalcade of the English Novel,* 1943; but it is now time for us to make a complete survey of her writings to arrive at a new estimate of her place in the history of the modern English novel.

---

8. Letter, May 11, 1960.
9. Letter, March 4, 1960.
10. Letter, July 17, 1961.

Thorncote, Rock Ferry, Cheshire. May Sinclair's birthplace.

May Sinclair's mother.

Frank Sinclair.

May Sinclair's home near Sidmouth, South Devon.

NEW WRITERS.

MISS MAY SINCLAIR.

IT is little more than a year since Miss May Sinclair's first book, "Audrey Craven," was published by Messrs. Blackwood and Sons. Her career as a novelist, therefore, is only beginning. But she can already show a considerable record of excellent literary work. Her first efforts were in the direction of poetry, and two volumes of verse were published. Many of her poems afterwards appeared in various periodicals, including the *Pall Mall Magazine*, the *Academy*, and *Temple Bar*.

The first published article from her pen appeared in the *New World* in 1893. It was on Hegelian Ethics. Miss Sinclair has not continued to write on subjects so abstruse, and has in fact done no more work in this line since she first tried her hand at fiction in 1895. She has, however, done several translations, among others Sohn's "Outlines of Church History."

Miss Sinclair's first short stories, "A Friendly Critic" and "Not Made in Germany," came out in *Macmillan's Magazine* in 1896 and 1897. She has also contributed occasionally to *Black and White*. "Audrey Craven" was remarkably well received when it appeared in May of last

From Photo by]   MISS MAY SINCLAIR.   [*Alfred Ellis*.

year, and the first edition was exhausted in a few months. By October a second edition was required.

Miss Sinclair's new book is to be published this autumn by Messrs. Blackwood and Sons, her first publishers.

The **Bookman,** *September, 1898.*

Salcombe Regis churchyard.

May Sinclair, ca. 1904.

MISS MAY SINCLAIR

By May Sinclair

THE DIVINE FIRE

The story of the regeneration of a London poet and the degeneration of a London critic. 14th printing. $1.50.

"Certain it is that in all our new fiction I have found nothing worthy to compare with 'The Divine Fire,' nothing even remotely approaching the same class." — MARY MOSS, *in the Atlantic Monthly.*

"I find her book the most remarkable that I have read for many years." — OWEN SEAMAN, *in Punch* (London).

"A full-length study of the poetic temperament, framed in a varied and curiously interesting environment. . . . Moreover, a real distinction of style, besides being of absorbing interest from cover to cover." — *Dial.*

The Atlantic Monthly Advertiser, *1904.*

May Sinclair, 1904.

At Mark Twain's seventieth birthday dinner, New York, December 5, 1905. From left to right: Not identified, John A. Mitchell, James Mac-Arthur, May Sinclair, Emily Post, S. M. Gardenhire, Hamilton W. Mabie.

May Sinclair, ca. 1907–8.

Portrait. The American, *August, 1908.*

May Sinclair as a suffragist outside the "Votes for Women" shop in Kensington, 1910.

May Sinclair, 1913.

At the writing hut at Stow-on-the-Wold, ca. 1920–24.

With Jerry, ca. 1924.

Original charcoal sketch, ca. 1920. Artist unknown.

The Green, Reeth.

May Sinclair, ca. 1930.

May Sinclair with Florence Bartrop, the 1940s.

The house in Bierton, Aylesbury, where May Sinclair died in 1946.

Florence Bartrop, 1960.

Medico-Psychological Clinic.

BRUNSWICK SQUARE,

LONDON, W.C.

The Medico-Psychological Clinic of London.

Part 2:
HER WRITINGS

10

Prose Fiction of the Eighteen-nineties

May Sinclair's first published prose fiction, a short story, "A Study from Life," the only work of hers to bear the complete initialed signature, M. A. St. C. Sinclair, appeared in *Black and White*, on November 2, 1895, after a long editorial delay. It is in the smart contemporary playscript form of which F. Anstey was the master.

Using a diamond-hard pen, she tells in two half-columns about an experimental novelist, Dora Fausett, whose intended subject for a novel, Frank Dysart, breaks off his friendship with her because he has become aware that she is not returning his love and has only been dissecting him for use as a character in a novel, and he announces his engagement to Maud Verney. From pure spite, Dora declares that she has always loved him, but when Frank wishes to resume his friendship and enjoy her alleged love, Dora answers with a chilling rejection. Writing quickly, she reduces the novel that she had planned to a short story and sends it off. Now Frank breaks his engagement to Maud and earnestly appeals to Dora to take him back. But the story has already been sent in, and Dora has no further interest in her curtailed dissection. Frank goes to the dogs, and Dora's story wins critical praise as an admirable "study from life."

The rather cruelly experimental novelist was to change sex to become Langley Wyndham in *Audrey Craven*. If Frank Dysart represents a fantasy fission of Anthony Deane, the name of Frank's fiancée, Maud Verney, is a fair stroke of psychic prophecy of the name of the girl to whom Deane became engaged three years later: Maud Versturme. May Sinclair's care to leave traces of the fictional original of the ultrafictional portrait—Frank Dysart becoming Fred

Donovan in the short story—shows her attention from the beginning to the psychological niceties of the creative process.

The second published story, "A Friendly Critic," appeared anonymously in *Macmillan's Magazine* for October, 1896. It is a clever comedy spung from her relationship with her own "friendly critic" and from her insight into his motive for trying to convert her into a writer of prose.

Its demi-Dickensian hero, Ormond Brownrigg, is vain of his neoclassical verses, which the editor of the *Piccadilly Review*, Horace Gibson, refuses to publish. He publishes instead critical essays on Swinburne, which Brownrigg writes with little pride in them, but whose merit Gibson holds high. Brownrigg's infatuation with an attractive member of their literary circle, Leonora Campbell, to whom he indites a couple of quatrains, enables Gibson to conspire with Miss Campbell to discourage Brownrigg from ever again writing verse and to encourage him to stick to his clear prose. Miss Campbell's sympathetic depetaling of Brownrigg's artificial flowers of verse parallels Deane's sympathetic dissuasion, as the verses amusingly burlesque May Sinclair's neoclassicism. Leonora Campbell speaks the key words: "I must say I think you've hardly done yourself justice in publishing very minor poetry, you who can write so delightfully in prose." Brownrigg's male disguise for the author is removed in this characterization of him: he was "as sensitive and impressionable as a woman, and had a charming way of blushing at little compliments like a young girl."

Her third short story, "Not Made in Germany," appeared anonymously in *Macmillan's Magazine* in January, 1897. It is a fluffy, sentimental comedy whose interest for students of literature is almost guaranteed by its setting, the Main Reading Room of the British Museum. Its tone is struck by the sentences, "The world, and therefore the British Museum, is built for boys and girls to make love in. And they are taught to think they can move heaven and earth." Two details that were to win emphasis in separate novels make their first appearances here: fur and violets, both of which the incompetent translator from the German, Nora Vyvart, wears.

Audrey Craven, published by Blackwood in October, 1897, is rooted in the late Victorianism of Thomas Hardy's *Jude the Obscure,* with one exception that shows May Sinclair to belong to the new generation. While she accepts the fact of heredity, she resists the Victorian surrender to it as the force of destiny and the judge passing doom upon the unfortunate inheritor. It is of the new age in its grasp on analytic psychology, in the artistic sureness and consistency with which it demonstrates the determination of unconscious motivation. It is as well

the first of the novels in which May Sinclair was to trace the process
of reaching for individuation.

Audrey's defective heredity can be read in her disillusioned father,
who is so doubtful that his daughter will mature normally that his
will postpones her financial coming of age until her twenty-fifth year,
and in her cousin, Vincent Hardy, who has talent as a writer but is
handicapped by a basic instability that leads toward erotic vice and
drunkenness. His only interest to Audrey in her unconscious search for
a substantial self is his greater strength of will. His passion for Audrey
and his determination that she will stabilize his vulnerable nature by
marrying him (after he has proved himself by roughing it in British
Columbia for a year and by writing a book about his experiences) do
not result in a union or in a marriage. May Sinclair does not accept
as inevitable a judgment that Hardy had passed upon the sickly cousins
of his novel of hereditary doom. Instead, she develops Audrey's unconscious striving for a stabilizing trellis to her weakly vine, or rather,
toward a psychological substance by infusion of another's strength. She
shows Audrey "falling in love" (while Vincent Hardy is in British
Columbia) with an artist, Ted Haviland, who is inspired by her trust
and her beauty to a finer art; then Audrey falls in love with a popular
naturalistic novelist, Langley Wyndham, who is in search of a model
from life who will prove in fiction that women are beastly, because his
fiancée jilted him; then, after Wyndham's annihilating exposure of
her is published and his fiancée relents, she falls in love again (that is,
into a state of dependency upon) a clergyman, Flaxman Reed, from
whom she hopes to win a climactic goodness by character injection.
But Audrey frightens the clergyman into the priesthood by confessing
how near she had come to sinning with Wyndham and by exposing to
the clergyman his own lusting for her. Even then Audrey does not suc-
cumb to any doom; she calmly marries a rich goose farmer, Algernon
Jackson, whom she had once held in contempt when she was yearning
for a finer, absorbed self.

The publication of Wyndham's novel, *Laura: An Idyll of Piccadilly,* is the subject of a debate between Percival Knowles, a critic, who
is indignant over the cruel exposure of a real personality examined in
a novel, and Wyndham, whose aim had been a truthful resection of a
weak character.

Ted Haviland's sister Katherine is the center of a theme that was to
reappear in *The Creators:* the effect that a woman's passion in love
has upon her art, and the effect that her engaging in an art has on her
womanliness. Vincent Hardy (the cousin whom Audrey jilts for a
more rewarding suitor) becomes dependent upon Katherine for his

will to live. He believes that the energy that Katherine expends upon her art lessens her womanliness. Lacking faith in Katherine, he lacks faith in himself, and he does not hold onto life.

Katherine's philosophy of art for sale undergoes a change that reflects the repeated counselings of that honest and shrewd friend of May Sinclair's, Anthony Deane. At first she believes that an artist must aspire to fulfill the highest classical standards of beauty, and that the market will follow him, and will reward him with a livelihood. Later she comes to believe that an artist must not go all out for perfection if he is to earn a living, but must learn to knead his compromise with the marketplace into the substance of his work.

Conscience motivates the characters importantly. Ted Haviland is sorry that he had laughed at Audrey for wanting *him* to plan the decoration of her rooms so that it would express *her* unique personality and her sense of beauty. Even the selfish Audrey is propelled by conscience to try to win Flaxman Reed's goodness for herself to make her life at last a worthy one. Langley Wyndham suffers a brief conflict between sorts of conscience. His scientific-artistic conscience urges him to experiment to the farthest point at which he can find out Audrey's breaking point of conventional restraint, while his social conscience deplores his taking advantage of a trusting woman. Percival Knowles, the critic, cannot forgive him for flouting the social conscience that holds it evil to expose to public mockery and to the victim herself the weaknesses in her nature. Katherine Haviland's conscience is firm as a rock in its dedication to those who need her, first, her brother Ted, and then the dejected and rejected Vincent Hardy.

With beautiful mastery over her character, May Sinclair keeps the reader aware of both Audrey's want of substance and her unconscious search for an infused substance. To Wyndham, Audrey reveals herself without an awareness of what she is saying: " 'You know—I have no firm faith, no settled opinions.' "[1] Through Katherine's perceptions, we realize how each new sought-for personality soaks into Audrey's behavior like a colored infusion into a colorless liquid.[2]

Audrey's basing her admiration for a man upon his artistic and intellectual abilities, his cleverness as a painter or a writer, provides a first instance of a motif that was to recur so repeatedly as to become a personal disclosure. A phrase here and there betrays the author's familiarity with metaphysics. Once the author says of Audrey, "The thing itself was the one thing that Audrey could not see."[3] There are

1. *Audrey Craven* (New York: Henry Holt, 1906) , p. 116.
2. *Ibid.,* p. 141.
3. *Ibid.,* p. 92.

other clues to self-revelation. Audrey plays loud and long to her cousin "wild Polish music [Chopin] alive with beautiful pulses of love and frenzy and despair."[4] Knowles and Wyndham say of her at the Dean's party, in the first chapter, that she is said to be looking for a religion, and that she had been talking transcendentalism, had complimented Flaxman Reed on the splendid logic of the Roman faith, and now was probably contributing valuable material to Broadbent's great work on the Fourth Gospel.[5] A contemporary current of literary theory, the documentary experimental realism that is Wyndham's method in 1896, is explicitly described.

The novel has high value as a psychological textuary. Katherine reflects that Ted's love for Audrey is a stupidity that came upon him like a madness.[6] Wyndham thinks Flaxman Reed a fraud: " 'Well—a self-deceiver. Isn't that the completest and most fatal form of fraud? He fights and struggles to be what he isn't and calls it renouncing self.' "[7] Wyndham is epigrammatic when he says, " 'To the pure all things are pure, but to the Puritan most things are impure.' "[8]

The most memorable tone of the style is its irony, which mostly sounds with a comical ring: "Miss Audrey Craven was not in search of a religion, but she had passed all her life looking for a revelation";[9] "If it came to the point, Audrey would boldly offer her own character for dissection rather than suffer conversation to be diverted to a less interesting topic";[10] "Audrey was not the first woman who has tried to be original by following the fashion";[11] Audrey's house in Chelsea is "screened by the narrow strip of railed plantation known as Chelsea Gardens";[12] of Audrey: "She pulled out the tremolo stop, and then spoke."[13]

The passage that describes evensong at St. Teresa's in Lambeth has the beauty that Virginia Woolf was to make more noticeable years later, the translation of musical sounds into designs of motion:

> The organ and choir burst into the anthem. It was a fugue; the voices seemed to have gathered together from the ends of the world, flying, pursuing and flying, doubled, trebled, quadrupled in their flight, they met and parted, they overtook and were overtaken. And

---

4. *Ibid.*, p. 20.
5. *Ibid.*, p. 3–4.
6. *Ibid.*, p. 153.
7. *Ibid.*, p. 130.
8. *Ibid.*, pp. 160–61.
9. *Ibid.*, p. 7.
10. *Ibid.*, p. 16.
11. *Ibid.*, p. 91.
12. *Ibid.*, p. 9.
13. *Ibid.*, p. 18.

now it was no longer a fugue of sounds—it was a fugue of all sensations. The incense rose and mingled with the music; the music fled and rose, up among the clustering gasjets, up to the chancel roof where it lost itself in a shimmering labyrinth of gold and saphire, and died in a diminuendo of light and sound.[14]

May Sinclair was now launched as a novelist whose creativeness was never to be satisfied with any one method, or content to go in any one direction for long. She had written a profound psychological novel containing a principal character whose unconscious compelled her behavior, and two chief analysts, Katherine Haviland, the painter, who projected the confident, loving, self-sacrificing aspect of May Sinclair and is awarded the author's highest credentials for the accuracy of vision and insight, and Langley Wyndham, the novelist, who projected her coolly professional ego-will.

A Hero of Fiction was published in *Temple Bar Magazine* in September, 1898, more than three and a half years after Anthony Deane had annotated the manuscript. It is a neatly designed little ironic novelette, melted down from the original fifteen chapters to eight. Every fault that Deane had bared with his sensible judgment was removed, and every suggestion incorporated. The dialogue is amusing, the text light and witty.

The pretty eighteen-year-old daughter of a scholar whose field is the philosophy of ethics has inherited her father's gift for turning experiences with life and books into fantasy; and Madge Tracey has imagined herself to be a variety of Saphos and Hypatias, and has imagined a middle-aged bachelor, James Wenham, whose only skill is for the game of backgammon, to be a great scholar in Greek literature and philosophy, and therefore a fitting mate to the poets and scholars she has fantasized herself to be. A modest young novelist who never talks about his work, Dick Verrall, loves Madge for her feminine qualities of youth, beauty, and health, and he recognizes her purity from any intellectual adulteration. Teresa Creichton, a gentle, wise spinster and an excellent cook, has marked James Wenham for her husband. The humble Wenham at first succumbs to Madge's flattery on his intellect and proposes to her; but conscience induces him to call upon Teresa to dispel Madge's fantasy that he is a scholar. Teresa is successful in disillusioning Madge and in breaking a foolish engagement. After resenting Wenham's fraudulent scholarship, Madge becomes enlightened enough to realize that her fictive mind had imagined the fraud. Freed from her fantasy, Madge accepts Dick Verrall, and

---

14. *Ibid.*, p. 127.

as a wife, she leaves all creating of fiction to her novelist husband. Teresa's love wins a good husband in the sincere, realistic James Wenham.

Madge is related to Audrey Craven in having no fixed nature, only a suggestible one, taking her cue from her reading. The logic with which May Sinclair was to expose the contradictions in the philosophical writings of fellow members of the Aristotelian Society (which they had hoped would not be noticed) she already applies in her comic reference to Madge being nineteen years old on her twentieth birthday. Teresa Creichton appears to be a first and carefully observed (but sympathetically rendered) sketch for a character who was to become the feline Mary Cartaret in *The Three Sisters*, because Teresa practices the same thoroughness in studying Wenham to prepare a perfect nest for his comforts, habits, and his fear of difficulties that Mary Cartaret was to resort to in stealing Dr. Rowcliffe from Gwenda. May Sinclair's mother's love for fur is worked into Teresa Creichton's gesture of playing with the tails of her sable cape.

Blackwood brought out *Mr. and Mrs. Nevill Tyson* in November, 1898, after some revisions of the original manuscript, as Zack's letters show, on the side of reticence. It continues surveying life inside the regions that *Audrey Craven* had begun to sketch out, and stays within the perspective of *Jude the Obscure* by blending the themes of a conflict-evoking heredity, innocent passion, and a strong but unconscious search for an ideal, and it departs from *Audrey Craven* and nods toward *Jude* in surrendering to a sense of inevitable doom.

It is a cause of wonder that this novel was published at all, because it treats the sexual relations of man and wife with an almost medical frankness. The openness with which May Sinclair represented both Nevill Tyson's animalism toward Molly and Molly's animal passion in response offers imposing evidence of her great moral strength and personal innocence. Her relatives were surprised by its contrast to the shy spinster whom they knew as one without any experience of passion. It is a cause of regret, also, that the less inhibited original was lost, because just as *Audrey Craven* represents May Sinclair's fear of her want of substance, and her turning to the creation of a novel as a consoling proof of artistic substance,[15] so Molly Tyson is her confession of the woman waiting inside her person to be excited into passion, and her equally honest foreboding of the kind of man who would excite her, with possibly tragic consequences for both. The dedication of the book to Janet Elizabeth Hogarth reveals the woman whose encour-

---

15. See *The New Idealism* (New York: Macmillan, 1922), p. 34, for a statement of the objective reality of a work of art.

agement May Sinclair most trusted to give her confidence in the psychological truth of this novel.

The conflict-evoking heredity resides in Nevill Tyson, heir of a tailor-uncle to an estate that gives him a place in Leicestershire's county society, and son of a tailor who had, under great stress of sensual temptation, abruptly switched from his commercial life to become an ascetic minister in a fervid Baptist denomination. The son, Nevill, had in his last year at Oxford been overcome by the same kind of powerful lust that his father had succeeded in overcoming, and his wildness had ended his scholarly career and his political ambition, and sent him on a rough adventuring in India, Texas, and the Soudan.

The innocent passion is that which a classical scholar's daughter, Molly, feels for Nevill. The marriage takes place despite her father's warning of Nevill's instability. Molly is determined to be the completely self-offering wife that Nevill seems to want. His conscious attitude toward his marriage is determined in part by the character of his unexplained mother, by his father's character, and by his first wildly sensual and humiliating affair at Oxford. The affair had caused him to believe that the ideal woman is unattainable, and that all that is possible is a shallow, animal relationship. His potential for worship he discloses when Molly suffers labor pains; then he adores her as the mother ideal; but his love turns to hate when he curses God for inflicting such cruelty on woman as the pains of giving birth. When Molly is still weak after her childbirth, he feels no pity; he blames her motherhood for having made her face and eyes so lacking in luster. He resumes his Madonna worship very briefly when her beauty comes back, but loses it as soon as he catches sight of her feeding her infant. Then he claims for himself the richness of her body that she is giving her child. To be the perfect wife, she gives in to his animal demand, gives up her feeding her child, and lets the infant die of the shock of being separated from her breast.

The truth appears to be that Nevill had chosen Molly unconsciously because his instinct (never made conscious) tells him that she does indeed conform to the standard of the ideal woman that he professes to worship, but which he perverts into a basis for feeling contempt toward all actual women, a contempt that is like Langley Wyndham's temporary one, a revenge upon the woman who hurt him.

Molly is too ingenuous to pierce through Nevill's warped, complex nature to discover his real longing. Her lack of critical perception prevents her understanding his intellectual self-viewing as an instrument of a cosmic force chosen to take revenge upon Molly for the hurt that the corrupting woman had done him. She does sense that when Nevill leaves her for an erotic adventure in London, his closest confidant, Captain Stanistreet (to whom Nevill has confessed his conviction that the ideal woman does not exist) knows the secret of Nevill's evident searching, and thinks that by being seen going about in public places with Stanistreet she will excite in Nevill a jealousy that would make him want to repossess her. She proves to be right, and she does recapture Nevill. But again she makes the mistake of giving herself so completely, body and mind, without a demand upon him, that she does not satisfy his disguised longing for an adoring relationship. When, after their orgiastic reunion, she confesses that she has been true to Nevill, never tempted by Stanistreet, Nevill breaks into a reality-effacing anger at her goodness by accusing her of having deceived him. The fire that threatens Nevill's life while he is helplessly drunk, and that scars most of Molly's body because she bravely puts it out, elicits a fleeting adoration. But he cannot face the simple truth that the reality that he has searched for instinctively and rejected intellectually awaits him in Molly, and he deserts her to become the tender officer to his dysentery-stricken men in the Soudan. Doom overtakes the two, with Nevill dying in battle in the Soudan, and Molly dying at home. He is memorialized as a hero; she is regarded by her friends as an abandoned woman who had been unfaithful with her husband's closest friend.

Mr. and Mrs. Nevill Tyson, then, relates to May Sinclair's theme of the search for individuation, in the ironic right choice by Nevill Tyson's unconscious of the woman who could mature his infantile sexuality but whose ingenuous desire to complete his conscious need assures his failure and causes her to fail as mother and as wife. It also illustrates one of the leading phases of her predominantly psychological art, that which demonstrates how human beings defeat their potential for individuation by turning away from chance-proffered insights into reality. Nevill, searching the Embankment for a prostitute on whom to expend the sexual energy that is revolted by Molly's scarred body, finds one, but is so upset by her imagined resemblance to the unscarred Molly, that he turns away from her.[16] He cannot bear the accusation of the insight that he had turned his loving wife into a prostitute, and is, as well, responsible for the loathsome scars.

May Sinclair's analytic mind well understood the complexity of the intellectual Nevill Tyson, reader of the Upanishads, theoretical idealist, actual animal seeking a spiritual sublimation: "Tyson the bundle

---

16. *The Tysons* (New York: B. W. Dodge, 1906), pp. 276–77.

of paradoxes, British and Bohemian, cosmopolitan and barbarian; the brute with the immortal human soul struggling perpetually to be."[17]

Tenderness lights up a passage that tells about the clever Miss Batchelor holding Tyson's child, which the mother has rejected:

> She let him explore the front of her dress with his little wet mouth and fingers. He had made a great many futile experiments of the kind in the last two days. Of those three worlds that were his, the world of light, the world of sleep, and the world of his mother's breast, they had taken away the one that he liked best—the warm living world of which he had been lord and master, that was the flesh of his flesh, given to his hands to hold, and obedient to the pressure of his lips. Since then he had lived from feeble hope to hope; and now, when he struck upon that hard and narrow tract of corduroy studded with comfortless buttons, he began again his melancholy wail.[18]

Miss Batchelor, "that extraordinary woman, condemned by her cleverness to perpetual maidenhood," seems like an explicit autograph paralleling the implicit one in Molly: "To some women a bitterer thing than not to be loved is not to be allowed to love. And when two women insist on loving the same man, the despised one is naturally skeptical as to the strength and purity and eternity of the other's feelings. . . . I did not say that Miss Batchelor loved Tyson."[19]

The name of Tyson's Leicestershire home, Thorneytoft, echoes the sad home in Cheshire where May Sinclair was born: Thorncroft.

I think we should spare a minute for a look at her reviews of other novelists of her time, the result of Anthony Deane's searching for work for her in London, so that we can have a guess at the standards that she was setting up to control her own artistry, to explain the case for her own recognition.

---

17. *Ibid.,* p. 293.
18. *Ibid.,* pp. 86–87.
19. *Ibid.,* p. 89.

11

The Reviewer and Her Standards
in the Eighteen-nineties

May Sinclair wrote altogether four reviews in the 1890s, three of them of novels. It is true that she could not slip into the relaxed mood of the chattily dignified commonplace that Anthony Deane tried to teach her by the example of his "Turnovers," but otherwise she was an ideal reviewer. She approached her subject with sympathy, had an instinct for discovering what was good, and was free from the common reviewer's lust for scratching hard and crowing loudly upon turning up some flaw. And she gave a neat form to her judgment.

Her review of Mary Pulling's *The Teacher's Text Book of Practical Psychology* (published in the spring, 1896, number of the *Cheltenham Ladies College Magazine*) is a masterpiece of which William James would have been proud. She appreciated the author's good sense in her discussion of the individual nature of apperception, in her relating habit to conduct and character; and she contributed a brilliant analysis of perception, recognizing it to be equally crucial to psychology and metaphysics.

Her reviews in the *London Bookman* in April of Richard Whiteing's *No. 5 John Street* and Lily Dougall's *The Mormon Prophet,* and of Beatrice Harraden's *The Fowler* in May of 1899, let us see that May Sinclair read the novelist in the novel. These are the requirements that she set up:

The novelist must have broadly sensitive perceptions, a broad area of feeling to discover shades and tones that are imperceptible to the ordinary person.

He should try to develop always deepening insight into human beings, and aim to contribute fresh revelations of the psychological mystery that motivates human behavior.

He must color the views that he represents with his personality, but the personal coloring must not lessen for the reader their impression of actuality.

The representation of life should be realistic without compromise, but conveyed subtly.

The novelist may take sides in representing a phase of life that contains matters of social problems; but he must not become a lone chorus delivering his opinions on a stage that is bare of characters.

He must not tolerate in himself any social prejudice whatsoever toward human beings. An important criterion of his merit as an artist is his ability to portray simple, ordinary people.

As a person he should continuously aim to broaden his philosophical comprehension of life; as an artist he should aim to reveal life steadily and as a whole, and avoid seeking out limited areas to provoke limited moods.

He should conceive his art to be not an instrument equipped with a few strings to be plucked, but a full keyboard on which he will reproduce the whole range of life's moods.

These were the standards that May Sinclair set up in her early reviewing and lived up to in her creative writing, to the end of her endurance.

12

The Novels: 1900-1910

Two Sides of a Question (March, 1901) contained two short novels of disappointed love: *The Cosmopolitan* (197 pages) and *Superseded* (130 pages).

The Cosmopolitan is a tragicomedy told in a gently ironic mood with technical finesse. Its two principals are a woman, Frida Tancred, who is the secretary of her self-absorbed father with whom she lives on an isolated country estate, and an artist, Maurice Durant, who, meeting her, misses the richness of her personality and her readiness to love him because he looks for a woman's obvious sexual character- istics and is disappointed by their apparent absence. He does see that she needs to get out of her sentimental yoke and encourages her to travel. After five years they meet again, when travel has brought to the surface what Maurice Durant, clever painter that he is, had lacked the insight to imagine. His justified love comes too late to win a re- sponse from her, and Frida sublimates her longing for an intelligent life in the gathering of wisdom in India and in supporting a bacterio- logical laboratory that is investigating methods of controlling the bubonic plague. She catches the infection from a coolie whom she is nursing, and dies. After her death Durant understands what it was that Frida had been interested in exploring and what it was that he had failed to see in her: the mystic beauty of life.

The logical conversion that was to become a mark of her style we read in a key sentence: "Frida Tancred had shown insight when she reproached him with his inability to see anything that he could not paint, or to paint anything that he could not see."[1]

1. *Two Sides of a Question* (New York: J. F. Taylor & Co., 1901), p. 194.

Little touches remind us of Anthony Deane's advice to May Sinclair to lighten her style. To the artist's sex-searching eyes, Miss Tancred's gown is like a chaperone: "In its imperishable prudery it refused to define her by ever so innocent a curve; all its folds were implicated in a conspiracy against her sex."[2] Colonel Tancred achieves a youthful air by wearing his sixty years as if they were an undergarment, well out of sight.[3]

Wisdom is pressed into a number of maxims: "A woman has no more formidable rival than her idea in the head of an imaginative man."[4] And the psychologist ever and again makes us understand the unobvious. When Durant suspects that Frida is falling in love with him, the author cuts in, "The fact remains that if he had loved her he would not have known."[5] Five years later, Frida tries to explain to Maurice what had caused her to suppress her love: " 'You are incapable, not of loving perhaps, but of loving a certain kind of woman the way she wants to be loved. You can't help it. As I said before, it is the difference in the point of view.' "[6]

In life, Anthony Deane had been the visitor who had helped to free May Sinclair's imagination to observe the world outside her mind. The yacht that May Sinclair's father sailed on the Mersey, the *Windward*,[7] reappeared as Frida's yacht, and her brother William's yacht, the *Torch*, berthed at Hull,[8] sailed again when Durant hired it from its owners. Frida's last letter to Durant was dated at Poona, where May Sinclair's brother Frank had died. The bacteriological laboratory in Bombay predicted the direction that led to the Medico-Psychological Clinic of London.

Superseded, telling the end of the life of a woman teacher in a girls' school in Regent's Park, London, is an ironic tragedy following the example set by George Eliot in the first of her compassionate portrayals of clergymen. Juliana Quincey, the oldest of the devoted teachers on the staff, worn by decades of correcting papers, tutoring slow pupils, and devising stimulants to arouse the lethargic, collapses under the strenuous new regimen, based on officially approved lists of cultural monuments and introduced by a progressive young headmistress to raise the standard of the school. A young gynecologist who treats Miss Quincey stirs up a sediment of a lifetime's unused love.

---

2. *Ibid.*, p. 8.
3. *Ibid.*, p. 11.
4. *Ibid.*, p. 3.
5. *Ibid.*, p. 67.
6. *Ibid.*, pp. 175–76.
7. Florence Bartrop.
8. Lloyd's Register.

His successful visits induce a false angina whose unconscious end is to make Dr. Cautley call again. The sight of the doctor in love with a young colleague of hers causes Miss Quincey's heart to stop its now hopeless beat.

Comedy and pathos build the tenderly ironic mood in which her portrait of an aging teacher is drawn. Movement often inspired May Sinclair to write buoyant poetry, as when she describes the dance toward freedom of the pupils when school is dismissed.[9] The poet is just as true in simple speech, as when Dr. Cautley and Rhoda Vivian confess that Miss Quincey had led to their finding and loving each other.[10]

Juliana Quincey's false angina is May Sinclair's first venture into psychopathology. A letter from Zack informs us that May Sinclair had backed up her intuitively creating imagination by studying a medical textbook.

The poet-soul of May Sinclair had labored long and stubbornly to keep its wick lighted. *Nakiketas and other Poems, Essays in Verse,* and occasional sonnets and songs had glared and flashed and flickered. A favorite poem, "Sapho," found its first sheltering lamp in *Audrey Craven,* and a "Song" was printed in *Mr. and Mrs. Nevill Tyson. A Debt of Honour* was never performed. *Tancred of Adan,* printed in part in a still unidentified periodical, had lacked the fuel to go on burning long enough to fulfill its plan; it might well have won the earliest success if its energy had not been consumed in the (I believe) contemporary writing of *Mr. and Mrs. Nevill Tyson.* Sometime in the 1890s, that poet-soul entered on its novitiate to gain a gratifying metempsychosis.

The Divine Fire, appearing in September, 1904, advanced May Sinclair from a writer of clever and daring and moving books to the author of an imposing novel that no one else in her time could have written. It rewarded the prepared reader with a view of the secret drama that May Sinclair lived in converting herself from poet to novelist, for this compactly articulated novel is an allegory of her conversion. Readers of its time enjoyed its elaborate finish, since they were accustomed to it from their reading of the Greek and Latin classics. Readers of this day, who are tuned to a more colloquial and contemporary fare may be slower in yielding to it. It has something of the classic strength of the *Odyssey,* which took years of changes in the telling to firm it, and generations of scholars to give it prestige. But as with the *Odyssey,* rereading flexes the surface and brings back

---

9. *Two Sides of a Question,* pp. 203–4.
10. *Ibid.,* pp. 331–32.

to its primal vigor the enormous energies and the profound changes in May Sinclair's innermost life, which she packed into it. It is one of the hugely revealing classics of the century, but it requires rereading to make its merits thoroughly enjoyable.

In genre, *The Divine Fire* is a psychological romance, less singing than Meredith's psychological romances, but, except for *The Ordeal of Richard Feverel,* richer and less self-conscious in its subtleties. It traces the parallel progress of the life of Savage Keith Rickman, son of a secondhand bookseller in London, as person and as poet, beginning with the time when he finds that echoing Greek verse in English gives him a dreamy escape from the grossness of his nature and a form of protest against the gross modernity of which he is a part. His affair with Poppy Grace, the music-hall singer, lets flesh and blood humanize his rhetoric and his ego-derived fantasy, and inspires him to a new phase, in which he hopes to meet ideal beauty in actual life. Poppy Grace also seems to have caused him to branch into the idiom and matter of common life. It is a pity that the three songs that Poppy sings, in chapters nine, ten, and forty-one, were not attributed to Rickman, because they have a mastery of the common touch that he is alleged to have shown in his *Saturnalia*. His new poetry of hope is the first version of a phenomenon that *Far End* was to feature: a writer's fantasy anticipating future actuality. Rickman's meeting the ideal, Lucia Harden, daughter of Sir Frederick Harden, shocks him into a period of barrenness, during which he fears he will never again be able to write. But the failure of his imaginative power is only temporary, a sign that his love for Poppy has died, and that the creativeness that depended on her embraces has died too. The onset of his new love, a love for an intellectually and socially ideal woman, takes on a physical intensity from the beginning, and his physically stimulated body inspires the poet to write again, this time a sequence of sonnets to Lucia, the classically disciplined expression of his love for an ideal woman met in life, but embraced in the imagination only; for Lucia is not won easily; she is a lady whose sensitiveness to the Cockney's vulgar background bars any thought of marriage. Rickman's engagement to Flossie Walker, fellow lodger in a Bloomsbury lodging house, represents a period of intensifying his ideal inspiration from the unattainable Lucia, but does not result in any direct influence upon his verse. His reunion with Lucia and the breaking by Flossie of their engagement leads to the climax of his writing verse drama whose inspiration by an actual woman and an ideal love is enhanced by its nearing the possibility of physical attainment. The verse drama is significantly entitled "The Triumph of Life."

When she visited America in 1905 as the much-praised author, May Sinclair told "Pendennis" of the *New York Times* that she had never met a poet until she met Richard Watson Gilder in New York.[11] In 1908, she wrote to him that she knew Rickman perfectly, even intimately, "since my acquaintanceship with him has never been in real life."[12] On both occasions she was pointing vigorously away from herself. She never confessed that she had published three of Rickman's sonnets under her own name, nor that she had quoted two lines from an unpublished poem and had referred to another. The sequence of "Nine and Twenty Sonnets," which becomes Rickman's testament of love for Lucia, was in life a collection of verses (planned to occupy fifteen spaces, of which only nine were filled) that she showed to Richard Garnett and hoped Lane would publish.

The allegory lies in the fact that a poet has been wrought into the principal character of a novel and also that the poet is the essential May Sinclair. Rickman moves to verse drama, but even in his climactic work he remains faithful to classical form and classical ideals. That delineation is true to the second meaning of Rickman: May Sinclair moved on; Rickman is only the relic of her classical past.

The narrative pattern of the romance issues from a triangle made up of the largely self-educated poet of the tradesman class, Savage Keith Rickman; a woman of a county family, the daughter of a baronet, whom he loves, Lucia Harden; and the lady's cousin, Horace Jewdwine, a lagging suitor, a don, a literary critic, and an editor who discovers Rickman but is too jealous to advance his interests when he observes how Lucia is impressed by his classically inspired verse. The setting is mainly the unromantic atmosphere of the book trade and of literary journalism in London from 1892 to 1901, but it also recreates the warm red hills overlooking Sidmouth in Devon.

The design is rich in contrasts. The relationship between the divine fire of love and the mortal fire of poetic creation for critical appreciation is a theme contained inside the social conflicts between the poet's early environmental legacy of Cockney speech and vulgar awkwardness, and his independent studying for verbal perfection in Greek and English and an ideal social goodness in which honor holds the highest place; and between his vulgar caste and Lucia Harden's sensitive traditional gentility.

The Divine Fire remains to this day in the forefront of English novels that try to penetrate beneath the cortically derived theories that Jewdwine and Rickman confidently exchange, to the psychic mystery

---

11. November 12.
12. *Book News Monthly,* February.

of the creative personality. It begins its explication by listing the separable segments of Rickman. There are seven, including an observatory of internal and external events, which gathers and comprehends raw experiences for the poet-self to organize into artistic life. It is this serene awareness that ponders the problem: "How on earth could you pull yourself together when Nature had deliberately cut you into little pieces?"[13]

May Sinclair combines her interest in the path to individuation with Rickman's evolution into a great poet by showing that Lucia's effect upon the aggregate of selves is to excise the young man about town, the shopman, the all-selves-affecting drunkard, and to encourage the amiable young man, the journalist, the student and recluse, the serene and perfect intelligence, and the poetic genius to work in a personal harmony. May Sinclair suggests this movement in the titles of the first and fourth books: "Disjecta Membra Poetae," and "The Man Himself." She further probes literary genius as a gift of the intellect, whose necessary emotional stimulant for emotive wordmaking originally comes from reading words describing imagined experiences written for another mind's reimagining without any reliance upon specific corresponding experiences outside the reader's mind. Direct encounters in life may then provide the incentive for literary creation on the basis that the reading has supplied. She moves her poet through three stages of stimulation: the elementary one of the purely intellectual or verbal; the advanced stage of sexual stimulation; and the climax of a union of intellectual, sexual, and social stimulation from the woman whom he can truly love: "Poppy had drawn him by his senses; Flossie by his senses and his heart; Lucia held him by his senses, by his heart, his intellect, his will, by his spirit, by his genius, by the whole man. Long after his senses had renounced their part in her, the rest of him would cling to her, satisfied and appeased."[14]

She almost insists upon the importance of physical excitement as a stimulant to a higher creativity, as when she describes Rickman on the night when he stands on Harmouth Hill overlooking Harmouth and feels the urge to write again: "He was not in the least deceived as to the true source of his inspiration. In all this, if you went back far enough, his body counted; his body which he had made a house of shame and hunger and desire, shaken by its own shivering nerves and leaping desperate pulses. But what of that now? What matter, since that tumult of his blood had set throbbing such subtle, such infinite vibrations of his soul. *That* was what counted. He could tell by it

13. *The Divine Fire* (London: Constable, 1904), p. 43.
14. *Ibid.*, p. 474.

the quality and immensity of his passion, by just that spiritual resonance and response."[15]

She also probes the literary work to make certain that its statements
of love are true. Lucia reads Rickman's sequence of love sonnets to her,
but she suspects that they may have originated in his compartmented
ego-genius, rather than in his feelings as a whole person; that his ego
had suggested to his body that it supply the feeling base he needed
to give the impression of truth to his writing, and that it had suggested to his verbally excelling mind that the dictated feelings were
really spontaneous feelings aroused by Lucia. Through Lucia's questioning, May Sinclair exposes the truth that the literary artist can
suggest himself with will and words into states of feeling that are not
the products of the stated causes. As a critic she can distinguish between
the word-induced and the life-born, between the willed emotion and
the life-sprung emotion.

As in *Sons and Lovers*, the problem of the male principal is given
the chief focus, although Miriam Leivers's problem is just as pressing
as Paul Morel's. May Sinclair gives Lucia's problem a far fairer proportion of emphasis than Lawrence gave Miriam's. Very briefly, Lucia's
complex problem originates in the repression that her social caste
exerts upon her mind and body's natural eagerness to mate with her
intellectual and spiritual equal. She does not have the personal experience with love to recognize the reality of Rickman's statements of
love, and she has not yet evolved the sense of responsibility to break
the social taboo after having nearly recognized the reality of her love
and his love, and to accept them as the basis for a realizable union.
She goes through a neurotic illness before she can accept her specific
responsibility for causing and accepting Rickman's love.

Horace Jewdwine also is given fair space in the elaboration of his
problem as a critic of literature and as an editor. While he is the editor
of the *Museion*, he is not expected to make a profit, and he can pro-
claim his honest, if narrow, opinions. But when he accepts the editorship of *Metropolis*, whose publisher expects a profit, he strangles his
honesty and rationalizes its death with clever and relevant theorizing.
May Sinclair sums him up with her trenchant brevity: "Even more
than for eminence he longed for power. He longed for it with the
passion of a weak will governed despotically by a strong intellect."[16]

His rationalizing is simple. Posing as a man of strength and decision,
he explains his point of view: " 'My dear fellow, modernity simply
means democracy. And when once democracy has been forced on us,

---

15. *Ibid.*, p. 249.
16. *Ibid.*, p. 413.

there's no good protesting any longer.' " He assures Rickman that he will go on protesting as a private citizen, but as a public critic, " 'I must accept a certain amount of defeat at the hands of the majority.' "[17] Privately he believes that the majority "has destroyed criticism by destroying literature."[18]

There is other literary discussion in the novel. The quick sketch of Herbert Rankin's popularity records the kinds of novels that readers wanted in this decade: "Drawing-room comedy, pathetic pastoral, fantastic adventure, slum idyll and mediaeval romance, it was all one to Rankin. An infallible instinct told him which genre should be chosen at any given moment; a secret tocsin sounded far-off the hour of his success."[19]

The sonnet form that was May Sinclair's obsession and Rickman's choice is defended: "He had chosen purposely the consecrated form that pledged him to perfection, bound him to a magnificent restraint."[20]

The constructive craftsmanship is in itself worth study for its firmness and for the subtlety with which it ties the many solid facts of the novel into an organic unit. Three devices give the progress of the psychological romance a fluent cohesion: the title motif, the playing of a musical composition, and the library which Sir Frederick Harden has secretly mortgaged.

The title is the start of a gathering ribbon that runs two strands, exaltation and light, through the story. "Divine" reappears continually in varieties of nouns, verbs, participles, and plain adjectives; and "fire" recurs plentifully with its synonyms of light and flame.[21]

The musical vinculum is Lucia's playing of Beethoven's Sonata *Appasionata*. She plays it first for Horace Jewdwine on the hot July afternoon when he shows her Rickman's first, more rhetorical version of "Helen of Leuce." She plays it then primarily as a love call to rouse the too complacent cousin-admirer, but her playing is also affected by her enjoyment of the verse drama and by her thinking about the poet.[22] A year later she plays it again after having met a most unusual cataloguer and scholar, whom she has not yet identified as the poet whom her cousin had discovered but out of jealousy not named to her a year before. She has been affected by the meeting with Rickman, and does not know that he is listening and that he is moved by her playing.[23]

---

17. *Ibid.*, p. 415.
18. *Ibid.*, p. 416.
19. *Ibid.*, p. 587.
20. *Ibid.*, p. 480.
21. See *Ibid.*, pp. 100–101, 409, 410, 462, 475, 487, 667.
22. *Ibid.*, p. 16.
23. *Ibid.*, p. 115.

Through the accident of finding a page of his verses in the library and so recognizing him as the poet whose work attracted her a year ago, she becomes eager to please him. He asks her to play for him, and Lucia knows without his naming it what piece he wants her to play. Once more she plays the Sonata *Appasionata,* deliberately pressing into its tones what he means to her.[24] Music enables Rickman to ask for and Lucia to give what neither could confess in the nakedness of spoken words. After five years of separation, without any messages passing between them, they meet in Mrs. Downey's lodging house in Bloomsbury. Rickman opens the piano in the music room and lights the candles on its brackets. He does not have to speak, and Lucia knows what he wants her to play: "The Sonata *Appassionata,* isn't it?"[25] This last performance sweeps away the hold of Rickman's pledge to Flossie and every barrier to his courtship of Lucia.

The mortgaged library is the third ligature, a realistic tie contrasting with the romantic ones, skillfully employed as setting, symbol, and cause of a series of dramatic decisions. The coincidence that Isaac Rickman's financial agent, Dicky Pilkington, holds the mortgage of not only Sir Frederick's estate but also of the library of fifteen thousand volumes and needs to have the library valued for sale to Rickman's, and that Lucia wants the library catalogued before she joins her father in Cannes, results in Rickman's coming to Harden Court in the open role of expert cataloguer hired by Lucia and in the secret role of valuer for his father.

The Harden library, as the expected legacy to a woman for the first time in twelve generations of Hardens, is a symbol of Lucia's heritage of culture; the mortgage on it is a symbol of her father's betrayal of responsibility to his only child.

The library becomes the setting in which Rickman and Lucia fall in love, and in which Rickman suffers profound humiliation for his Cockney mispronunciation of Homer. It becomes the setting for his resolution that his betraying blunder in speech shall be the last. The library becomes the symbol to Rickman of his own class of tradesman, of Lucia's heritage and scholarship, of his mastery of the scholarship Lucia also has mastered, and of the common ground with Lucia by which he might make an improbable but faintly possible entrance through his creative genius, which she had discovered in the library, to the class in which, born in exile, he would feel at home.

As Rickman's love possesses him, the library becomes the symbol of

24. *Ibid.,* p. 181.
25. *Ibid.,* p. 445.

his ideal love for Lucia, as that of a man of the highest honor. The failure of Rickman's attempt to persuade Horace Jewdwine to buy in the library to keep it in the family makes of the library a means of exposing Jewdwine as unworthy of Lucia. Mr. Rickman's refusing to listen to his son's plea that he either withdraw as purchaser of the library or offer a fair price for it makes the library a partial cause of Rickman's leaving his father's business and his tradesman class forever. Because his book-learned son no longer advises him on old books (Keith had offered to help his father without pay and without any connection with the firm, and had been refused), Mr. Rickman falls into hard times. He jeopardizes the library by mortgaging it to Pilkington for the sum that Keith had named. Increasing troubles bring on his death, and his death makes Keith heir to a half-partnership in the original Paternoster Row shop selling religious books. The four thousand pounds that Keith receives from the sale of the half-partnership pays off the principal of the mortgage on the library, but not the accumulated interest owed Pilkington. Rickman's resignation as reviewer from *Metropolis* after Jewdwine has switched reviews to favor a powerful friend, makes it doubtful if he can save the library before the note falls due. Pilkington's leniency and the starvation that brings him to the notice of friends enable Rickman to regain the library for Lucia. At the close, the library is a symbol of the material and spiritual union whose first moves had taken place as romantic dreams among the titles of imagined realities.

When we turn again to certain characteristic convictions and interests, we notice the insistence on Rickman's body being the source of the joy of his soul, pointing the way to the theme of *The Helpmate*.[26] The conviction, repeated to friends and interviewers, that her English readers were less kind than her American ones is at least half asserted in Rickman's answer to Lucia's saying that she is jealous of the whole world's love for her husband-to-be: " 'Of the British public? It doesn't love me, Lucy, nor I it.' "[27]

May Sinclair's interest in philosophy ventures to disclose itself in only incidental passages, most of them lightly ironic, as when Rickman cites Coleridge to make the point that the Harcombe Valley, which he and Lucia are surveying, has no reality but what they give it;[28] or when Lucia offers Rickman space and time for his writing by asking him to consider acting as her secretary in Italy;[29] or when Dicky

---

26. *Ibid.*, pp. 194, 249.
27. *Ibid.*, p. 661.
28. *Ibid.*, p. 145.
29. *Ibid.*, p. 178.

Pilkington explains that the only pursuit of reality is the pursuit of profit, because finance hands one a reality that one can grip firmly, while art can hand one only a picture of it;[30] or when Flossie Walker's mind is read as, wondering how to bring Rickman to some positive decision, she is "in the stage of doubt so attractive in philosophers and women, asking herself: Is knowledge possible? And if so, what do I know?"[31]

Her interest in the unconscious as an area of emotional and decision-making behavior is expressed in the grammar of qualifying terms without any directly substantive word. Lucia Harden does not know either how attracted or how stimulating she is to Rickman: "She had no thought of being Mr. Rickman's inspiration; her attitude to his genius was humbly reverent, her attitude to his manhood profoundly unconscious."[32] When she meets Rickman five years later and learns that he is engaged to Flossie Walker, she relaxes her reserve toward him: "Unconscious of her sex, she had remained unconscious of her power; she had trusted (unconsciously) to the power of another woman for protection."[33] May Sinclair described the possibility of a conscious effort to suppress an old habit pattern producing an unconsciously enacted and opposite effect. Early in his stay at Harden Court, Rickman, who has been dreading a lapse of aspirates, is surprised to hear that Lucia has read Euripides and other Greek dramatists in their original language: " 'And Aeschylus and Sophocles and Aristophanes—?' Mr. Rickman became embarrassed as he recalled certain curious passages, and in his embarrassment he rushed upon his doom—'and—and—'Omer?' "[34]

She had also a sophisticated comprehension of the dream as a medium for transmitting messages from the unconscious to the conscious, a medium in which, if the message violated a convention, conscience granted it diplomatic privilege, as it might grant, say, to literature; "it is only a dream." Less than a fortnight before Lucia is to leave for Cannes to join her father, she dreams that she has started for France and has three times missed her train. In the dream she reaches the platform of Harcombe Station, wearing only a nightgown. The train is waiting, and Rickman announces that he is taking charge of her journey as her private secretary. She stands talking to him without embarrassment even though she is clad transparently. She is sleeping lightly enough to know that she is dreaming, but she can avoid recog-

30. *Ibid.*, pp. 244–45.
31. *Ibid.*, p. 349.
32. *Ibid.*, p. 184.
33. *Ibid.*, p. 505.
34. *Ibid.*, p. 103.

nizing the message of her dream wish to stay with Rickman and have him manage her life, because it has the obvious unreality of the dream. She is wakened by a cold wind and the rattling of a loose window in the library below, and going downstairs, she finds that Rickman has worked late and fallen asleep in front of the fireplace. She rebuilds the fire and draws his coat closely over him, while he pretends he has not been wakened. The dream has relaxed her usual reserve; she has not ignored its message completely.[35]

Lucia's hysterical paralysis is the second instance of a woman's retreating into a neurotic helplessness because she cannot decide upon the action that would dissolve a great stress. Later novels would contain more instances.

The logical converse (which was not a trick of style to produce an easy epigram, but a true manifestation of her habit of balanced thinking to test a point of view) appears about a dozen times in this novel. In the first chapter it is, "Lucia might not have the intuition of genius, but she had the genius of intuition;"[36] in the last chapter it occurs in dialogue. Rickman is the first speaker, Lucia the second: " 'I'm afraid I wasn't always faithful to my dream.'—'Because your dream wasn't always faithful to you.' "[37]

Many critics gave May Sinclair credit for the good taste with which she handled risqué materials. She combined a prim propriety with a total fearlessness in telling the truth about the people whom she had created. She postponed her panic over what she had written (as we saw by peeking into her workbooks) until after it was published. Rickman remembers his real feelings in his *Saturnalia* period: "His notion of pleasure was getting drunk and making love to Miss Poppy Grace; the love he made was better described by a stronger and coarser monosyllable, and he used his imagination to glorify it."[38] She says all she needs to say about Flossie's limited appeal to Rickman when she tells us what he sees as he catches her in her especially donned overall dusting his rooms to pose at domestic aptitude: "But so far from concealing her, the overall, tucked in and smoothed out, and altogether adorably moulded by her crouching attitude, betrayed the full but tender outline of her body."[39]

May Sinclair's descriptive art gives sensitive life to a facial expression, the impression of a room, the exciting microcosm of a city street, or the exhilarating discovery of beauty in a panorama. Rickman's

35. *Ibid.*, pp. 190–94.
36. *Ibid.*, p. 12.
37. *Ibid.*, pp. 666–67.
38. *Ibid.*, p. 137.
39. *Ibid.*, p. 363.

saying that God leaves the edges rough sometimes when he is making a big thing provokes the first betrayal in Lucia's face of sympathy for Rickman the person: "Something like a faint ripple of light passed over her face under the obscuring veil it wore for him."[40] The beauty of Sidmouth, from esplanade to the red cliffs, comes home to us in several chapters picturing the seaside town of Harmouth.[41]

The scenes in conversation show May Sinclair's great improvement in form. Perhaps she studied the plays of Pinero to achieve the subtlety in fragmentating dialogue for the utmost dramatic emphasis that distinguishes *The Divine Fire* from *Audrey Craven,* where she had worked more for the witty remark than for showing minds engaged in a closely woven discussion.

Irony, whether of wit or of action, was one of her strong moods. She says of Horace Jewdwine, "His own taste in women was refined almost to nullity."[42] And of the Harden family, "It was a tradition in the family that its men should be scholars and its women beauties, occasionally frail."[43] Lucia's grandfather, the Master of Lazarus College, believed that "the feminine intellect was simply a contradiction in terms."[44] Lucia sees her father only "in his moods of unnatural sobriety."[45] The popular novelist Rankin, who waits for the starving Rickman to show up at dinner late, "was also hungry, as hungry as a man can be who has three square meals every day of his life."[46] Rickman resigns from *Metropolis* because Jewdwine has switched two of his reviews, one favorable, one condemning, and he does not expose the editor. So Fleet Street believes that he has sold out his honesty to Jewdwine: "And now the fame he would have among them was the fame of a literary prostitute, without a prostitute's wages."[47]

Satire on social conditions is scarce, but when Lucia first becomes interested in helping the brilliant classical scholar and shopman find more congenial work for him, he explains the difficulty: " 'Most doors seem closed pretty tight except the one marked Tradesmen's Entrance.' "[48]

Her comic mood, which only a few critics noticed, freely interposes its entertainment.[49] The comic scenes are original in tone, underived

---

40. *Ibid.,* p. 104.
41. See especially *Ibid.,* chaps. 14, 21, 32, 33.
42. *Ibid.,* p. 36.
43. *Ibid.,* p. 125.
44. *Ibid.,* p. 126.
45. *Ibid.,* p. 128.
46. *Ibid.,* p. 588.
47. *Ibid.,* p. 570.
48. *Ibid.,* p. 177.
49. See Ibid., chaps. 9, 18, 24, 32, 64.

from any of the many models of comedy current, like Anstey, Jerome, Jacobs, Ridge, Grossmith, and Pain. The health and heartiness of Dickens were not unknown to her.

The modulations of flame and light and divinity on the theme of the divine fire result in poetry that is on the whole happier than the poetry that once was confined to verse. She developed a gift for the poetry of metaphor and simile that compares favorably to that of Thackeray in *Henry Esmond*, like the metaphor on the chamber of the mind where the life and death of love is experienced: "For in the house of Love there is only one chamber for birth and for dying; and into that clean, unfurnished place the soul enters unattended and endures its agony alone. There is no Mother-soul to bear for it the birth-pains of the new life."[50] The tone of the poetry can turn comic-grotesque, as with the figure that Rickman chooses to describe his fear of betraying his Cockney upbringing: " 'A man who has once murdered the Queen's English always feels, you know, as if he'd got the body under the sofa. It's like homicidal mania; the poor wretch may be cured, but he lives in terror of an attack returning.' "[51]

It would be unthinkable to consider a May Sinclair novel without paying tribute to its perception into human behavior, for example, the agony of self-awareness that Lucia's presence in the library causes Rickman at first, when his breathing makes him the unquiet center of the room: "In the surrounding stillness, the blowing of his nose became a monstrous and appalling act."[52] Kitty Palliser, Lucia's friend, notices that Lucia's footman, who adores Lucia, waits on Mr. Rickman as if he positively loved him, and so she guesses at Lucia's repressed affection for the cataloguer.[53] With this hint May Sinclair guides the reader to Lucia's problem: to find a path to consciousness for her deep unconscious love. Kitty tells Rickman, " 'People in trouble don't change to other people. They only change to themselves.' "[54] Sir Frederick's death discloses to Lucia her disastrous financial position. She cannot tell whether or not she can forgive him: "Lucia was too young for the great forgiveness that comes of understanding."[55] Flossie Walker obtains two pleasures from her engagement to Rickman: "It may be a triumph to make one man supremely happy; but the effect is considerably heightened if you have at the same time made another

---

50. *Ibid.*, p. 139.
51. *Ibid.*, p. 449.
52. *Ibid.*, p. 100.
53. *Ibid.*, p. 122.
54. *Ibid.*, p. 217.
55. *Ibid.*, pp. 220–21.

man supremely wretched."[56] Sidney Spinks is the wretched man.
Flossie is "wise enough to know that in contending with a chivalrous
man a woman's strongest defence is her defencelessness."[57] Sidney
Spinks worships Rickman as his ideal and tries to emulate him; "and
like all imitators, he exaggerated the master's manner."[58] One of the
ladies lodging under Mrs. Downey's roof, Ada Bishop, a typist (who
charges a shilling a thousand words), has observed men long enough
to know something about them. She tells Flossie that gentlemen never
know their own minds when there are two to choose from, and "gentlemen don't care to look at a girl who's as flat as two boards back and
front."[59] Jewdwine warns Rickman not to leave *Metropolis:* " 'The
event will prove.' " Rickman answers with the deflating acuteness of
Aldous Huxley: " 'It won't prove anything. Events never do. They
merely happen.' "[60] Of Rickman, whose resignation leads to his starving so that he might save the Harden library for Lucia, May Sinclair
says, "His sufferings would have been unendurable if any will but his
own had imposed them on him in the beginning."[61]

The deepest revelation is, I think, the allegorically expressed one.
But quite as direct is the characterization of Rickman as "one whom
the gods torment with inspired and hopeless passion."[62] Kitty Palliser's
hat is decorated with Parma violets in the fashion of 1892.[63] Accepted
as a lover, Rickman says to Lucia, "Do you know, Lucy, you've got
violets growing among the roots of your hair?"[64] It must seem to be
making much of a trifle to be noticing violets, until in *The Combined
Maze* the perfume and the name assume the omnipotent force of
destiny. May Sinclair was the Lucia whose nerves shrank from giving
pain and who suffered if she caused even slight inconvenience to
others, as when Lucia enters Mrs. Downey's dining room late, apologizing, " 'I'm so sorry, I'm afraid I'm rather late.' "[65]

All that remains for the present-day student to hold in his hand as
a remnant of the morocco bindings and tooling in gold that adorned
William Sinclair's books (the originals of the Harden library) is a
slender private accounts book, also bound in morocco and stamped
with a name in gold: *W. Sinclair, Esq.* The unusual name *Jewdwine*

56. *Ibid.,* p. 395.
57. *Ibid.,* p. 520.
58. *Ibid.,* p. 533.
59. *Ibid.,* p. 467.
60. *Ibid.,* p. 567.
61. *Ibid.,* p. 580.
62. *Ibid.,* p. 132.
63. *Ibid.,* p. 116.
64. *Ibid.,* p. 665.
65. *Ibid.,* p. 430.

may have come from a reading of Samuel Butler's life of his grand-father, for the irremovable second master of Shrewsbury School, whom Dr. Samuel Butler bore as his cross, was named, with only a slight difference, "Jeudwine."

I wonder if May Sinclair's dislike to hear *The Divine Fire* praised as her greatest work was not in great part due to her sense of guilt over having used herself so exhaustively to supply the essence of the two principal characters and over having romanticized them beyond the limits of the realism that she drew for her later novels.

The Helpmate (August, 1907), the second of the novels about a problem marriage, opens with a postshock scene that sets the mode of the clearly objective and conscious dramatic means that traces the story of an unconscious influence. In describing the wife as the cause of the problems in a marriage, it strikes a balance of sexual faulting with *Mr. and Mrs. Nevill Tyson;* by moving to the denouement of a partial insight into reality, it strikes a balance of hope for a solution as against despair.

The shock situation occurs on the fourth day of the honeymoon of Anne and Walter Majendie, when Anne overhears some women in the hotel at Scarby discussing the scandal of her husband's affair of seven years before with a Lady Cayley. The shock destroys the image of Walter's goodness, which was based consciously on his gentle treatment of his sister Edith, who is bedridden with a spinal disease, and unconsciously on Anne's religious training, her early adoration of a minor canon of the cathedral and her association of love with the worship of God and with a saintly goodness in a person. She had once dreamily expected to marry the canon, and the fantasy ideal of worship for him remained as the control in her unconscious over the choice of the man she would marry. The fantasy that she had married a sinless man covers the fact that Anne is a healthy animal, a natural mate and a natural mother, except for that demand for a Christ-like mate. The scandal threatens to expose her own healthy animalism, because it forces her to identify herself with Lady Cayley, an attractive animal to have been her husband's mistress once upon a time. To avoid facing her healthiness, she begins to loathe her body and to impose a new image on Walter, the cause of her self-loathing, as that of a sinner from whom she must withhold herself to regain her illusion of saintliness. The happiness of her three days of unconscious sensualism she presses back into her unconscious, because to face its reality would threaten to expose the truth about herself. She consciously withdraws into a saintlike communion with God as her spiritual husband, so justifying her arrogance toward her physical husband.

Walter will not tolerate any feeling of guilt over an affair that is seven years dead and meaningless now. He is adoringly kind to Anne, believing her to be a saint, and repressing any suspicion that she enjoys her spiritual arrogance, the downing of her healthy body.

The unconscious that permits Anne to indulge in a conscious fantasy of union with God is also the home of her instinct to fulfill herself as a woman in love with the man who can fulfill her as a mother. These two sources of command are in perpetual conflict during the nine years that follow the opening shock situation, when Anne is twenty-seven and Walter thirty-two. The sight of her husband in church on a Sunday morning, and the sound of his moan of longing excite her, and her excitement turns into a repressive sense of shame.[66] On her birthday Walter takes Anne for a picnic to Westleydale Woods. Anne's picking up a child to hold it to her breast releases her wish for a child of her own, and she surrenders to Walter's lovemaking in the open air. For only a moment, and only to have her sudden need for motherhood satisfied, she understands that Walter has a need for her. If she had known of Walter's sinning years ago, she would never have accepted him, but for the moment she is glad that his sister Edith had not carried out Walter's wish that she tell Anne; for then, she would not have had this moment of giving in to her wish for motherhood. For only during this moment is that wish dearer to her than her sainthood.

A child is born, Peggy, who becomes Anne's barrier against Walter's passion.

Anne's forbidding her home to a hopeless admirer of the paralyzed Edith, Charlie Gorst, because he is a sinful man, leads to Charlie's becoming involved with a pretty flowershop assistant, Maggie Forrest. And Charlie's involvement leads to Walter's visiting Maggie, first to free Charlie from an embarrassing tie; then, bowing to the pressures of his thwarted passion for Anne, of Maggie's captivating resemblance to Anne in the way she lifted her lip, and Maggie's unselfish gentleness and gratitude to him, to accept the offer of her body's comfort to him. Walter's health from now on Anne mistakes to be the sign of his growing in grace, a growth that she believes she is sharing with him.

A doctor's discovering that Peggy has a valvular heart disease shocks Walter into an abrupt renunciation of his affair, which has run three years. Lady Cayley's visit to Anne to deny that she is the woman who has been gossiped about as Walter's mistress, and her naming Maggie, breaks the news to Anne, and Anne's thoughtless tears in the presence of her daughter leads to Peggy's death from the shock of thinking that her father must be dead for her mother to be crying. Anne's blaming

66. *The Helpmate* (New York: Henry Holt, 1907), p. 52.

Walter for the death of Peggy sends Walter into a long drinking bout away from Anne, and Lady Cayley's offer of a renewal of the past causes Walter to suffer from a stroke.

Only when Walter lies paralyzed is Anne's spiritual pride, her need to triumph over the man who had tempted her, appeased. Now, helped by her virtuous feeling of compassion, her physically healthy self for the very first time admits the truth that she had hitherto repressed: that she loves Walter's body, and wants that body to recover; that loving Walter's body, she had loved God best.

She cannot admit her own animal nature. She remains "the saint in love with her own sanctity"[67] that Lady Cayley had seen her to be. She bestows upon herself a triple crown of glory for goodness in confessing her sin against Walter and God, in forgiving Walter the past, and in being ready to forgive him even if he had surrendered to Lady Cayley (he had not). She is still a religious devotee, but she has been shocked again, from being a proud and cruel wife into being a kind and forgiving wife; and she is a healthier person because she has gained the peace of a reconciled self. The minor canon has been at last displaced by the gentle husband whom she had nearly crucified to death, and whose helplessness forced her sensuality into a compassion that freed her from the tyranny of her self-righteousness.

The play of the unconscious is exposed without psychological cant. The repression of the three days of happiness is phrased in Lawrentian language years before Lawrence: "In herself, too, below her kindling spiritual consciousness, in the unexplored depth and darkness of her, its work remained."[68] Consciously she says, "I can't love him, I can't love him—unless God makes him fit for me to love." But "Sleeping, she dreamed that she was in his arms."[69] The impulse to submit finds its voice when Anne makes an offer: " 'All the same, Walter—.' " She lifted to him the set face of a saint unresisting the torture. " 'If you compel me—.' " But Walter will not accept that offer, for he wants a surrender in love, not with resentment.[70] "At times, when the high spiritual life died down in sleep, she slipped from her trouble, and turned, with her arms stretched towards him where he lay. In her dreams he came to her with the low cry she had heard in the wood at Westleydale. And in her dreams she was tender; but her waking thoughts were sad and hard."[71] She dreams a dream set in Westleydale that tries to tell her that her good angel is love, and that love

67. *Ibid.*, p. 403.
68. *Ibid.*, p. 86.
69. *Ibid.*, p. 91.
70. *Ibid.*, p. 191.
71. *Ibid.*, p. 195.

would bring her the peace that cold saintliness is not giving her.[72]

The philosophical point of the book is phrased in Anne's remembering something that Edith had once told her: "That there is no spirituality worthy of the name that has not been proven in the house of the flesh."[73] Ethics and rationalization are intertwined in the conclusion to which Anne comes, the very same position that May Sinclair had advanced in her dialectical poem "Guyon" in *Essays in Verse*, and in her Hegelian essay of 1893: "It was a great and terrible mystery, that the sin of his body should be the saving of her soul."[74]

But May Sinclair was also aware of readers who might be more interested in the point of view that a family physician might take to a wife who did not understand what she was doing to her husband in repelling his need of her. Lawrence Hannay, Walter's business partner, tells her very patiently what she has done wrong, and ends, "If you want to get down to the root of it, it's as simple as hunger and thirst."[75]

May Sinclair is everywhere the completing dramatist without whom the psychology would not be more than preserved nerve tissue, and the philosophy arid abstraction. Anne's encounter with Lady Cayley at the Hannays' tea,[76] Peggy's molding her mother's face with her fingertips to smooth the tragic brow to tenderness and to draw the closed lips into a smiling curve,[77] Lady Cayley's self-clearing visit to Anne,[78] and Anne's confrontation that breaks Walter's nerve[79] are some of the scenes that raise her to a high rank as a dramatist in the novel.

The narrative construction shows an improved mastery of the chain-reaction series to create an unbroken momentum of inevitability, and the first use of inset patterns to support the summit significance. The relationship of the Lawson Hannays illustrates in miniature the prescriptive point of the relationship that the Majendies lack. It is the physical matedness of the two that has saved the erratic Lawson Hannay from wrecking himself; Mrs. Hannay is the right wife for Lawson, however common she seems to Anne, because she is a strong helpmate, which Anne is not. Dr. and Mrs. Gardner hold their place as an ideal of married happiness: two people who are in love because of the radiant mutual attractiveness of their minds.

We appreciate May Sinclair's sense of balance in her overall picture

72. *Ibid.*, pp. 206–8.
73. *Ibid.*, p. 427.
74. *Ibid.*, p. 428.
75. *Ibid.*, p. 423.
76. *Ibid.*, chap. 12.
77. *Ibid.*, p. 252.
78. *Ibid.*, chap. 31.
79. *Ibid.*, chap. 35.

of life in noticing that Edie's paralysis is not neurotic but organic, and in observing the contrast inside the novel in the fantasy lives of Lady Cayley and of Anne. Lady Cayley knows that her fantasy is invention, and she exerts herself to believe the illusion and to make others take it for apparent reality.

Formal philosophy shows through once or twice, as when Dr. Gardner teases his wife: " 'Don't you see that these pragmatists are putting the cart before the horse? Conduct is one of the things to be explained. How can you take it, then, as the ground of the explanation?' "[80]

The ironic wit entertains without losing its sympathetic effect. Walter amuses the Eliotts' dinner party with a description of a local ex-member of Parliament making his maiden speech: " 'I take it that speech was so maidenly that it shrank from anything in the nature of a proposal.' "[81] Walter Majendie has turned Mrs. Eliott's intellectual salon into a comedy theater with such aplomb that Miss Proctor wants to lure him away. The result is that "Mrs. Eliott remained uncomfortably seated on her dilemma."[82]

As a sample of the spell that May Sinclair puts upon the visual imagination one should read the passage in chapter twenty-seven that shows Anne brushing her hair for the night while Walter watches. The passage blends the painter's joy in the beauty of color and light, and the dancer's feeling for graceful movement, with the frustrated responses of Walter's body.[83]

The style discovers the center-reaching metaphor in sentences as well as in longer passages. On the night when Anne hears about the old scandal she cries "with hot eyes that drank the tears of their own passion."[84]

The comically irreverent outburst that was to reappear in later novels occurs for the first time when Walter tells about the aunt whose ardent religious disciplining weaned him from religion. By Palm Sunday she was so exhausted from her Christian endeavors that she would fly into a passion that lasted until noon on Easter Day: "For quite a long time he had believed that that was why they called it Passion Week."[85]

The logical converse crops up a score of times to challenge the reader's intellect, and to suggest the author's habit of balancing points of view. Anne had thought that the Eliotts' dinner party would convert

---

80. *Ibid.*, p. 220.
81. *Ibid.*, p. 72.
82. *Ibid.*, p. 75.
83. *Ibid.*, pp. 304–5.
84. *Ibid.*, p. 6.
85. *Ibid.*, p. 49.

her husband. The chapter ends: "Mrs. Eliott's dinner party had not saved him; on the contrary, he had saved the dinner party."[86]

As a woman fighting to establish herself in society in spite of her unconventional past, Lady Cayley is a very lively migrant from the dramas of Pinero and Jones, and a forecast of her tragic balance in Kitty Tailleur, who dreamed of daring. Her name is an obvious borrowing from Pinero's most famous play of the genre of the "woman who dared."

A division between father and mother had already been the theme of a poem, "Margery," in *Essays in Verse*. Florence Bartrop told me that she understood from May Sinclair that the contrasting personalities of her own parents suggested the story of the Majendies. Majendie is a disappointed man who wanted to go to Oxford and who had been forced to leave the books that he loved to support himself in a shipping office. Anne is ashamed of her husband's business and makes her way as often as she can to the garden green of Thurston Square: "Sitting in Mrs. Eliott's drawing-room, she forgot that the soul of Scale on Humber was given over to tallow, and to timber, and Dutch cheeses. But for her constant habit of depreciation, she could almost have forgotten that her husband was only a ship-owner who had gone into the horrible partnership with Lawson Hannay."[87]

Scale on Humber we may take for Hull, and Scarby, two hours away by rail, for Scarborough. A hint of the camera that registered the original scenes out of which the novel was so powerfully realized is Peggy, who loves her father more than she loves her mother, and who senses her mother's lack of love for him. The name Majendie appears in *Lethaby's Sidmouth Journal and Directory for 1882–1891*.[88] It was that of a family living in Hill's Cottage in Salcombe Regis in the years when May Sinclair and her mother lived in that village. Hull, of course, was often visited by May, because her brother William managed a provisioners' store there from 1879 until his death in 1896.

The third novel of marriage, *The Judgment of Eve* (America, 1908; England, 1914), rivaling Mrs. Gaskell's *Cousin Phillis* in brevity and in cruel pathos, is short enough to have been published in a single issue of *Everybody's Magazine* and as a supplement in book form to *The Lady's Realm* in December, 1907.

It opens as a provincial idyll of humorous romantic love. With rhythmical and emotional charm it moves through deepening shadows of irony until it ends in pitiful tragedy. The main irony results from

---

86. *Ibid.,* p. 77.
87. *Ibid.,* pp. 269–70.
88. Kindly shown me in the Sidmouth Museum by its director, P. W. W. Ninnes.

the unromantic marriage to which Aggie Purcell's romantic choice condemns her. The prettiest girl in the Cotswold town of Queningford, she rather favors spinsterhood over marriage as alternative promises of contentment; she does not have strong vitality. And she chooses a gentle solicitor's clerk from London, Arthur Gatty, because he shares her tastes in music, painting, and Browning, and is humble in his manner, over John Hurst, a strong young farmer, who must be cruel to kill pigs and lambs for food. Aggie dreams that she would go on living the life for which her schooling in romantic literature has trained her.

From a tranquil romantic girl, she grows into a passionately devoted wife. Arthur declines into an irritable, unimaginative, static clerk, accepting the frustration of being a tolerated failure. Aggie's sentimental education survives long after her physical energy has been drained by housework and by children. Arthur, after working hours, wants only oblivion. Despite the doctor's warning that her body is not strong enough, Aggie bears child after child, keeping from Arthur the secret of her risk out of her pity for his need of her body as the only relief left to him from despair. Even after he learns of the risk to her life, his weak will and habit of self-indulgence swallow his caring. Her eighth pregnancy at last breaks Aggie's hold on life. Just as Anne's belated compassion and insight keep *The Helpmate* from flaring into satire, so Arthur's numbed agony at the realization that Aggie has been the giver and he the selfish taker keeps this novel from pointing to bitterness. The irony of Aggie's mistaken choice is clinched by the contrast with her sister Susan's happy marriage with the robust farmer whom Aggie had feared. John had accepted the doctor's warning after Susan's first child was born that she must have no more children. He had been the gentle, considerate husband that Arthur had promised but had lacked the will to be.

The difference between the two men is lodged in Aggie's thoughts as she remembers a book and a passage in it that her vicar had underlined twice. The passage is the text of the novel: "If there is aught spiritual in man, it is the Will."[89] The importance of the will had not been included in Aggie's curriculum.

Arthur's regression from love to sensuality is told in Lawrentian imagery three years before Lawrence's first book appeared: "The man had passed over into the sensual darkness that is seldom pierced by pain. Of the pleasures that had once borne him, buoyant and triumphant, on the crest of the wave, none were left but such sad earthly

---

89. *The Judgement of Eve* (New York: Harper, 1908), p. 105.

wreckage as life flings up at the ebbing of the spiritual tide."[90]

One could hardly guess at the author's serious knowledge of philosophy from the ironic reference that Arthur makes to a lecture that the young couple have just heard, on appearance and reality. As they sip their cocoa at home, Arthur lucubrates, " 'Only think, how people wreck their lives just because they don't know the difference between appearance and reality! Now we *do* know. We're poor, but we don't care a rap, because we know, you and I, that that doesn't matter. It's the immaterial that matters.' "[91] They glory for a short time in the splendid reality of their love, which they picture on the walls of their Camden Town house in the Burne-Jones photogravures bearing the titles "Love leading Life" and "Love Triumphant."

This serious book is no exception to the rule that almost every book of May Sinclair's has its chuckle: "Nature, safeguarding its own interests, had whispered to Aggie that young ladies who live in Queningford are better without intellects that show."[92] An autobiographical note identifies this Queningford as Fairford in Gloucestershire.

A passage of special value as poetry creates the moment when Arthur perceives his thoughtless cruelty to the woman he has loved and hurt beyond reparation. The thought becomes a death sentence from which his wife's last testimony wins him pardon: " 'It would have been better' said this new self, 'if I had been unfaithful to her. *That* wouldn't have killed her.'—As if she had heard him through some spiritual sense, she pressed his hand and answered him. 'Thank God,' she whispered hoarsely, 'that you've always loved me.' "[93]

Kitty Tailleur (June, 1908; American title: *The Immortal Moment*) presents a version in the form of a novel of the motif of a woman with a past daring to hope for a respectable marriage, which Pinero and Jones had already made familiar in their compassionate social problem dramas. Its structure, built with a single setting and a centered design, resembles that of a play, and eight of its chapters compare well with the dramatic dialogue of those masters of the social problem enacted in tense scenes. The opening mood, a gay readiness for holiday-making, ensures ample room between contrasting moods for a powerful resonance to the tragic clang with which the dilemma is resolved.

In a southern coastal resort hotel, the pretty Mrs. Kitty Tailleur becomes the subject of gossip through the subtleties of appearance and

---

90. *Ibid.*, pp. 66–67.
91. *Ibid.*, p. 40.
92. *Ibid.*, p. 7.
93. *Ibid.*, p. 120.

behavior that uninnocent men recognize as the signs of a negotiable
woman. An innocent widower, Robert Lucy, taking a holiday with his
sister Jane, and not yet joined by his two small children, feels immediate pity for her, champions her against the gossips, and proposes
marriage. His sister's approval of Kitty as a new sister-in-law blesses
the proposal. Robert's conscious desire for Kitty is his wish to have a
pretty mother for his children; his unconscious interest in her, like
Pinero's Mr. Tanqueray for Paula, springs from his intuitive reading
of Kitty as a woman who would satisfy the sexual needs that his late
wife had thwarted. Kitty is thrilled to be loved by a man, not just
hired. She says of him to Jane, " 'He is the first nice man who—who
hasn't been what men are.' "[94]

The prospect of a new and decent life so heightens her beauty that
when the man who has kept her, Wilfrid Marston, a man of importance in the War Office, calls upon her at the hotel, his jaded appetite
revives, and he uses his diplomatic craft to recover her for himself.
He pretends to regret the fraud that she would practice on her fiancé
if she did not confess her past to him. Her meeting Robert's two
children, whom she had dreaded as her nemesis, and her being allowed
to carry in her arms the five-year-old Barbara tip the scale toward confessing. She ends her full confession by agreeing with Robert that he
cannot marry her, on the children's account. His promise to care for
her, but again on the children's account with austere propriety, breaks
her half-hope of a compromise in an affair. Still the diplomat, Wilfrid
Marston offers to compensate Kitty for the marriage he had caused
her to lose by proposing to marry her himself. His offer only gives her
the motive for proving that her own purification by love is final. His
proposal has not changed him as Robert Lucy's proposal had changed
her; he still cares only for her body, not for her goodness. Kitty tells
Marston, " 'I couldn't get away from *it*. You'd keep me in it. It's
what you like me for—what you're marrying me for. You haven't married, all these years, because you can't stand living with a decent
woman. And you think, if I marry you, it will make it all right. All
right!' "[95]

The motivation of all the people is justified with May Sinclair's—
and Pinero's—customary thoroughness in depth. After her arrival at
the hotel, Kitty Tailleur moves in convincing gradations from prostitute to prospective wife. At first she is the bold flirt, shaking a fur
piece off her shoulders so that she may meet the best-looking man at
the hotel. In her first conversation with Robert she chaffs him roughly

---

94. *Kitty Tailleur* (London: Constable, 1908), p. 126.
95. *Ibid.*, p. 303.

to insure their intimacy with the least loss of holiday time. She is surprised by the change that she notices in herself under the influence of Robert Lucy's respect and tenderness and of his sister Jane's friendliness, and she begins to long to live their kind of life. Then she becomes unsure of herself and of keeping Robert's love: " 'Oh, Robert, you do *really* think I'm nice?' "[96]

The conscience that Wilfrid Marston invokes to keep her for himself is strong, like that of most of May Sinclair's protagonists. It was her conscience that caused her to dispense with the hypocrisy which other women of the underworld assumed as part of their protective disguise, and so it was her conscience that made her desirable to the intelligent sensualist, Marston. It was her conscience, which she inherited from her clergyman father and her strict mother, a conscience that later separated her from her parents, that made her afraid she might be an unworthy stepmother to Robert's children.

The clearest example of a theatrical apprenticeship to Ibsen is the return of attention to the place that becomes the site of the tragic climax. The place is the cliffside enclosure where Robert Lucy and Kitty meet three times, the last time for his proposal, the place from which Kitty jumps to her death.

The translation of sounds into images of visible movement is an expression of the poet's way: "Kitty was excited and her voice went winged. It flew upwards, touched a perilous height and shook there. It hung, on its delicate, feminine wings, dominating the male voices that contended, brutally, below."[97]

Kitty's respectable companion, Grace Keating, is observed for a psychological revelation. A "little click in Miss Keating's throat" signals her having told a lie.[98]

Analytic sketches of Jane Lucy, who is five years younger than her brother Robert, match some of the author's characteristics: "Jane was always on the look-out for things happening." "Jane was the thrall of her own sympathy."[99] "She was always entering surreptitiously into other people's feelings. . . . People had a way of telling her their secrets, and Jane preferred not to be told. All she wanted was an inkling, a clue: the slenderer the better."[100] Jane Lucy was to develop into Jane Holland, the novelist in *The Creators,* with her philosophy of gathering materials unchanged.

The Creators: A Comedy (September, 1910) is an analytical novel

---

96. *Ibid.,* pp. 245–46.
97. *Ibid.,* pp. 19–20.
98. *Ibid.,* p. 98.
99. *Ibid.,* p. 4.
100. *Ibid.,* p. 5.

about writers, mainly novelists, and their marriages. The style seems to have undergone a stringent discipline to purify it of what one of its characters calls "the literary taint," meaning rhetorical sentimentalism. Its setting is London, and its time is precisely dated from 1902 to 1910, directly following the time of *The Divine Fire*. Its titular claim to comedy rests upon a strong starting will to write with detachment about the kind of people who were in life as precious to May Sinclair as her own heart's blood, to tell the truth about their intelligence, their devotion to their god, their genius, their improvidence, their honesty, their egotism, their loyalty to each other and forbearance with each other, their unwitting cruelty, and their infinite capacity for sacrifice. The opening will to stay immune to sentiment often gives in to the need to confess love, but the style never leaks feeling from the substance.

There are three marriages of writers: a novelist, George Tanqueray, to a servant in his lodging house in Hampstead, Rose Eldred; a woman novelist, Jane Holland, to a publisher and member of a large and philistine family, Hugh Brodrick; and a poet, Owen Prothero, who is tubercular, to a translator and writer of light novels, Laura Gunning. The underplayed criterion of comparison is the feminine test of a husband's faculty for realizing and loving the whole person of the woman whom he has married.

Jane Holland and George Tanqueray are joined by what is for both of them their most intimate friendship, and divided by their separate marriages. Jane writes compassionate, tender novels, and wins a celebrity that George does not gain with his brilliant but harshly realistic novels. Jane is warm and friendly; George is a recluse, contented with a few writer friends, of whom most are women, and Jane is the closest to him. His charm easily attracts people, and he invades them quickly with his rapid perception; but he cannot bear being himself invaded and glides off as soon as he has gathered the few materials that he needs to set his imagination creating its own living materials with realistic conviction. He is a great admirer of Jane's genius, her most effective stimulant and advisor; Jane thinks him the greatest living novelist.

Jane's love for Tanqueray contains a strong physical element, yet his great flaw in her eyes is his nature to isolate his sexual appetite from his intellectual sympathies. When she sees him "on the first mad hunt with love"[101] her conscience checks her from making any move that would capture him. Tanqueray is actually obsessed with Jane, but her

---

101. *The Creators: A Comedy* (New York: Century Co., 1910), p. 9.

cleverness frightens him, or rather, frightens the separate sexualness of him. Not encouraged by Jane, he lets his searching sexual impulse fasten on his landlady's niece, the healthy, pretty, gentle, uneducated Rose Eldred, and he marries her. After playing with Rose during their honeymoon, he ignores her on their return to Hampstead, to lose himself in his interrupted writing. He is acute in reading people whose mysteries he wants to take from them to give life to his novels, but Rose is no material for his fiction, and he is not even aware of the social dilemma that he has forced upon her by persuading her to marry out of her class, or of his cruelty in forbidding her to fill her time with household work, in forbidding her to disturb him as he writes all day and half into the night, in forcing her to sleep alone, in opposing her wish for a child.

Jane, disappointed by Tanqueray's sexually defined choice, marries a successful newspaper publisher who has decided to found a literary monthly and who, admiring Jane as a writer, falls in love with the woman embodying the writer. Jane's situation as a wife and mother introduces a problem: whether or not a woman novelist to whom the quality of her writing, not her happiness as a person, is the supreme desideratum, should marry. Jane gives full compassion and much of her energy to Brodrick's numerous and demanding family. As a result of giving up several months in daily attendance upon a sister of Hugh who suffers from a fatal cancer, Jane loses a daughter in a stillbirth. She gives up a whole year from her writing to cure her younger boy of his screaming terror. She tries to make Hugh understand the restlessness that has disturbed her because her urge to write has been blocked: " 'There are women—angels naturally—who become devils if they can't have children. I'm an angel—you know I'm an angel—but I shall be a devil if I can't have this. Can't you see that it's just as natural and normal—for me?' "[102]

The third marriage is that of the tubercular poet Owen Prothero and Laura Gunning, writer of light novels. This is a marriage of mutual compassion. Prothero is sorry for Laura's struggle to write while her bankrupt, senile father rustles newspapers noisily, so that she has to drop her creative writing and turn to translating for their support; and Laura pities the sickly and courageous romantic whose verses sing about man's joyful communion with God, while critics and readers go about their most ungodly ways. Owen's love for Laura is the finest love of the three men; much finer than Tanqueray's for Rose or for Jane; and finer than Hugh's; for it is a divine fire, love not

---

102. *Ibid.*, p. 327.

for Laura's body alone, or for her body and her heart, but for the whole nature of Laura, and Laura knows it: "And she knew that it was not her body alone that he sought for and held, but the soul that was her womanhood. It stood before him, a new-born Eve, naked and unafraid on the green plots of Eden. It looked at him, and its eyes were tender with desire and pity. It was tremulous as a body inhabited by leaping light and flame.—She knew that in them the flame burned singly. . . .—It was not so even with Jane. Jane had taken into her life an element of tumult and division. The Lord her God (as Tanqueray had once told her) was a consuming fire. Married she served a double and divided flame."[103]

The theme of sexual separateness recurs toward the end, when Tanqueray appeals to Jane in Devon to elope with him. Jane is strongly tempted, but her conscience reminds her of the claims of Rose upon George and of her family upon her, and she does not trust George or herself to keep the sexual desire from overwhelming them. " 'George,' she said, 'you know women as God knows them; why didn't you know me? Can't you see what I am afraid of? What we're all afraid of? What we're eternally trying to escape from? The thing that hunts us down, that turns again and rends us.' "[104] J. B. Priestley had turned that theme into a play, *Ever Since Eve.*

To sum up the three marriages, we see that two out of the three are problem marriages. Only Laura Gunning and Owen Prothero enjoy the perfect marriage of mind and body and spirit that had been celebrated in *The Divine Fire.*

A pendant to the marriage situations is the story of Nina Lempriere, the novelist whose heredity has instilled in her strong passionateness. She embodies the two major themes: the danger to the personality of an overwhelming sexual passion, and the handicap that marrying imposes on the woman writer. Nina first loves Tanqueray, and then Prothero. Her undemanding devotion loses both, the first through his mental closeness to Jane, the second through his mental and physical union with Laura. Her part in the total pattern is that of an optional other-self of Jane Holland. Nina Lempriere's remaining a virgin coincides with her writing novels of such emotional power that she comes to believe that her virginity had conserved the passion that she would have expended upon the man whom she might have married, and that it is the secret of her power. She says to Jane, " 'Look here. . . . I *believe,* if any woman is to do anything stupendous, it means virginity. But I *know* it means that for you and me.' "[105]

---

103. *Ibid.,* pp. 317–18.
104. *Ibid.,* p. 475.
105. *Ibid.,* p. 106.

Her solitude makes her probe deeply into the soul of the writer's creativity: " 'Doesn't it look, Jinny, as if genius were the biggest curse a woman can be saddled with? It's giving you another sex inside you, and a stronger one, to plague you. When we want a thing we can't sit still like a woman and wait until it comes to us, or doesn't come. We go for it like a man; and if we can't get it peaceably we fight for it, as a man fights when he isn't a coward or a fool. And because we fight we're done for. And then, when we're down, the woman in us turns and rends us. But if we got what we wanted we'd be just like any other woman. As long,' she added, 'as we wanted it.' "[106]

In this novel there is a broadening of the craft of moving the action of the novel through unconscious motivation. In *Audrey Craven* and in *The Helpmate* the course had been a relatively straightforward progress limited to the principal character. In *The Divine Fire* interest in the unconscious had been directed to a secondary character. But in *The Creators* there is an interweaving progress of unconsciously guided action unified by the principle of obliqueness of effect. When Jane Holland's mind clears after she has digested the surprise of Tanqueray's marrying Rose, she recovers the sequence of causation of which the marriage was the effect. She realizes that, in spite of the self-discipline with which she had suppressed an impulse to take advantage of Tanqueray's erotic hunting urge, on the evening of the dinner in her rooms with which she celebrated the great success of a novel, she had unconsciously signaled her passion for him strongly enough to encourage his lusting further, and to direct him to Rose and his misalliance.

Hugh Brodrick is another object of oblique suggestion. His housekeeper in his Putney Heath home is a distant cousin of the wife of his brother John. Gertrude Collett idealizes Brodrick, turning her responsibilities into the devotions of a spiritual bride. He has become fascinated by Jane's writing and by her personality. When Jane falls ill while she is writing a novel for his *Monthly Review*, he has her transferred to the shelter of his home. Gertrude Collett becomes jealous of Jane and afraid of the wild, queer blood she supposes Jane to have inherited to judge by her outspoken writings. Gertrude is troubled so much that she unconsciously agitates Brodrick. By intensifying his emotion with her distress, she sharpens his compassion for Jane into passion. Here is May Sinclair's analysis of the unconscious communication that influences Brodrick:

For Gertrude lived and moved and had her sentimental being in Brodrick. Thus she laboured at her own destruction. So preoccupied

---

106. *Ibid.*, p. 105.

was she with the thought of Brodrick that her trouble, travelling along secret paths of the nerves and brain, had subtly, insensibly communicated itself to him. He grew restless in that atmosphere of unrest. If Gertrude could have kept, inwardly, her visible beautiful serenity, Brodrick, beguiled by the peace she would have wrapped him in, might have remained indefinitely quiescent. But he had become the center of a hundred influences, wandering spirits of Gertrude's brain. Irresistibly urging, intangibly irritating, perpetually suggesting, they had prepared him for the domination of Jane Holland. But Gertrude was not aware of this.[107]

She is even "unaware that her emotions had any root in flesh and blood."[108]

Indirect suggestion acts upon Jane too. Tanqueray has become so anxious lest Jane's independent art should become a captive of Brodrick's *Monthly Review,* and Jane be overwhelmed by his numerous relatives as the result of her accepting his hospitality during her illness, that he warns her against falling in love with her publisher. The result of his warning her against temptation is to encourage her frustrated love for Tanqueray to move further toward an already progressing and hitherto unconscious affection for Brodrick. Gertrude Collett's fear pushes Brodrick into proposing, not to Gertrude but to Jane, and Tanqueray's anxiety pushes Jane into accepting the proposal.

Another striking instance of suggestion lets us see how Jane sheds the numbness that stopped her writing after Tanqueray married. She happens to be walking on the Broad Walk in Kensington Gardens when a little boy runs into her so violently that he upsets himself. Jane scolds him for the indignity he has done her, but when she hears him crying out to his mother that he was a steam engine and could not stop, the child's pain pierces the numbness that was smothering her own pain, and lets her suffering flow out to lose itself in the distress of the little boy. The intensity of the boy's imagination and the shock that had made her notice it reawaken her own imaginative concentration. Suddenly the held-in idea of a novel about a character named Hambleby leaps into life and drives her as insistently as the child's imagination had driven him. Her first thought thereafter is about the relief it will be to be creating Hambleby instead of suffering from the mental paralysis that has anesthetized her against Tanqueray's marriage. She does not seem aware of the act of identification that made her imagination once more a steam engine, the source of infinite, irresistible power.[109]

107. *Ibid.,* p. 255.
108. *Ibid.,* p. 256.
109. *Ibid.,* pp. 109–11.

Although we see Jane pouring imagined reality into her novel about Hambleby, we learn nothing about the mysterious relationship between the writer person and the written persons, a revelation that was not to be made until *Far End*. The only link (and it is a very slight one) is contained in the name of the clerk who is to undergo hardship: Hambleby repeats the stressed vowel and the rhythm of the name Tanqueray, the man whose hold on her mind Jane is consciously trying to break, and whom she is unconsciously determined to punish with a thwarting fate. The description of Hambleby,[110] a suburban bank clerk, fits the germ idea of the principal male in both *The Combined Maze* and *Arnold Waterlow*.

A substantial penetration into the author's life is that which describes Jane's state of mind when she becomes absorbed in a novel that drains her energies away from her family. The world in which she lives her physical life recedes; the world of her vision becomes the solid life; the souls of her characters are the souls that she becomes one by one. The spiritual warmth with which she lives the lives of her characters makes her feel unfaithful to her husband and her child: "Bodily unfaithfulness seemed to be a lesser sin."[111]

Joined to the moments that show us the author in being are statements that form a writer's testament on the theory of the literary imagination. Jane agrees with Tanqueray's conviction that the novelist should look, but not stare at life:

> His device was "Look and let go." . . . Your senses, he maintained, were no good if you couldn't see a thing at the first glance and feel it with your first touch. . . . The fruitful genius was feminine, . . . humble and passive in its attitude to life. It yearned perpetually for the embrace, the momentary embrace of the real. But no more. All that it wanted, all that it could deal with was the germ, the undeveloped thing; the growing and shaping and bringing forth must be its own. . . . It was only the little men that were the plagiarists of life; only the sterile imaginations that adopted the already born, and bargained with experience to do their work for them.[112]

Owen Prothero sees personal flaws in Tanqueray's practice of his theory: " 'Tanqueray sees so much inside other people that he can't see inside himself. What's worse, I shouldn't think he'd see far inside people who really touch him. It comes of perpetually looking away.' "[113] He thinks Tanqueray was cruel to have married so pure and simple

---

110. *Ibid.*, p. 112.
111. *Ibid.*, p. 347.
112. *Ibid.*, pp. 15–16.
113. *Ibid.*, p. 183.

a woman as Rose Eldred: " 'He doesn't see anything. He doesn't even know she's there. How can he? His genius runs to flesh and blood, and he hasn't room for any more of it outside his own imagination. That's where you are with your great realists.' "[114]

Jane has to relearn the lesson that her writing art is a jealous god demanding sole loyalty: "You had to come to it clean from all desire, naked of all possessions. . . . For the divine thing fed on suffering, on poverty, solitude, frustration. It took toll of the blood and nerves and of the splendour of the passions. And to those who did not stay to count the cost or measure the ruin, it gave back immeasurable, immortal things. It rewarded supremely the supreme surrender."[115]

Tanqueray is very wise in warning Jane, after she has gotten well into her novel about Hambleby, that she must not fall in love with her protagonist: " 'You can't know people, you can't possibly hope to know them, if you once allow yourself to fall in love with them.' "[116]

Jane staunchly disagrees with the theory that Frances Heron, who is to become her sister-in-law, has about writing. Mrs. Heron is certain there are things that an artist cannot feel without having had experience at first hand, as of bearing a child. Jane replies, " 'I know what she knows—I was born knowing. But if I were married, if I had children, I should know nothing, nothing any more.' "[117] And again, " 'Experience? Experience is no good—the experience you mean—if you're an artist.' It spoils you. It ties you hand and foot. It perverts you, twists you, binds you to everything but yourself and it. I know women —artists—who have never got over their experience, women who'll never do anything again because of it.' "[118]

Tanqueray knows that attention to the social self may paralyze the writing self, and that is why he says to Jane, " 'If I don't like to see you celebrated, Jinny, it's because I want to see you immortal.' "[119] And again, " 'Celebrity's all very well at the end, when you've done the things you want to do. It's a bad beginning. It doesn't matter quite as much if you live in the country where nobody's likely to know you're celebrated till you're dead. But if you *will* live in London, your only chance is to remain obscure.' "[120]

The perspective of the novel tries to be comic, but the substance of comedy is scarce. For the first and only time after her sketch in

---

114. *Ibid.*, p. 195.
115. *Ibid.*, pp. 116–17.
116. *Ibid.*, p. 124.
117. *Ibid.*, p. 267.
118. *Ibid.*, p. 268.
119. *Ibid.*, p. 125.
120. *Ibid.*, p. 177.

Black and White, May Sinclair ventured into the mood of sophisticated comedy. Working at a novel, Jane has taxed her emotional capital so heavily that she has had to repulse Hugh's sexual needs; but when she is finished with it she surprises him by playing the hussy to make up to him in abandonment the pain she had caused him during her withdrawal. It is a good scene, beginning with " 'I'm tired of being made love to. I'm going,' she said, 'to fling off all maidenly reserve and make love to you.' " She teases Hugh: " 'It gives you, doesn't it, an agreeable sense of impropriety at your own fireside.' "[121]

There is just one sample of the comic irony that anesthetizes its victim while amusing the occasional lapser into the enjoyment of cruel wit. Jane thinks, "You couldn't have too much of Gertrude, for there was, after all, so very little to have."[122]

Personal revelation in the novel centers on the character who Evelyn Underhill knew would be recognized as May Sinclair's self-projection, Jane Holland. Jane's confidence in her abilities is no more audacious than any writer *must* feel to carry on. Verbal self-depreciation is only a sedative relieving the strain of actual audacity: "she worked divinely, shaping unashamed the bodies and the souls of men. There was nothing in contemporary literature to compare with the serene, inspired audacity of Jane Holland. Her genius seemed to have kept the transcendent innocence of the days before creation."[123] Unashamed—serene, inspired audacity—transcendent innocence—they are all true of May Sinclair's writing, as frank and true as Aldous Huxley's self-analyses as Knockespotch and as Mary Thriplow. True of her also is Jane's knowledge of the partition of the sexes in herself: "Through it all, through all her dreadful virility, she had always been persistently, and preposterously feminine. And lying quiet she was more than ever what George Tanqueray had said she was not to be—a mere woman."[124]

May Sinclair prophesied too well for herself and for Jane Holland when she described the relentless intensity with which Jane Holland wrote, and the penalty that her body would pay in time: "It had been relentless enough in its youth; it would be terrible in its maturity. The struggle, if she struggled, would tear her as she had never yet been torn. She would have to surrender, or at any rate make terms with it."[125] A final passage of prophecy is that spoken by the poet, Owen Prothero, as he descants on the virtues that may reside in a diseased body. He interprets the action of disease " 'as a partial discarnation of the spiritual

---

121. *Ibid.,* chap. 51.
122. *Ibid.,* pp. 407–8.
123. *Ibid.,* p. 11.
124. *Ibid.,* p. 448.
125. *Ibid.,* p. 449.

energies. It's a sign of their approaching freedom. Especially those dis-eases which are most like death—the horrible diseases that tear down the body from the top, destroying great tracts of brain and nerve tissue, and leaving the viscera exuberant with life.' "[126] The passage reads as if it were inspired by George Eliot's "The Lifted Veil."

Four of the five novels of this decade alone justify a place in the English gallery of literary fame. And there was still to come a rich harvesting from two more decades.

---

126. *Ibid.*, p. 216.

13

Other Writings: 1900-1910

Short Stories

All four short stories in this "undecade" are in a mood of deep irony. The point of "The Return of the Prodigal," in *Blackwood's Magazine*, January, 1902, is the imbecility of planning a bountiful surprise for one's family instead of keeping in touch with it to learn its needs. A mother and her two daughters in a suburb of Liverpool are waiting for their alcoholic son and brother whom the mother had helped sacrificially ten times to recover from financial failures. During the fifteen years of his absence he has not let them know of his change to sobriety, nor of the five million dollars he has made as a pork packer in Chicago, only that he is coming home. To sound out their mood, he eavesdrops in the garden. Instead of hearing jubilation, he hears a united wailing; and he returns to Liverpool with his gifts, as imbecilic in his sober vanity as when he had been a drunkard. The dream origin of the story blurs the lines of stated fact in a mist that distances them from an acceptable reality, even though the resolution is logically explained.

The writing in "The Fault," which appeared in the *Century Magazine* in January, 1908, is of a finer grain. Its irony hinges upon an innocent woman's losing her lover by repeating the gesture of an evil woman in the lover's past. Gibson married a woman whose long golden hair he loved to stroke. One day he came home from the office early, to find a good friend of theirs standing over his wife, stroking her hair, and to see his wife raise her arms to embrace the overhanging head. Four years after the divorce, Gibson meets Phoebe Richardson, who takes turns with her two sisters pushing her invalid father, a retired general, about in his bath chair. When one day hè sees how tired she looks, he orders her to relax in a long chair. As she obediently stretches back in the chair, she feels her combs loosening and reaches up to put them firmly back in place. Through her arched arms, Gibson sees the horrible scene again, and he leaves her. The hurt to Phoebe is softened with a Barriesque air of fantasy, for Phoebe wonders if she had invented Gibson's love for her.

Both Gibson's wife and Phoebe have a habit of twisting a curl of hair, the wife when she is bored, Phoebe when she is thinking seriously. Florence Bartrop told me it was a habit that May Sinclair had too, to vent her boredom.

McClure's Magazine published "Wilkinson's Wife" in February, 1908. Its irony rests upon Wilkinson's adoring the wife, and then the memory of the wife, who had frustrated his every wish and will while she lived. The narrator can find nothing in Mrs. Wilkinson's appearance, manners, mind, or character to explain her charm for Wilkinson, his self-immolation to her sadism. An image with which his wife is made real describes her mouth: "a mouth that pulled on an invisible curb."

"The Gift" appeared in the *American Magazine* in August, 1908, and in the *Fortnightly Review* in September. In its texture of impressions and intuitions of feeling it is Jacobean without being imitative. A woman writer, Freda Farrar, believes that her gift owes its birth and its survival to the encouragement that she has received from the literary master Wildon Caldecott. A long-time friend of Caldecott, Julia Nethersole, confides to Freda the story of Caldecott's unhappy marriage and his fear of women, and then instills in Caldecott the suspicion that Freda is passionately, although unconsciously, in love with him. Freda's sincere profession of gratitude for his literary gift to her, aimed to quiet his fear of any physical desire, frightens Caldecott, who has been misled by Julia, and he stays away from Freda, whose death, without any physical cause, is recognized to have had a psychic reason: it is the withdrawal of the master's spiritual nourishment that had inspired her writing. Caldecott is gradually awakened to the ironic truth that Julia, his protector against feared women, is in physical love with him, and has misled him about Freda from jealousy.

"Freda," like the "Frida" of *The Cosmopolitan,* is an alias for May Sinclair of the earliest years of the century: close to poverty, shy, often ill, dependent on some fellow-writer for courage to carry on. Wildon Caldecott seems to be Henry James, whose dedication to the art of fiction won May Sinclair's great respect. But Freda finds fault with Caldecott for having run away from the women who frightened him with their affection; she thought it was his duty "to stay by those women, and see them through—if he was honorable." In the introduction to *The Judgment of Eve and other Stories,* May Sinclair wrote, "I am aware that 'The Gift' betrays its *(naifly* obvious) inspiration. This is perhaps the reason why I like it best of all." She had reason as well to be proud of its technical perfection.

Satirical Dialogue

"Man and Superman: A Symposium" featured the Friday installment of the holiday book number of the *New York Times* on December 1, 1905. It preserves the mood of persiflage with two of the ten characters, a father and his twelve-year-old son, who pun and applaud each other's puns, while the rest fulfill May Sinclair's intent to satirize Shaw as a philosopher about women.

The main battle is fought between the Bernard Shaw Enthusiast, who thinks *Man and Superman* the last word on the subject of love, and goes to the root of the nature of love; and the Student of Human Nature, who agrees that it goes to the root, but in exposing the root to find out how it grows, Shaw kills the flower, and "the flower is the thing we live or die for."

Literary Essays

Miscellaneous Essays

"The Eternal Child," in the *New York Bookman* for July, 1906, recommended to American readers two novels for children by Mrs. Allen Harker, because the representations of children were unusual in that their behavior and their thoughts were purely of childhood, uninvaded by the moods of the sadder and wiser grown-up. Mrs. Harker's style had a simplicity "as unbroken and as quietly happy in the morning sunlight as a smooth English lawn," and the books were an outpouring of their author's philosophy: "No one can take from us the good times we have had." May Sinclair praised American readers for being quicker than English readers to attempt the untried, and for having "a greater love for the spontaneous, the unabashed, the all-exploring."

"Three American Poets of Today" appeared in September, 1906, in both the *Atlantic Monthly* and the *Fortnightly Review.* Its starting theme is the disregard that all three poets—William Vaughan Moody, Edwin Arlington Robinson, and Ridgely Torrence—shared for Walt Whitman's manifesto to young American poets to escape tradition, "to welcome with open arms everything that exists, simply because it exists, extracting from the baldest prose the divine essence of poetry." All three, instead of being revolutionary, were "born aristocrats in literature, careful of form, and fastidious to a fault in their choice of language."

Moody, in whom she heard the spirit of Swinburne, did not seem to be a product of America. In most of his poems his *cri du coeur* was "drowned by the music of an overfull orchestra." She found his best work to be his lyrical drama, *The Firebringer* and *The Masque of Judgment,* in which, thanks to his discipleship to the Greek tragedians, of whom Euripides was the most honored, he masterfully blended the old religions and the new metaphysics. His Americanism had two phases: his reaction against "the dominion of material immensities," and his hope that in time America would reconcile the breach between nature and spirit.

The art of Robinson, in whom she heard the spirit of Browning, she read as a union of a dramatic view with a lyrical mood. She thought his "The Night Before" worthy of standing beside Browning's "A Soul's Tragedy" and Meredith's "Modern Love." His style was solid, somber, gray on gray, marred by few purple patches.

She felt that Ridgely Torrence had not yet found himself, and she saw in *El Dorado* the faults of youth: fluency, feverishness, and audacity; its effect was spectacular rather than orchestral; its characters concealed their souls under wreaths of flowerlike imagery.

"George Meredith" appeared first in the black-bordered pages of the *Author* on June 1, 1909, a fortnight after Meredith's death, and it was also printed in the *Outlook* for June 19. It is both a point-by-point refutation directed at Meredith's unfavoring critics and a positive statement of his qualities. May Sinclair faults him for his weak sense of a specific locality. She places him as one reacting against the simultaneous counterpressures of Victorian realism and Victorian sentiment. He was the first to see that sentiment, not conscience, made a coward of the novelist; that sentimentalism was the flower of sensuality and the subtle source of spiritual corruption. He recognized that sentiment was the mother of all shams and hypocrisies, and the nurse of monstrous illusions. In *Diana of the Crossways* he declared himself prophet of the Real, of truth without sham. May Sinclair accepted his definition of fiction as "the summary of actual life, the within and the without of us."

His poems sprang from his joy in nature, in the splendid energies of life. Meredith's overwhelming personality often comes between his creations and his readers, but the man, we learn, is admirable, because he is fearless and passionately sincere. He believed that philosophy, meaning heuristic brain-stuff, was the cure for the sickliness of a sentimental world.

For Meredith the natural love of men and women was the sanest and most sacred of all things. Tragedy came to men and women only when they betrayed nature's immanent deity. He knew and dared to tell the whole truth about a woman.

May Sinclair found him to be great as a dramatist and as a psychologist, and therefore as a novelist. And however prominent the philosopher might be, the novelist was always in command in the novels. She was certain that Meredith would live, and be rediscovered for his incomparable vitality.

Critic of the Brontës

May Sinclair knew Charlotte and Emily Jane Brontë's secret world of lonely, suppressed passion, and their longing for the strong man whose mind would mate with their minds; and she had their superbly disciplined intellect. Her rapport with Anne was weaker. Ernest Rhys could have made no wiser choice than when he invited her to write the introductions of the Brontë novels, with the exception of *Agnes Grey,* for Everyman's Library.

Her first introduction, appearing in September, 1907, was to *Wuthering Heights*. It relied upon a consideration of Emily Jane's poems to uncover the secrets of the novelist, which were the secrets of her critic too. Critic and novelist differed most radically in that Emily was apparently obsessed by a longing for death.

May Sinclair interpreted the frustration that tortured Catherine Earnshaw, over her dilemma of having willed the life of the spirit with Edgar Linton without having been able to kill the passion of her body for Heathcliff, as being less of the flesh than of the spirit. She found joy in Emily's freedom from rhetoric, from the symbols and abstractions that came natural to Charlotte; in Emily's fresh concreteness, in the calm phrasing of the intense and clean passion that governed the lives of her principals.

In February, 1908, Everyman's Library issued two more Brontë titles. May Sinclair saw *Jane Eyre* to be without a traceable descent, its author's style shaped by no single dominating influence, her mind original in its views. In it Charlotte Brontë broke with certain proprieties and conventions of contemporary society and its imaginative literature: that a governess must know and keep to her place, a plain woman must accept her plainness as a final bar to passion, a beautiful woman must be socially magnetic, and that no woman dared to be awakened to the fullness of her womanhood by anyone but her husband. She thought that perhaps the trials that a governess remembered had left with Charlotte both a resentment against the beautiful idle woman and a callousness to the charm of other people's children. It was Charlotte's innocence of the stage that made it hard for her to control her tendency to be melodramatic, and it was innocence of life that made her treatment of fierce animal passion so brutal, so unconvincing. Her style had sometimes "the Teutonic quality of loaded power, of almost violent symbolism. Image follows upon image, and sentiment rushes in where passion fears to tread."

May Sinclair abhorred the zeal of biographers in pressing the identification of originals in life upon their fictional shadows, and insisted that "the genius has little need of actual experience as the man in the street understands it." She pointed to the new mood in comic courtship that emanates from the early scenes of teasing in which Jane and Rochester indulge, and appreciated the power that Charlotte, like her sister, manifested in creating the atmosphere of a place: "Not even Emily, whose style is sinless, excels her in passages of sheer description." The unique greatness of the book was not established by any test of thoroughgoing realism, but by the test of the quality of its passion. She judged Charlotte to be the first English novelist to handle the real thing in its essential purity: "In Charlotte Brontë's hands passion becomes a thing of strange innocences and tendernesses and terrors, rejoicing in service and the sacrifice of self. A thing superbly unaware of animal instinct; a profound and tragic thing that bears at its heart the prescience of suffering and of death."

Shirley also came out in February. May Sinclair suggested three causes of the twilight confusion in the novel: the deaths of Branwell, Emily, and Anne; the adverse criticism of *Jane Eyre* for its melodrama and for its defiance of the conventions; and the self-criticism with which Charlotte tried to correct her faults.

Charlotte wanted to reach greatness through realism, but her temperament was in conflict with the current demand for realism, and the conflict made her excessively self-conscious and restrained, and forced the poetry, with its passionate rhythm and exuberant imagery, out of her writing. Her greater degree of simple realism in this novel was still subject to the "old recurrent trick of the five adjectives on a string of commas." When the poetry came back toward the end of the book it was tainted with the rhetoric of the French poets before Verlaine, which M. Heger had imposed upon her: "Emily threw it off; she told M. Heger plainly that she saw 'no benefit to be derived' from his method. If only Charlotte could have done the same." In its content

Shirley showed an advance over *Jane Eyre*. Charlotte seemed eager to prove that she knew there were other things besides passion in which she was interested: business, labor troubles, and the position of women. Shirley Keeldar, a charming and competent businesswoman, is the first such figure in English literature, and as startlingly original as Jane Eyre: "She is the sister of Meredith's women, of Cecelia Hackett, and Diana and Carinthia Jane." Shirley's foil was Caroline Helstone, whom Charlotte deliberately punishes for the sins of which Jane has been accused. Charlotte remained under the spell of the masterful and arbitrary man; Rochester reappeared in elements of Helstone, Yorke, and Robert and Louis Moore. In her final judgment May Sinclair granted *Shirley* no higher rating than "a collection of glorious, palpitating fragments."

Mrs. Gaskell's *The Life of Charlotte Brontë* came out in June, 1908. May Sinclair felt that Mrs. Gaskell had made a major faulty decision when she accepted the stories about Branwell's immorality and made of Branwell the demoralizing influence upon Charlotte, the cause of the coarseness that she admitted, without any defense, spoiled *Jane Eyre*. She gave the highest praise to Mrs. Gaskell's thorough and delicate portrayal of the home life of the Brontës, her picture of Haworth, of the churchyard, "terribly full of upright tombstones," and of the parsonage at which no one ever called. It was impossible to get at the life of a great woman without understanding her family, because a woman's life is inseparable from her family, and her work is often inexplicable without her family's being taken into full account. This Mrs. Gaskell understood. May Sinclair's analytic perception picked out of the biography the foreknowledge of destiny in Charlotte's dream life; Charlotte's recurrent dream of holding in her arms a child whose cries she cannot still seems a symbolic augury of her fate to die in childbirth. The biography was a classic, "great with the greatness and completeness of fulfilled tragedy."

Villette appeared in the series in March, 1909. May Sinclair established three main views: that Emily, through her *Wuthering Heights,* was the most liberating influence upon Charlotte; that *Villette* is an imagined, not a journalized, creation; and that it is the first in the history of the analytical novel in English. May Sinclair destroyed Clement Shorter's theory of the biographical sources of *Villette* on the bases that it ignored the real mystery of imaginative creation, and that the biographical argument, as physical and psychological evidence proved, was only wishful conjecture. It was a refutation that Fannie Elizabeth Ratchford was to reinforce in her *The Brontës' Web of Childhood.*

May Sinclair named the moment of illumination that liberated in Charlotte the passion that is created as such an intensely personal experience in *Villette* to have come not in Brussels, from M. Heger, but in Haworth, from Charlotte's surprised reading of *Wuthering Heights*. The protracted cry of the agony of longing and frustration that comes from Lucy's heart "was a new voice in literature," the revelation of all that mid-Victorian reticence sought to hide. May Sinclair thought Lucy Snowe to be the most finished and psychologically unerring portrait that Charlotte Brontë ever drew; "the germ of the real" that gave her life being an innocent natural germ that came from within herself. With every book Charlotte advanced toward the "searching analytic light" that was to shine in Meredith and glare in Henry James. *Villette* was the first novel to give to psychological analysis the place it holds in the English novel.

The Everyman series published *The Professor* in February, 1910. Two thirds of its introductory essay was quoted from the introduction to *Villette,* in which it was used to disprove Clement Shorter's case and to support May Sinclair's. The novel was interpreted as evidence of Charlotte's original intention to be a quiet realist, suppressing the passionate and poetic tumult that throbbed in her imagination. The construction is the best in the three books, the style free from exaggerated and strained metaphor, its descriptive powers already formidable, its touch delicate, and its tone comparatively serene and idyllic. But it lacks the passion that was Charlotte's truest mood.

I wish that May Sinclair had commented on Charlotte's error in disguising a woman's nature inside a man's body and forcing male experiences upon that nature. I agree that *Wuthering Heights* freed Charlotte: from the fear of being feminine.

The last of the Brontë novels to be published in the series, *The Tenant of Wildfell Hall*, did not appear until April, 1914, and its study of an alcoholic was to rasp May Sinclair's feelings to a unique impatience with Anne Brontë. But her criticism of Charlotte and Emily seems to me the most perceptive of all Brontë studies.

Philosophical Textuary

Thoughts from Goethe is a booklet of aphorisms that the Hampstead bookseller Sydney C. Mayle published in August, 1905, in the Priory Press series. It is thirty-one pages of octavo (4⅛ x 7¼ inches), with an Introductory Note signed by "M. S.," which informs us that a few selections were taken from Professor Blackie's *Wisdom of Goethe*, from Professor Huxley's translation of Goethe's *Essay on Nature*, and from Carlyle's translation of *Wilhelm Meister*, and that the rest of the booklet was either originally translated or revised from existing translations, mostly of the *Conversations With Eckermann*. May Sinclair (For Richard Garnett's letters identify her as the compiler) ended her introduction by explaining, "I have chosen chiefly those 'Sayings' which show him in his speculative mood, as the man who, like Plato's ideal philosopher, was 'forever longing after the Whole of things, both human and divine.'"

During the year in which Janet Hogarth (later Mrs. W. L. Courtney) taught at Cheltenham Ladies College, 1889–1890,[1] she met May Sinclair, and learned that her "only loves were Plato and Goethe."[2] Since she had recently won a First Class in Philosophy at Oxford,[3] Miss Hogarth could be relied upon to appraise her friend's intellectual idols. Apart from the two poems on Goethe that were included in her *Essays in Verse*, the aphorisms in this booklet are the only direct evidence of Goethe's conducting to her some of the mystical force that we hypothecate as "formative influence." The pamphlet records ideas that she held to be worthwhile because they seemed true to her, and ideas that she respected because Goethe believed them to be true. They are unsystematic ideas about the nature of religion, of God, of nature, and of art, and the relationships of both artist and art to the universe and the mystery of its unity. Here are a few samplings of the ideas, in the most compressed form, to suggest the mood of the book and perhaps the materials of the conceptual foundation on which May Sinclair built her life as a writer and her imagined world:

Art rests upon a kind of religious sense, a deep seriousness.

The source of all evils in our modern literature is lack of character in individual scholars, writers, and critics.

The classic is sound, and the romantic sick. The antique is classic not because it is antique, but because it is strong, fresh, joyous, and sound.

What does originality mean? As soon as we are born the world begins to work upon us, and so it goes on to the end. What can we call our own except energy, strength, and will.

In art and poetry personal genius is everything. In the great work the great person is always present as the great factor. To appreciate the presence of a great somebody in any work of genius, the critic must himself be a somebody. A work of art will always be defective

---

1. Letter, Miss Mary Sager, Secretary of the Guild, January 22, 1963.
2. Janet E. Courtney, *The Women of My Time* (London: Lovat Dickson, 1934), p. 52.
3. Letter, Miss Mary Sager, November 8, 1962.

when any of the functions that go to make a complete man have been absent from its production.

It is with talents as with virtues; one must love them for their own sake, or utterly renounce them.

Everything that gives us intellectual freedom without self-mastery is disastrous.

The fabric of our life is formed of necessity and chance. Man's reason stands between them, and may rule them both.

Freedom consists not in refusing to recognize anything above us, but in reverencing what is above us. By reverencing it, we raise ourselves to it. By recognizing the higher thing we manifest that we bear it within ourselves.

One must *be* something in order to *do* something.

There is some higher influence, some moral order, that favors the steadfast, the active, the constant, the controlled and controlling, the human, the devout.

It is foolish to deplore earth's limitations. What we are here for is to give permanence to the perishing.

It is by the power of his "must" that a man shows what is in him. Any fool can live by caprice.

Our whole art consists in giving up our life that we may live.

Strictly speaking, everything depends on the feelings. Where they are, the thoughts are also.

Ingratitude is always weakness of a kind. I have never known men of ability who were ungrateful.

First and last, what we require of genius is love of truth.

Productiveness of the highest kind, great thought, remarkable discovery, are not in man's powers, but unexpected gifts from above, the pure efflux of divine grace, the *daimon,* or the genius of life which does with man what it pleases. Man is an instrument in the higher government of the world, a vessel found worthy to receive divine influence.

The end of all living is life.

Verse

Old verses were published in a table book, *The Hampstead Annual 1902,* and in *The Divine Fire.* The only new verse published in this "undecade" was a paraphrase, "Fragment of a Hymn to Apollo," which appeared in *Literature,* the Saturday journal edited by H. D. Traill, on February 10, 1900, and reprinted in *The Cheltenham Ladies College Magazine* for Autumn, 1901. The Greek text, arranged by Dr.

A. Thierfeld from an inscription found on a stone at Delphi in 1893, was printed in a parallel column with the paraphrase, which was spaced into three stanzas of 21, 19, and 14 lines. May Sinclair's management of the meter can be enjoyed at its best, I think, in stanza II.

> Hail to thee, mighty
> City of Athens!
> She the unconquered,
> She in her armour
> Bucklered and girded,
> Tritogeneia,
> Holds thee in safety,
> Fenced with th'inviolate
> Bound of thy plain.
> Kindle, Hephaestus,
> Flame for thine altar,
> Holy the offering,
> Holy the fire!
> Then shall young bullocks
> Burn, and the fragrant
> Orient incense,
> Writhing and soaring,
> Wreathe the immortal
>   Olympian hall.

During this "undecade," May Sinclair rose in stature not only in the novel, but in every other major form of writing that she tried: the short story, criticism of her contemporaries, and criticism of the Brontës.

14

The Novels: 1911-1920

The *English Review* had already published a short story of the occult in 1911 before it printed complete in May, 1912, the psychical romance *The Flaw in the Crystal*.

The frame pattern is a love story of anguished platonic lovers, a spinster, Agatha Verrall, and a married man, Rodney Lanyon, whose wife, Bella, has suffered for some years of their ten of married life from crazily jangled nerves. Agatha and Rodney have met on weekends in a quiet village in Bucks, fifteen miles from London, she to rest from too intense a sympathy for Rodney, he to get away from his wife. In Sarratt End, Agatha learns of her psychic power to heal herself, and after she is well she uses it from a distance to heal Bella, so that Rodney may be well too.

The inner story is a complex design of psychiatric, psychic, and mystical significances, some of whose lines of motive could be translated into the psychoanalytical terms of identification and assimilation. It is set going when a friend of Agatha's, Milly Powell, begs her to help her husband, whom she has brought to Sarratt End. Harding Powell is insane, shrinking in darkened rooms, terrified of life. Agatha agrees to help, and using her telepsychic powers, brings rest and sanity to the insane man. Her concentration on Powell so weakens her communion with Rodney that he stays away, and Powell's exorcised evil complex seeks out Agatha's weakened mind to make it its unresisting host. While she is possessed, as it were, by Powell's evil complex, she experiences a mystical vision, outdoors, of the evil of the earth, and is terrified by it.

The attack upon her by Powell's evil element helps to force out from under its cover of a platonic sympathy with Rodney Lanyon her physical longing for him. The Spirit with which she holds a dialogue teaches her that the power to heal—the self or other selves—requires a human vessel that is strong and flawless as crystal, and that it is flawless only when it holds no selfish desire, no physical longing for love. Agatha battles Powell's evil complex from the fear that if she is overcome by it, it will overcome Rodney too. So she realizes that her fear is the result of her hidden love. She can become serene and undefeatable only by giving up the cause of her fear. Outer and inner stories are joined when Rodney visits Agatha again. Bella is cured, and he is happy. But the sight of Agatha's exhaustion moves him to such a sympathy for her that he begs for her love in a passionate union. Agatha holds out against him and against her own powerful longing for him, and through her willing the sacrifice of a desired love, she makes herself strong again.

Evelyn Underhill, as she read the manuscript, could not understand why, after Harding Powell relapsed, Agatha would not apply her healing art once more. The reasons are that Agatha has discovered her healing power to come from her personal, not from a universal, spirit; and that she would be wasting it to help a nature that she has discovered to be evil in reality, a spurner of the divine. She therefore turns back to Milly the responsibility of building up her husband's mental health. Rodney, happy now as a husband, and reconciled to Agatha's goodness, will help get the best medical attention for Powell.

The method by which the will to heal can tap its spiritual resources is developed with plausible realism. It prescribes a state of lowered sensation and of sinking into a visualized darkness whose serenity removes the walls that normally defend the self and allows the will to draw upon its psychic power.[1] May Sinclair's requested letter in the *New York Times* and the letter of Dr. James H. Hyslop are signs of the interest that her handling of psychic materials roused at the time.

Agatha Verrall is kin to Jane Holland when her mind is read for her restraint toward Rodney Lanyon: "To have tried to get at him would have been, for Agatha, the last treachery, the last indecency."[2]

A turn of style that was to become characteristic of May Sinclair is her exercise of both the discipline of logic and of the Anglo-Saxon tradition of coupling negatives: "She was never not prepared."[3] Characteristic is her seeing the mouth as an image of wings: "The corners

---

1. *The Flaw in the Crystal* (New York: Dutton, 1912) , p. 159.
2. *Ibid.*, p. 7.
3. *Ibid.*, p. 5.

of her eyes and of her beautiful mouth were lifted; as if by—he could find no other word for the things he meant but wings."[4]

The book as a whole is written like a sustained poem, in the taut musical style of a composition whose every beat is being counted, its tempo swift for narrative eagerness, and slow for a dreamy mood.

It is *not* the first novel to describe a psychic experience, in which the healing of mental distress is of importance, in which a repressed emotion is brought out of the unconscious under the stress of a painful situation and is recognised as the cause of the trouble, and in which the principal woman character renounces a love that would violate the conventional morality, which her conscience respects. It *is* the first novel in which May Sinclair describes a woman in love with a married man.

The Combined Maze, a realistic novel of the psychological-psychoanalytical genre appearing in February, 1913, has compassionateness, fine artistry, and an original design relating fresh discoveries in human conduct. The germ of the story was already forecast in *The Creators,* when the novel about a suburban clerk possessed Jane Holland's imagination so compellingly that it drove away the deep pain that Tanqueray's marriage caused her: "She saw his Girl, the Girl he inevitably would have. She was present at the mingling of that blond soul with the dark flesh and blood of the Girl. She saw it all; the Innocence of Hambleby; the Marriage of Hambleby; the Torture and subsequent Deterioration of Hambleby; and, emerging in a sort of triumph, the indestructible Decency of Hambleby."[5]

The Combined Maze weaves together three life stories: the story of a decent chivalrous clerk in a furniture dealer's in Oxford Street, Ranny Ransome, who wrecks his chance at happiness on an episode of sexual madness; the story of a bookkeeper at a draper's in Oxford Street, Winny Dymond, a self-disciplining woman of shrewd insight and maternal protectiveness, whose decency costs her the man she loves; and the story of a Hertfordshire farmer's daughter, Violet Usher, who comes to work in gay, man-crowded London, a sexually greedy bitch who does not want the marriage and children that her body is splendidly equipped to cope with.

The novel is set mainly in Marylebone and Wandsworth, and calendared from the spring of 1902 to September, 1912. The title refers to a Corybantic gymnastic dance performed by men and women of the London Polytechnic Institute in Marylebone. It expresses joy in the courting impulse, the dancers pairing, intersecting, circling, wheeling,

---

4. *Ibid.,* p. 15. See also p. 184.
5. *The Creators: A Comedy* (New York: Century Co., 1910), p. 112.

serpentining, meeting, whirling, parting, running all the while to symbolize the energetic Wheel of Life. It is a wholesome design, a reminder that passion is good if it is kept within restraint. But actual life has no such orderliness. It sweeps together men and women who do not bear an equal responsibility for keeping the discipline of the whole to which the members of the Polytechnic Institute submit themselves. Ranny and Winny are members of the Institute and disciplined members of the team. Violet is only a spectator whose lust resents discipline.

The design, which emanates from Ranny Ransome, develops the forces of heredity, association, and suggestion that cause Ranny to fall into the trap of Violet's sexuality. The deepest source of his weakness is the emotional instability that he has inherited from his father, a pharmaceutical chemist and a chronic, furtive alcoholic. At sixteen Ranny refused to work for his father and became a clerk in a furniture warehouse. He rebelled against his father's flabbiness by developing a fine athlete's body at the Polytechnic. From his mother he inherits a romantic ideal of decency and honor, and he loves his mother with an intense desire to be the consoling substitute for the disappointing father whom Mrs. Ransome religiously protects with the illusion that he suffers from headaches, and is a good man, not an irritable drunkard. His mother's sentimental decency is the heritage in chivalry that binds him to the woman who has trapped him, and so is an almost equal cause of his ruin, although it is also the trait that the woman who loves him loves most in him.

The sequence of unconscious suggestion is convincingly drawn. Ranny, at twenty-three, kisses his mother, his face in the nape of her neck, and because she apparently uses a violet-scented soap or a violet perfume, he asks her, " 'Do you bury yourself in violets all night, or what?' "[6] As she strokes his hair, she remonstrates with him, " 'If you had a sweetheart, Ran, you'd leave off makin' a fool of your old mother.' "[7] He remembers that he has never kissed the seventeen-year-old gymnast, Winny, whom he has come to regard with a patronizing tenderness for her grace on the parallel bars and in the dances, and he buys a sachet of violets as a birthday gift for her. The word Violet is embroidered on the white satin cover. But he never gives it to her out of fear of the consequences of getting serious with her on a salary of eight pounds a month. His suppression toward Winny leaves him free for a sexually experienced farmgirl, Violet, an assistant in the draper's shop where Winny works, and whose name is reinforced in its sugges-

6. *The Combined Maze* (New York: Harper, 1913) , p. 56.
7. *Ibid.*, p. 57.

tion by her use of violet perfume on her clothes and her hair. The transfer of affection from his mother to Winny to Violet is complete, except that Violet can draw only the sexual phase of it from Ranny, because it is the only phase of affection that she knows. The violets theme represents only one of the carefully drawn paths of neural force and chance with which May Sinclair tells the story of a ruinous marriage.

The most scrupulous accounting of motives for decisive actions and the clinching of meaning through explained insight is supported by an extraordinarily subtle use of artistic foreshadowing such as even Hardy did not surpass in his *Tess*. There are many simple but effective judgments of technique involving time and internal balance. Again, character description obtains elemental clues from the mouth: from the mouths of Violet; Leonard Mercier, her lover; Ranny; the curate who preaches against lust; and Winny.

The style reaches beyond its habit of classical refinement to include the tone of simple, uncultured life. The people speak their natural colloqualisms and, when it describes them, the style absorbs the imagery with which they speak and think. May Sinclair's natural writing discipline aimed at the sharp, uniquely perceptive image. Clarity and uniqueness of impression presuppose subtle analysis, but colloquial speech and idiom, however essential they are for naturalness and the truthful ring, are not the ultimate tools for these effects. So, she was happy when she could find a gentle way of expressing a coarse fact: the solicitations of streetwalkers, which Ranny ignores, she calls "salutations of the night."[8] She was happy too when a fresh image soared out of her creativity: "the gas-stove, furred with rust."[9] She was reading and thinking Freud and Jung and talking over psychoanalysis with Dr. Jessie Murray, and probably studying much other psychological literature that was being published by the distinguished staff of the Medico-Psychological Clinic, and yet her style was not pockmarked by her reading. "Field of vision" is the only psychological term I detected, and that should not be objectionable to the lettered ear. She guarded herself against cant when she phrased Ronny's unconscious response to the stress on their bodies that their uniforms gave to the women gymnasts: "He was not aware how aware he was of their coming, nor how his heart thumped and throbbed and his nerves trembled at the tramp, tramp of their feet along the floor."[10]

The fair amount of humor tends to vanish from memory, as does the

8. *Ibid.,* p. 4.
9. *Ibid.,* p. 204.
10. *Ibid.,* p. 10.

great amount of it in Hardy, because it is not tightly bound to the main theme, but a turning of the leaves brings it back. Poetry sounds through the whole novel in alternations of outer and inner song. Symbolism appears dramatic and unforced.

May Sinclair's feeling, perhaps even her conviction, in this novel of what is right conduct for a woman in love is expressed in Winny's attempts to keep Violet and Ranny together, and her approving Ranny's taking Violet back after her escapades. The woman does right to submit to the loss of a love that she craves, to renounce every impulse of the will to challenge a decision that has come from the rule of honor. There is plenty of ironic exposure of the sentimental illusion, but the sacrifices of their happiness that Ranny and Winny make are sacred offerings, expressions of the need of the soul, exempt from any ironic smile.

A minor theme in this year of the publication of a better-known but not a better novel, *Sons and Lovers,* is the jealousy that Mrs. Ransome feels when Ranny announces that he is now financially able to divorce Violet and marry Winny. Violet has not robbed her of a son. But Winny "was so made as to be all in all to him, so made as to draw him to her all in all. . . . A mother Winny was and would be to him far more than if she had used her motherhood to bear him children."[11]

There are signs of the influence of other writers in this book, the most important one, I suspect, originating in the two Clayhanger novels. Ranny holds an attitude toward a woman that is new in May Sinclair's novels; he feels toward Violet as Edwin Clayhanger feels toward Hilda Lessways, the sense of a certain woman's being a mystery to which he must yield for his destiny of magical romance. And there is a new concern for an inner ecstasy beneath the outer bustling energy of a woman in love: Winny's secret devotion to Ranny, his home, and his children. Ranny's relationship to his family, his humorous penetration into the illusion-making of his uncle and aunt, read like miming of Arnold Bennett.

With the writing of this novel May Sinclair also appears to have adopted a method of systematic research for material that had not already come to her as chance experience. The most intimate personal confession is one ascribed to Winny. Ranny has said to her, " 'To look at you anyone would say you'd nursed a baby all your life!' " To which the author adds, "So she had—in fancy and in dreams."[12]

The Three Sisters (1914), a dramatic psychological-psychoanalytical novel, is set in the cluster of villages in the area of Swaledale and

11. *Ibid.,* pp. 351–52.
12. *Ibid.,* p. 174. Florence Bartrop.

Arkengarthdale in Yorkshire that May Sinclair came to love during her stays in Reeth. The nine years of the story are not dated; in the first year the doctor drives a trap, in the last year he drives an automobile. Her intensive study of the Brontës during the years just before she began on this novel must have inspired both the novel and the setting. Wisely, she picked a fresh region, far to the north of Haworth, and far from the Hull that she visited to see her brother William's family.

The Three Sisters bears no sign of imitating a single trait of the Brontës. The three daughters of the vicar are not the three Brontë sisters. The closest borrowing from Brontëan actuality is the Reverend Cartaret, the vicar who has fathered three sturdy daughters of contrasting personalities, gone through two bereavements, and wedded a third wife with high social connections and a tough will to live, who has deserted him and his intolerable virility, to take refuge among amiable friends in London. The vicar has become a frustrated demon, powered with the life force that had once emanated from the young farmer-blacksmith genius whom Cambridge had transubstantiated into a clergyman. Perhaps the final syllable of the name of Dr. Steven Rowcliffe should be added as a Brontë echo.

The several dramas in the novel develop from the vicar's having taken his family from a pleasant southern seaside town to exile in the harsh Yorkshire village of Garth, because his youngest daughter Alice, 23, had scandalously run after a man. He had made the move to punish the daughter who exposed so indecently the heredity that she owed to her father. The oldest daughter, Mary, is 27, and the middle daughter is Gwendolen. There is only one eligible male in the vicinity, young Dr. Rowcliffe, a native son who left a hospital practice in Leeds to serve his own people. The plot is developed with the skill of Jane Austen, and its moves are traced to psychoanalytic depths.

Alice's determined-upon illness gains its effect, to cause Dr. Rowcliffe to call. The doctor begins his study of the family with a perceptive mind. He sees that motherhood would cure Alice. He loves Gwendolen for her fine intellect, and her character for its evident health and integrity. He regards Mary as a smiling fraud, an actress playing to spectators. Gwendolen's leaving for London to give up her own desire for Steven so that Alice can have him gives the sly Mary her chance to play the role of perfect prospective wife, and Steven is trapped by the woman whose nature he had read. After marriage Mary does not give up her study of Steven, to make him a prisoner of habit in the comforts with which she cradles him. His awakening out of his domestic torpor does not amount to anything, for he has lost the will to go back to Leeds to resume his research, even with Gwendolen's help.

Alice has her need satisfied by the lusty young farmer Jim Greatorex, whom she marries after she is pregnant. She becomes a contented mother, and transforms Jim into a very tender husband.

All six characters act out the dramatic events that throb with vitality. Gwendolen, the most complicated, is an unacknowledged romantic. She fears becoming vulnerable to Steven's physical magnetism, like Alice the hysterical man-hunter, and she needs to exalt Steven as a doctor who is willing to sacrifice his life for any patient before she can let her admiration go out to him. But sacrifice is her standard, not only for others; and it is the command that she obeys herself when she leaves Garth to give Alice her chance at the only marriage she can think of. She is not entirely unperceptive of Steven's weakness of character; she can see that he does not really want to marry an intellectual woman.

Steven's strength is his intellect. His weakness lies in the ego, which depends on a woman's admiration, and in his will.

Jim Greatorex, lusty as a bull, can distinguish between the relieving and the fulfilling experiences of passion, and between the sentimental and the real relationship. He can be satisfied only by the real and the fulfilling. Having insight into his own feelings, he can read the feelings of others. Distant as he is from Gwendolen in matters of the intellect, he is close to her in his perception of real feelings. He is the only one at the end who sees, or cares, how alone Gwendolen is, and who understands that her suffering from disappointment is the secret of her intense joy in the flowering thorn on Greffington Edge.

The novel is so rich in its materials that it can be read in a number of ways. It is a family novel, whose parent-vicar visits upon his daughters the punishment for having desires that he has bequeathed to them. The poetic novel tells the story of Gwendolen's frustrated love for an unworthy man and her compensation in a heightened perception of beauty in nature.

The psychological-psychoanalytical novel is the most substantial. Conscious thoughts and insights into the unconscious are given an equal artistry of representation. Jim Greatorex acts as intuitive analyst when he convinces Alice that she is afraid to leave her home and come with him, not from fear of him, but from the greater fear of her father.[13] When Alice hears of her father's stroke, she suffers agony from the fear that she has caused his certain death, or his loss of mind. The birth of her child dispels her fear, for the fear from which she has suffered was a substitute for a composite of fears that she could not face and bear her child too: "So, without Ally being in the least aware

---

13. *The Three Sisters* (New York: Macmillan, 1914), p. 288.

of it, Ally's mind, struggling toward sanity, fabricated one enormous fear, the fear of her father's death, a fear that she could own and face, and set it up in place of the secret and dangerous thing which was the fear of life itself."[14] Only in the passage that tells what unconscious influence has undone his conscious reading of Mary's insincerity—the red-haired nurse in the hospital at Leeds, the buried image of Mary's own red, well-burnished hair—does May Sinclair use such cant words as *inhibitions, suggestions,* and *association.*[15] In Leeds, Rowcliffe had enjoyed the nurse's admiration, but ambition had fended it off. There is no cant, however, in the account of Rowcliffe's conscious resentment against Mary for having stolen him from Gwendolen, a mask for his unconscious boredom with her.[16] May Sinclair dramatizes Rowcliffe's boredom in an unconsciously expressive movement of the kind that she was to elaborate in her next novel: "He crossed his legs and the tilted foot kicked out, urged by a hidden savagery. The clicking of Mary's needles maddened him."[17]

The novel moves to a beat, from its opening scene, creating the gray stone village of Garth and its vicarage standing above the churchyard, to its last scene, inside the vicarage, where the vicar and Gwendolen await the ten o'clock prayers from which two of the previous captives have escaped. The pointillism that was not noticed until *Mary Olivier* makes inconspicuous appearances in short chapters, in broadly spaced sections within the chapters, in paragraphs of a single sentence, and even in the separation of the last paragraph in a chapter. The spacing helps to keep the musical beat going.

To balance the pointillism, a fresh care knits successive chapters together, with continuances, repetitions, similar or contrasting images, to create such an impression of continuous movement as one may enjoy in watching a perfectly choreographed and perfectly performed ballet. The concentration is so intent on the drama as image and as reality that the linking devices are felt only subliminally and detected only in a special reading for technical means. Each chapter is ended with a neat appropriateness that is only one detail in May Sinclair's striving for perfection as an artist. The style has her sensitive, vivid simplicity. Beautiful is the descriptive passage that follows a spectator's eye-movements over the interior of the schoolhouse on the concert night,[18] and newly born is the image of teary eyes: "her eyelashes were parted and gathered into little wet points."[19]

---

14. *Ibid.,* p. 294.
15. *Ibid.,* p. 242.
16. *Ibid.,* pp. 314–15.
17. *Ibid.,* p. 314.
18. *Ibid.,* p. 120.
19. *Ibid.,* p. 15.

Most often the moments of poetry are little services in worship of a place; their subjects, the grayness of Garth village,[20] the early moonlight on the village of Morfe,[21] thorn trees flowering in the moonlight of Greffington Edge.[22] The dialogue is peeled of all excess; it is as pure as art can represent an external movement between minds. Time is a measure of happiness during the visits of Dr. Rowcliffe; a symbol of power, the vicar's; and a symbol of the failure of power. The prayers time, ten o'clock every evening, which flowing Time faithfully serves to the vicar as a symbol of his power as clergyman, father, and warden, gives way, after his stroke, to a clock moved by his helplessness and a clockface marked in medicine time, bedtime, and by the hours of his various other needs.[23]

It is when we study the elemental character themes striating this novel that we realize how personal a revelation this novel is. Much of that revelation is contained in Gwendolen: "She took to metaphysics as you take to dram-drinking. She must have strong, heavy stuff that drugged her brain. And when she found that she could trust her intellect she set it deliberately to fight her passion."[24] Alice plays the music that May Sinclair had played and kept to the end: the Sonata *Pathétique,* and the *Grand Polonaise.*

In a penciled draft of a note for Marc Logé, May Sinclair identified Morfe and Rathdale as Reeth, and Garth and Garthdale as Langthwaite in Arkengarthdale. Dr. William C. Speirs recognized the main setting as the Arkengarthdale where he had practiced for fifty-six years, and Greffington Edge as in reality Fremington Edge.[25] Reyburn is Richmond, about eleven miles from Reeth.

May Sinclair made two radical adjustments for the attack on *Tasker Jevons: The Real Story* (1916; the American title became *The Belfry*). The first was inventing a character to be her narrator and stylist; the second was that the narrator is a man. The mood is as realistic as the subtitle says; the result is a superb heroic comedy, rich in ironic effects.

Tasker Jevons is a new version of *The Divine Fire* brought strictly up-to-date. The romantic orthodoxy of *The Divine Fire* made the poet's genius and his love interdependent. The modern realistic version shows the writer's genius, after his first short book, to be autonomous. *Tasker Jevons* updates *The Divine Fire* in another regard: Jevons can not only make beauty, but he can also market it very profitably. As a writer whose accurately calculated practicality manages his literary

20. *Ibid.,* pp. 1–2.
21. *Ibid.,* pp. 58–59.
22. *Ibid.,* pp. 320–21, 388.
23. *Ibid.,* p. 305.
24. *Ibid.,* pp. 351–52.
25. Letter, July 5, 1964.

genius to success, Tasker Jevons is May Sinclair's version of Gissing's Jasper Milvain and of Bennett's farcical Henry Shakespeare Knight.

Prospectively, the novel shows May Sinclair verging on the family novel whose major theme will be the conflict between the family and a rebellious daughter. Here the family setting and the daughter are subordinate to the heroic comedy of Tasker Jevons. In the next novel the family was to fill out to the proportions of a major interest, the rebellious daughter still being held to a co-principal role, as a preparation for the next character novel.

Tasker Jevons is the story of the marriage of a novelist genius, James Tasker Jevons, who needs to escape from memories of his father's cruelty and from the deadly dullness of his father's office, a registry of births, marriages, and deaths in a parish in Hertfordshire; and a woman of society, Viola Thesiger, who needs, except for her love for her soldier-brother Reggie, to break out of the stifling family respectability of Canterbury close, and who, venerating the written word, chooses the literary genius with a vulgar heredity as her hero. Ironic is Jimmy's wanting, above everything else in the world, to be accepted by the graciously snobbish family whom Viola's nerves cannot endure.

The heroic comedy shows us Tasker Jevons uniting his two careers, one as a writer and public figure, the other as husband and social aspirant. He plans his achievement of greatness as a writer step by step, allowing each step forward its calculated time for completion. His first novel will win attention by being deliberately nasty. His second will be a penitential obeisance of wanting to please. The third will be the grand attack, the kind of book he really will enjoy doing. It would be his best book and create a taste that he could enjoy satisfying over and over. His plan succeeds, his third novel wins the treasured American market, and Jevons expands his business of writing to do every kind there is, to become "an engineer of literature."[26]

Once he can buy whatever his vulgar tastes choose—whether it be a white car trimmed in black, or a house in Mayfair furnished like a Tudor baronial hall—and exhaustion from his strenuous writing relaxes the inhibitions on his vulgarity, Viola's nerves find marriage with Jimmy unendurable. Although she can care for no one but Jimmy, his vulgarities become too much for her social sensibilities, and she leaves him.

When the war breaks out, Jimmy tries to enlist; his leaky heart causes his rejection for regular service. He refuses to become a war correspondent; he wants to be a doer. At last he is accepted by the

---

26. *Tasker Jevons* (New York: Boni & Liveright, 1916), p. 194.

Belgian Red Cross as an ambulance driver, and Viola joins the service too to be near him. The war makes possible the grand scene at Melle, where Jimmy rescues Viola's brother Reggie from the burning town hall, loses a hand, and denies himself the last anesthetic so that the wounded Reggie may have its comfort. So, the war brings husband and wife together for a hero's welcome in the Canterbury close, and a bed in the holy of holies of the Thesiger household, Reggie's room.

For her narrator May Sinclair chose a journalist, Walter Furnival, who had been an unsuccessful suitor to Viola but who does well in winning her sister Norah, whose nerves are always calm and whose temperament radiates good humor. Furnival's taking the war correspondent's job that Jevons had declined enables him to follow Jimmy's activities throughout the war and to testify to his devoted, patriotic joy in its adventurous side. Well aware that she had used the war to resolve the marital problem, May Sinclair has Walter Furnival say at the end, "Don't ask me what would have happened to them if there hadn't been a war." But the critics who caviled at her for invoking so gigantic a narrative device as the war to heal what they saw as only an insoluble problem of cultural differences, forgot that the basic magnetism between the two had never been weakened, and that the war did change social attitudes radically. Jevons knows his own stigma: "the damnable tendency to do the sort of thing your father does,"[27] and knows what Viola needs in him: "I'm the queer, unexpected thing she wants and will always want."[28]

The identified narrator enables May Sinclair to relax her tight compression in style for a familiar masculine relationship with the reader. The strict beat gave way to an air of journalistically vivid but unhurried personal reporting. Dialogue that had been stripped to dramatic bareness became conversation interspersed with commentary. May Sinclair had to hold a close discipline over her natural analytic style to secure the relaxed effort. She let her sense of humor go in Furnival's describing a scene incidental to Jimmy's moving into his Hampstead cottage. Jimmy had bought a four-poster bed, which the carpenter who was to install it discovered was four inches too tall for the ceiling. Accustomed to changing his environment when it did not suit him, Jimmy ordered the carpenter to raise the ceiling four inches. The carpenter asked permission instead to cut two inches off each leg and off each post for a total cost of four shillings, instead of an estimated forty pounds and unpredictable results.[29] There is a delightful Wode-

27. *Ibid.*, p. 167.
28. *Ibid.*, p. 107.
29. *Ibid.*, p. 116.

house arrangement of running a poetic vine up a prose trellis in a sentence that refers to Canon Thesiger's first reception of Jevons in Canterbury: "It must be said of the Canon that he nothing common did or mean upon that memorable scene."[30]

May Sinclair guided the journalist to build the beautiful internal balancings that are one of her structural skills, and she let him have his moments of poetry. A tender one is Viola's explaining her pride in Jimmy's love: "Nobody but Jimmy really thinks me nice. Nobody but Jimmy knows how nice I *am*."[31] The book's comfortable unhurriedness downily covers the neat knitting that May Sinclair always performed. Even the Canterbury Cathedral chimes have their place as balance and as prophecy of Furnival's success with Norah, after he had loved and lost Viola to Jevons and the Belfry at Bruges. The dreadful worst is already sighted in 1909 when Jimmy got a cramp in his writing hand, his right, and Viola warned him to rest. Jevons answered jollily, " 'Easy on. They won't amputate it.' "[32] Every move is sighted, every ingredient in an episode of dramatic interest is readied.

In making the Melle Town Hall episode acceptable, May Sinclair did just what Hardy did when he combined the mnemonic resource of refreshing the reader on a certain chain of circumstances with the persuasive one of expressing his philosophy of the willfulness of chance. Jevons had tried so hard to win the acceptance of all the Thesiger family, for Viola's happiness and his own, and he had failed to win over Reggie: "And now, without any effort, or any calculation, or foresight, by a stupendous accident, he had found happiness and peace and certainty. The thing was so consummately done, and so timed to the minute, that when you saw him there enjoying it, you could have sworn that he had played for it and pulled it off."[33] But every move toward the meeting has been prepared.

The ironic effects range from the hilariously comic to the poignant. Psychological discoveries are phrased with informal casualness and without any pressure of medical authority. A simple coincidence is the fact that *Tasker Jevons* is the second novel in succession to range over a nine year's span of action. This one is dated from 1905 to 1914.

A listing of facts about James Tasker Jevons gives away the personal acquaintance whom May Sinclair drew upon as a model. His identity as a writer is most perceptively given away in a passage in which Furnival analyzes the personality and the novels of Jevons: "The

---

30. *Ibid.*, p. 128.
31. *Ibid.*, p. 143.
32. *Ibid.*, p. 157.
33. *Ibid.*, p. 329.

whole thing for him was as obvious as any business transaction (he had the sort of mind for which business transactions *are* obvious). He had studied the public he set out to capture. He presented the life it knew—the moving, changing, fantastically adventurous life of the middle classes. Until Jevons rushed on them and forced their eyes open, you may say at the point of the bayonet, the middle classes didn't know they were moving and changing and being adventurous. Nobody knew. It was Jevons's discovery." And every reader of *The Card* would recognize its hero (born in the same year as its author) from something Jevons says, " 'You can do anything, Furnival,' he said, 'if you're only funny enough!' "[34]

Jevons's experiences in trying to attach an outfitted Motor Ambulance Corps to some Red Cross group were, of course, those of Dr. Hector Munro, whose daring in retrieving wounded under fire was transferred to Jevons. The name for a rebel, Thesiger, was not arbitrarily chosen. It was the name of the actor Ernest Thesiger, a friend of May Sinclair's, the grandson of the first Lord Chelmsford and of the heiress of the last Duke of Dorset. In his autobiography, *Practically True* (1927), Thesiger wrote, "Had I been content to move in respectable circles, my way would have been easy. But I craved to know such dreadful people as painters, actors, writers, and musicians, and they were not on the family visiting list."[35] Furnival's club in Dover Street was the Albemarle, for which Furnival sponsors Jevons, as May Sinclair sponsored Arnold Bennett. The areas in Belgium that Furnival covered were exactly those which May Sinclair served, observed, and wrote about in her *Journal of Impressions in Belgium*.

The description of Jevons's voice as having a Cockney accent and the placing of his father's home in "some parish down in Hertfordshire"[36] are evidence of a conflict, which the manuscript verifies. Into a space left broad and vacant May Sinclair wrote "St. Mary's, Poplar" as the home of Jevons's father. That would account for the Cockney accent, but would spoil the mood and structure of the novel; for if the father had been left in Poplar, accessible to Viola as well as to Jevons, May Sinclair would have had to elaborate the Jevons side of the implied balance of family conflicts. She would have sacrificed some of the tone of comedy and would have weakened the purpose of the design, to draw the way Jevons willed going, and his father's home was not on Jevons's road to fame. The typescripts have the Hertfordshire address. May Sinclair's special editor with Hutchinsons, Miss Aphra Wilson,

34. *Ibid.*, p. 154.
35. *Ibid.*, p. 2.
36. *Ibid.*, p. 7.

performed devoted service in rectifying errors that only the galley proof reveals.[37]

At last, twenty years after she published her first novel, May Sinclair ventured on her first full-scaled portrait of a family, *The Tree of Heaven* (1917). It is her only comprehensive survey of social history as members of the Harrison family, whose head is a dealer in fine woods, engaged in it, starting in 1895 and ending in 1916. The appropriate motif for that period she phrased, "If you had youth and life you were in revolt."[38]

She took back full responsibility as the unproclaimed narrator and as a woman, and softened away all intellectual hardness. The strongest single internal cohesive force flows from the thoughts of the mother of the Harrison family, Frances, who is only thirty-three in 1895, a year older than May Sinclair in that year. Yet May Sinclair skillfully withholds from her the central authority that would tempt the reader to make her opinions his chief points of reference. Unfailingly contemporary, she installs her sympathy inside the three oldest children. Irony, which had saturated *Tasker Jevons* (*The Belfry*) as a man's book, is allowed only passing expressions. Sentiment largely takes its place, the sweet tang of a tonic of comfort and courage to those who sought for strength in a world strained by war. Published when the war had still a year to go, it assumed victory without brashness in the confident spirit that Lawrence Stephen preached to Michael Harrison when he said, "Victory is a state of mind."[39] May Sinclair had absorbed the aims of the Medico-Psychological Clinic, and let them guide her art to do good like a medicine, at no expense of truth. No wonder the students of the Orthopsychics Society had read it as literature and as therapy. During the next war, novelists with a similar understanding of man's need in time of despair wrote *Time Must Have a Stop* and *The Razor's Edge*.

Three generations provide the characters for the drama of revolt and the contrasts of change. Mrs. Fleming is the strong-willed mid-Victorian mother of Frances Harrison that May Sinclair had known in her own mother. She is forceful in her antifeminism, had fought Frances when that daughter broke away from her home to marry Anthony, and then respected her for having had the stronger will and won the success of wedding a prosperous man. Her own husband had been a bankrupt, and is dead. She is contemptuous toward the daughters who had been afraid to break away, Aunties Louie, Emmeline, and

37. Florence Bartrop. Hutchinsons records were destroyed by fire-bombs during World War II; letter, Dorothy Tomlinson, April 14, 1960.
38. *The Tree of Heaven* (New York: Macmillan, 1917), p. 163.
39. *Ibid.*, p. 340.

Edie. Frances Harrison is permissive toward her children, letting them choose their careers so that she might keep their love, although inside herself she dreads changes in them and in the world in which they live. The Victorian prejudice that she holds in favoring her sons against her daughter helps to form Dorothea's revolt to feminism. Anne Brontë had earlier caught the same incentive to feminism in her *The Tenant of Wildfell Hall.*

There are four revolutions to which May Sinclair gives major attention and two revolutions that she barely notices as she tells the story of the Harrisons. Dorothea, who takes a First Class in Economics at Newnham College, joins in the political and intellectual revolution of feminism as a member of the Women's Franchise Union. Michael goes to Cambridge and graduates from Oxford; he becomes a member of a literary and artistic group intent on creating new verse and other new art forms. Nicky, who attends Cambridge, becomes an automotive engineer and contributes to the technological revolution, designing a Moving Fortress, a tank. A fourth revolution is the moral revolution. Vera Harrison, wife of Bartholomew, the hypochondriac brother of Anthony Harrison, becomes involved in that by virtue, if that word may be allowed, of having a child by a lover, Captain Ferdinand Cameron, and, after Ferdie's death, of being the mistress of the Irish Nationalist poet, playwright, novelist, and editor, Lawrence Stephen. The two subordinately referred-to revolutions are the Irish Independence movement and the strike of the building trades. Anthony, as a timber merchant, takes the latter revolution calmly, believing that it cannot go on forever, because building must sometime start up again.

The most elaborately dramatized revolution is the feminist one, in which Dorothea first becomes active when she attends the organization meeting of the North Hampstead Branch of the Women's Franchise Union in the autumn of 1910. Although she is earnestly willing to help the cause, she will not give up her soul to the hungry pack: "She would stay, on the edge of the vortex, fascinated by its danger, and resisting."[40] The uninhibited rioting up and down the country of the Women's Franchise Union causes her to leave its ranks: "Dorothea's soul had swung away from the sweep of the whirlwind. It would never suck her in."[41] She continues her loyalty to the unmilitant Social Reform Union, until the death in war of the man whom she loved, Frank Drayton, who hated all revolutions—he had stopped the mutiny of a native battery in India by laughing in the faces of the mutineers[42]— makes Dorothea regret the opportunities that she had wasted: "I could

40. *Ibid.,* p. 124.
41. *Ibid.,* pp. 232–33.
42. *Ibid.,* p. 144.

bear it if I hadn't wasted the time we might have had together. All
those years—like a fool—over that silly suffrage. I could bear it if I
hadn't been cruel to him. I talked to him like a brute and an idiot. I
told him he didn't care for freedom. And he'd died for it. He remembered that. It was one of the last things he remembered. He said 'It's
your War—it's the biggest fight for freedom.' And he's killed in it."[43]

Michael takes part in the literary revolution to break away from
tradition, to be a voice of the self, not an echo of any herd. He experiments with "live verse" to create new forms, new effects, to combine
a clean picture with the inner reality. In Paris he learns about Jules
Reveillaud and his theory that poetry, steeped so long in painting and
music, needs to be rescued by sculpture, to acquire the lineal sharpness
and hardness of stone, the clean hard reality.[44] Michael's thoughts often
flow as the stuff of poems; he sees pine trees falling in a forest and
gives them the power of thought about their destiny.[45] Lawrence
Stephen, editor and patron of the young revolutionaries, knows that
the young men distrust him "because he refused to destroy the old
gods when he made place for the new."[46] The single aim of the various
revolutions, feminist, literary, technological, moral, Irish, and perhaps
even the building trades revolution, was freedom.

Counterrevolutionary movements also fall within May Sinclair's
scope of this period of revolutions. The aims of the German revolution
were the neatness, the orderliness, the impersonality of the centralized
social state. Nicky's designing a Moving Fortress feeds the counterrevolution that was the war for democracy. His marriage to Phyllis
Desmond—the stage designer who was left with an unborn child, carelessly fathered by her fellow revolutionary against moral convention,
Headley Richards, the play producer—is his effort at counterrevolution
against immorality. Dorothea is counterrevolutionary in resisting the
suppression by the feminist leaders of her right to decide to abstain
from violent action. Michael is counterrevolutionary in opposing the
hunter's killing instinct of certain fellow revolutionaries who crave to
erase the old masters and who harry all writers who dare to rebel on
their own. To Michael, an artist has meaning only as a private soul.
For a long time he is a counter-counterrevolutionary in resisting the
popular pressure to fight for democracy. Lawrence Stephen, at first a
revolutionary in his ambition to be a thorn in the side of England,
whose land he prefers to live in over the Ireland whose spirit alone he

---

43. *Ibid.*, p. 317.
44. *Ibid.*, p. 185.
45. *Ibid.*, p. 189.
46. *Ibid.* See chap. 17 in particular; p. 239.

worships, realizes that Ireland cannot win her freedom unless England is safely free, and he joins in the counterrevolution against the German state.

The war, which affects every single character's life, is viewed from both sides, hostile and acceptive, but the climactic position is a declaration of faith in it. Frank Drayton calls it "the biggest fight for freedom";[47] Lawrence Stephen views it as "a bigger fight for a bigger freedom" than the fight for Ireland's independence;[48] and Michael, after siding with the literary revolutionaries in defending the Germans for shelling cathedrals that happened to be in their way of fire, sees it at last as "the Great War of Redemption."[49]

Those readers who expected to find sexual naturalism found it in Vera's new zest for Lawrence Stephen after he put on a khaki uniform: "It'll be like living with another man."[50] Confirmed readers found the psychological discoveries that they had come to expect. Sentiment, perfectly controlled, gives thrilling intensity to many passages reaching the power of poetry. A gently spread pointillism gives sections of chapters the effects of points of feeling, of poetry, the spaces being left for imaginative expansion and fusion. Time is not a beat but a flow, and dialogue once more the essence of intent and communication. The style is an astringently restrained consummation of sense with reality. Nicky's suffering from earache is described as being not continuous: "Now and then a thin wall of sleep slid between him and his earache."[51]

Irony breaks through the checking wall in this novel as on rare occasions sentiment flowed into *Tasker Jevons*. Ironic is the sight of the four Fleming women, who have worn black in mourning for the father who had died in 1895, as they cross to the West Heath on a visit to the Harrisons, their black appropriate to the deaths of Nicky and Michael, their present mission being to watch Anthony drive to the station the third son whom he is offering his country, John.

The psychic element lurks in the delicate creature of fantasy that is Veronica Harrison, daughter of Vera and Captain Ferdie Cameron, who sees her father's image when he dies, and uses the same tele-psychic gift that Agatha Verrall had practiced to cause Dorothea, who has been arrested for demonstrating and is in a cell in Holloway Gaol, to feel the beatific sensation of being at peace in a convent cell.

No novel of May Sinclair's has so much description of, and so many judgments upon, social conditions and social values. The leading social

47. *Ibid.*, p. 315.
48. *Ibid.*, p. 339.
49. *Ibid.*, p. 377.
50. *Ibid.*, p. 346.
51. *Ibid.*, p. 38.

lesson of the book is the lesson of the inevitability of change, in a country, and in people. Frances Harrison is an example of that lesson. In 1895 she resisted every form of intellectual disturbance from minds like Ibsen and George Moore, and she had no love for England or for its people, adoring only her family. By 1916 she has exchanged her physical passion for her husband and her children for a mystique that becomes her great reality: England. It is of the nature of the climax that the children reach too as their characters develop: a metaphysical discovery of reality. For Michael it is the poetry that he is trying to make, the most real thing there is.[52] For Dorothea it is the fusion that love makes of Frank and herself.[53] For Veronica it is her psychic gift, which is so real that she thinks it is God.[54] For Nicky, and later for Michael, it is the ecstasy that comes only in the heat of battle.[55]

The self is the most important of the psychological themes in the book, counterweighting the aggressive force of the collective vortices. It runs all the way from Michael's explaining at the age of seven why he does not want to go to Rosalind Jervis's party—"At a party I can't feel all of myself at once—like I do now"[56]—to Dorothea's resenting the herd pressure of the militant feminists.

May Sinclair was too close to, and too fond of, her friends among the imagists and vorticists and other poets and painters to allow us to make any identifications at all of originals. Morton Ellis would destroy all the poets of the past, and let poets write only what no one else could imitate. Austin Mitchell would break up the syntax to give language a fresh start. Henry Nevinson, in his *Last Changes and Chances,* records a note that he made of a meeting in Yeats's chambers in Woburn Buildings, at which Yeats said that all reading of contemporaries and imitation of them was bad.[57] In his *Wyndham Lewis,* Hugh Kenner describes Lewis as having by 1914 resolved never again to write a phrase that would betray any hint of literary antecedents.[58] The one unretouched portrait of an original in the book, Florence Bartrop told me, is Timmy, May Sinclair's cat Tommy, which she gave to Nicky.

In her enthusiastic description of Réveillaud's theories and Michael's aim as a poet, May Sinclair confessed how strongly the theories of the imagists had impressed themselves upon her.[59] More and more she

---

52. *Ibid.,* pp. 185, 398.
53. *Ibid.,* p. 313.
54. *Ibid.,* p. 359.
55. *Ibid.,* pp. 369, 395, 396.
56. *Ibid.,* p. 18.
57. *Ibid.,* p. 123.
58. *Ibid.,* p. 276.
59. *Ibid.,* chap. 14.

adopted their aims for her own prose style. An experiment in imagistic prose occurs in the first two pages of chapter nine, giving Michael's impression of Cheltenham.

Deep in their personal and family revelations are the fantasy of the woman with psychic gifts, Veronica Harrison, the realistic feminist, Dorothea Harrison, the gunner, Frank Drayton (who has served in the Royal Artillery in India and who teaches gunnery at the Royal Artillery Arsenal at Woolwich), the drunken Uncle Maurice, the baby-deprived, almost insane Aunt Emmeline, and John Harrison, who has a mitral murmur.

Mary Olivier: A Life (1919) is the apprenticeship-to-life novel toward which May Sinclair had been moving ever since *Tasker Jevons,* and the novel that she regarded privately and mentioned publicly as the novel of which she was proudest. Like Jasper Jevons's third novel, it was the one that she wanted most to do, the one that she wanted to repeat with variations, the one that she hoped her readers would acquire a permanent taste for. She set it in her own generation, calling her self-projection by her own name, and disclosed the never-before-told secret of her birth year, in the date on Mary's christening cup, 1863. She also hinted at the cause of Mary's father's death as alcoholism and gave the accurate year of her own father's death, 1881.

The pattern of the life of a gradually recognized woman poet is centered in a full family group, including parents, three brothers, the mother's sister and brother-in-law, and the brother and two sisters of her father. This family group is supplemented by the portraits of four more families, the Waughs, the Kendals, the Herons, and the Sutcliffes, and by many more persons whom Mary meets and who affect and mark her social and spiritual pilgrimage.

For it is a pilgrimage, the pilgrimage of a daughter to freedom from her Victorian family's sentimental imprisonment, without any weakening of love and compassion or any shirking of responsibility. The biographical design elaborates in five books Mary's growth from her second year to her forty-seventh. The pointillism that May Sinclair had been practicing quietly is brought to a studied perfection through chapters of irregular length divided into sections that are sometimes split up by spaces marked with a dotted line. The new pointillism was discovered because it changed from gentle daubs that spread their light to splinters and episodes of needle sharpness, pure smelted experiences of a character, whose pointed meaning pricks sensibilities and brain for an immediate effect before the fusion.

The narrative moves forward in *current retrospection,* without any anticipative hints to establish drift, without any leaps forward to create mediate terminals of a present progress or to prepare for dramatic satisfaction. Mary's impressions, feelings, thoughts, and circumstances as they have just occurred are all we know in any moment of narrative time. The preparation, we realize when we look back, has been as meticulous as always, but there is no auctorial anticipation.

The mood is astringent toward every impulse of the creative ambient to react sentimentally to its own creation. Mary Olivier's throbbing sentiment is left strictly as her primary experience. Her secondary consciousness records what it sees and hears without any such sympathetic vibration as the unidentified narrator of *The Tree of Heaven* allowed herself to indulge in, but its effect approximates the fullness and objective conviction of an omniscient teller. It reports Mary Olivier's perceptions, actions, feelings, impressions, fantasies, thoughts, and dreams in *oratio recta* and *oratio obliqua*, in formulations of introvocative (second person), ectovocative (third person), and egovocative statements.

There is little decoration of period furniture to act as calendars. Except for sparse references to a speech by John Bright, to Gladstone, to the Battle of Sedan, to Marshall and Snellgrove's, to Barnardo Homes, Maskelyne and Cooke's, the reality of the late Victorian household comes alive solely through the behaviors of the people.

There are two principal settings, Ilford in Essex, and the fictional Morfe in the Garthdale of Yorkshire, which had been home to *The Three Sisters*. Both regions are given a real and beautiful life such as Anthony Deane once had pleaded with May Sinclair to aim for.

The innermost energy that atomizes into *Mary Olivier* is the awareness that an imaginative, strong-willed, intellect-blessed girl, the sister of three brothers of weaker will, experiences of her own passionate, feminine self, and of her family, whom she loves, but who she learns is hostile to her growth into individual womanhood. Its broader drama is made out of the conflict of the girl and woman with her dearly loved family; and the overlapping themes composing that drama are the defense of the self, Mamma, the Will, truth, religion, sentiment, love, intellectual beauty, making poems, the psychic gift, the concept of reality and philosophy as a guide to it, and the experience of reality.

The central drama is the war between Mamma and Mary, a war between the will to impose itself upon people and the will to assimilate ideas for growth of the self and the discovery of truth and reality. Only as Mary's will creates poems does she try to impose her will upon unidentified people. Little Mamma holds her family in her power by being gentle and looking weak, and by letting her children see how she suffers when they disobey. She freely flicks the Victorian lash of parents on their children: " 'I'd rather have seen you in your coffin than married to Maurice Jourdain.' "[60] And " 'If that's what comes of your publishing I'd rather see your books were sunk to the bottom of the sea. I'd rather see you in your coffin.' "[61] Mary, whose deepest motive seems to have been to please Mamma, at last publishes a poem in a magazine in 1900. Mamma reads it and has nothing to say. Irony tints the years of senility when Mamma becomes a little girl trying as hard to win Mary's praise as once Mary had tried to win hers. After Mamma's death Mary dreams of her; she understands why, on waking, she passes from a mood of pain to one of relief.

In religion the war is over the difference between belief and compulsion. Jehovah was such a hater of other gods, while classical gods cared for things one liked best: "trees and animals and poetry and music and running races and playing games," and one did not *have* to believe in Zeus. "That was the nicest thing of all."[62] The end of the doctrinal war is Mary's discovering by way of the freshness and strangeness of the Greek New Testament that "the Kingdom of God is within you." God was the hidden self. Christ's followers did not understand his teaching and after his death made him into a God.[63] Mary's religion came from discovery; Mamma's religion was a worship by compulsion.

Sentiment, which had flowed freely in *The Tree of Heaven,* is now a potential enemy of a mind aiming to win freedom. Mary must not care too much about how her mother feels about her unbelief: "The part that cared was not free. Not free."[64] Mary is so hungry for her mother's declaration of love: " 'How'm I to know you love me if you won't say it? . . . Oh—oh—oh—I love you so much I can't bear it; you little holy Mamma.' "[65] But Mamma refuses to give comfort in a lie.

Moving through the continuous war between Mamma and Mary is the story of Mary's other surging of love, from the first love for her brother Mark when she is thirteen, to her love for the Greek scholar Richard Nicholson, when she is thirty-nine, whose mistress she becomes rather than have him think that he can gain her only by proposing marriage.

Mary begins to write poetry as an outlet for her unsatisfied longing for love. She teaches herself elementary Greek and absorbs the rhythms and sounds of Homer, Aeschylus, Sophocles, Aristophanes, Euripides. Her first tranlation is of the *Orestes* of Euripides. Later she writes a

---

60. *Mary Olivier: A Life* (New York: Macmillan, 1919) , p. 229.
61. *Ibid.,* p. 349.
62. *Ibid.,* pp. 78–79.
63. *Ibid.,* pp. 319–20.
64. *Ibid.,* p. 170.
65. *Ibid.,* p. 69.

verse drama, composing the verses in her mind on the moor at Morfe, a drama about a son's hereditary destiny.[66] Her translating the *Bacchae* into the chanting rhythms of Walt Whitman leads to her recognition as a poet when she is in her forties.[67] Richard Nicholson inspires her in that work with his encouragement.

Truth is the moral and intellectual issue in the war over religion. Mary cannot confess a belief that she does not hold to be true. She is fourteen when she discovers the indifference of people toward truth and realizes that her own search would make a lonely journey. Mamma asks her if she has ever asked God to help her unbelief. Mary answers, " 'No. I could only do that if I didn't believe in my unbelief.' "[68] She refuses to read prayers, and Mamma accuses her of setting herself up in her silly self-conceit against the truth. Mary thinks that accusation through and decides that *her* personal quest for truth matters: "It mattered more than anything in the whole world, the truth about God, the truth about anything, just the truth."[69] Mary's reading of Spencer, Ribot, and Maudsley makes her understand Spinoza's concept of the intellectual love of God; even ugly facts that are true have an enchantment about them because they are true.[70]

Mary learns that only if truth is revered can there be a real self. She knows that if she obeyed her mother in thought and feeling completely she would be lying the whole time: " 'Hiding my real self and crushing it. It's your *real* self she hates—the thing she can't see and touch and get at—the thing that makes you different.' " And " 'I used to wonder what the sin against the Holy Ghost was. . . . It's that. Not adoring the self in people. Hating it. Trying to crush it.' "[71]

Her reading in Spencer, Haeckel, Ribot, and Maudsley made her despair of being successful in building a real self; Ribot taught that only biological laws were real, and Maudsley that a person's ancestors fixed his ineluctable destiny. Mr. Sutcliffe frees her from her fear of scientific determinism, assuring her that she *is* a separate self and need not be afraid of any doom just because her Aunt Charlotte is crazy.[72] After Mark is dead, Mary discovers that Mamma never cared for Mark's self: "It was her son—*her* son she loved, not Mark's real, secret self."[73] Defense of the self requires an unending battle.

Will is the foundation of the building of the self. Mr. Sutcliffe sup-

---

66. *Ibid.*, pp. 298–99.
67. *Ibid.*, p. 339.
68. *Ibid.*, p. 169.
69. *Ibid.*, p. 197.
70. *Ibid.*, pp. 288–89.
71. *Ibid.*, pp. 249–50.
72. *Ibid.*, p. 294.
73. *Ibid.*, p. 305.

ports Mark's initial advice to her to trust in her will when he says, "Find out what you want, and when you see your chance coming, take it. Don't funk it."[74]

Mary exerts her psychic gift on a number of occasions, as when she pits her will against Richard Nicholson's will that her mother die after a stroke, so that her mother might live;[75] when she wills to end her wanting Richard and to end Richard's wanting her;[76] and when she wills the removal of all that stands between her will and her discovery of God as the ultimate reality.[77]

Mary's fervent search, one that includes all other strivings, is for the full experience of reality. Her first encounter with it happens when she is seven and is walking in Ley Street, in Ilford. A white light diffuses a waterlike quality over the fields and road and over her home, and she is overwhelmed by a feeling of pure happiness. Her reading in philosophy and poetry refines her understanding so that she can discover God to be the ultimate reality, the ultimate maker of happiness. This is her discovery after her mother has died and Richard Nicholson, too impatient to wait for her, has married an old love: perfect happiness comes not from people or things, but from somewhere inside, and accepting God's will as the will of the self brings the miracle of perceiving beauty, feeling happiness, freedom, and the consciousness of God—the complex miracle of Reality. There is a halt, a moment of doubt before the end: "Supposing there isn't anything in it?" It is the doubt of a player holding his hand on a chess piece, to consider the risk that the move might turn out to be disastrous. But the doubt clears. Certainty energizes the halted hand to make the move: "There isn't any risk."[78] Happiness through sacrifice became a closed question in this novel. The question was to be reopened in later novels.

Mary's reading in philosophy and in the sciences for intellectual help toward the discovery of reality makes the novel the dramatic embodiment of the metaphysical pilgrimage that appeared in 1917 under the title *A Defence of Idealism*. And the writing of *Mary Olivier* must have stimulated some of the thinking that led to *The New Idealism* in 1922.

The philosophical substance of the book, important as it is, rides lightly, sharing all the creative and aesthetic graces that match the best writing of May Sinclair in both experimental and traditional forms. There are some half dozen passages of verbless vorticist prose, many

74. *Ibid.*, p. 258.
75. *Ibid.*, pp. 350–51.
76. *Ibid.*, p. 367–68.
77. *Ibid.*, p. 377.
78. *Ibid.*, pp. 379–80.

freshly invented similes and metaphors, and delicate choices of arresting images. There are many passages of poetry, many vivid insights by a child's mind and descriptions of a child's keen senses. There are comic things, and tactful renderings of risqué matters. May Sinclair uses her ingenuity to slip unconscious revelation past Mary's self-awareness, as when Mary blames Dorsy Heron's taking her to the workhouse to see an old woman who was dying as the cause of her dream of her mother dying: "Why can't I dream about something I *want* to happen? Why can't I dream about Richard?"[79]

Musical favorites reappear, the *Fantasia Polonaise,* the Sonata *Appassionata.* May Sinclair told Florence Bartrop that *Mary Olivier* was substantially her life story, excepting only the love episodes; the brothers were true. Mark is an imperfectly anagrammed but closely factual Frank. The faith-jumps that Mary performs into Mark's and Jim Ponsonby's arms May Sinclair said she had taken with Frank. Like Mark, Frank was home on leave from 1884 to 1885,[80] and the album of photographs that Mark and Frank brought from India was one of May Sinclair's inheritances. Mark's sword, which must have been Frank's, appeared already in *Mr. and Mrs. Nevill Tyson* and in *Tancred,* the verse drama that Mary was composing when a letter broke the news of the death of Mark. The copy of a letter that May Sinclair wrote to Marc Logé, her translator, gives a list of the chapters that she declared were autobiographical.[81] Roddy, the brother who drew pencil sketches of battle scenes and sailboats, was Joseph Walter, who drew the same sketches in May Sinclair's music albums. May Sinclair told Florence Bartrop and her niece Wilda that Roddy was the character she most loved in all her novels. Roddy's feeling ashamed of staying at home, "living on Mamma's money"[82] is a clue to Amelia Hind's having supplied the capital that enabled William Sinclair to establish his shipping business in Liverpool and live for some years like a gentleman. Emilius, father of Mary, describes himself as an insurer of ships, instead of the shipowner that William Sinclair was.

A hint for the family name that masks that of Sinclair came from a man whose regular daily appearance not at the Buck, but at the Black Bull, in Reeth, enabled any observer to set his watch at four

---

79. *Ibid.,* p. 352.
80. Letter, J. O'Connor, Royal Artillery Institution, Woolwich, May 16, 1960.
81. Chap. 6, sections i, ii, iv; chap. 9, sections i, ii, iii; chap. 9, sections i, vi; chap. 12, section i; chap. 13, sections ii, iii; chap. 16, sections i, ii, iii; chap. 21, sections i, ii, iii; chap. 24, sections iv, viii; chap. 25, section iv; chap. 27, sections v, xi (Herbert Spencer, Darwin, Haeckel) ; chap. 28, section i; chap. 30, section i; chap. 35, section ix; "All this description of the *inner life* is autobiographically as accurate as I can make it."
82. *Ibid.,* p. 181.

o'clock. Mr. Oliver was a regular, not a hard, drinker.[83] Mr. Sutcliffe originated in Professor Gwatkin, and Professor Lee Ramsden must have been Professor Henry Morley. Richard Nicholson is a fantasy based upon Richard Aldington, who was about thirty years younger, not six years older, than May Sinclair.

A table of contents for the manuscript discloses the care with which May Sinclair sharpened each section to its point of meaning, for each section of each chapter bears a title. To have prefixed its title to each section would have given the effect of a mosque whose every minaret was hung with a sign. But the new edition, which *Mary Olivier* deserves, should include that series of titles at the safe distance of the table of contents.

The Romantic (1920) is the second novel to visit the battlefields in Belgium, which May Sinclair saw in 1914. It is her first frankly psychoanalytical novel, a species of love story told as a character mystery that is climaxed by a dramatized combination of the analysis of the principal character and the psychotherapy of the affected, almost equal secondary character. I believe that only Rebecca West in her *The Return of the Soldier* and J. D. Beresford in his *God's Counterpoint* (both 1918) preceded her in developing a novel out of an instance of psychotherapy.

The central situation is the love of a sexually healthy and intensely romantic woman for a man of physical beauty, for whom she invents, to rationalize her passion, a beautiful mind, and whom she gradually discovers to have, instead, a psychopathic personality. The external drama gradually reveals the psychopathic personality of John Roden Conway. The internal drama presents two concurrent conflicts within Charlotte Redhead. One conflict, resulting from the disillusionment in which an affair with a married man had ended, engages her will as it suppresses her strong sexual instinct. The second conflict is between her accumulating knowledge of Conway's sickness and her persistent sentimental attitude toward him, which fights to sustain a lovable illusion. The two conflicts are interdependent, since Charlotte's sentimental love for her illusion of Conway has as its motive making him the object of her will to suppress her sexual instinct; that is why she agrees to his offer of a platonic love. The unconscious motive for her sentimental love is his physical beauty, the goal of her repressed sexual instinct. Her repressed physical longing and her need to idealize him to make the repression worth the strain obstruct her insight into Conway's psychopathic nature. The open narrative interest, then, is in the

---

83. Dr. W. C. Speirs, letters, July 15, July 17, 1964.

psychiatric mystery of Conway's nature as it is experienced through Charlotte's illusion-fantasizing personality. The covert interest is in the complex inner life of Charlotte. We learn once more what we were told in *Mary Olivier,* that sentiment may be the breeder of illusion and an enemy to the discovery of unpleasant truth. We also notice the common interest of *The Tree of Heaven, Mary Olivier,* and *The Romantic* in a character's adventuring toward reality.

The structure opens with a prologue that explains what sort of sexually experienced person Charlotte Redhead is, and how she happens to fall in love with John Roden Conway and to agree to a platonic relationship. It ends with an epilogue in which a psychotherapist both analyzes Conway's behavior and frees Charlotte after Conway's death of her repressed love for him, which has disguised itself as an atoning dedication to the wounded Belgian soldiers whom he had betrayed with his cowardice.

The world of the novel is one of monomental experience. Charlotte's secondary consciousness acts as an external penetrant mind reporting her experiences, and May Sinclair introduces two doctors into the story to fortify the reader's certainty of understanding. Dr. Billy Sutton's impressiveness in Charlotte's eyes establishes him as a dependable judge of Conway, and Dr. Sutton's building up the authority of Dr. Donald McClane as a psychotherapist overcomes her earlier resentment and leads to her giving him the confidence that enables him to effect a cure. These two doctors importantly clarify a story that is experienced largely through a romantic and illusion-prone mind.

The style is a miracle of compactness, yet it is not stark in substance nor stiff in movement. A woman's feeling for rhythmical writing and a sensitive eye for the image that will flash the thing seen make the movement supple, the form trim. May Sinclair had even less trouble than George Meredith had in coaxing psychology and poetry to be congenial stylemates. Poetry is always near, in sustained passages, in brief figures, in choices of the luminous image. The sound of a ship's bow at sea is heard in "the boat went steadily, inflexibly, without agitation, cutting the small crisp waves with a sound like the flowing of stiff silk."[84] Of the nature of verse is the choric repetition of the one-word paragraph, "Turn," to describe Charlotte's looking in four directions away from Gibson Herbert, with whom she stands waiting for his train on the station platform at Stow, after his single night, his last, of furtive crawling back to Charlotte.[85]

In accord with the treatment of John Conway's character as a mys-

---

84. *The Romantic* (New York: Macmillan, 1920), p. 49.
85. *Ibid.,* p. 4.

tery whose revelation makes a story, May Sinclair three times uses the detective story device of grouping, in sets of three, facts that advance Charlotte's understanding to date.[86] The brevity, two hundred pages of generous type, conceals the taut, fine lacework of construction. There is no showmanship in this novel, but a supreme conscientiousness of craft dramatizing the pathology of Conway—who drives a Red Cross motor ambulance—that causes him to dream playing the hero, to abhor sex, and to act the cruel coward in times of stress, all the effects of his secret impotence.

The conflicts of Charlotte are deliberately underplayed as discoveries to be come upon by the reader who cares for internal drama and the little ironies of a woman's dual search for illusion and reality. Beautifully clear is Charlotte's physical obsession with John,[87] and clear her need to disguise this interest from herself by inventing for him a beautiful mind instead.[88]

Dr. McClane's psychotherapy on board the ship taking them back to England is tactfully gentle. He helps Charlotte save face, to spare her humiliation over her error, by saying, "In a sense the real John Conway was the man who dreamed,"[89] for the real Charlotte also is a dreamer, a dreamer of love, a romantic. Dr. McClane explains that her conscious hatred of Conway is the expression of a love that has been pressed into the unconscious. She must dislodge her hatred to lose her unconscious love, and she can do that by forgiving Conway his cruelty and his cowardice as the involuntary expressions of an inner insane force. So Dr. McClane frees Charlotte to be able to love again, to love the normal, gentle Billy Sutton.

The model for Dr. McClane was certainly Dr. Hector Munro, in whose skill as a psychotherapist May Sinclair had so much faith that she subsidized a Field Ambulance Corps for him as a means of helping him become better known.[90]

I had thought the name "Redhead" an awkward choice until *Kelly's Post Office Directories of Cheshire* from 1857 to 1864 brought up again and again the name of the Reverend Thomas Fisher Redhead, the perpetual curate of the Sinclairs' parish church of St. Peter, Rock Park, Rock Ferry. The inn at Stow-on-the-Wold where May Sinclair stayed is introduced in chapters one and two.

The Romantic runs in its original typescript form up to the last quarter of chapter eight. From then on (page 85 of the printed text)

86. *Ibid.*, pp. 28–30; 32–35; 136–38.
87. *Ibid.*, p. 27.
88. *Ibid.*, p. 28.
89. *Ibid.*, p. 201.
90. Mrs. Belloc-Lowndes, *A Passing World* (London: Macmillan, 1948), p. 196.

there is some rewriting, which was done after Richard Aldington (who read a carbon typescript of the novel in March, 1920) found that May Sinclair had lauded Charlotte's heroic presence of mind in rescuing two machine guns from the advancing Germans by loading them into her Red Cross ambulance, without realizing that the action flouted the Hague Convention and would earn Charlotte no military decoration.[91] May Sinclair immediately wrote out the substitutions and interpolations to be made in the typescript, which was already being set up, and sent them with this letter:

1 Blenheim Rd.
N.W. 8

March 29, 1920
Dear Mr. Flower
    It has been pointed out to me that the machine gun incident in chapter viii of The Romantic was a breach of the Hague Convention!
    It must be put in its right place. Would you kindly see that the enclosed additions and corrections go to the printers at once?

Sincerely yours,
May Sinclair

The incident was retained, but Charlotte was rebuked for the violation instead of honored.

In each novel of this decade of assured recognition, May Sinclair pressed to the limits of her reach to find and clarify her discoveries of human nature. Each novel was different in theme and style and structure. Each novel asked the critic to employ every cell of his brain to match the author in giving imagined actuality to her phrasings of what was real to her. She well knew that the poet who experimented had to risk being ignored or being hounded. She must have felt that she was risking oblivion by being the always exploring, freshly experimenting novelist.

---

91. Letter to me, February 17, 1960.

15

Other Writings: 1911-1920

Short Stories

May Sinclair became as fine a craftsman in the short story as in the novel; her moods cover a wide range.

"The Intercessor," the first of four stories published in 1911, appeared in the *English Review* in July. It is an occult horror mystery set in a Yorkshire farmhouse and fantasized under the spell of Emily Brontë, with help from her also in the use of on-the-scene narrators. A researcher into county history becomes the intercessor between the returning ghost of a child and its pregnant, frightened mother who had not returned the child's affection. The story, which is eighty pages long, has power. "Appearances," in the August *Good Housekeeping* (and the December, 1913, *Fortnightly Review*) is set in Cannes, and tells about the amateur psychotherapy performed upon a too easily aroused man by a woman who only looked "fast." "Miss Tarrant's Temperament" ran in *Harper's* through August and September. It is a brilliantly written society story about a beautiful woman who needs to tantalize men, and who cannot give back a genuine affection for the affection that she excites in men. "Between the Lines" appeared in *Harper's* in December. It is a humorous story of suggestion and countersuggestion, involving neurasthenia, repression of the libido, the power of an ideal, and the DuMaurier-like theme of the possible recovery of an ancestral memory. Simpson, the artist, helps the young-looking Major Lumby escape marriage to a huntress-matron of a hospital for nervous diseases by suggesting that he imagine himself hopelessly in love with a married woman.

249

There were three stories in 1913. "Khaki," in the September *English Review*, is set during the Boer War. It commemorates a bank clerk who had been laughed at by clever artistic people in Chelsea for his military theories, but whom the war proved to be indeed a military genius and a hero. "Compensation," in the October *Good Housekeeping*, is a comic bonbon, a Maugham-like tale of a widow whose confession that her age is fifty shocks a suitor who thought her only thirty. She declines his now brave proposal, and the two relax into a mere friendship without fear of age. "The Wrackham Memoirs," in the December *Harper's*, tops caustic satire upon a popular novelist of great vanity and a lust for posthumous fame with a surprising sentiment. The novelist's daughter releases her fiancé from her original demand that he edit the absurdly pompous memoirs of her father as her love moves from her father to her fiancé. Florence Bartrop believed the novelist was intended as an impression of Hall Caine.

Two stories appeared in 1914. "The Collector," in the *Century Magazine* for January, is a farce about a society woman who collects popular people and who persecutes a novelist celebrity until he locks himself in the bathroom in her home, from where he dictates his terms of freedom from further pursuit. Watt Gunn seems to be a trial sketch for Tasker Jevons. "Red Tape," in *The Queen* for November, deserves being collected. It is a graceful comedy spun out of inherent pathos about two middle-aged people who prepared when war came to enlist as medical aides, but were turned down as being too old. The pattern of moods is exquisitely varied. The comic spirit that May Sinclair expressed so well in her social life appears in the advice of Miss Delachervy's chemist, who recommended her to buy a bone, not a celluloid toothbrush, to take to the front, because a bomb would be almost certain to ignite the latter. Authentically May Sinclair is Miss Delachervy's announcement, "I shall stay in London to protect my cat."

"The Pin-Prick," in *Harper's* for February, 1915, is a compassionate story set in such a studio of flats as May Sinclair had lived in. A painter, May Blissett, shy, the victim of much family sorrow, kills herself from loneliness, from starved affection.

"The Frewin Affair," in the January, 1917, issue of *Woman at Home*, is a comedy about a woman with a sense of humor who plays a trick upon the husband member of a very complacent, superior couple who live for themselves and urge upon others their formalized life. To teach him the surprises that the spontaneous life may offer, Margot Cautley takes Mr. Frewin on a drive in her car and apparently runs out of gas: "A two gallon can chock-full of petrol doesn't retire of its own initiative into an impenetrable bower of heather and bracken." "Portrait of My Uncle," in the *Century Magazine* for January, is a subtlely told analytic story of a married couple who exchanged hatred and torture, and yet remained in love and wholly dependent on each other.

"Fame," appearing in the *Pictorial Review* on May 10, 1920, is an ironic comedy of the literary life. It brings back Walter Furnival as the tireless biographical detective who assembles the materials that result in a best-selling unkind version of Liston Chamberlin's life, and who later learns the kindlier truth about his subject from the novelist's divorced wife, who had loved and understood him and his need for freedom. "The Bambino," published in the *Athenaeum*, September 24, is the harrowing story of Jack Archdale's marriage to a beautiful but stupid woman whose careless handling of her child damages its brain to idiocy.

The sad mood of seven out of these fourteen stories of the decade unfairly leaves a deeper impression upon the memory than do the entertaining moods of the other seven.

Feminism and Fair Play

On March 28, 1912, a physician, Sir Almroth Wright, wrote a letter filling three columns of the London *Times* and diagnosing the feminist movement as a disease, its aim "to convert the whole world into an epicene institution . . . in which man and woman shall everywhere work side by side at the self-same task and for the self-same pay"—an unrealizable goal. A woman doctor who was to become a member of the Medico-Psychological Clinic, Dr. Agnes Savill, replied in the *Daily Mail* on April 2.[1] Another reply came in the form of a booklet, *Feminism*, dated March 31 and published by the Women Writers Suffrage League in May, 1912. It argued for the immediate and the historical justice of the revolution implied in the granting of women's suffrage.

May Sinclair attacked Sir Almroth's case for "the hysteria bacillus" by naming women leaders of both the militant and the nonmilitant suffrage groups who did not bear any marked signs of hysteria, neurosis, or degeneracy. She cited Dr. Savill's reply in the *Daily Mail* to refute Sir Almroth's contention that men and women could not work side by side. Sir Almroth had overlooked the psychic factor that makes human beings different from animals: proximity discourages rather than encourages distraction from work. Sir Almroth thought that only the intellectual woman, whom he thought to be emotionally atrophied,

---

1. Letter, T. E. Amos, librarian, *Daily Mail*.

could work with men. He did not know that the woman whose sexual instincts are not conspicuous is often the most complete, because she has a will and a control over those instincts. The physiological emergencies to which he thought women were inherently subject were not the monopoly of women, or the monopoly of unmarried women. The truth was that the suffrage societies were not recruited almost entirely from the ranks of the unmarried, but had a remarkably large proportion of married women and of married women who were mothers.

May Sinclair ridiculed Sir Almroth's classifying medical women with the artificial intellectual: "There is no class in whom the springs of human sympathy, of pity and maternal tenderness are more enduring than in these handmaidens and servants of Science."[2] She ridiculed Sir Almroth's conclusion that when a woman's life force is frustrated the inevitable consequences are hysteria, neurosis, and manifestations of degeneracy. Frustration could mean a rechanneling of energies into an intense experience of life or into artistic creation. Not hysteria, but love was at the root of the suffrage movement.

It was the excess number of women that drove women into the labor market. Many women already had to support themselves, their children, their fathers, brothers, and husbands. Men did not mind having women work under them if their work was cheap. They deliberately undervalued women's work to keep it cheap. Men's having the vote affected their wages, and women were justified in wanting the vote to secure fairer wages. Equal rights would make real efficiency the test of value.

May Sinclair would not justify, defend, or condemn feminine militancy, but she thought that history would justify it, as it had defended similar violence. History had always regarded political violence as a thing apart and tended to assign the final responsibility to the governments that provoked it.

That she was not an antimale feminist she proved in an essay, "A Defence of Man," in the *English Review* for July, 1912 (and in the *Forum* in October), which modified rather than rebutted Cicely Hamilton's essay, "Man," in the April number of the *English Review*. May Sinclair proudly told of having been brought up with boys until she was twenty-seven. She credited men's risk of danger and endurance of hardship with having made comfort and civilization possible. Nature's economy had made man the procurer of the material means of life and so condemned him to an inferior spiritual role, to inferior sexual feelings and sexual morality, while Nature had allowed women

---

2. P. 27.

to develop profounder feelings, a finer moral splendor, a superior sexual restraint. The contemporary race for wealth was not aiding the spiritual improvement of men, and yet men had been the founders of religions and pioneers of spiritual progress.

Wherever men and women worked together, women had acquired men's virtues. In the equal comradeship that suffrage would give women, men could absorb the superior morality of women. Men's fear of being swamped by the *Nimmerweibliche* through suffrage was groundless. Nature had too much need of the *Immerweibliche* to cause her extinction. Raising man to an equal pedestal of morality with women through suffrage could safeguard the future of the race with the greater temperance and equal morality that feminism was fighting for through the vote.

An article commissioned by *Collier's Magazine,* "Women's Sacrifices for the War," appeared on November 21, 1914, and was repeated in *Woman at Home* in February, 1915. It has value for its descriptions of wartime services by women and as May Sinclair's confession of faith in the war. In detail she told how the many suffrage societies turned to recruiting, distributing milk to expectant mothers, doing Red Cross work; caring for refugees, providing employment for women, saving girls from white slavery, feeding the poor, and caring for children. The war proved that a great many jobs held by men could be filled in an emergency by women. The women had proved they would not collapse into preferring peace at any price, but wanted the war to be fought to a victorious finish. If the war should last long and take a heavy toll of men, it would settle for all time the question of women's ability to fill men's places.

May Sinclair insisted that the part women had taken in the war was not sacrifice, but service. Her feminism was ardent, but it was not sex warfare. The heart of it was simply the plea to England's conscience to play fair by awarding to women the political power that their social services had won them the right to exercise.

The War and Its Aftermath

In May, June, and July of 1915, the *English Review* published a total of thirty-seven pages of what was entitled "The War of Liberation: From a Journal." It was a truncated version of the book of 239 pages, *A Journal of Impressions in Belgium* (also 1915).

A Journal of Impressions in Belgium is the personal and pseudonymous expansion of the "Day Book" that May Sinclair kept as the secretary of Dr. Munro's Motor Ambulance Corps serving with the Belgian

Red Cross. It is frank, imaginative, and unaffected, as it recounts her arrival at Ostend, where all the terror that she had imagined the war would hold for her vanished, except for the fear the women in the party had of drunken Uhlans. In Ghent the members of the ambulance unit, five women and nine men, began to realize each other's individuality, and then dissolved their individualities to form the ambulance unit that had two good British Red Cross ambulances at its command to serve the Belgian Red Cross.

The wards of the wounded in the Flandria Palace Hotel became a world of transcendent pain, in which May Sinclair discovered that the torment of others could bring peace to the self-tormented. A wounded German, brought in on a stretcher and booed by Belgians, dissolved the hatred that she had prepared herself to feel.[3] The refugees at the Palais des Fêtes had no pride, scorn, or hate for the enemy. The misery of the homeless was so deep that one dared not feel as one watched them. May Sinclair thought of herself not as a member of the corps but as one of "the stunned sleepers in the straw who cannot feel."[4]

When an ambulance carried her into the middle of an artillery duel, she felt an exaltation and a sense of reliving something gone through many times before.[5] She thrilled over the prospect of Germans attacking a village and of her carrying the wounded. She felt only "the clean and fiery passion, and the contagious ecstasy of war."[6] When she took two stretcher bearers to look for a wounded man who was said to be near Lokeren, she felt a steadily mounting happiness: "While it lasted you had the sense of touching Reality at its highest point in a secure and effortless communication, so far were you from being strung up to any pitch."[7] When she found the horribly wounded Flamand, he became for her "the most beautiful thing I have ever seen. And I loved him. . . . He was my first wounded man."[8]

She was assigned to nurse a young English officer whom none of the staff gave a chance to live. Resembling her own Agatha Verrall, Veronica Harrison, and Mary Olivier, she willed her patient to be still and without pain, without morphine. He finally did lie still, without signs of pain, and he slept without morphine. She willed her own sensations to go, and images to go, "until only a clear blank darkness" remained, within which she willed and prayed that he should get well.[9]

3. *A Journal of Impressions in Belgium* (New York: Macmillan, 1915), p. 44.
4. *Ibid.*, p. 59.
5. *Ibid.*, p. 147.
6. *Ibid.*, p. 157.
7. *Ibid.*, p. 168.
8. *Ibid.*, pp. 169–70.
9. *Ibid.*, pp. 219–20.

' The commandant had taken with him Freud's *Psychopathology of Every-Day Life,* and May Sinclair packed it along with all his other belongings when the retreat from Ghent began, in the wake of the Belgian army. In Bruges she escaped her obsession for returning to Ghent by looking at the Belfry.[10] In Ostend she was led away by a nurse from a ward in the *Kursaal* in which a man was screaming because his leg was being amputated without an anesthetic.[11]

The personal confessions draw us very close to the author. She even recalled the game of football that she played with her big brothers in the garden. They let her kick off and run with the ball, and let her kick goal after goal, but moved her aside for the scrimmage.[12] She remembered having "lived through a good many terrible nights in sick-rooms."[13]

The wide-open realistic vision, the feeling for irony and the comedy of the incongruous that the realistic vision gathers in, a unique directness springing from a personal, not a literary communication, the casual touches of the artist sketching instantly intelligible pictures—these elements make *A Journal* a deep experience and provide us with the factual materials for fictional projections.

A postscript to *A Journal* appeared as an article "Worse than War," in the August, 1920, number of the *English Review.* In it May Sinclair recalled a prophecy that a war correspondent had made in Ghent in October, 1914, of a nightmare of pestilence that would follow the war and be worse than the war. He had been right. An air of hopelessness was brooding over a Europe that had been brought to its knees and to the lowest levels of living filth, physical degeneration, starvation, and exhaustion by the Allied blockade.

A whole-hearted patriot, she did not attack the strategy of the conquerors. Compassion for the enemy in time of war must not make one a traitor to one's own people. But since the enemy was brought to a subanimal level of illness and weakness, military necessity had lost its point. Help must be given quickly and adequately. The Allies had to show human compassion to prove their moral stature. They had to do all they could to prevent disease from spreading over all the boundaries and striking the victors with cholera, malaria, tuberculosis, and typhus. They had to prevent anarchy from developing out of hunger and desolation. They had to help Europe if they were to preserve their own economy. Without the blockade, the Allies would not have won

---

10. *Ibid.,* p. 266.
11. *Ibid.,* p. 271.
12. *Ibid.,* pp. 105–6.
13. *Ibid.,* p. 216.

the war. Without the work of the Relief Commission, they could not win the peace. She foresaw that if the exhausted nations were not helped to regain their capacity to work, Germany, with her immense capacity for recuperation and industry, would absorb the impoverished and exhausted peoples around her. If she did absorb them, there would be the danger of "a war more terrible than any we have yet seen. Nobody with the smallest intellectual prudence would assert that such a war is impossible or even very improbable." That was why she appealed for a pooling "of all peoples and nations and languages, of conquerors and conquered, in one regenerating work of charity." She ended with a special plea for the "Save the Children Fund."

This little piece contains solid evidence of the humanity and the prescience that May Sinclair joined to her perceptiveness, and of the sanity that she had recovered after experiencing the controlled fury of war.

Psychology and Philosophy

Dorothea Beale had been the first to guide May Sinclair to the road of psychology to reach her goal of philosophy. Dr. Jessie Murray further encouraged her to add to her intuitive touch for human psychology the light of psychoanalysis.

The first report we have of what she assimilated from that new study is contained in a two-part article, "Symbolism and Sublimation," which was published in the *Medical Press,* August 9 and 16, 1916. Her primary object was to review Jung's *Psychology of the Unconscious,* which Beatrice Hinkle had translated. In Part I she explains the now familiar process of repression and the taboo, the relationship of the psyche to the libido, the repressive role of the psychic censor, and the method by which the psychoanalyst uses the symbols that the libido supplies in dreams and fantasies and free associations to break through the censor, which prevents the sublimation of the libido to take place on the necessary level of consciousness. The whole evolution of man had involved a lifting up of the libido out of the unconscious into the conscious and in the direction of intelligence. The symbol is the bridge by which the libido moves from past to future. The psychoanalyst's interpretation is the light by which the psyche sees the bridge: "A libido readapted to the higher purposes of the psyche is a libido adapted to reality."

In Part 2 May Sinclair commented freely on the theories of Freud, Adler, and Jung, and offered her estimate of their separate values. She accepted the displacement of the original theory of the sexual shock as the cause of a neurosis by the new theory of regression. She believed sublimation to be the only effectual form of self-assertion and redress. She also felt that both Freud and Jung underrated the value of repression, which at some period must have been of advantage to the race. At his best, the ascetic was the guardian and often the source of the spiritual tradition. A great deal that passed for repression was really sublimation, or attempts at it.

Something of the encouragement that Jung may have given her to the writing of *Mary Olivier* appears in a passage that discusses Jung's treatment of the conflict with the mother: "That conflict begins in childhood and is waged most fiercely on the threshold of adolescence. It must be fought to a finish and the child must win it or remain for ever immature. If the parent wins ten to one the child becomes neurotic." She thought that the final chapters of the *Psychology of the Unconscious,* those on deliverance and sacrifice, were of absolute importance: "The idealist will find in them the answer to his feverish questioning. He will find that throughout man's history man's goal has always been one and the same thing: Sublimation; the freedom of the Self in obedience to a higher law than preceding generations had laid upon him."

She was early in noticing what Hugh Crichton-Miller was to fix as a truism in his *Psycho-Analysis* in 1933: that so much in Freud revolted and depressed, while Jung consoled and encouraged. She ended with a distribution of credit. Freud had built no solid bridge between his psychoanalysis and his psychotherapy. Jung had built that bridge with his discovery of the function of the symbol. Yet Freud the pioneer had hacked his way through a hitherto impenetrable dark forest and had left a straight path for those who followed.

A review in the *Medical Press* on May 16, 1917, of Dr. Charles A. Mercier's *Causation and Belief* drew upon May Sinclair's reading in Mill, Green, Russell, and Kant, and rejected Mercier's sequential view of causation in favor of Russell's insistence on the configuration of the Whole and Kant's triple dialectic, which held that the causal relationship had no meaning apart from totality. A second book by Dr. Mercier, his *Spiritualism and Sir Oliver Lodge,* she reviewed in the *Medical Press* on July 25. She applauded Dr. Mercier for exposing the unscientific nature of Sir Oliver Lodge's experiments to show the survival of existence after bodily death, and deplored the increase in unscientific authority being advanced by scientific names. She also faulted Dr. Mercier for ignoring the facts of telepathy and clairvoyance. A number of errors of fact and a typographical error that she had missed in the proof of her review provoked a reply from Sir Oliver that was printed on August 8, together with her humble, gracious, but not abject apology, which ended her contributions to the *Medical Journal*.

A judgment, even an adequate description of her *A Defence of Idealism*, published in August, 1917, will have to come from those who have made formal philosophy their life's work. The reviews by philosophers were notably respectful to her thinking and admiring toward her imaginative style. The words "A Defence" in the title correctly express a characteristic of much of May Sinclair's critical writing. In her Introduction she recognized her fate with respect to this book: "It does look like personal misfortune or perversity that, when there are lots of other philosophies to choose from, you should happen to hit on the one that has just had a tremendous innings, and is now in the process of being bowled out."[14] She felt that the new realists were wrong in believing that twentieth century pluralism was the philosophy of the future; she believed that the new idealism would be born again.

She regretted having to differ with those whom she profoundly admired: Samuel Butler, M. Bergson, William James, Bertrand Russell, and William McDougall. She charmingly apologized for the beautiful demolition that she inflicted upon William James's Pragmatism. But what could she do? "I believe in Pragmatism as a branch, and a very important branch, of casuistry. I do not believe in it as a philosophy. It is a method and not a philosophy. It is not even a philosophical method. Pragmatism is one long argument ad hominem, and it is nothing more."[15]

She wrote as a person expressing her mind, employing every spark and flash and flare of her imagination to light the concepts of her intellect. As an analyst of method she called William James to order for having classified the idealistic monists as "tender-minded," and the pluralists as "tough-minded," for prefacing his use of reason with a six-shooter of prejudice that made his audience plump for Pragmatism before they heard a word of evidence.[16]

She explained that she wished to disentangle what was true in realistic pluralism from what was merely fascinating, so that not every hope and belief in a hereafter might have to be surrendered. She had similarly tried to disentangle what was untrue in Idealism from what she believed to be sound and enduring, and to state her adversary's case in each instance to his best advantage.

She defended her inclusion of mysticism because of its importance to psychology, and because she thought that students of comparative

14. *A Defence of Idealism* (London: Macmillan, 1917), p. vii.
15. *Ibid.*, pp. ix–x.
16. *Ibid.*, p. xi.

religion should keep it under consideration to determine whether it marked a reversion or a progression in the search for reality. Among those friends whose help she acknowledged were Evelyn Underhill, authority on mysticism, Cecil Delisle Burns, authority on the new realists, and Mrs. Susie S. Brierly, the experimental psychologist.

Personal references keep the reader who is primarily a student of the novelist aware of the very human being who was giving life to the abstractions of the intellect. Panpsychism made her think how pleasant it was to believe that her cat had designed his "fine black coat of fur" for himself.[17] Materialism, with its method of arguing cause and effect as a sequential relationship, could point to the effects of poison being introduced into the blood, like the profound coma of Bright's disease,[18] which she had witnessed when her brother Harold died of it in Gresford in 1887. The faith of Professor McDougall and Professor Thorndike in the supremacy of neural habit associations to the exclusion of psychic factors of desire and choice determining the movements of animals reminded her of how her cat had proved to her the dominance of psychic associations over neural ones.[19] Her genteelness she betrayed when she translated Anatole France's "le coup de pied au cul" as "a kick in the ribs."[20] In the chapter on the new mysticism she described how the pluralists and pragmatists abhorred a monist. In their eyes, "he is like a man with a history of drink in his family."[21]

She interpreted the vision of beauty that a lover experiences as a laying hold on eternal life, and the act of loving as a lover's finding "his own innermost reality." There was even a higher state of certainty than the state that the lover achieves: "Almost every other hero knows it: the exquisite and incredible assurance, the positively ecstatic vision of Reality that comes to him when he faces death for the first time. There is no certainty that life can give that surpasses or even comes anywhere near it. And the world has been full of *these* mystics, *these* visionaries, since August 1914."[22] The beauty that she had seen in Yorkshire and had pictured in *The Three Sisters* came back to her in her last chapter, "Conclusions," which describes the moment of heightened psychic intensity in which one perceives reality: "moments when things that we have seen all our lives without truly seeing them, the flowers in the garden, the trees in the field, the hawthorn on the hillside, change to us in an instant of time, and show the secret and

17. *Ibid.*, p. ix.
18. *Ibid.*, p. 87.
19. *Ibid.*, pp. 108–9.
20. *Ibid.*, pp. 251–52.
21. *Ibid.*, p. 273.
22. *Ibid.*, p. 302.

imperishable life they harbour: moments when the human creature we have known all our life without truly knowing it, reveals its incredible godheads; moments of danger that are moments of sure and perfect happiness, because then the adorable Reality gives itself to our very sight and touch."[23]

Wit abundantly entertains us as we follow the finely sentient, relentlessly firm probing of a particular philosophy. She laughed at Mr. McDougall's theory of psychophysical parallelism as suggesting a relationship like that of an unhappy love affair, "with the reciprocity all on one side."[24] Of pragmatism she wrote, "What God hath joined let no pragmatist put asunder."[25] And of Russell's theory of the separable relations of whole and part she wrote, "What analytic logic hath put asunder, let no man join."[26] She laughed at the new realists' argument that subject and predicate were separate and independent, so forcing monistic idealism to surrender its most sacred tenet:

> Idealism, seeking unity before all things, is supposed to have assumed faithfulness in the union of subject and predicate. Realism, on the look-out for plurality, finds, on the contrary, that subjects are polygamous and have many predicates, while there never was a predicate yet that could remain faithful to one subject for very long. The rose is red, but so is the dawn and so is Bardolph's nose. And, unless you adopt the realistic theory of universals, you are in danger of arguing that the nose and the rose are not red, because redness is not a rose nor a nose. In short, the relations of most subjects and predicates are temporary and fortuitous, and their behavior, from the point of view of monism and monogamy, an open scandal. Therefore, the pluralist argues, you had much better agree with him that relations are irreducible and independent entities, and that so are their terms.[27]

To a philosophically uncommitted reader, May Sinclair argued brilliantly and entertainingly that Idealism offered at least as probable an explanation of the tie between the physical object perceived and the psychic phenomenon of perception as could any system of philosophy by the expedient of producing the mind as the consummator of this union.

Brontë Criticism

In 1912 May Sinclair published *The Three Brontës*. It is a brilliantly written informal essay interpreting and valuing the Brontës

23. *Ibid.*, p. 379.
24. *Ibid.*, p. 126.
25. *Ibid.*, p. 158.
26. *Ibid.*, p. 212.
27. *Ibid.*, p. 231.

as persons and as artists. Always she draws upon her own experience as a creative writer and upon her own humanity as a person sending her intuition into the depths of her subjects. Only Anne did she fail to understand.

May Sinclair saw Patrick Brontë as an egoistic, morose, rather savage father, who was also a good companion and a good teacher when his daughters were small. She covered her deeper insight with a sentimental cloak, "poor and unhappy and innocent old man," while she drew on his failings for *The Three Sisters.* It is strange that she should have overlooked his influence as a model of the Brontë obsessing male.

For the children their imagination was a world of greater reality than their home; it was an escape from being a clergyman's daughters; and yet Haworth was the homeland of their affections and of their inspiration. Away from Haworth they were homesick almost to madness, for their parsonage, the churchyard, and the moors. Charlotte was the one who was divided between Haworth and her passion for knowledge. She was proposed to, but preferred freedom and the passion for knowledge. Death struck at the sisters in a series of personal blows: Branwell's death hastened Emily's, and Emily's hastened Anne's death. Charlotte went to her marriage afraid, warned by premonitions. There was no real corruption in Branwell, May Sinclair insisted; his worst vice was his sentimentalism. Emily infused Anne with her contempt for all creeds, and Anne fearfully gave in, to suffer secretly from religious doubt.

Charlotte was warmly emotional but eccentric in showing her emotions, as at the party that Thackeray gave in her honor, where she spent most of the evening talking to the governess. She loved children: "It must have been an agony to have to look after them, especially when the rule was that they were not to 'love the governess.' "[28] Her dream about a little crying child whom she could not still was a premonition that she gave to Jane Eyre. She was free from the sentimentalism of the Victorian age, and her conscience was, next to her genius, the largest and most delicate part of her.

Haworth established Charlotte's genius, and Haworth rescued Emily from the sterile rhetoric of M. Heger. New in *Jane Eyre* was a good woman of no sensual charm, who felt a passion glorified above the plane of the animal, and who was no moral prude but abstained from judging a man who displayed his mistresses. The reading of *Wuthering*

---

28. *The Three Brontës* (London: Hutchinson, Hutchinsons Booklovers edition, 1938) , p. 66.

Heights made all the difference in waking Charlotte from half-aliveness to full life. May Sinclair destroyed the theory of a tragic passion by Charlotte for M. Paul Heger. The realistic characters in *Villette* were created from "the germs of the real."

May Sinclair praised the fragment entitled *Emma* as continuing the new greatness that *Villette* had reached. Only by indirection did she speak her real opinion of the Reverend Nicholls, whom she found it hard to forgive for having killed off Mr. Ellis and Matilda. She saw that Charlotte's poems were the raw materials for her novels, and that only in her novels was she a poet.

Emily loved all living things, yet seem removed from all, and she had an intense repugnance for external contacts. She loved the young and helpless Anne, the helpless Branwell, and the moors. Her soul was self-sufficient. The secret of her greatness was her sense of the reality behind the illusion. The pantheism she held came from her self, and she was as much a mystic as a pantheist. She gave her pure passion to life, and life gave her nothing in return; but her very destitution made her genius rich and virile. She relied on none of the consolations of religion.

May Sinclair examined the Gondal poems to show that they were indispensable to a comprehension of Emily: "For supreme in the Gondal legend is the idea of a mighty and disastrous passion, a woman's passion for the defeated, the dishonored, and the outlawed lover; a creature superb in evil, like Heathcliff, and like Heathcliff tragic and unspeakably mournful in his doom."[29] Zamorna became Heathcliff. Emily was all the people and all the moods in the Gondal cycle.

In examining *Wuthering Heights* May Sinclair discovered the essence of the marriage philosophy of the Brontës when she noticed that in marrying Edgar Linton, Catherine sinned by separating her body from her soul. Sharing major importance with the theme of the adoration of the earth was the tragedy of a spirit haunting the human lover whose soul she was. May Sinclair thought that only Thomas Hardy compared to Emily in picturing a place so vividly. Emily had one supremely simple style, unloaded with figures, but her construction, May Sinclair thought, was the worst ever, its faults overcome only by the fact that Emily's dramatic instinct never failed her.

Significantly confessional is May Sinclair's saying that Charlotte was "one of those novelists who do not write novels before they are nearly thirty,"[30] and that Charlotte did not know after her sojourn in Brussels

---

29. *Ibid.,* p. 196.
30. *Ibid.,* p. 100.

that her right medium was prose.[31] May Sinclair had found Mrs. Gaskell's *Life of Charlotte Brontë* in her father's library and read it a score of times: "For the first time I was in the grip of a reality more poignant than any that I had yet known, of a tragedy that I could hardly bear."[32]

May Sinclair felt closest to Charlotte, and worshiped Emily. It is true, as she complained, that too much has been written about the Brontës, but her essay is among the indispensable studies of genius by a genius.

After reading in the *London Times* of July 29, 1913, four letters written by Charlotte Brontë to M. Constantin Heger following her second return from Brussels in February, 1844, May Sinclair wrote an indignant essay on "The New Brontë Letters" that was published in the *Dial* on November 1. She deplored the invasion of Charlotte's privacy and incautiously confessed that she had been wrong in declaring any element of real passion by Charlotte for M. Heger improbable. Despite her judgment that the letters did not express an acknowledged love, her fear that Charlotte might have felt passionate longing clouded her perception of the truth that they were literary sublimations of gratitude.[33] The uneasy essay became the preface to a new issue of *The Three Brontës* in March, 1914.

The last introduction in the Everyman Library, to *The Tenant of Wildfell Hall*, published in April, 1914, is a mixture of critical assaying and impatience, much sharper in its treatment of Anne than were the references to her in the Brontë book. In that, although denying her genius, she had at least felt compassion for Emily's protégée. Still, May Sinclair grants what her temper would have denied to Anne. *Agnes Grey* she describes as portraying the suppressed and frustrated woman squirming in her intolerable prison house, and espousing a woman's right to love, at any rate in literature, as she saw fit. *The Tenant of Wildfell Hall* advocated revolt against the woman's vow of obedience, even against the marriage laws: "Mrs. Huntingdon is, if not the first, one of the first of the long line of insurgent modern heroines." The slamming of her bedroom door was the first such slamming in English fiction. But outside of that reverberating sound May Sinclair found not a thrill in all its lamentably dull pages.

---

31. *Ibid.*, p. 103.
32. *Ibid.*, p. 235.
33. Rebecca West wrote to me, October 24, 1962. "The publication of the Heger letters was a tragic and terrible blow to May—like a personal bereavement. She had wanted so much to think of the Brontës as virgin priestesses of art." But May Sinclair's original insight was supported by Fannie Elizabeth Radford in her *The Brontës' Web of Childhood* (New York: Columbia University Press, 1941).

The subject of *The Tenant* was a very sensitive one for the critic: the story of a vicious, mother-spoiled male, an alcoholic, unfaithful to his wife, cruel to his child. And Anne and May Sinclair were too much alike. Anne too was a gentle volcano, a quiet little person whom no one but her sisters would suspect of knowing so much about cruelty and of having the courage to describe it with such specific details and with such a calm control. And Mrs. Huntingdon is very like May Sinclair. She has a fine intellect, a keen interest in the psychology of association, a hatred of drunkenness seen in family privacy, a hatred of the effects of it on character. May Sinclair thought her a "fearful figure of intellect and integrity," lifeless because Anne had no genius to give her life. May Sinclair further disliked her for having a furious propensity to preach as Anne's spokesman. For May Sinclair, the novel that Victorian readers found second only to *Jane Eyre* in absorbing interest was merely "the first presentation of that Feminist novel which we all know."

Criticism of Her Contemporaries

A strong emotional response to the work, the loyalty of friendship to the author, and a fighting need to champion writing that met with prejudice inspired May Sinclair's criticism of her contemporaries. Her article on "The Gitanjali," in the May, 1913, number of the *North American Review,* was written at the flood tide of her responsiveness to Eastern mysticism. In it she traced the literary ancestry of Tagore to Chandidas, Chaitanya, and all the Vaishnava poets. She thought his devotional poems a blend of music and rhythm finer than Swinburne's with Shelley's metaphysical subtlety and intensity. Some of the passages recalled Walt Whitman, that "robust and boisterous Vaishnavist of the Western West," without his boisterousness. He resembled Whitman too in that his adoration of life was not greater than his adoration of death.

The dualism inherent in Christianity caused the Western mystic to regard the visible world as abhorrent and unholy. The Eastern mystics denied the visible world's existence, and therefore held no hatred or horror of it. Tagore bridged the natural gulf that the Western mind felt between the common human heart and the transcendent being. The veil of Maya, the illusion of the world, permitted a full view of the reality, a perfect oneness. May Sinclair repeated a part of her review in the chapter on "The New Mysticism" in *A Defence of Idealism,* with more emphasis on Kabir's sharing the Christian metaphysics of dualism.

Her rapture did not last, as a passage in *Mary Olivier* showed;[34] but it was wonderful while it lasted.

"Two Notes" in the *Egoist* for June 1, 1915, defended H. D.'s poetry against Harold Monro's article "Imagists Discussed." May Sinclair called H. D. "the most significant of the Imagists," her poems able to stand within their own school "for sheer emotion, for clean-cut and perfect beauty." She admitted that H. D.'s poetry lacked passion, and thought that the reaction from the passion and the sentiment that passed for passion in the nineteenth century was inevitable: "And isn't it almost time to remind us that there is a beauty of restraint and stillness and flawless clarity?" She praised H. D.'s success in the "clean, naked, sensuous image" carrying emotion without rhyme, but not without rhythm. She defended the aim of the imagists to scrap imagery, to make the image form and substance, presentation, not representation, reality itself, not a symbol of it. She found plenty of individual differences among imagists—Amy Lowell, F. S. Flint, Richard Aldington, H. D.—and doubted that a formula could include them all. The imagists were true believers in transubstantiation. She pleaded that in their "hour of heroic immaturity" they be spared from further attack, and allowed to practice their sacramental act of writing poetry.

May Sinclair wrote the Introduction for a book of *vers libre* by Jean de Bosschere, *The Closed Door,* published in September, 1917. The French text was translated on parallel pages by F. S. Flint, and illustrated by its author, the illustrator of *Uncanny Stories.* She praised the poems for their mystic vision, their mastery of symbolism and sublimations. Her praise at this far-removed time seems greatly excessive, an outflow of her passion for Belgium, for de Bosschere was a *flamand.*

"*Prufrock:* and Other Observations, a Criticism," is a beautifully written defense and interpretation published in the December, 1917, number of the *Little Review,* which advertised itself as "the magazine that is read by those who write the others." May Sinclair opened her critique with claws out for the reviewers who had dispraised the volume, in particular Arthur Waugh, who had called T. S. Eliot a "drunken Helot." She accused the critics of attacking him not for his work, whose finest she ranked with Browning's, but because it had appeared in the unpopular *Blast,* and because his genius disturbed comfortable and respectable people. Mr. Eliot wrote in no tradition. He headed straight for reality without corners or curves. Some of the realities he saw and wrote about were ugly and unpleasant, but there was no reason why he should not do such things if he did them well

---

34. *Mary Olivier: A Life* (New York: Macmillan, 1919), p. 277.

enough. His supposed obscurity for some readers came from his swift movement; he was actually as clear as daylight. She defended Eliot's right to choose his subject and his concern for reality, and praised his original technique.

"The Novels of Dorothy Richardson," an essay in the *Egoist* and in the *Little Review* for April, 1918, considered the first three novels in the Pilgrimage series, to justify the method and to declare its success. May Sinclair opened her case by asking that the philosophic cant of the nineteenth century be thrown off so that the twentieth century artist could be judged by new critical terms. She agreed with J. D. Beresford's opinion that Dorothy Richardson had just plunged right into reality, and thought that the precedents for her plunge had been set by the deGoncourts and by Margeurite Audoux. She saw a growing tendency to plunge, and judged that Dorothy Richardson had not plunged deeper than James Joyce in his *Portrait of the Artist as a Young Man*.

Dorothy Richardson's method was to avoid narrative, situation, drama, explication, omniscience, and the study of character. She limited herself to Miriam Henderson's knowledge and to her powers of divining, and so accepted the limitations that life imposes on us all. She let life just go on and on, and that meant "Miriam Henderson's stream of consciousness going on and on." All that mattered was Miriam's consciousness; the flow of time outside it did not matter. There is apparently nothing in Miriam's life to justify living, and yet she is happy: "What really matters is a state of mind, the interest or the ecstasy with which we close with life."

"The Reputation of Ezra Pound," appearing in April, 1920, in the *English Review* and in May in the *North American Review*, shows May Sinclair to be the champion and enthusiast that her friendship compelled her to be and the critic who admitted limitations that she would never have allowed in her own writing, but which she tolerated as a true poet's license.

She recognized the offense that Pound had given to the establishment by withholding respect from respectable persons, by voicing an arrogant indifference to many of the admired masterpieces of his day, by associating himself with unpopular movements. She also called attention to his ardor in making known the work of Gaudier-Brzseska, Joyce, Wyndham Lewis, and T. S. Eliot, instead of gaining recognition for himself. She thought him the most individual poet of his century, although he was not original. He had rejected the literature of the Edwardian and Georgian eras to absorb the three diverse literatures of the Langue d'Oc, old China, and Augustan Rome, and snatches at

Anglo-Saxon, Sappho, and the Greek epigrammatists. She thought the Chinese poets the most beneficial of all the influences that he sensitively absorbed, and Propertius the closest fitting of all his masks.

He could have won popularity by doing the familiar thing with exquisite dexterity. Instead, he "adopted the mark of fantastic intellectual Inhumanism," and defended his rebellion by saying that the great passionate human themes had lost their direct appeal; many associations and repetitions had altered them. If he had not involved himself with *Blast* and the *Little Review* and had not spoken his honest opinions of his contemporaries, he would have had a kindlier reception from the critics.

The quotations that May Sinclair chose caught the exquisitely right touches of his genius, in timing a pause, in tuning a cadence, in leaving an image with one rather than pressing it upon the mind's eye. The campaign to establish Ezra Pound as a major poet has been won. It should be remembered that May Sinclair fought for him powerfully at a very critical moment of that campaign, when Pound might very well have defeated himself.

Verses

The champion of the imagists and others turned to verse to solace the deep hurt that she suffered when Dr. Munro dismissed her from his Ambulance Corps. Instead of writing in the traditional forms, she now invented free patterns of her own.

She wrote three sets of verses about the corps, of which only the first and third, as far as I know, were published. The first set, "Field Ambulance in Retreat, Via Dolorosa, Via Sacra," appeared in *King Albert's Book,* which Hall Caine edited and dated Christmas, 1914. It paints, rather than tells, in twenty-seven lines of free verse the beauty of a Flemish road and of the harvest fields, and the sadness of a regiment of infantry retreating as the Red Cross ambulance rushes on:

You know nothing of beauty and of desolation who have not seen
That smile of an army in retreat.

The third was first titled "Ave! (To a Field Ambulance in Flanders)," and then retitled "Dedication (To a Field Ambulance in Flanders)," dated March 8, 1915, and placed ahead of the Introduction to *A Journal of Impressions in Belgium.* In its thirty-nine lines of free verse it confesses May Sinclair's shame over having been separated from the Ambulance Corps, and her envy of the members who continued to face the goddess Danger. Rhythm, image, and feeling lift the subject to a religious plane, part Greek, part Christian.

Her best poetry of the decade appeared in September, 1920, in Thomas Moult's magazine *Voices:* "Childhood," three lyrics of childhood experiences, irregular in measure, rhyme, and rhythm, with a fine control for piercing effects. Two of the lyrics tell of an open clash between the child and her family (meaning her mother); the third confesses a rebellion that was silent.

The first poem, "Visionary," is set in Rock Ferry and tells us of the child's clash with the family when, at the age of four, she insisted that she had seen God in the sky and was put to bed for her naughtiness. "Prison-House" is the recantation of the same little girl at seven:

> I was only four, you know.

The third lyric, "Fright," tells of the desolation of the little girl because her mother will not speak to "her little lamb" and lets her go to bed without a word or a kiss:

> I climb the last stair
> Where the gas burns always low;
> In the big dark room my bed
> Stands very small and white—
> God—God—are You there?
> I feel with my hands as I go;
> The floor
> Cries out under my tread;
> Somebody shuts the door;
> Somebody turns out the light
> At the head of the stairs;
> And I know
> That God isn't anywhere,
> And that Mother will die in the night.[35]

These lyrics are worth saving for English poetry and for the memory of May Sinclair.

Literary Theory

In her Introduction to *The Judgement of Eve and other Stories*, dated February 13, 1914, May Sinclair excepted "The Judgement of Eve" and "The Wrackham Memoirs" from the canons of the short story and specified them as examples of a form of the novel that results from the novelist's boiling down his materials to their simplest possible

---

35. Quoted by permission of Thomas Moult.

expression. A novelist could justify such a compaction only "if the subject requires it."

She discusses oblique narrative as having "severe and embarrassing limitations," but where motives were obscure and doubtful, where the interest lay in things as they appeared to the teller, or as he interfered in a situation, then the method was expedient. It had eternal fascination "for those who love to deal in half-lights and obscurities, in things insubstantial, intricate, and ill-defined." In the last paragraph she announced that the book was a manifesto of "a transition period, the passing to a more intense and concentrated form."

Related to this manifesto is a sketch for an essay on the modern novel, difficultly legible as written on the back of three pages of the manuscript of *The Tree of Heaven*. It defined the function of the novel, "to represent life, . . . to view life in the form of a story," and required the artist to be willing to leave the beaten track, the materialistic road that leads to a known destination, through cities of ghosts and cemeteries of the dead, and that is maintained by the vested interests of traditionalism, to pioneer on a new road. The art of the new century must choose its own roadways. The projected essay was certainly a testament of her faith and her practice.

Publicity

The materials in her literary remains prove that May Sinclair, who was a member of the Board of Management, wrote the *Special Appeal in Time of War* for the Medico-Psychological Clinic, undated, published October 8, 1917, giving a full description of the clinic's program, and the *Report* of the clinic, again describing its work and appealing for financial support in 1919.[36]

Miss Laura E. Price, a student and part-time secretary for the Society for the Study of Orthopsychics discovered a copy of another piece of work that she believed to have been prepared by May Sinclair: *Prospectus of Educational Arrangements* (Society for the Study of Orthopsychics, 1919). An interesting paragraph in this pamphlet reads: "The student of character commences with a study of his own psychology, through Psycho-Analysis, which forms the principal part of the first year's work but is continued throughout the course. As soon as the student has acquired sufficient aptitude in the study of his own psychology, he is given under supervision opportunity for the study of others; cases are assigned to him at the discretion of the Directors."

---

36. See American Philosophical Society, "May Sinclair and the Medico-Psychological Clinic of London," *Proceedings*, August, 1962, for a full account.

16

The Novels: 1921-1927

May Sinclair opened the last decade of her writing life with her first comic novel, a masterpiece, *Mr. Waddington of Wyck* (August, 1921). The prevailing mood is unsympathetically comic, but the psychological dissector of a Meredithian county gentleman who is stuffed with the wadding of conceit turns into a sympathetic sharer of his suffering from the shock of discovering himself to be unloved by all but his mother.

The narrative glides in scenes of entertaining conversation, for which May Sinclair has no superior. The comic tone is modulated in amazing effects of counterpoint and variation. Most of what happens takes place in Lower Wyck Manor, Mr. Horatio Bysshe Waddington's home, to give the reader the snugly comfortable feeling of being seated in a theater to savor the comedy of a man's full exposure. His egoism is his greatest sin, his excessive comfort in being himself, in taking for absolute truth the illusion that he is the central serious interest of the world he observes. He is only half right. He is the comical, not the serious, central interest of the world that he observes, the world that observes him. And the discovery of the truth becomes unbearable. May Sinclair further uncovers the secret of his unhappiness that provides the terminal aesthetic experience.

Horatio Bysshe Waddington—lord of the manor of a Cotswold village, descendant of three hundred years of respected Gloucester-shire Waddingtons and sire of a sixteen-year-old schoolboy, Horace, who has his mother's lust for laughter—is in his fifties. He has no sense of humor, and no tolerance for laughter, despite the eighteen years of it that his wife has gotten out of his saturation with his mirror-reflected self. He has dismissed one secretary, his wife's clever journalist cousin,

Ralph Bevan, who was helping him with his "Ramblings in the Cotswolds," and has engaged a second secretary, Barbara Madden, the
daughter of a friend of Mrs. Fanny Waddington. Barbara is far more
tactful in concealing Mr. Waddington's incompetence as a writer
from him.

The most delicious comedy, and pathos too, develops out of Mr.
Waddington's reaching for the romance that he has never experienced.
Two women become the objects of his ambition. The first is a widow,
Mrs. Elise Levitt, who has played to his need to enjoy the sense of
power by obtaining wartime and postwar favors for her son Toby. She
next obtains from him tenancy in a cottage that he has luxuriously
renovated without asking her to pay rent. Finally, she leads him up the
garden path to the expectation of romance, until, seeing that he will
not pay cash down, she sets him reeling with her plangent laughter.
Her attempt to blackmail him brings Barbara Madden to his rescue.
Certain that Barbara must be in love with him to have saved him from
Mrs. Levitt, he now turns to Barbara for his hope of romance. His
preparations for an elopement with her, including the purchase of
magenta pajamas with a design of orange forked lightning, lead to a
second and more serious setback: Barbara's hilarious laughter. And
that laughter wounds Fanny, his wife. Fanny had hoped that Mrs.
Levitt would give Horatio some romance, and then wished that Barbara might have been kind instead of cruel toward her husband.
Fanny's regret has two sources; one is in Horatio. Horatio had felt for
the first time a real caring for someone other than himself when he
cared for Barbara. The second is her facing the truth that Horatio
had been her laughable sorry third choice, whom she married because,
as Ralph Bevan explains to Barbara, she had been "a mortal woman
and she wanted a husband and children";[1] and she had never given
him the love he needed. Only his mother loved him, and at the end,
it is to the mother that the frustrated Horatio runs. Fanny says, " 'He's
going back to his mother to be made young again.' "[2] Through all her
years of marriage, Fanny's sense of comedy had been more powerful
than her sense of pity; and she had failed to keep him young through
love. Horatio was the joke that Fanny had played upon herself.

The historical perspectives in comedy in this novel point to Meredith's *The Egoist* and to Jane Austen's *Emma*. The conceit of Mr.
Waddington is sufficient evidence of the former, and the many instances
of illusions illustrate the latter. So even Barbara Madden, penetrating
as she is, along with Ralph Bevan, into the truth about Mr. Wadding-

1. *Mr. Waddington of Wyck* (New York: Macmillan, 1921), p. 128.
2. *Ibid.,* p. 315.

ton, is badly mistaken at first in thinking that Ralph is in love with Fanny, and that Fanny is willing to surrender to Ralph.[3]

A dramatic scene magnificently elaborated as comedy uses the symbolic motif that Henry Fielding had employed in *Tom Jones* for a sentimental effect. Horatio sits with Elise on a sofa, her skunk fur piece lying between them, serving less as a barrier than as a sort of ouija board for his real messages of desire and her simulated ones. As his fantasy pictures Elise living in a bijou of a house awaiting his passionate visits, he unconsciously strokes the long tails of her fur, and her hand joins in the play of stroking the fur to lead him on.[4]

To make certain that the reader will not overlook the stuffiness suggested in Horatio's family name, May Sinclair once uses its key word to describe Horatio "wearing a royal blue wadded silk dressing gown."[5] Technically admirable is the author's having two collaborating observers and commentators upon Horatio, his wife, and his son Horace; they are the literarily sensitive Ralph Bevan and Barbara Madden, who between them expertly modulate the proportions of comedy and sympathy. But May Sinclair also intervenes to control the mood, most unsubtly when she applies the words "fatuous" and "fatuity" to certify Mr. Waddington as a butt for laughter. She did not repeat this crudeness in a later comedy.

A number of decorative motifs appear, to combine symbolism with characterization. Fanny is given a butterfly image, and a humming that is significant when sounded and when silenced. Mr. Waddington is given a sudden hopping about, to express his rocketing impulse of youthfulness and his absurdity.

The descriptive writing is squeezed to the essence of image and meaning. There is a line about the Cotswolds in winter: "all white, netted with the purplish brown filigree-work of the trees."[6]

The war that was called Great lightly sifts into this story of the year 1919. Ralph, a journalist, had lost his job and gone to war, been gassed, and had suffered a concussion from a shell-burst. Barbara had served as a secretary in a department in the War Office. Mr. Waddington had been a special constable, a member of special tribunals, and had driven his car about the countryside on zealous missions. Mrs. Levitt had pleaded with him for her son's exemption from war service and for his employment in a safe wartime job.

---

3. *Ibid.*, p. 12.
4. *Ibid.*, p. 190. See also Maurice Johnson's delightful treatment of the device of Sophia's muff in his *Fielding's Art of Fiction* (Philadelphia: University of Pennsylvania Press, 1961), pp. 129–38.
5. *Ibid.*, p. 283.
6. *Ibid.*, p. 259.

Traces of family and personal happenings are freely transmuted into art. Barbara tries to check Horace's cruel comic feeling toward his father by saying, "If you found your father drunk under a lilac bush I believe you'd go and fetch me to look at him."[7] Brought into the comedy is one of the most serious interests in May Sinclair's life, her brother Frank. Elise is the widow of a captain in the gunners, Frank Levitt, who had served in Poona.[8] Barbara's exhilaration in being driven swiftly up and down hill in a motor car was one of May Sinclair's joys. The Impromptu by Schubert that Fanny hums[9] must have been No. 2 of *Quatre Impromptus*, Opus 142, for its beat matches Fanny's humming beat, as May Sinclair's own album of Schubert lets us see. The ending, Horatio's going to stay with his mother, sounds a call that May Sinclair had already confessed in her early poetry, in the dedication of her first novel, and in her frank psychograph, *Mary Olivier,* and was to sound in the ending of her next novel; the wish, unfulfilled in life, for a return of love from the mother whom she loved, who made her look and feel young.

Wyck is Stow-on-the-Wold, and Ralph has a room at the White Hart Hotel, May Sinclair's home-away-from-home. The manuscript reveals that the original title was *Fanny Waddington's Husband,* which, while it would have made a subtle ironic contrast to Mr. Waddington's point of view that he possessed Fanny, and others about him, would also have been a mistake in hinting that Fanny's mind was importantly entered into, when it was not. The present title is in more direct agreement with the purer mood of comedy than with the subtler mood of comic irony.

Life and Death of Harriett Frean (January, 1962) is the negative balance to *Mary Olivier.* It tells of the life of a daughter who submitted to her Victorian parents' will to make her a good child; who let them persuade her with their genuine but intolerant love to feel only their feelings, and who let them kill her potential for developing a self and becoming a loving and loved wife. Renunciation of love brings no sublimation, for there is no nobility about wrecking three other lives besides aborting one's own. There may be a certain suicidal nobility about Mrs. Frean giving up her chance of being cured of cancer through an operation performed in time because she would not use the hundred pounds it would cost and lessen Harriett's small income left by the rashly speculating Mr. Frean.

Its mood is mellow-surfaced, variously tinted ironic satire. It would

---

7. *Ibid.,* p. 151.
8. *Ibid.,* p. 148.
9. *Ibid.,* p. 1.

be unfair to expose the corrupting center without appreciating the surface of trustful love, the peace of family unity, the air of kindness, the drama of passion, the comic play among women friends.

Its compactness puts it into a special class of dwarf novel, bodied with the complete and complex organization of a full biographical novel. It sheds a cool luminousness that is energized by its consumption of a glowing, then a decaying, vitality. Its field of experience is bounded by Harriett's awareness, which her secondary consciousness reports from the outside. Possibly as a gesture disguising the personal origins of the might-have-been, May Sinclair sets the time of the story about twenty years before the dates of Mary Olivier's successful struggle against family suppression. The time spans from the 1840s to 1912, when Harriett is not yet sixty-nine.

Symbols light the way of meaning and the drift of the story from the opening to the close. The first symbolic episode describes Harriett's mother reciting the nursery rhyme about the pussycat that went to London to see the queen. Just as the queen was passing, a little mouse came out of its hole and ran under the chair, and that is what the pussycat saw. Harriett was to be distracted from her will to succeed as an individual by her instinctive child's impulse to love and obey and submit to her parents.

Harriett's doll, Ida, becomes a symbol. Harriett doesn't want to let her playmate, Connie Hancock, cuddle and fondle it. Her mother orders her to let Connie play with it. Harriett is so hurt by her mother's order that she pretends that Ida has died, coffins it in a pasteboard box, and lays it away in a drawer-cemetery of a wardrobe. Ida is the self that Harriett wanted as a child to preserve as her own. By inflicting a polite renunciation upon her, her mother caused her to bury that self and accept her mother's choice of a new doll, Emily, as its substitute. We remember that May Sinclair's mother's name was Amelia.

Harriett thereafter lives for her mother's approval. After she has been deprived of her tea at a school treat because her mother mistook another child's used plate standing in front of Harriett as the sign that she had finished her plate and was waiting for a second helping, her mother gives her the maxim that is to guide Harriett's life: "It's better to go without than to take from other people. That's ugly."[10]

Harriett's schoolfriend Priscilla Heaven, unhappy, selfish, neurotic as a child, becomes engaged to a bank clerk, Robin Lethbridge. Robin's visits to Harriett's more pleasant home end in his falling in love with Harriett, and in Harriett's finding him a stimulating lover. But her parents' lesson of renunciation causes her to refuse him, despite his

---

10. *Life and Death of Harriett Frean* (New York: Macmillan, 1922), p. 15.

foreknowledge of great unhappiness with the neurotic Prissie. The happiness that Harriett feels over having given up Robin to her friend Prissie is seen to be the falsest kind of sublimation.

Robin's marriage is a disaster. Prissie's repressed awareness that Robin does not love her leads to a hysteria that paralyzes both her legs and so forces Robin to give her, through pity, the attention he cannot will to give her through love. The suppression of Harriett's loving self turns her into a cruel demon who finds relief over Prissie's paralysis and exaltation over having been the means of Robin's achieving an ideal self-denying love for Prissie. Harriett's renunciation leads not only to Prissie's paralysis, but also to Robin's degeneration. After Prissie's death and Robin's marriage to Beatrice, her nurse, he becomes as fretful and demanding upon Beatrice as Prissie had been to him. Harriett's frustration makes her cruel even to her loyal maid Maggie, whom she discharges for nursing her illegitimate baby. It becomes Harriett's fault that the baby dies.

The sane balance to Harriett's sentimental sickness is provided by Beatrice's niece, Mona Floyd. Mona accepts a man who had broken his previous engagement, and answers Harriett's rebuke by pointing out the unhappiness that her conventional sentimentality had caused to three people besides herself.

Harriett has never become a self, with feelings that are her own. At sixty-eight she is proud to learn that she is suffering from the same malignancy that her mother had died of, and she is exalted to think that in every stab of pain she is living her mother's life again.

The symbol returns to tell its tragic meaning when Harriett, emerging from her operation, hallucinates having borne a dead baby. She thinks, "It's sad—sad to go through so much pain and then to have a dead baby."[11] A naked irony exposing the self that died in her mother's image speaks the climax, when Harriett smilingly salutes her visitor at the hospital, her friend Connie Pennefather, as "Mamma."

Analysis is taken over by the characters. Robin's second wife, Beatrice, fully explains to Harriett the origin of Prissie's hysterical paralysis.[12] Harriett's mind is read to explain why she rejects a cat as a companion: "A cat was a compromise, a substitute, a subterfuge."[13]

The style is throughout a glory in lithe beauty and precise freshness. There is poetry in the scene of the illusionary happiness of the Frean family,[14] and in the image of a beauty that Harriett cannot bear, Maggie's feeding her baby: "And sometimes she saw Maggie unbutton her

---

11. *Ibid.*, p. 133.
12. *Ibid.*, p. 97.
13. *Ibid.*, p. 116.
14. *Ibid.*, pp. 31–32.

black gown in a hurry and put out her white, rose-pointed breast to still his cry."[15]

The relief of comedy offers a smile in this somber book when Lizzie Pierce tells how the Pennefather boy proposed to her: " 'My *dear*, he kept on doing this' (Lizzie did it) 'as if he was trying to sit on himself to keep him from flying off into space like a cork. Fancy proposing on three tumblers of soda water! I might have been Mrs. Pennefather but for that.' "[16]

There must be many passages in the book that bear flakes of memory. Harriett's home in a London suburb could have been the Ilford of life and *Mary Olivier*. Harriett and her mother have been happy in Sidmouth: "She remembered the red cliffs, the sea, and Aunt Harriett's garden stuffed with flowers."[17]

Anne Severn and the Fieldings (November, 1922) is a number of kinds of novel, each kind admirably right. It is a family novel, subtly grouping its members into alignments of loyalty. It is a novel of love that erratically grows into a stable passion. It is a novel of self-discoveries and positive individuation. It is a psychological novel contrasting differences among persons in facing reality and exposing the suggestive powers of associations. It is a psychiatric novel describing two psychoneuroses from analysis to cure. And it is a novel about farming in May Sinclair's favorite Stow-on-the-Wold region that she called Wyck. I think it, and not *Mary Olivier*, is May Sinclair's greatest self-fulfilling novel. Her soul needed the fulfillment of a passionate love, and this novel answers that need. The larger number of characters tenanting this novel forbade the extreme shearing away that she practiced on *Harriett Frean*.

Its method is mostly dramatic dialogue of close sequence. The point of view is an all-comprehending one, although the judgment of the author upon her characters is rare. The literary nervous system by which each character lives, changes, and is related to other characters is possibly May Sinclair's greatest triumph in craftsmanship to support her greatest triumph in creativity.

The head of the family, Robert Fielding, is absorbed in managing the large family estate at Wyck-on-the-Hill. His wife, Adeline, a beautiful woman, demands affection, but evades her responsibility to help and love those members of her family who need both care and love, and she can be malign in her selfishness. Only the oldest of the three sons, Eliot, is from the very beginning emotionally stable and percep-

---

15. *Ibid.*, p. 100.
16. *Ibid.*, p. 34.
17. *Ibid.*, p. 68.

tive. He becomes a doctor, researching in bacteriology. The second son, Jerrold, inherits his mother's nature of ignoring unpleasant reality. The youngest, Colin, has the weakest nervous system, inheriting both his mother's fear of unpleasant reality and her craving for attention. Into this household of boys comes Anne Severn as an adopted sister. She is the daughter of the widowed John Severn, an Indian commissioner, a friend of Robert Fielding, and the fiancé whom Adeline had jilted to marry Robert. Anne brings with her strength of body and mind an infinite capacity for loyalty. The relationships of these six people drive the basic narrative dynamics of the novel.

Eliot's love for Anne is calmly channeled into bacteriology, for Anne's unwavering choice from childhood on is Jerrold. Jerrold is tender to her as a boy and big brother, but his reality-evading and fearridden nature makes his individuation a long, pain-suffering, pain-inflicting course. Even after he has fixed his choice upon Anne, her association as a nurse with his dying father, and his sense of guilt over having been a coward in ignoring Anne's warning that his father was ill turn his love into revulsion.

All the young people are drawn into the war: Eliot in the RAMC, Jerrold and Colin in the army, Anne as member of a Field Ambulance Corps. Colin is discharged as a victim of shell shock in 1915, and Anne, dismissed from the Ambulance Corps, becomes his nurse. Jerrold, recovered from his revulsion against her, returns to court Anne, but his mother, who has married John Severn after her husband's death, malignly misleads Jerrold into thinking that Anne and Colin are lovers, to avoid having to take over the care of Colin. Jerrold's marriage to Maisie Durham, who had fallen in love with him when he was in the Indian Civil Service, produces a brief barrier to the passion that unites Jerrold and Anne, temporarily and furtively at first, then, through Eliot's informing Jerrold of their mother's having deceived him about Anne, and through Maisie's strength in facing the reality that Jerrold and Anne love each other and in her renouncing Jerrold, finally and openly.

Three people arrive at a truer state of selfhood. Anne's intelligent nursing of the psychoneurotic Colin enables him to stand alone. Jerrold finds his best self, his real self, which loves his father's lands and gives them care, and which at last loves Anne better than himself. And Maisie is freed from both the unconscious dominance by a truth that she had feared to face—Jerrold's not loving her—and from the illusion that masked it from her awareness, her false angina.

The steps by which each situation forms and is resolved are developed with the greatest care to produce complete conviction. The power of association that had already been an important force in *The Combined Maze* was used in a pivotal dramatic scene to reverse Jerrold's longing for Anne, and in subtler episodes. When Mrs. Fielding caresses the back of Anne's neck to welcome the little adopted girl, her fingers stroke among the roots of Anne's hair. At once Anne thinks of her mother and jerks her head away to preserve the memory of that particular caress as exclusively her mother's.[18] Years after, when Jerrold caresses her in the very same way, the distance in time from her sorrow and her absorption in her love for Jerrold give the caress a dreamy, mother-centered thrill.[19]

The psychological-philosophical summit by which the maturity of the characters is judged is the experience of reality. That may come as a sensing of an authentic release in passion, as the development into a strong and individual self, or as the discovery of a truth that has been overlaid by an illusion. Maisie repeats to Anne what Eliot had taught her: " 'He said it was the test of everybody, how they took reality, and that Jerrold had had to learn how, but that you had always known.' "[20] For Anne and Jerrold, reality is the ecstasy of love finding love. For Maisie reality is the misery of love finding only pity.

The relaxed phrase is so rare as to be noticeable. One quip, not really true, tells what women in London say about Eliot Fielding: " 'Dr. Fielding isn't interested in people, only in their diseases. And not really in diseases, only in their germs.' "[21]

May Sinclair's innocent family love once more became the emotional well for her most powerful love story, the story of Anne's marrying her adoptive brother who had been to India. By studying it here we can begin to understand what a disturbing obsession, because of its very innocence, it must have been to her peace of mind, and what a stimulation to her creative art.

A copybook in her literary remains, "Notes on Farming, Stow-on-the-Wold," proves the care with which May Sinclair learned the things that Anne needed to know to be a successful farmer and manager of the estate while the brothers were off to war.

A Cure of Souls (January, 1924) was her second long comedy. Intimations of Trollope ascend from it—not the Trollope whom May Sinclair used to read to her mother, but a Trollope aged and shocked by the spoliation of his world, yet retaining his gifts for satire, comedy, aesthetic sensitivity, drama, character portrayal, and dialogue of un-

18. *Anne Severn and the Fieldings* (New York: Macmillan, 1922) , p. 7.
19. *Ibid.*, p. 201.
20. *Ibid.*, p. 319.
21. *Ibid.*, p. 90.

surpassed naturalness of effect. The narration is as omniscient as Trollope's. The setting is the Queningford in Gloucester of *Judgment of Eve.*

In *Mr. Waddington,* May Sinclair had allowed some of her characters to be spokesmen for the comic viewpoint; here she keeps the control of the comedy mostly in her own hands. She introduces one character, the canon's sister, Charlotte Roper, as an authoritative informant on the canon's nature, on his history of having been spoiled by his mother and of his once having been in love with a woman who loved him. And Mrs. Roper is perceptive of other people; she instantly recognizes the intense passion inspiring Agnes Lambert's arduous parish work.

There is no unity of mood in this comic satire. The dominant motive that sanctions laughter at the Reverend Canon Clement Purcell Chamberlain is his selfishness, but the laughter has many notes in its scale, from the defensive laughter of the equally guilty reader to the laughter of derisive outrage. The selfishness of his joy in the pleasures of the eye and body is often described in pure poetry. The comedy of the canon is more poignantly satirical, more frankly outraged than anything in *Waddington.* It ends in a gentle, ironical exposing of the loss of self-confidence by an aesthetically but not humanly sensitive intellectual whose conscience has been forced to face the reality that he has betrayed to his greed for sensuous selfishness a calling that has perquisites of great beauty, but whose reason for being is service to mankind, and that is made possible only by the gift of caring for others. May Sinclair seemed to remember and to regret the brusque treatment with which she had begun her comedy of the Waddington whom she called fatuous when she wrote about the canon, "His worst enemy couldn't say that he was fatuous."[22]

The comedy is developed in a succession of instances, all pressing the charge of his selfishness, of his not caring about others, only for himself. Out of fairness to her subject, May Sinclair suspends the comic mood to explain through his sister Charlotte that the canon's mother had built her boy's world for him so that he had never learned that he must share it with others. In spite of his senior curate's confessing that he had lost his faith in God, he tries to persuade Jackman to stay in orders, to spare his having to prepare sermons. He replaces his junior curate, who prods him with reminders of work that needs to be done, with an old friend who longs for the inertia of a country curacy. He is afraid of marrying a war widow, Mrs. Kitty Hancock, because

22. *A Cure of Souls* (New York: Macmillan, 1924), p. 27.

of the boisterous vigor of her five children. He uses the personal adoration for him of one of his two parish visitors, the nervously unstable
Agnes Lambert, to save himself parish visiting and another curate's
pay, so that he may hire a butler and a first-rate gardener. His marriage
to a widow with a restful disposition and a genius of a cook dispels the
comic mood because it breaks Miss Lambert's fantasy of a spiritual
love and cracks her nerves.

The canon brings disaster to Kitty Hancock's sister, Mrs. Sylvia
Rivers, by advising her to confess to her husband the secret of her
having had a lover while her husband was away on military service.
His immediate motive for the careless advice is to get her out of the
house because a delicious fragrance tells him that a chicken is roasting
in the oven for his dinner and is just about done. He does not know,
and does not care that Sylvia is a coward, and would rather run away
with her lover than dare to face her husband with the truth.

His comic selfishness and selfish cruelty are balanced by admiration
for his fundamentally good mind, his attempt to be honest in his worship, his fine urbanity, his magnificent command of public occasions,
and his flawless preaching of orthodox sermons that urge his people to
do what he is too indolent to do; and by compassion for his having let
his mind fall into sloth.

Kitty Hancock becomes engaged to marry the curate whose eagerness
to serve the parish had caused the canon to have him transferred. Un-
forgivingly outraged by the ruinous advice that the canon had given
her sister, she lists to his face the charges that crack the canon's mask
of self-worship and force him to face his real self. He is honest enough
to admit that she is right. The widow whom he has married, Molly
Beauchamp, consoles him and advises him to leave for a region where
he could dream undisturbed. He now knows that "he would have no
peace or comfort until he had given up his cure of souls."[23]

The style is musical in all its tones of different moods, comedy,
irony, satire, and sense enjoyment. It creates poetry in the phrasing
of some clearly held emotion, like the canon's pride in his church: "He
was like a husband who has no more passion for his wife yet finds pleasure in watching her effect on other men."[24] The right word again
and again resonates with its extraordinary aptness. The canon has
been hurriedly advising Mrs. Rivers while the chicken is in the oven:
"As he returned there came towards him from the open kitchen the
smell of roast chicken singed: ruined beyond redemption."[25] "Redemp-

23. *Ibid.*, p. 324.
24. *Ibid.*, p. 126.
25. *Ibid.*, p. 305.

tion": the perfect image as he would see it for his profanation.

Agnes Lambert offers a variant to the mystical religious reality motif that had given *Mary Olivier* its sublime climax. Here it is given a minor place and subjected to a realistic analysis. Agnes Lambert's searching for God is exposed as an attempt to sublimate an unconscious sexual yearning for the canon into a spiritual ecstasy that is only a feverish flight. Mary Olivier's search for God had been consciously willed and was successful. But Agnes Lambert, despite her use of the self-emptying technique that Mary Olivier had employed,[26] is only a mental case, and Dr. Lawson blames the canon for having made her that.[27]

The dialogue that is the principal method of narration is expert beyond praise, matching Pinero's genius for eloquent reticence. The canon and his wife have recently returned from their honeymoon. The clock strikes ten, their eyes meet.

> "I think——"
> "Shall we——?"
> She rose and he followed as she went, slowly, with her rolling, padding motion, upstairs.[28]

The controversy over the placing of the War Memorial was recognized by the people of Stow-on-the-Wold as a local happening, although their rector was totally unlike Canon Chamberlain. The canon's name, spelled Chamberlayn, is of the highest social status in Stow. The canon was, I think, drawn from narrowly selected and perhaps unkind impressions of Anthony Deane, who also came in time to love society rather better than parish duties, which he gave up to become an editor, and then chaplain to King George V. The character of Alice Vachell, whose pallor came from passion for Canon Chamberlain, not from weakness, seems to me a thumbnail self-portrait.

The Dark Night (May, 1924) returns to a faith in the mysticism that had been questioned in *A Cure of Souls*. It is a romantic novel written as a lyrical memoir in thirty-three canticles of free verse. It opens with a hymn to a tree:

> There is a beech tree in my garden,
> It stands in a green grass-plot, on a little mound,
> A woman's smooth torso, grey-glistening,
> > seamed with black wounds
> Where the rain weeps. . . .

---

26. *Ibid.,* p. 222.
27. *Ibid.,* pp. 282–85.
28. *Ibid.,* p. 273.

The story is told with careful foreshadowing of growth into fulfillment, and it is pure poetry in rhythm, image, and feeling. It is set partly
in Stow-on-the-Wold, and mainly in the little white house and garden
in St. John's Wood that were home to May Sinclair.

It is the story of Elizabeth, who loved God, and who fell in love
with Victor through reading his verse and, when she met him, fell
more deeply in love with him. Just before they are to be married,
Victor confesses that he has become frightened by the cage that marriage would be for him. He must stay free, or his gentleness would
turn savage and his singing would end: "I am a beast, untamed, that
must go alone." He leaves England, travels in Italy, and then returns,
because he cannot live without Elizabeth, to accept marriage and her
support.

An adopted daughter of a cousin of Elizabeth's, Monica, captures
the vulnerable Victor away from Elizabeth, and jealousy and hatred
cause Elizabeth to lose touch with God and to feel desolate in her
spiritual loneliness. Compassion prompts her to give her house over
to Victor and Monica and their child, and once more God fills her darkness with his light. Victor, whose sight has been his greatest joy because
of his love for color, suddenly goes blind. Monica deserts him for a
rich lover. Through his blindness, Victor learns to share with Elizabeth
the experience of seeing God.

Externally, the novel is related to *The Tree of Heaven* by the presence in Elizabeth's garden of a real tree of heaven, not an ash, and
internally through its being as a whole such a poem as was attributed
to Michael Harrison, except for its terminating in faith. It is related
to *The Helpmate, The Flaw in the Crystal, Mary Olivier,* and *A Cure
of Souls* by Elizabeth's ritual of emptying her soul of sense in the dark
and letting herself be flooded by a spiritual essence. Classical meters
seem to have inspired the free use of the spondee and the molossus.
The sixth canticle reminds us of Amy Lowell's "Dinner Party."

Arnold Waterlow: A Life (September, 1924) is something of what
May Sinclair in an interview said she intended it to be: a male counterpart of *Mary Olivier*. Arnold is born in the same year as Mary, 1863,
and he has to pit his will against his mother's hard will. But it is much
more complex in its implications; in fact, it is as much a converse as a
counterpart of *Mary Olivier*, for May Sinclair was continuously re-
examining her ideas about values in life.

It is a converse in that its principal reaches the bottom, not the top,
of the pyramid whose summit is success in either art or intellectual
achievement. Arnold sacrifices his ambition to lead the intellectually
realized life in order to realize a vision of the reality of God. The ques-

tion that May Sinclair does not state but that the reader might ask is whether or not Arnold's experience is an illusion. On the summit is a minor figure, Max Schoonhoven, pianist and composer. The middle figure is the violinist Rosalind Verney, who gives her body and her energy to be stimulated for her art by Schoonhoven and to further his career.

Their strength of body and will to reach a set goal determines the success of the characters. Max Schoonhoven has an inflexible will. Rosalind has the will to become a perfect violinist and sacrifices Arnold's happiness to obtain Schoonhoven's stimulation to reach her goal, but her will and her body are weaker than Max's. Arnold's will of the intellect to achieve an intellectual fineness surrenders to the command of his psyche to sacrifice himself to an unloving, demanding woman. Effie Warner, the intellectual mate and physical mistress of Arnold during Rosalind's absence with Schoonhoven, is so weak in body and will that she gives up her hold on life to make Arnold's taking back the deserting and deserted Rosalind easy for him.

As a counterpart to *Mary Olivier*, the novel repeats a deep love for the mother and a conflict with the mother's intense driving will, the development of the mind, the search for love, the sacrifice of the intellectual equal and beloved, and the progress to the vision of a psycho-metaphysical God, although it offers somewhat different terminations to those paths.

There are elements of *The Combined Maze* in this novel too. The husband gives up his chance at a true mate of mind and body to take back his errant wife, and the true mate agrees that it is the only thing he can do, as a matter of honor. In *The Combined Maze*, although Ranny Ransome recognizes that a common streak in himself has drawn him to the common Violet Usher, he takes her back out of his intuition to honor his marriage as a sacrament, not as the climax of an elaborate metaphysical mystique. Arnold thinks that he is finding God by taking back his wife. Only his dreams suggest a more physical motive. In *The Combined Maze* the good woman sacrificed is independently strong and survives the separation. Effie Warner dies, and Arnold recognizes that he is responsible for her death: "He had done what he had to do; but it had been he who had done it, and it had killed Effie."[29] Yet Effie is the woman about whom he could think, "He had never come across a mind that went with his so surely and swiftly."[30] He could defend his affair with her to his patron Mr. Godden by saying that it was far more immoral of him to marry Linda than to go to Effie, " 'Because

29. *Arnold Waterlow: A Life* (New York: Macmillan, 1924) , p. 430 .
30. *Ibid.,* p. 327.

Linda didn't want me and Effie did.' "[31] He could think of her: "Her mind was joined to his mind as her body to his body, never to be put asunder,"[32] and before Linda comes crawling back, "Effie's love was the only perfect thing that he had known, the only thing of which he could be certain that it would last for ever."[33]

The mood of the book is very complex. It contains a rejection of the intellectual life—which Effie Warner represents to perfection—a calm acceptance of the death of the loved one that this rejection causes, and a vehement assertion of the belief that only through the sacrifice made under the prompting of a sense of honor is it possible to achieve a transcendent vision of the reality of God. The only justification that May Sinclair offers for the sacrifice of Effie—apart from the reality of God that Arnold is desirous of experiencing—is that Effie has no belief in God as a reality. But she gives no hint that Rosalind could join him in this metaphysical union either.

A curious ingredient in this complex novel is a friend of Rosalind's, Mary Unwin, who is a persistent influence upon Arnold. She defends Rosalind during her first affair with Max Schoonhoven and again when Rosalind runs away to Max after the death of her baby: " 'Max is simply an illness she gets. She can't help it.' "[34] And she persuades Arnold to believe that Effie had to die if he was to have his vision of God.[35] Mary Unwin's reason for entering the novel seems to be to protect the artist Rosalind, and to check the movement toward rebelling against convention that Arnold had expressed to Mr. Godden: "We had to make up our minds between being happy and being thought respectable. Effie doesn't care what people think."[36] Mary Unwin is a regenerated Mary Olivier, reviving the contemplation of the beauty of sacrifice, the sanctity of the marriage tie, and the promise of the vision of the reality of God. May Sinclair created Arnold Waterlow as a boy whose mother's influence was to make him fall in love with a woman who would, like herself, make him feel unimportant, and to bend him to regard suffering and sacrifice as the highest virtues; but Mary Unwin seems to have been introduced to ensure that Arnold would carry out the sacrifice and have the reward of a metaphysical aura. There is a curious affinity between Mary Unwin and May Sinclair too. The house that Mary Unwin's sister lends to Effie and Arnold for their holiday[37] is identifiable as The Quest, in which

31. *Ibid.*, p. 354.
32. *Ibid.*, p. 367.
33. *Ibid.*, p. 412.
34. *Ibid.*, p. 303.
35. *Ibid.*, p. 439.
36. *Ibid.*, p. 353.
37. *Ibid.*, pp. 374–75.

May Sinclair and her mother lived in Sidmouth; and the house where Mary Unwin shelters Rosalind until Arnold should invite her to return to him[38] is clearly Hillsides, where May Sinclair lived in Stow-on-the-Wold.

Arnold's rationalizing his love for a woman who, like his mother, does not return his love is taken from Spinoza: "He who loves God cannot endeavour that God should love him in return."[39]

I think that May Sinclair implied a lowering of the intensity with which she upheld the supreme holiness of the self in *Mary Olivier* and described the tragedy of its obliteration in *Harriett Frean* when she allowed Effie to die—Effie, who had explained to Arnold the difference between them: " 'I've got a personal preference for being really myself; you've got a personal preference for being swallowed up in God.' "[40]

May Sinclair made no attempt to explain a contradiction to Mary Unwin's and Arnold's belief that the sacrifice of Effie was needed for Arnold to win a vision of God. Arnold has a vision of God while he is staying with Effie in Sidmouth: "his whole being was filled with a poignant, exquisite and unearthly bliss."[41] It is clear—but not to Arnold —that it was love that had enabled him to see the reality of God—love for his mother when he was four, love for Effie at Sidmouth. The possibility that May Sinclair herself doubted the climactic vision of reality that Arnold Waterlow experienced is suggested in a later novel, *Far End*. There the novelist Christopher Vivart says of Anne Bywater, whose story represents the story of *Arnold Waterlow*, "She's worse to do than Peter. You see I'm not absolutely sure of her."[42]

Episodes in some of May Sinclair's novels have a symbolic value that can be isolated. In the very first scene Arnold accepts the image of a birdcage reflected in the window of his room as that of a real birdcage hanging outside his room. He will risk being subject to the human destiny to take the illusion for the real. His single perception into an optical illusion—the illusion that the side wall of the house in East Ferry, as he looks up at it, is about to topple on him—gives him the illusory confidence that there is nothing to fear from anyone or anything. The episode is given a whole chapter, five, as a measure of its importance. A description of a dream that Arnold has of Rosalind when she is away with Schoonhoven suggests that Rosalind's hold upon Arnold is an elementary sexual one,[43] for Rosalind appears in his

38. *Ibid.*, p. 443.
39. *Ibid.*, p. 256.
40. *Ibid.*, p. 335.
41. *Ibid.*, p. 379.
42. *Far End* (New York: Macmillan, 1926) , p. 100.
43. *Arnold Waterlow*, p. 302.

dream as the little girl who introduced Arnold to the sexual act[44] and also as the girl who made a fiercely aggressive attempt to seduce him.[45]

Metaphysical ideas are perfectly absorbed into the narration. In chapter thirty-five Effie argues as a realist and Arnold as an idealist on the highest plane of reflective dialogue as art; the scene is a great improvement over the similar dialogue in "Guyon," one of the verse essays in *Essays in Verse*. The compression of the writing of this large book allows many of its passages to stand as poems, truer in pitch than the early lyrics. The appearance of God in a cloud over the esplanade in East Ferry[46] and the fearful night that Arnold suffers after his mother failed to kiss him goodnight[47] were formed into verses as parts of the "Childhood" series. Rosalind's playing of a mazurka becomes a ballet in sound.[48] Arnold dreams of Effie, who is dead: "He could see the clear drift and dip of the sheet above the ankles."[49]

The moment of comic relief is an irreverent one, which Arnold contributes after a Bible lesson: "If nobody wants the Holy Ghost I'll have him."[50] He is sent to bed a whole hour early.

Other traceable actuality than that already mentioned infuses the novel. East Ferry is the Rock Ferry of Cheshire. Joseph Waterlow's yacht "Windward" was William Sinclair's; so was his alcoholism. Linda's studio in Edwardes Square was May Sinclair's. The ship *Buen Juana* mentioned in chapter one was William Sinclair's *Beann-Uamha*.

The Rector of Wyck (April, 1925) is a combination of family novel, philosophical novel, and psychological novel (stressing heredity and noticing the process of religious conversion). Its time span is set from 1882 to 1917. Its point of view is omniscient and includes the author as commentator. The method is dramatic, and the overall mood is relaxed and kindly. It continues to show May Sinclair reacting creatively to her own works in making this novel a penitential obverse to *A Cure of Souls*. It offers continued evidence of an antiintellectual reaction and a full reversal of her previous advocacy of a metaphysical approach to reality and to God.

The principal character dramatizing the antiintellectual reaction is Martha Fenwick, who becomes Mrs. John Crawford, the rector's wife. She is a London girl whose father is a successful barrister with offices

---

44. *Ibid.*, p. 98.
45. *Ibid.*, pp. 180–81.
46. *Ibid.*, p. 21.
47. *Ibid.*, p. 101.
48. *Ibid.*, p. 200.
49. *Ibid.*, p. 436.
50. *Ibid.*, p. 68.

in the Temple. As a young woman she is passionately interested in books and in people who do publicized things, like painters, poets, composers, politicians. She has looked forward to marrying a clever, free-thinking journalist, Philip Attwater, who writes for *The Parthenon* and *The Age*, but she is not depressed when he picks her less ambitious, unintellectual, restful sister, Susan.

In Cheltenham to attend a wedding, she meets a fascinating young tennis player. On one thing she has made up her mind: she will not marry a clergyman. When the young tennis player turns out to be the new curate and, like Philip Attwater, a Balliol product, she confesses to him her total disbelief in religious observances and in a God, but John Crawford has seen that she has compassion, and religion is for him the practice of compassion—the practice of compassion is religion. They marry.

John Crawford disregards the dialectics of Christianity for its practice: "Christianity isn't so much a creed to be stated as a life to be lived. It's a personal experience or it's nothing."[51] Matty surrenders her intellectual curiosity for the sake of love and faith. As a contrast to Canon Chamberlain, the rector of Wyck is a tireless provider of comfort to his people and an organizer of activities to hold their interest in the goodness of life. His income is too small for him to be able to travel. When he inherits some money from his father, two-thirds of the income goes to his alcoholic brother's family in Liverpool, while he goes without a pony and governess-cart, the *Spectator, Punch,* and new clothes.

Matty's brother-in-law, Philip Attwater, the professional intellectual whom she had first thought of as her husband, is the main target of the novel's antiintellectual irony. He is an agnostic, a great advocate of baring the truth fearlessly, that is, without fear of the pain others may have to suffer. To his mind, "Charity's what we do for other people to please ourselves."[52] On a visit to Wyck he accuses Matty of being a hypocrite because she is testifying to a belief that she cannot know. The pain that he causes her by making her agree he justifies with his motive: to restore her innocence, her intellectual honesty. When he boasts that the secret of his own intellectual emancipation is his being immune from illusion, he exposes his arrogance to the point of absurdity. John grants Philip that truth depends upon the point of view, and asks him to let Matty be free to find it in his company rather than in Philip's.

Only once does Matty break out of the arduous routine of being

51. *The Rector of Wyck* (New York: Macmillan, 1927), p. 79.
52. *Ibid.,* p. 9.

the rector's wife, and the cause is a compound of irritation over the petty gossip that is the vice of village life and a subtle illness that seems to be her suppressed agnosticism twitching under the surface of her compromise through love for John. She takes the cure of visiting the clever society in London, which she had revelled in as a young woman. In the company of Philip and Susan she observes the intellectual London of 1912 buzzing with cubism, vorticism, and the fourth dimension. She is repelled by its cerebral aridity, its bareness of human feeling. Her former hero, Philip, is laughed at by the younger generation as a paralyzed relic of the past. The intellectual dust that has not yet been exposed is judging the intellectual dust that is being swept away, and Matty wilts in the dust cloud. The world of the wordy is so far away from the common-sensible, humanly emotional practice of life to which she has become accustomed in her parish work, and she returns to the proved reality of her home and her husband, permanently cured of her flare-up of romanticizing the intellectual life. John never wavers in his acceptance of the duties that face him, in his simple interpretation of religion as love for all humanity.

The family chronicle stresses heredity. In the older child, Millicent, there seems to be reborn Matty's subdued agnosticism and there is added to it a reaction against her mother's sentimentalism, which had let love subdue the freedom of the intellect. Millicent is practical, intelligent, well-organized; she lacks only the gift of loving. At the Cheltenham Ladies College she is inspired by the Principal to make social service her career, and she finds a place in a secular mission in Poplar that is proud of avoiding all religious bigotry. After her mother dies, her father, broken by grief and loneliness, asks her to stay with him, but Millicent is immune to any sentiment that would divert her from her socially important career.

The boy, Derek, is born with an innately destructive personality, inherited from his father's family. John's father had been a drunkard, as is Uncle Charles, John's brother; and Derek repeats the family weakness that had skipped John. His excuse for drinking is that he resents the ease with which his family is good, and the pressure of that goodness trying to shame him into being like them. He is only standing up for himself in resisting that goodness. He does well at farming, and dies a hero in the war.

The war inspires John Crawford to preach England's righteous cause, and Philip Attwater to preach pacifism and to write mildly seditious pamphlets. He lives "in the glorious expectation of imprisonment that never came."[53] The best thought that Attwater can gen-

---

53. *Ibid.*, p. 231.

erate when he reads the unfinished sermon that John had been writing when he died—the sermon that declared God was incarnate in humanity forever, laboring, suffering, dying, and living the atonement in each human being—is the comment, "I wonder if he knew how unorthodox he was."[54]

The reversal of an earlier position on the primacy of the intellect as a stimulant to love is declared in Matty's explaining to her mother why she accepted John as her husband, when it was Philip whom she had first thought of: " 'I loved Philip with nothing but my mind. I love John with all there is of me.' " She does not care if John is clever or not: "It's not his mind I am in love with. . . . It's him—him—him. There isn't anybody like him."[55]

The constructive craft is as careful as ever. Dialogue is supreme in a variety of moods. Comedy has its customary moments. Analytic revelations, even in this sentimental novel, prove May Sinclair's perceptive grounding of action in motive. Matty's conversion by John is subtly analyzed as well as poetically dramatized. Derek's hell of sexual stress in adolescence is shown to be at the core of his tormenting Milly, the tabooed image of the girl he is in love with.[56]

John is the spokesman for the philosophy that harmonizes with the intent of the book, as when he explains the existence of evil in God's world: "Evil comes from man's free will and from the free will of the devil, but it's better that man and the devil should be free than that they should be bound even to be good—wound up like watches to go right. By overcoming evil, here and now, some day we shall be free only to be good. If there is a God. But if there isn't a God, then we are tied to evil for ever and ever. The world without God can never be free to be good."[57] He defends his faith against the charge that it is based on ignorance: "We don't know, that's why some of us believe."[58]

Characters out of earlier books, at earlier ages, make us more aware of the Cotswolds as the setting: Mrs. Waddington and her son Horatio, Sir John and Lady Corbett, Dr. Ransome, Robert Fielding and Adeline.

Actuality trickles through the book. The Fenwicks live in Ormonde Terrace, Regent's Park, where May Sinclair received a thrilling letter from George Gissing in 1897. Anthony Deane had been a curate at Cheltenham, where he met his Maud, and he had been an enthusiastic tennis player. In a letter to May Sinclair, dated February 4, 1894,

---

54. *Ibid.*, p. 258.
55. *Ibid.*, p. 32.
56. *Ibid.*, p. 150.
57. *Ibid.*, p. 75.
58. *Ibid.*, p. 79.

from Barcombe Lewes in Sussex, he had written, "Christianity, although it provides (as some of us think), a simpler, nobler, more logical belief than any other school of thought,—is a mode of life rather than a mode of thought, is a Fact rather than a creed." May Sinclair, then, had been a dissident, like Matty. St. Ursula's in the novel offers a plausible impression of the program and the appearance of St. Hilda's East, which the Guild of Cheltenham Ladies College had built in 1895, during the time of the novel. The building described in chapter fifteen was probably Mildmay House, which no longer exists.[59]

Far End (August, 1926) is a novel about a psychological novelist, his marriage, his writings, his affairs, and his home in the country. His novels are shown to be expressions of elements of his total self. And since Christopher Vivart is a part of May Sinclair, his novels also express elements of May Sinclair. The form is of the closely trimmed species. Much of the substance is dialogue at its best. The point of view is omniscient.

May Sinclair begins as the interpreter of actions, but soon turns over the showman's part to the novelist's wife, who is a wholly reliable analyst. *Far End* continues the vein in which *Arnold Waterlow* had been conceived: admitting the importance of the intellect, but denying it primacy as an instrument of individuation. *Arnold Waterlow* is ingrained with doubt over the sacrifice Arnold makes of the woman who completes his intellectual and emotional life. *Far End* forestalls all doubt by marrying the novelist to a woman who completes both phases of his needs and who defeats the two temptresses to passion. It continues the theme of individuation, picking it up in the mature years of the principal, and carries it to success. It repeats *Arnold Waterlow*'s preference for married love to rebellious passion, but discontinues, as had *The Rector of Wyck,* the thesis that a vision of reality requires a vision of God. The principal's achievement is his understanding of the reality of his wife's love for him, and of the reality of his dependent love for her. The novel displaces the philosophy of Idealism and the sublimation of love, with realism and the enjoyment of love. The discussion of abstract ideas does not deal with metaphysics, but with the technique of the novel.

When we meet Christopher Vivart at his family home, Far End, in an unnamed county, he is engaged to Hilda Courtney. At thirty he is already an active novelist. Hilda's love is a mature respect for his mind joined with a healthy mating love for his body. Christopher's love is a child's need of a motherlike source of approval, a reliable loyalty, an

---

59. Letter, F. Wyatt Joyce, M.A., Former Warden, St. Hilda's East, December 2, 1963.

intelligent advisor. When he discusses the novel that he has just finished, *The Transgressors,* he unself-consciously reveals the impulses
that he is giving a preliminary run in his imagination, and so prophe-
sies how someday he will act, and Hilda in her comments reveals her
nature and foretells the trend of her behavior toward his action. *The
Transgressors* is about a marriage that dissolves because the wife, Diane,
loses interest in her husband's body, and another woman, Maisie,
draws him away from his indifferent wife. Hilda sympathizes with
Maisie and thinks that Diane had been asking for it. Kit's sister Cicely
argues for the older view of patience and sublimation. The husband
in the novel, Bertrand, expresses both Christopher's potential for
breaking the marriage tie at the urging of strong physical love and his
endowment with a conscience, for at the end of *The Transgressors*
Bertrand thinks of Diane, his wife, with tenderness, reserving for her
an ideal love that seems finer than his passion for Maisie. Christopher's
declaring that Bertrand would not have left Hilda for Maisie foretells
his giving up Mona Ryland to keep Hilda. Christopher's comment,
"Technical unfaithfulness, unfaithfulness of body . . . is different from
entire unfaithfulness of body and soul,"[60] foretells the rationalization
with which he will defend his physical infidelity with Mona Ryland
and prepares for a second sort of infidelity, infidelity of trust.

Vivart's next novel, *The Idealist,* written after his marriage, is
comic in mood. It is about a philosophical idealist, who has finished
his great book and is preparing to set off on a lecture tour of America
when he reads a book that converts him to realism. His secretary, who has absorbed his idealistic philosophy, begs him to publish
his book, go on his lecture tour, with her, and publish his conversion
later. He asks his realistic wife, upon whom he depends for all his
real-life decisions, what he should do. She advises him to confess the
truth of his conversion, of course. *The Idealist,* proclaimed as Vivart's
finest book, tells us about his ultimate dependence upon his wife, and
also implies a decrease in May Sinclair's ardor for the cause of idealism.

The war breaks out. Vivart is wounded in 1917, and recovers. Cicely's
husband, Maurice Calverly, is reported missing. Cecily thinks that she
hears Morry calling her and runs to the door. She falls dead on the
threshold. News of Morry's death confirms the psychic message that
Cecily had received. The tragedy causes the Vivarts to leave Far End
for Hampstead.

The next novel of Kit's is the experimental *Peter Harden,* whose substance is confined to what the principal character is aware of. *Mary
Olivier* would be the parallel in May Sinclair's experimental career.

---

60. *Far End,* p. 20.

The birth of a second child, a crying baby, who exhausts Hilda's energies, causes Vivart, after ten years of depending on Hilda to do his typing and to encourage him, to hire a quiet room and a typist. The typist, Mona Ryland, excites his physical passion with her adoration of his work and his person. Hilda discovers the affair, and wins him back by withholding her body, which Kit wants still, and by withholding her mind and counsel, which Kit still needs. She takes him back with full forgiveness.

The new novel that Mona had typed, *Anne Bywater: A Life,* is a female *Peter Harden*. Like May Sinclair, Vivart is a balancing novelist; only, as a male, he reverses the order of the sexes. The next novel, *The Hypocrite,* is not described, but its title suggests that it comes out of the double life that Kit led when he gave his body to Mona, while his mind expected Hilda to retain her full love of mind and body; that is the section in *Far End* covering chapters sixteen to twenty-two.

The second affair of Kit's introduces him to a young-looking widow, Mrs. Audrey Templeton, who has read his novels avidly and who isolates Kit from his wife by assuring him of her very special sympathy with his work and by giving him the incense of praise that he seems to need from another than the customary source. This situation was prepared for in *The Idealist,* in which Professor Broadbent's secretary tried to make him believe that whatever his wife might mean to him, it was really she who was his mental mate. Mrs. Templeton's discussion of *Anne Bywater* makes it out to combine *Mary Olivier*'s philosophical and spiritual search after reality with *Anne Severn*'s theme of the natural priority of a passionate adulterous love over a marriage that lacks reciprocal love, which fits the preterminal stage in the complicated *Arnold Waterlow*.

Christopher guards himself against a repetition of giving pain to Hilda with a physical passion by insistently interpreting Mrs. Templeton as a spiritual admirer, an imagining, not a performing, lover. Mrs. Templeton makes us even more sure of May Sinclair's new attitude when she asks Kit if Hilda shares that vision of ultimate reality that Anne Bywater longs for, implying that *she* certainly does. The ironical context in which the reference is made to what once had been sacred implies that the vision was sacred no more. Kit's reading the manuscript of *The Hypocrite* to Mrs. Templeton and his dedicating it to her before Hilda has seen it hurts Hilda deeply. He rationalizes his intimacy with Mrs. Templeton by explaining that there is no affair, only a companionship of minds, and his mind is absolutely his own to do with as he pleases. Hilda reminds him of his former argument that the mind, not the body is what counts in fidelity. Because he has not been physically unfaithful, she lets him have her body; but because he has been unfaithful in his mind, she withholds all sharing.

Thoughts of Far End and the peace that it gave them before Cecily died induce them to return there with their children, and the move fully heals their breach. The individuation that Vivart wins is due to the love and the applied intelligence of the mature, the already individuated Hilda.

Many analytical passages, told in dialogue, give insight into the novelist's secret person. Again May Sinclair displays her interest in the effects of suggestion upon behavior, especially the unintended effects.

The discussions about the technique of the novel, which Vivart and the well-read critic Grevill Burton engage in, reveal May Sinclair's actual humility over her theorizing. Grevill Burton deflates the airy abstractions that Vivart rhapsodically argues, as when he points out the literal impossibility of Vivart's theory of the authorless, immaculate novel: "You tell the story, you make things happen."[61]

The psychic moments belong to Cicely. The comic break from analytic seriousness occurs in the sample of dialogue that Vivart quotes from *The Idealist,* a breakfast conversation between Professor and Mrs. Broadbent. It begins with Mrs. Broadbent asking, " 'Can I offer you a slice of your consciousness?' "[62] Mrs. Templeton's interpreting *The Idealist* to Vivart, " 'I see you growing up, wise and a little sad,' "[63] seems, like Mrs. Broadbent's quip, another phrasing of disillusionment.

The impression continues to persist with me that May Sinclair read Pinero and learned something of his mastery of the spontaneous effect in dialogue, through the use of the resumed sentence, and the broken-off sentence repeating a question and answering it. The gesture with which Mrs. Templeton, when she is all alone, repudiates Christopher's kindly interpretation of her nature as one who might sin only in her imagination, is pure Pinero.[64]

My analytic identifying Vivart's *Anne Bywater* as a fictional representation of *Arnold Waterlow* gains support from the typescript of *Arnold Waterlow.* "Bywater" was the name written into the spaces left blank up to chapter eighteen. "Waterhouse" was the next trial at a name before "Waterlow" gave the satisfying click.

The Allinghams (March, 1927) was the last of May Sinclair's family novels. In the ductile ease of its style, and in the sensitive orchestration of its aesthetic effects to the very end, it is technically the best. Its onlooking is omniscient, its major form of telling superbly shaped

61. *Ibid.,* p. 81. See the whole chap. 14.
62. *Ibid.,* p. 35.
63. *Ibid.,* p. 171.
64. *Ibid.,* p. 176.

dramatic dialogue, its attitude realistic. It is placed in Berkshire; its time starts moving in 1893 and stops in 1910. The subject not apparent on the surface, but working at the roots of the narration, is one that May Sinclair had developed in six novels already: the influence, hit or miss, of heredity.

The Allinghams, like the Harrisons of *The Tree of Heaven,* are prosperous. Unlike them, they have a neurotic problem base. Grandfather Stephen Allingham lives with a doctor; his mind mourns the passing of an unidentified self: " 'Stephen's gone away. Poor Stephen's gone away. Does anybody know where Stephen is?' "[65] Grandmother does not live with him. Grandfather's father and an aunt had been mad too; a brother is an alcoholic. His son, William, the head of the family now, shows no mental weakness; he efficiently manages a large family estate inherited from an uncle. He has followed his father's pattern by marrying a woman who seems to feel no affection, only possessiveness, and that more toward the girls than toward the boys.

Grandfather's failure to have won love supplies the cue for the narrative theme unifying and contrasting the lives of the six grandchildren: their search for love.

The oldest, Margaret, the most tautly strung, is sickly sensitive to hurt and hateful in her defensiveness. What she feels as love is a lust like that of a starving wild animal for unresisting prey. When she is thirty-two the courtship of an innocent curate explodes the nervous system that has not been accustomed to affection into a violent insanity. So Margaret loses what she had been searching for and found, because she has never been able to develop a capacity for love that trains on caring for others.

Wilfrid, two years younger, completes his studies at Cambridge. His dream of becoming a general by way of Woolwich and the Royal Artillery is dismissed by the discovery of a mitral valve incompetency. He takes a course at the Cirencester Agricultural College to be of help to his father and luckily finds a mate in Charlotte Nevern, his sister Mollie's closest friend at the Cheltenham Ladies College. Charlotte overcomes his worries about his family's taints in a delightful scene of realistic romance.[66]

Stephen is the poet in the family. He too goes to Cambridge, and his poetry is printed in the *Cambridge Review* in 1899. He translates the chorus from the *Bacchae* of Euripides. He betrays something of Margie's tense, possessive lust when he falls in love with the middle-aged wife of an Indian Army officer, Mrs. Vera Asprey, and expects her

65. *The Allinghams* (New York: Macmillan, 1927) , p. 28.
66. *Ibid.,* chap. 18.

to divorce her husband to become his wife. He argues that because she loves his mind she should love his body too. He cannot understand her lack of physical passion and her sense of responsibility toward her loyal prosaic husband. She cures his passion for her by putting in his way her daughter Violet, who has beauty, talent as a linguist, and a genuine response to poetry, and who is thrilled to be attractive to a good poet. His poem written in childhood, "The Blue Flower,"[67] is a delicate lyric of traditional rhyme scheme, and his "Frustration,"[68] in free verse, a moving confession of despair.

Mollie is intelligent, sympathetic, clear-headed, patient, loving, loyal, and incapable of inflicting pain. She gives up her ambition, after studying in Dresden, to become a concert pianist, because Mamma would be unhappy if she left home. And because Papa does not want his little girl to rough it with Richard Eden in Canada as the wife of a farmer in training, she loses five years of happiness; but she does marry Richard on his return.

Robin, brilliant in mathematics, is infected with the alcoholic taint, and is removed by his father from Cambridge as punishment. He is lucky to find a farmer's daughter, Rose Denison, who gives her beauty, strength of body, strength of will, and a steady love to help him become a successful farmer. His mother's sister, Aunt Martha Lambert, shames his father into giving the boy a farm in Wiltshire instead of sending him to Canada to be out of sight as a disgrace.

The climactic mood of the book is awarded to the youngest child, Angela. After Stephen shows her Susan the cat with her four kittens pawing her breasts, Angy knows what she wants from life: the happiness of being a mother. The taint affects her in that she is romantically intense, defiantly indiscreet, wholly trustful of her impulse. She finds the object of her love and her completion as a mother when she is sixteen and meets the handsome Captain Cartaret who is home on leave from India. His wife is India-baked to haggardness. There are no clearer scenes in the English novel than those in which the skilled and merciless seducer plays upon the innocent romantic girl who is in love for the first time. Angy is pregnant when Captain and Mrs. Cartaret must return to India. While Cartaret was her lover, Angy was a splendid actress of innocence, the soft victim of a skillful master. Her parents' threat to separate her from the child that is to be born turns her into a tigress of a mother. Her Aunt Martha Lambert, her sister Mollie, and her sister-in-law Rose come to her defense, and she leaves home to have and keep her child. The shock to her parents of

67. *Ibid.*, pp. 41–42.
68. *Ibid.*, pp. 341–42.

Margie's being taken away from them by her insanity softens them to decency, and they welcome Angy and her child home, so that they may again have a child in the house. Angy has fulfilled her need for motherhood, and feels no shame, only pride in the father's personal charm and his Distinguished Service Order, in the passionate love that had brought so wonderful a possession to her. The almost perfect self-ishness of her seducer makes no impression on her mind. Angela shows us May Sinclair renouncing renunciation, deriding sublimation, even when the beloved is a contemptible seducer who has violated his mar-riage troth. He has given Angela the child she needed to complete herself.

In a relatively obscure position is the theme of the love of minds, or a love for a mind as the basis of physical love. That theme is made drama in the love that Mrs. Vera Asprey feels for Stephen Allingham as a poet, and in the full love that her daughter Violet has for Stephen. The serious theme is burlesqued by the excuse that the senior Mrs. Allingham gives for her lack of any compassion for her husband: " 'Oh, my dear Mary, if it had been anything but that, anything but his mind gone. If it was dipsomania, if he was mad with drink and hurt me I could have borne it. It's the worst of all things that could have hap-pened. His dear mind that I loved.' "[69]

This last of May Sinclair's family novels affords a special insight into the self-exposing nature of objective characterization. Each of the six Allingham children represents a segment of the complex personality that was May Sinclair, as well as being artistically and individually a whole person. Margie is the intense, affection-craving, inwardly turned element that dominated the years in which May Sinclair tried sublima-tion through sonnets. Stephen is the metaphysics-reading, downs-loving literary genius who found her way to celebrity. Mollie is the musically gifted, soundly intelligent, family-sacrificing, loyal friend that her family and her writer friends knew. Robin is the genius for abstract thinking, disguised here as mathematics. His renunciation of mathe-matics for farming is another gesture at renouncing the intellectual life. Angela is the passionate, beauty-worshiping element of May Sin-clair that wanted to give love without care for conventional taboos, and who, like Mollie, hated giving pain to others: "I love people. Just people with their funny ways and their hidden secret lives that you can never get at. They fascinate me."[70] Of that spirit Mollie Tyson and Anne Severn had already been made literary flesh. And two quite subordinate characters contain more of the whole of May Sinclair. One

69. *Ibid.*, p. 28.
70. *Ibid.*, p. 268.

is Aunt Martha Lambert, the defender of the children against their gently possessing yet tyrannizing parents. A second is Charlotte Nevern, the girl whom Wilfrid marries; she is resourceful in balancing each statement of Wilfrid's pessimism over his heredity with a logical consideration that gives him courage to found a family with her.

The elusive processes of literary inspiration, creation, and reaction are analyzed in the experiences of Stephen. His overlying reaction following creation is self-doubt. He is certain when his verses are bad, but he is uncertain when they are not bad. The rector of Burton Salome, Mr. Verrall, soundly advises him, "Your own literary conscience is the final appeal."[71] To Stephen is committed whatever discussion there is of formal philosophy. For him all reality is reduced to beauty, and beauty is what is hidden under appearances; it is part of the being of God. He says, "It's the business of art to disentangle the reality from the appearance and show it. The art which is the truth of the presentation will be in the beauty, not in the ugliness. That's why beauty is truth. The rest is a question of technique."[72]

Sexual behavior is described frankly. In contrast, moments of poetry glow often; they are most tender when love is the central emotion. Again, the control over the modulation required in the passing from chapter to chapter is unsurpassed in the English novel.

The last creative work of May Sinclair, *History of Anthony Waring*, was published in August, 1927. (Her subsequently published volumes of short stories were collections of earlier work.) It is a classically disciplined novel, dramatizing a kind of pathetic Everyman, a good, well-meaning, intellectually clever but socially unintelligent male, an only child, as he bumbles through life from his fourth year in 1854 to his death of a heart attack in 1913. It has the same structure as *Harriett Frean*, stripped to the essence of description, thought-flow, and dialogue. It is about both the career of Anthony Waring and his marriage.

His choice of a career is the army, but his solicitor father cannot afford Sandhurst and Woolwich, and starts him in his own law office. At school Anthony had been fascinated by Homer, Euripides, and Aeschylus. The legal language he has to read and write tortures a mind trained to simplicity and clarity by the classics. A legacy from an aunt enables him to succeed in a substitute ambition: to work with writers, because he idealizes them. He starts as an invoice clerk with a firm of publishers and in time becomes a literary advisor and a recognized reviewer.

The course that leads to his marriage starts with his playing horse.

71. *Ibid.*, pp. 150–52.
72. *Ibid.*, pp. 157–58.

He whips himself to reach full speed, and when he falls and gravel cuts his legs he does not cry, because horses do not cry. His mother wonders why he whips himself so hard, and he explains that his horse likes it, and he knows, " 'Because—he's me.' "[73] His mother counters his tendency to inflict suffering on himself by playing with him the game of lion. When he rushes at her she screams to show her fright and to make him feel invincible. But his mother falls ill, and when Minnie the maid not only shows no fright at his game but rebukes him for making a noise while his mother is so ill, he loses the lion's heart that his mother had tried to train in him. His mother had also taught him gentleness toward the weak by making him feel pussy's rapid frightened heart when he forced it into his play cart.

After his mother's death his aunt becomes her brother's housekeeper. A former headmistress of a girls' school, she exerts a strict discipline that uncovers in him a capacity for savage hatred. Her sudden switches from congeniality to irascibility confuse him; his mother had been so sunny, had made him feel so strong and confident. Dying, his aunt confesses that the pain of her cancer had made her irascible at times.

Anthony's experiences with love are painful. Mabel Randall jilts him when the man whom she loved agrees to marry her. His obtuseness is not appreciating how rare is the gentle sympathy with which an undemanding mistress, Louise Leray, who says she is a dressmaker, loves him, causes him to dismiss her impatiently and cruelly when he discovers that she is a prostitute. He has forgotten the lesson that his mother had taught him, to be tender to the weak, and the lesson that his aunt had taught him, to be fair-minded, to balance bad with good.

He is thirty when he falls in love with the imagined mother-image of Ellen Mildmay, who had nursed him during his severe pleurisy. His father warns him that she has a cruel temper, but the imagined mother-image overrules the warning. Ellen proves to be jealous of Anthony's job as literary advisor and reviewer, and jealous of everyone who is friendly with him. Ellen is a perfect nurse when there is illness; a demon when all is well.

Anthony's reunion at forty with a school friend, Austin Freeman, who has brought his wife from India back to England, to leave her while he returns, gives Anthony great joy and great sorrow. India has dulled Austin's mind and turned his temper into hating nearly everything. Jenny's mind is still eagerly alive, and Anthony's mind excites her mind and her body. Ellen's savage jealousy of their friendship makes it impossible for Jenny to continue visiting Anthony's home after her husband has gone back to India. They know that they could

---

73. *History of Anthony Waring* (London: Hutchinson, 1927), p. 14.

not resist becoming lovers if they were to meet alone in Jenny's house; and Jenny wants to stay loyal to Austin, and Tony wants to stay loyal to Austin's trust in him. Tony is more sorry for Ellen than for himself: "Because she doesn't know how to be happy."[74] Jenny returns to India.

As time wears on, Ellen obsessively rehearses the broken relationship, and to justify her hatred of the two who had loved, she cruelly insists on believing that Tony had been unfaithful with Jenny. Her final stab of jealousy pitches Tony forward with a heart attack into the arms that once had been the symbol of the longed-for mother.

For the first time in all the novels of May Sinclair the nurse figure is dogmatically religious, meanly jealous, a destroyer of happiness, a nurse from the lust of power over the dependent.

Analysis told as drama helps to give the characterization the strength that always is May Sinclair's. Ellen asks, after Tony has proposed to her, " 'Are you quite sure you love me? It isn't that you're just dependent on me with being ill?' "[75]

The style of the book changes in its course, like the style of Stephen Hudson's *Prince Hempseed* (1923). At the outset it has the simplicity of a child's reader; it advances into the mature style that carries analytic insight when Anthony is seven and Aunt Sarah becomes housekeeper and teacher. Tony's frustrated existence is sketched in the lines of his mouth: "A stern upright stroke was marked at each corner of his mouth, as if he had worn a bit, witness to his habit of holding himself in."[76]

Pain and death can evoke poetry. Mr. Waring suffers from influenza: "He felt as if his body were stuffed with swollen lungs, as if his lungs stuck to his sides and were torn from them with every breath in agony."[77] As he dies, "The groaning breath rattled in his throat like a cable running out."[78] Rhythm and repetition can stir the mood of poetry, as when Tony asks Minnie if he is not going to kiss Mamma good night? " 'No. Not tonight, Master Tony.'—And not the next night, nor the next, nor any other night."[79]

Naturalism in sex has its moment when Tony interrupts an embarrassed gentleman in Louise's room,[80] and comedy has its grinning irreverence when the boy Tony remarks, " 'Jesus has cake for tea *every* day.' "[81]

---

74. *Ibid.*, p. 160.
75. *Ibid.*, p. 116.
76. *Ibid.*, p. 174.
77. *Ibid.*, p. 139.
78. *Ibid.*, p. 141.
79. *Ibid.*, p. 22.
80. *Ibid.*, pp. 100–101.
81. *Ibid.*, p. 8.

Irony is so blended with pathos that it can seldom be separated. It starts on the Sunday evening when Mamma sits at the piano and sings, " 'There's a Friend for little children . . . Whose love can ne-ever die.' "[82] It remains pure when Tony discusses the publishers' dilemma to sell for survival, that they may publish some beauty: "The most you can do is to publish so much of what it likes that you can afford to bring out a beautiful thing now and then. We can't do it all the time."[83]

The actuality of life trickles through the novel. Aunt Sarah is very like Dorothea Beale in her teaching of history as an exercise in balancing good with bad, bad with good. Ellen's arguments to convert the unbelieving Tony to an orthodox Christianity[84] are an echo of Mrs. Sinclair's voice. Tony and Ellen start their honeymoon at Sidmouth. Mr. Waring's office is in John Street, Bedford Row, where May Sinclair's solicitor, Richard S. Garnett, also had his office.

The novel as a whole came out transcendently clear in its first form. The first of two manuscript drafts gives the total writing time as twenty-five days. It gave no sign of being the end. Its spire of meaning could well have been only a stage in May Sinclair's modulation of moral values. It defends renunciation, virtuous restraint, as the higher good; but it faces the consequences of a goodness that balks love. The wages of that goodness are not sublime happiness at all, but anguish and death to the loving.

In *The Creators* Jane Holland had felt the relentless grip of her art upon her energies and had foreseen the penalty that she would have to pay for her total surrender to it. *Thoughts from Goethe* showed that May Sinclair knew the elements of creativity: energy, strength, and will. *The Judgment of Eve* had made will the greatest virtue, as had also a book that May Sinclair must have read, Arnold Bennett's *The Human Machine*. She had allowed her art to possess her wholly, and had chosen her will to drive her without a curb until it exhausted all her energy and her strength. *History of Anthony Waring* was the end for her, although existence was to go on for another nineteen years.

---

82. *Ibid.*, p. 7.
83. *Ibid.*, pp. 149–50.
84. *Ibid.*, pp. 110–11.

17

Other Writings: 1921-1931

Short Stories

The thirteen new short stories of the period began with a sophisticated comedy; the trend then moved toward pathos, with irony a constant effect, and death a requisite for the occult stories that crowded into these years.

The amoral irony of "Lena Wrace," appearing in the *English Review* in February, 1921, and in the *Dial* in July, is as sophisticated as Maugham's best in the genre. Lena Wrace, accomplished mistress of a number of men, hires an unattractive secretary, Ethel Reeves, to avoid the risk of a rival for the affections of her distinguished lover, the painter, actor, and writer, Norman Hippisley. The death of Hippisley reveals the surprise that Ethel Reeves, in revenge for Lena's contempt, had made herself far more interesting than Lena to him. The spreading story of her secret affair wins Ethel a popularity that outshines Lena's.

"The Return," appearing in *Harper's* in May, 1921, is a gracefully unfolded, irony-prinked story told by Simpson, but left out of the collected *Tales*. A London bank-clerk poet, Gerald Marriott, whose volume of *vers libre* has been praised by important reviewers, visits his home in a village in Dartmoor (his father is the rector, and his mother is proud of her literary family), expecting that his especially bound volume with its enclosure of admiring reviews will win his family's belated recognition of his talents. Instead, the family reduces him to the same "miserable little slobbering shivering wretch they hunted and hounded," preferring the sweet sentimental poem, "Roses and Shadows," by his older brother, Herbert, because it is traditional in form and in worship of his childhood home. The story is a thing of genius as it confesses May Sinclair's deep experiences with parental dogma and prejudice, with the powers of reviewers to fell and lift, and with the conflict pitting free verse, aiming at a rocklike firmness of strength and truth, against the soft sentimentalism of traditional verse.

"Heaven," in the *Fortnightly* for September, 1922, is an occult comedy about a son who, having allowed himself to be dominated by his mother's will all his life, becomes at last uneasy in the heaven of his mother's choice. A hypnotist gets through to him and frees him for an independent search for reality.

"Where Their Fire is not Quenched," in the *English Review* of October, 1922, is a horror story telling the punishment in the world of afterdeath of a woman who in life had given up her body, which craved a spiritual completion, to a limited sensual affair with a married man. Every earlier spiritual relatonship is corrupted in retrospect, and she suffers a perpetual imprisonment in the loathed embrace to which she had yielded in life.

The ending effect of "The Victim," in the *Criterion* of October 1922, is a gentle spiritual esthesia, although its substance is macabre. The victim of an untraced murderer visits the killer as a spirit to thank him for having saved him from financial embarrassment and from an oncoming illness, and further surprises him with the consolation that the woman he loves knows that he is the murderer, but loves him and will marry him.

"The Nature of the Evidence," in the *Fortnightly* of May, 1923, told in a pleasant oral style, also moves out of the macabre to a spiritual esthesia. A dead wife returns to prevent the consummation of her scholar-barrister husband's second marriage, and give him an ecstasy far greater than that of sex, an ecstasy of the whole being, not just of the body.

"Jones's Karma," in the *Criterion* of October, 1923, comically proves a Mahatma's point that an individual has both freedom of will and the necessity of enacting his Karma. Perfect freedom is being indifferent to a pair of opposites. Perfectly indifferent between a delicious dinner and a bowl of rice, the Mahatma sits down in front of the dinner.

"The Villa Desirée," in *The Ghost Book,* an anthology appearing in October, 1926, is related to *The Flaw in the Crystal,* and is told in the form of a mystery tale. The evil complex of a widower, separating from his body, frightens his prospective bride out of the same villa in which it had frightened the first bride to death before the man had come to her.

Three of the stories in the volume *Uncanny Tales* had not, as far as I know, been published in periodicals. "The Token" glides with great beauty from a compelling realism into the occult as it tells about an invalid wife who is never sure while she lives that her physically frustrated scholar husband loves her. It is a rage of frustration that he directs upon her when he sees her cleaning a little paperweight Buddha. After her death, her spirit watches him as he works in the library. When she sees him smash the Buddha that had touched off his deeply regretted rage, she has had her token of his love, and is appeased.

After the son in "If the Dead Knew" is provoked into bitterness toward the memory of his mother by a doctor's criticism that she had mollycoddled him, his mother's spirit visits him to confess her pain at his unkind thoughts of her, and he is depressed by guilt. His fiancée's assuring him that he had always loved his mother is followed by a second visit from the now affectionate ghost who restores his peace of mind.

"The Finding of the Absolute" is a metaphysical comedy picturing an idealistic heaven in which each soul creates his own world, space and time being such absolutes as Kant had dreamed of, and Immanuel Kant is one of the philosophers in residence. An interesting domestic contribution is a glimpse of May Sinclair's black cat, Jerry, dancing.

"The Pictures" had not been published before its appearance in *Tales Told by Simpson* (May, 1930). It is a caustic study of a male model who paints and who deludes himself into thinking that he is an undiscovered genius.

"The Mahatma's Story," published in *The Intercessor and Other Stories* (September, 1931; 1932 in America), is a fable. Two painters, the unsuccessful one of whom attributes the other's success to luck, interchange identities and circumstances in an agreed-upon experiment under hypnosis. Changed conditions do nothing but apply different pressures upon the unchanging inner selves, the successful painter even improving, to meet a tougher challenge.

There was no evidence of any weakening of the critical discipline that holds creativity from error, and only in the move toward occult and abstract themes was there a hint, not quite a sign, that the reservoir of warmly personal feelings upon which creativity draws was running low.

Psychology and Philosophy

"Psychological Types," in the *English Review* for May, 1923, offered a lucid statement of Jung's theory of types and some challenges. After listing the functional subdivisions of each type and praising Jung's definitions of them, May Sinclair asked, where, in this scheme, was truth? "There will be no whole of truth, only the half truths expressed by the two mutually opposing attitudes," that is, the conscious and the repressed. God became only a "function of the unconscious, namely the manifestation of a split-off sum of libido which has activated the God-*imago*." She insisted that Plato's philosophy was extroverted, not introverted; that romanticism must be introverted, not extroverted; and that neo-classicism was certainly as extroverted as realism. She thought that Jung did not sufficiently show how dominant and repressed attitudes were reconciled in the normal individual, nor how the symbol worked in normal psychology. She congratulated the translator, Dr. H. Godwin Baynes, on "his brilliant and scholarly rendering of a most difficult text."

May Sinclair's purpose in writing *The New Idealism* (April, 1922) was to study the new realism as developed by Whitehead, Alexander, Russell, Boodin, Laird—all of whom she admired and enjoyed—to judge how far the old idealism should be revised so that it should not be altogether lost. It "must once more be empirical, critical, reactive. . . . It must somehow contrive to reconcile the universe of things with the universe of thought, without doing violence to its palpable objectivity. It must cease to make nonsense of the plain principles of physical science, and of the plain man's progress in the world of so-called physical realities; and it must be proof against all attacks based on the behavior of that world."[1]

What professional philosophers thought about this highly professional volume has been set aside for a study of May Sinclair's image, but there are elements in it that any student of literature may enjoy. One entertainment comes from the tireless sensitivity with which May Sinclair's feminine fingers probed the cloth of argument that massive figures of authority had woven. They tested each seam, slipped through wide gaps in the sewing and thin areas of the lining, and then audaciously draped the garment over the author's figure to let us behold some amusing exposures of his nakedness. The literary artist applied her analytic genius to extracting meanings, phrase by phrase, sentence by sentence, shuttling over all as each meaning was extracted, to expose the clashings of sense.

The student of her life can enjoy the references she makes to the planning of her day, à propos of Professor Whitehead's theory of event-moments as the true realities in nature, a nature in which space,

---

1. *The New Idealism* (New York: Macmillan, 1922) , pp. 13–14.

time, and matter are only adjuncts of events, and events are related
to a time system by parallel layers and layers of durations of these moments. She lists her activities to contradict the theory: "Take, for example, the duration of my day. The duration of my working times
(10 a.m. to 1.30 p.m., and 5.30 p.m. to 7.30 p.m.), and the durations
of my meal times (8.30 to 9 a.m., 1.30 p.m. to 2 p.m., 5 to 5.15 p.m. and
8 to 8.45 p.m.) are 'parts of the same duration' which is my day; yet
so far from being parallel they are successive; they fit into alternate
places in the completed order of my day."[2]

He can enjoy her reference, à propos of the theory of the essence
of reality existing apart from the object itself, to the 53 bus that she
took in Piccadilly Circus to return to St. John's Wood, and her testimony that her total experience was a part of her consciousness and
allowed no grounds for assuming any real essence of a bus or of the
Circus outside consciousness.[3] She describes herself writing at her desk
and looking about her study, to prove the need to separate time from
space by the very limitations of the conscious act of perceiving.[4] She
describes her dream, "of dressing for a party, of opening endless cup-
boards and endless drawers, turning over innumerable garments, rejected for some dream reason, and finally setting out, clothed in nothing but a simple handkerchief."[5] It is all relevant to her argument that
time is a moving dimension.

The easy allusiveness of her style animates the abstractions of her
thought, as when she finds the perfect image for consciousness as the
realists abstract it: "a pure, featureless transparency let down between
subject and object, and dividing them, if it can be said to divide what
was never joined and never could be joined."[6] She draws attention to
her feminineness and her vulnerableness to the weapons of men when
she confesses, "Even now I cannot get over my fear that Professor
Whitehead's mathematics may yet do something to me that I shouldn't
like."[7] She makes us think of Professor Broadbent in *Far End* when
she confesses the influence upon her of Professor Alexander's *Space,
Time and Deity:* "You are almost overwhelmed by the temptation to
forsake all and follow him."[8] She finds a dramatic image to say, "There
is no use calling in an empirical quality to help an *a priori* reality
in distress."[9]

2. *Ibid.*, pp. 103–4.
3. *Ibid.*, p. 121.
4. *Ibid.*, p. 228.
5. *Ibid.*, p. 251.
6. *Ibid.*, p. 32.
7. *Ibid.*, p. 162.
8. *Ibid.*
9. *Ibid.*, p. 177.

The student of satire can enjoy the logic with which May Sinclair harasses the accepted giants. Pondering Professor Broad's statement that "in all probability nothing that is perceptible is real," she wonders why, then, he goes to such pains to make his unperceived real the counterpart of the perceived?[10] After examining the assumptions of critical realism, she resolves them into meaning that "we know the reality we can't know by means of knowledge that we haven't got."[11]

In her Introduction she had modestly admitted, "I do not imagine for one moment that my own idealism is watertight, or that no doubt will ever trouble me as to the truth of its assumptions. All metaphysics are highly problematic, and the idealist is not more bound than other people to furnish a watertight system. Enough if his theory does not leak too much; he cannot *prove* anything any more than other people."[12]

Her conclusion was that there was a need to assume "an ultimate consciousness to sustain the universe in the absence of any other; to hold Time and Space together and resolve their contradictions; to unite the personal perspectives of the finite selves." The last paragraph declares the rightness of satisfying the religious consciousness, saying with restraint what *Mary Olivier* had confessed lyrically: "Every finding of new truth, every creation of new beauty; every victory of goodness, every flash of spiritual insight and thrill of spiritual passion is, while it lasts, a communion, here and now, with God."

May Sinclair's address to the Aristotelian Society on February 5, 1923, was published in the *Proceedings* in 1923. It repeats the matter of chapters nine and ten in *The New Idealism* with sharpened clarity. She argues that the realist's theory that objects exist independently of consciousness is empirically untenable, and resubmits her thesis of the two states of consciousness. Primary consciousness "is all immediate sense perception, all feeling and willing . . . the sudden flash of the instantaneous present." It is all remembering, dreaming, and imagining. "It includes all conceptual knowledge; it is the stream of thought, of all thinking that has thought for its current object, provided that reflection, judgment, inference or reasoning have not cried a halt."

Secondary consciousness is "the awareness of awareness . . . the play of thought round and about its object." Primary consciousness is not distinguishable from its object; it affirms nothing but the presence of its object. Its object, its content, is "in an indivisible unity with itself."

---

10. *Ibid.*, p. 81.
11. *Ibid.*, p. 138.
12. *Ibid.*, p. xii.

Secondary consciousness distinguishes between consciousness and its object, but it cannot save the object for independent reality. "Primary consciousness has swallowed it before secondary consciousness can get a look in." Secondary consciousness is the consciousness that the realist says can be distinguished from its object. It is as dependent on primary consciousness as realism requires consciousness to be on its object. But its object is primary consciousness. The realist declares that the green on the table cover is *there,* and not in his consciousness, his judging consciousness. Secondary consciousness rightly judges the green of the table cover to be an object distinct for its judging, but green is there only because primary consciousness can perceive it.

The status of an atom or an electron May Sinclair relegated to a world of independent reality beyond both primary and secondary consciousness, for the idealist does not take the human consciousness to be the sole supporter of the universe.

The concept of secondary consciousness was intended to let idealism reach closer to realism, but not to surrender to it.

Criticism of Her Contemporaries

May Sinclair's essay on "The Poems of F. S. Flint" in the *English Review* of January, 1921, begins by recalling the poems of Flint and Pound in the first *Imagist Anthology* of 1913, since when Pound had tended "more and more to an obscure and complex intellectual subtlety, Mr. Flint becoming steadily simpler, clearer, and more profoundly human."

She traces the development of Flint from his *Net of the Stars* of 1909, when he sang his discontent with the old measures to old measures, through his *Cadences* of 1915, when he found "unrhymed cadence," on to 1920 and to greater skill in the new form; and she illustrates his development by quoting the poems that he wrote in those three periods on swans. Imagism meant "a return to reality, to direct vision." In his last swan poem, in *Otherworld,* of 1920, Flint gave only the "pure image," and the poet had become the "pure perceiver." She was certain that the cause of his developing as a poet was his breaking with tradition. The imagists, the first revolutionaries in poetry since Wordsworth, had a goal similar to Wordsworth's manifesto of freedom from mechanical language and freedom for the language as men really spoke it; theirs was "to restore the innocence of memory, as Gaugin restored the 'innocence of the eye.' "

May Sinclair called Flint England's best authority on modern French poetic literature, an admirer of the already known and respected, an explorer of the unknown who deserved to become known, and an excellent translator from the French.

"The Poems of Richard Aldington," in the *English Review* for May, 1921, identified the two uncomfortably joined halves of the poet: his absorption, before the war, of Greek poetry and its ideals of beauty, and his conscience-compelled view of his own time from the war on, a world he could not love. He wrote about modern ugliness from inside the Greek world of joy in life. Beauty hurt him because its position in the modern world was dangerous and impermanent. He had been thwarted when he tried to reconcile Greek beauty and modern life.

May Sinclair thought his *Myrrhine and Konallis* "a sequence of the most exquisite love poems in the language," but his war poems were too calm, lacking the vital quality of D. H. Lawrence's poems of war. She approved his using prose rather than English verse in translating from the Greek, and named Walter Savage Landor as the prose poet to whom Aldington owed an immense debt. She thought that the Greek half of Aldington had ripened to a precocious maturity, while the modern half had not even approached maturity. She liked the clearness and directness of sincere speech that was his style, and his getting "more sheer music into his unrhymed cadence than any other contemporary writer of vers libre."

In "The Novels of Violet Hunt," in the *English Review* of February, 1922, May Sinclair recognized that the critical image of being clever and hard had been fixed to Violet Hunt by her novels in the early nineties, even though she was never on the side of hardness, always for the tender and suffering. She picked her strongest mood as that of the psychological realist, and thought that her *White Rose of Weary Leaf* should have placed her "high in the ranks of tragic realists." *Unkist, Unkind* leaned toward the gruesome and uncanny. *The Celebrity at Home* and *The Celebrity's Daughter* were delightful comedies, *The Last Ditch* had smartness, and *Tales of the Uneasy* were powerful stories of the uncanny, expressing the author's true bent. The women Violet Hunt created with complete conviction were *demivierges,* women who must feel the thrill of danger before they can feel passion. May Sinclair praised the perfect form of *White Rose of Weary Leaf,* and recommended tolerance of formless novels like *Their Lives* and *Their Hearts,* because they were without affectation. She recommended the novels of Violet Hunt not for their beauty, but for their sincere and austere truth-telling.

The publication of H. D.'s book of verse, *Hymen,* in 1921, gave May Sinclair a chance to rework and amplify her original "Two Notes" in the *Egoist* (June, 1915) into a typescript article of thirty-seven pages, "The Poems of H. D.," which she sent to the *Dial,* whose editors started on page 20 of the typescript and thereafter cut heavily to produce the article, which appeared in February, 1922. The *Dial* article reviewed H. D.'s whole development as a poet: "There is, perhaps, no contemporary poet who has a finer sense of outline, none who can so constrain rich sensuousness to supersensuous form." H. D. never stood still after achieving formal perfection, but kept altering the texture of her poems. In her earlier poems she was the perfect imagist. In her later manner, a profound vision caused her to overload the image. But what it lost of sharp simplicity, it gained in depth and range. The obscurity that critics had carped at in some of her poems was in the mind of the critic: "There is nothing in contemporary literature that surpasses these later poems, at first sight so splendidly dim, at last so radiant, so crystalline. An austere ecstasy is in them."

In March, 1927, an almost complete version of the typescript was published in the *Fortnightly Review*. Commenting specifically on "The Tribute," it praised the *vers librists* for having revived beautiful assonance as a substitute for rhyming. May Sinclair thought assonance more satisfying than the "tight, clipping recurrent rhyme. It is a hint, a dawn of rhyme that hangs back, letting the rhythm pass on till the one closing rhyme clinches all."

Introduction

Romer Wilson's *Martin Schüler,* originally published by Methuen in 1918, was published by Knopf in New York in February 1928[13] with an introduction by May Sinclair, then well known to American readers.

May Sinclair glanced at all of her novels and assured her readers that Romer Wilson had shown maturity in this her "wonderful first book." She had succeeded in giving her musical genius an individual truthfulness in presenting his tastes, his behavior, his creative processes, and his life lived intensely on the borderland between sanity and insanity. Martin Schüler violated the sensitivities of others to give himself that space from social pressures which he needed for freedom to create. He created his music by letting the conceived idea sink into his personal depths until it came out of them with the rush of spontaneous creation. The descriptions of interiors and of natural scenery were extraordinarily vivid; the portraiture was beyond praise.

Reviews

The only contribution to Brontë criticism in this decade was a review

---

13. Letter, Katherine Hourigan, January 21, 1965.

of Alice Law's *Patrick Branwell Brontë* in the *London Bookman* of May, 1924, entitled "Who Wrote 'Wuthering Heights'?" May Sinclair treated the case for Patrick Branwell's being the author of *Wuthering Heights* with the kindest patience; but she could not believe that Emily allowed a work that was not her own to bear her name, that Branwell's vanity would have let a book of his bear his sister's name, or that Branwell's mental powers during the winter of 1845 were equal to the great creative task. May Sinclair's kindness was harshly treated in Miss Law's letter of rebuttal.

Perhaps the personal admiration that Florence Bartrop reported Sinclair Lewis to have had for May Sinclair led to her being invited to review *Babbitt* on the first page of the *New York Times* "Book Review" section on September 24, 1922. The review belongs to her best creative analysis.

She began by recalling that in *Main Street* the street is the protagonist, an organism whose active cells are people, and whose action is to resist, conquer, and absorb the foreign elements that invade it. *Babbitt* fixes attention on "one superb central figure," whose main effort is to give value and distinction to his nonentity with flattering illusions. Like the heroine of *Main Street*, he was a contradiction between floppy self-importance and futile discontent. And yet May Sinclair found Babbitt lovable. She admired the wholly created presentation, free from analysis and dissection. In style, construction, and technique, the novel outdid its predecessor. Its effect upon its readers would be that no one would recognize himself, but everybody would recognize somebody else.

Her review of E. L. Grant Watson's *The Desert Horizon* in the *Literary Digest International Book Review*, in June, 1923, discerned Watson's success in making the Australian bush real, and his error in giving a literary translation in place of the actuality of the thoughts and feelings of the bushman, Martin O'Brian.

In her review of Henry Justin Forman's *Sudden Wealth,* in the November, 1924, number of the *Literary Digest International Book Review* she praised the "sharp, clear reality" of the person of a socialist, George Pollock, who married a millionaire's disinherited daughter and then inherited money anyway through the breaking of the father's will. She pointed out the technical flaw of switching the interest to a nephew and his love affairs in Paris, but the concluding touch she thought fine and subtle.

Publicity

Although the hospital secretary was understandably unable to find a remaining printed copy in 1968,[14] a penned draft that May Sinclair kept of "Appeal for the Elizabeth Garrett Anderson Hospital Fund," dated 1926, proves the continuance of her active concern for medical welfare. The draft eloquently invites support for this "hospital founded by a woman [in 1866], for women, . . . staffed entirely by women," offering "the very highest medical and surgical skill" to the very poor. It deprecated any prejudice against the hospital as a feminist institution, for the good done for a woman spread through her family into a good for the whole community.

---

14. Letter, J. A. Missen, April 8, 1968.

18

Her Place and Her Meaning

Literary fame is an image that has survived the eternal human battle between the critics who affirm and support an author and those whose need is to deny and destroy him.

The history of May Sinclair's image from 1892 to the present forms a bulky record of calm appreciation, superlative admiration, vexed dismissal, and intermittent cries of wonder and indignation that her genius was overlooked. It is a study in the varieties of human tastes and capacities for imaginative recreation. But the history of the image has no useful point now. We must do our own reading, from beginning to end, and form a fresh image, the truest representation that we are able to give of what we ourselves have experienced.

I believe that May Sinclair deserves a place of honor in the main tradition of the English novel of the first quarter of the century; a considerable testimony of current and historical criticism would grant her that place.

She did not win it solidly in her time because much of the current critical reviewing was out of touch with the tradition of the English novel that would have admitted her to a place of honor, and some of it held her womanhood against her. Much current reviewing did not understand that traditionally the English novel puts no limits on a writer's freedom to learn all that is to be known about human beings, in actuality, in philosophy, and in the sciences, and to tell what he has learned; and that it does not limit his freedom to reach as deeply as he is able to reach within himself to control the flow of his creative spirit in style and craft. She knew that the instinct of tradition is to extend its life through growth, and that traditionalists in literature are mistaken worshipers who would make a mummy of it. Her gentleness and her womanhood were of no help to her. While traditionalists surrendered to the irreverence of George Moore and D. H. Lawrence and James Joyce, they stood firm against gentle May Sinclair, who never attracted a cult or court to champion her cause.

One venture of hers that irked the traditionalist critics of before 1915 was her representing some of the unromantic manifestations of the sexual instinct in quite decent human beings, not as exposés, nor under the conventional veil of moral reproach, but with compassion. It was a compassion that Anne Brontë had shown in *The Tenant of Wildfell Hall,* and Emily Brontë had not even thought it necessary to voice in *Wuthering Heights.*

When the insights of Freud and Jung filtered into the medical and the popular imagination, she again exasperated the traditionalist critics by assimilating some of those insights into her novels as reasonable confirmations of her own intuitive creativity. With her careful studies of childhood as either a formative or a predictive period of an adult's life, she even irked critics who had apparently forgotten about *Jane Eyre* and *David Copperfield.* The critics who objected to the psychoanalytic insights that they could identify had not noticed her plentiful use of intuitive psychoanalytic insights in *The Divine Fire,* whose romanticism they applauded rapturously. They argued that they did not object to her presenting pathological behaviors; they only disputed her right to explain them in psychoanalytic concepts and to show them being cured. The presence in her novels of doctors who authoritatively explain a mental illness constituted for them an unforgivable violation of a law that they had set up: science and literature belong to separate worlds, and science must never be allowed the freedom to turn literature into a clinic. Those critics who defaced her image have, of course, long since been swept aside by the flood of economic, political, medical, and engineering realism—that is, science—that the novel has absorbed because novelists have refused to honor any No Trespassing signs, and readers have thirsted increasingly for scientific substance in their novels, not merely in what has been named "science fiction," but in the regular novel. Look, for example, at James Barlow's *Liner.*

Apart from the traditionalist critics, May Sinclair could depend upon the favor of those readers who shared her interest in what psychological science, with its eternal object to be of greater help to man, could tell them about human behavior. The first quarter of this century, and a decade or so beyond, was a very serious and hopeful time to live in and write for, a time when people were curious about the self they were supposed to manage and to be responsible for, a time when public school and high school students still read Plato, and knew what Socrates had taught—a time that encouraged Aldous Huxley to repeat the Socratic counsel so that man, knowing the truth about himself, could live in symbiosis with his fellow men and with nature. That thirst for self-knowledge and reality was the last popular urge of its kind in this century.

May Sinclair already had in the marrow of her writing bones an impassioned reading of the Greek poets and dramatists, of Plato, Goethe, Mrs. Gaskell's *Life of Charlotte Brontë,* and probably the novels of the Brontës and George Eliot, not to mention her readings in the English poets and dramatists and in English and German idealism, when she began to write her novels in the eighteen-nineties. Her work is unique, in its parts and as a whole. The unique flavor of her art is in part derived from the distinctive essences that her imagination distilled out of its absorption of the Greek world with its passion for mortal beauty and intellectual inquiry; of the Christian world as a life of sacrificing mortal for immortal beauty; of the Buddhist world that made life a beautiful illusion leading toward vanishment in a goal called God, and out of its study of the closed world of the mind peering tirelessly to locate the self related to the infinite potential of animal pulsings and adjustments by the will, and its study of the open world of economic, social, and personal actualities, relationships, and realities. And all these a study of Goethe's mind had given her the confidence to try to contain in a varyingly reconciled whole.

She belongs in that channel of the English novel that flows from the confluence of the more romantic and compassionate current of the Brontës, Mrs. Gaskell, and George Eliot, and the more realistic, more ironic, more intellect-displaying current of George Meredith, George Gissing, Walter Pater, George Moore, and Samuel Butler. She is related, too, to the somber Trollope of *The Last Chronicle of Barset, The Prime Minister,* and *An Eye for an Eye.* Her interest in heredity relates her to the Hardy of *Tess of the D'Urbervilles* and *Jude the Obscure;* but her philosophy rejects the doom of destiny, holding out only for a biological heritage that may or may not appear in an individual, and whose threat may be challenged and defeated by a resolute will.

The placing of May Sinclair in this broad channel of her traditionally accepted forebears must not ignore the claims of such partial contemporaries, older and younger, who have not yet been given a sure place: such serious writers as Mrs. Humphrey Ward, "Lucas Malet," Mrs. W. K. Clifford, Violet Hunt, "Zack," Ada Leverson, J. D.

Beresford, W. B. Maxwell, Sheila Kaye-Smith, Elinor Mordaunt, E. M. Delafield, and Rose Macaulay.

My complete sympathy with all three writers would place May Sinclair on a level with Virginia Woolf and the Arnold Bennett of all but his four greatest novels. My more moderate sympathy with D. H. Lawrence as a novelist moves me to rank her body of novels above his.

The core of meaning running through May Sinclair's novels is a person's progress toward becoming an individuated self, against forces outside the person, such as family, class, and convention, and inside the person, such as racial, hereditary, and singular forces. It is the meaning of *Adam Bede,* of *The Mill on the Floss,* of the despised as well as the praised portions of *Daniel Deronda,* of *Marius the Epicurean,* and of *Robert Elsmere.* Over the whole course of her work May Sinclair does not tip the balance romantically in favor of a person's resoluteness of will or of his reaching his goal.

Her study of metaphysics focused her attention on the idea of reality, and her innate concern for the subjective level of life led her to make the search for the experience of reality an important theme for psychological narrative. She developed the subjective phase of what had been from the time of George Gascoigne's novel an almost objective, certainly a dramatic theme: a person's achieving the perception of reality in the form of insights into others, into himself, and into human values. It was the goal of that nonmetaphysical novelist, Charles Dickens, in *Martin Chuzzlewit, David Copperfield,* and *Great Expectations.* Even her temporary enthusiasm for the stream of consciousness method sprang from her belief that because it tried to limit itself to the subjective level, it came closest to the actual experience of reality.

Her attention to illusory beliefs was stimulated by her intuition for the psychoanalytic attitude and later by her study of psychoanalysis rather than by her reading in metaphysics. Ernest Jones put the case tersely in a televised interview, answering Lionel Trilling's question as to the aim of psychoanalysis: "Truth, on the basis of reality." The conscious exposure of illusions has been an inseparable twin in the realistic novel with the goal of insight into reality. There is no more delightful example of it than Jane Austen's *Emma,* nor has there been a more persistent aimer at illusions within May Sinclair's writing time than Somerset Maugham. He, however, took no notice of the unconscious as a source of illusions. May Sinclair shot her shafts as straight as did Samuel Butler through the illusions on which Victorian parents built their authority to break their children's separate selves. Butler recognized the directive power of the unconscious in art and in life without knowing the term *psychoanalysis.* Maugham won popularity and esteem. Samuel Butler has not really won either honor. There must be something about an English novelist's reminding his readers of the dictatorship of the unconscious that disqualifies him for popularity; but it should not deprive him of esteem.

I offer some qualities of hers to test May Sinclair's right to a place of honor among the novelists of her time, and therefore of all time: an unseduceable integrity as an artist; substantial fresh discoveries of human behavior, of women and of men; an increasingly perfected dynamics of causation leading to an inevitable ending and a clear spire of meaning; characters who are entered to their conscious and unconscious depths, and so thoroughly comprehended as to become irrefutably real; careful, credible dramatic preparation, and the bold use of episodes as symbols to establish the drift; ingenious ligaturing of chapters; a style recognizable as hers alone, free from all clichés, rare in its slips into analytic cant, delighting with fresh images, inspired figures, and varied rhythms, and not allowing a word or a phrase to evade a supremely sensitive critical scanning; care in each novel to balance moods or modulations of a mood; freshness from book to book; an increasingly disciplined, selfless economy of means; dramatic dialogue at its best; many flashes of wit and the adequate relief of tension through comedy or irony; the recurrence of a theme (like the study of a life, or of lives, in a family setting) managed so as to surprise the reader with the variations that it has undergone; a unique honesty and fairness in reexploring earlier insights with a fresh development and a fresh conclusion to offer a balance of possibilities; and not least, the frequent excitement and even exaltation that we can identify as the lift of poetry.

The anonymous critic in Kunitz and Haycraft's *Twentieth Century Literature* was perceptive when he wrote of her, "She is almost a major novelist, who had the misfortune to be too early for her destined public." The only quarrel I have with that estimate is over the word *almost*. I have confidently placed her among the major English novelists from Samuel Butler to Storm Jameson, and have given her to my students to read. Their critical approval leads me to hope that this champion of new writers when they were young will find champions among the present day youth. If they will read her they will find her a superb craftsman in the novel, and a stimulating guide to their exploring by way of the literary imagination the felt movements and attitudes of the self, which forms and firms, or forms and reforms under the masks of the identity.

Bibliography*

Novels

Audrey Craven. London: Blackwood & Son, 1897; New York: Henry Holt, 1906.

Mr. and Mrs. Nevill Tyson. London: Blackwood & Son, 1898; New York: B. W. Dodge, 1906 (published in America as *The Tysons*); New York: Henry Holt, 1907; London: Constable, 1909; serial publication under original title in *Ainslie's Magazine*, May, June, 1906.

The Divine Fire. London: Constable, 1904; New York: Henry Holt, 1904.

The Helpmate. New York: Henry Holt, 1907; London: Hutchinson, 1912; serial publication in *Atlantic Monthly*, January–September, 1907.

The Judgment of Eve. New York: Harper, 1908; *Everybody's Magazine*, September, 1907; London: supplement to *The Lady's Realm*, December, 1907.

Kitty Tailleur. London: Constable, 1908; New York: Doubleday, Page & Co., 1908 (published in America as *The Immortal Moment; The Story of Kitty Tailleur*); London: Hutchinson, 1923.

The Creators: A Comedy. London: Constable, 1910; New York: Century Co., 1910; serial publication in *Century Magazine*, November 1909–October, 1910.

The Flaw in the Crystal. New York: Dutton, 1912; *English Review*, September, 1912.

The Combined Maze. London: Hutchinson, 1913; New York: Harper, 1913.

---

* For a fuller bibliography see the *Bulletin* of the New York Public Library, 74, no. 7 (September, 1970): 459–67.

The Three Sisters. London: Hutchinson, 1914; New York: Macmillan, 1914.

Tasker Jevons. London: Hutchinson, 1916; New York: Boni & Liveright, 1916; New York: Macmillan, 1916 (published in America as *The Belfry*).

The Tree of Heaven. London: Cassell, 1917; New York: Macmillan, 1917.

Mary Olivier: A Life. London: Cassell, 1919; New York: Macmillan, 1919; London: J. Lehmann, 1949.

The Romantic. London: Collins Sons and Co., 1920; New York: Macmillan, 1920.

Mr. Waddington of Wyck. London: Cassell, 1921; New York: Macmillan, 1921.

Life and Death of Harriett Frean. London: Collins Sons and Co., 1922; New York: Macmillan, 1922; serial publication in *North American Review*, December, 1920–March, 1921.

Anne Severn and the Fieldings. London: Hutchinson, 1922; New York: Macmillan, 1922.

A Cure of Souls. London: Hutchinson, 1924 [January]; New York: Macmillan, 1924.

The Dark Night. London: Cape, 1924 [May]; New York: Macmillan, 1924.

Arnold Waterlow: A Life. London: Hutchinson, 1924 [September]; serial publication in *Home Magazine*, October, 1923–July, 1924; New York: Macmillan, 1924.

The Rector of Wyck. London: Hutchinson, 1925; New York: Macmillan, 1925.

Far End. London: Hutchinson, 1926; New York: Macmillan, 1926.

The Allinghams. London: Hutchinson, 1927 [March]; New York: Macmillan, 1927.

History of Anthony Waring. London: Hutchinson, 1927 [August]; New York: Macmillan, 1927.

Collections of Stories

Two Sides of a Question. London: Constable, 1901; New York: J. F. Taylor & Co., 1901; London: Hutchinson, 1923.

The Return of the Prodigal, and Other Stories. New York: Macmillan, 1914.

The Judgement of Eve, and Other Stories. London: Hutchinson, 1914.

Uncanny Stories. London: Hutchinson, 1923; New York: Macmillan, 1923.

Tales Told by Simpson. London: Hutchinson, 1930; New York: Macmillan, 1930.

The Intercessor, and Other Stories. London: Hutchinson, 1931; New York: Macmillan, 1932.

Uncollected Stories

"A Study from Life" [By M. A. St. C. Sinclair]. *Black and White*, November 2, 1895.

"A Friendly Critic" [Anonymous]. *Macmillan's Magazine*, October, 1896.

"Not Made in Germany" [Anonymous]. *Macmillan's Magazine*, January, 1897.

"A Hero of Fiction." *Temple Bar*, September, 1898.

"Red Tape." *The Queen*, November 14, 1914.

"The Return." *Harper's Magazine*, May, 1921.

Volumes of Poetry

Nakiketas and Other Poems [By Julian Sinclair]. London: Kegan Paul, Trench & Co., 1886.

Essays in Verse. London: Kegan Paul, Trench, Trübner & Co., 1891 [published January, 1892].

The Dark Night [a novel in verse]. London: Cape, 1924 (limited signed edition, and limited edition) ; New York: Macmillan, 1924.

Philosophy

"Descartes" [By Mary Sinclair]. *Cheltenham Ladies College Magazine*, no. 5 (spring, 1882).

"Studies in Plato." *Cheltenham Ladies College Magazine*. I "Was Plato a 'Dualist?'" no. 27 (spring, 1893); II "The Platonic Sociology." no. 29 (spring, 1894); III "The Philosopher-King." no. 31 (spring, 1895).

"The Ethical and Religious Import of Idealism." *The New World*, December, 1893.

A Defence of Idealism. London: Macmillan, 1917; New York: Macmillan, 1917.

The New Idealism. London: Macmillan, 1922; New York: Macmillan, 1922.

"Primary and Secondary Consciousness." *Proceedings* of the Aristotelian Society, New Series, 23, no. 7 (1923) : 111–20.

Dialogue

"Man and Superman: A Symposium" [Satire on Bernard Shaw]. *New York Times,* December 1, 1905.

Character Sketch

"A Servant of the Earth." *Woman at Home* (1899). Reprinted in Annie Matheson. *Leaves of Prose, with Two Studies by May Sinclair.* London: Stephen Swift, 1912.

Brontë Criticism

Introductions to volumes in the Everyman Series published by Dent (London): *Wuthering Heights* (September, 1907); *Jane Eyre* February, 1908); *Shirley* (February, 1908); *Mrs. Gaskell's Life of Charlotte Brontë* (June, 1908); *Villette* (March, 1909); *The Professor* (February, 1910); *The Tenant of Wildfell Hall* (April, 1914).

The Three Brontës. London: Hutchinson, 1912; second edition with a new Preface, 1914; Boston: Houghton Mifflin, 1912.

"New Brontë Letters." *Dial,* November 1, 1913 (became the new Preface to the second edition of *The Three Brontës.*)

Literary Criticism of Her Contemporaries

"The Eternal Child." New York: *Bookman,* July, 1906 (on the novels of Mrs. L. A. Harker).

"Three American Poets of Today." *Atlantic Monthly,* September, 1906; *Fortnightly,* September, 1906 (on Moody, Robinson, and Torrence).

"George Meredith." *Author,* June 1, 1909; *Outlook,* June 19, 1909.

"The 'Gitanjali': or Song-offerings of Rabindra Nath Tagore." *North American Review,* May, 1913.

"Two Notes: I 'On H.D.,' II 'On Imagism.' " *Egoist,* June, 1915.

"The Poems of H. D." *Dial,* February, 1922; *Fortnightly,* March, 1927 (the latter is a fuller version of the original manuscript).

"Prufrock: and Other Observations." *Little Review,* December, 1917.

"The Novels of Dorothy Richardson." *Egoist,* April, 1918; *Little Review,* April, 1918 (reprinted as Introduction to *The Pointed Roofs.* New York: Knopf, 1919.

"The Reputation of Ezra Pound." *English Review,* April, 1920; *North American Review,* May, 1920.

"The Poems of F. S. Flint." *English Review*, January, 1921.

"The Poems of Richard Aldington." *English Review*, May, 1921.

"The Novels of Violet Hunt." *English Review*, February, 1922.

Introduction to Romer Wilson. *Martin Schüler*. New York: Knopf, 1928.

Textuary

Thoughts from Goethe. London: Priory Press Booklets, S. C. Mayle, 1905.

Translations

Rudolf Sohm. *Outlines of Church History*. London: Macmillan, 1895, 1901, 1904; Boston: Beacon Press, 1958, 1962.

Theodore von Sosnosky. *England's Danger, The Future of British Army Reform*. London: Chapman & Hall, 1901.

Feminist Writings

Feminism. London: Women Writers Suffrage League, 1912.

"A Defence of Men." *English Review*, July, 1912; *Forum Magazine*, October, 1912 ("A Defense of Man") .

On World War I

"From a Journal." *English Review*, May, June, July, 1915 (the first published version of the next title) .

A Journal of Impressions in Belgium. London: Hutchinson, 1915; New York: Macmillan, 1915.

Translations of Her Work

L'immortel moment. Translated by C. Mottot. Paris: Tallandier, 1912.

Un romanesque. Translated by Marc Logé. Paris: Plon-Nourrit et Cie, 1922.

Les trois soeurs. Translated by Marc Logé. Paris: E. Ramlot et Cie, 1932 (published February 22, 1933) .

Index